# Apache
# Server

*Rich Bowen, Ken Coar, et al.*

*A Division of Macmillan USA*
*201 West 103rd Street, Indianapolis,*
*Indiana 46290*

# Unleashed

# Apache Server Unleashed

## Copyright © 2000 by Sams Publishing

International Standard Book Number: 0-672-31808-3

Library of Congress Catalog Card Number: 99-65691

Printed in the United States of America

First Printing: February 2000

03    02    01    00        4   3   2   1

## Trademarks

## Warning and Disclaimer

**ASSOCIATE PUBLISHER**
*Michael Stephens*

**EXECUTIVE EDITOR**
*Don Roche*

**ACQUISITIONS EDITOR**
*Angela C. Kozlowski*

**DEVELOPMENT EDITOR**
*Susan Shaw Dunn*

**MANAGING EDITOR**
*Charlotte Clapp*

**PROJECT EDITOR**
*Christina Smith*

**COPY EDITORS**
*Margaret Berson*
*Gene Redding*

**INDEXER**
*Chris Barrick*

**PROOFREADERS**
*Bob LaRoche*
*Kaylene Reiman*
*Tony Reitz*

**TECHNICAL EDITOR**
*Brian Powell*

**TEAM COORDINATOR**
*Pamalee Nelson*

**MEDIA DEVELOPER**
*Dan Scherf*

**INTERIOR DESIGNER**
*Gary Adair*

**COVER DESIGNER**
*Aren Howell*

**COPYWRITER**
*Eric Borgert*

**EDITORIAL ASSISTANT**
*Angela Boley*

**LAYOUT TECHNICIANS**
*Ayanna Lacey*
*Heather Hiatt Miller*
*Stacey Richwine-DeRome*

# Contents at a Glance

# Contents

# About the Authors
## Lead Authors

**Rich Bowen** lives in Lexington, Kentucky, with his woof, wife, and waif: his 65-pound puppy, Java; his beautiful and talented wife, Carol; and the sweetest girl in the whole world (Zanna said so, so it must be true), Sarah Rhiannon. Rich works for DataBeam Corporation, a subsidiary of Lotus Corporation (a subsidiary of IBM), where he is the Linux Geek, Just Another Perl Hacker, and Intranet WebSlinger. (He's working on getting those titles on his business card.) Rich has been running Web sites on Apache since the initial release in 1995 and was running Web sites on the NCSA HTTPd before that. At the moment, he's running Apache at `www.databeam.com`, `www.rcbowen.com`, and on his little IBM ThinkPad. Rich is a founding member and Grand Poobah of the Lexington Perl Mongers (`http://lexington.pm.org/`). In his spare time, Rich enjoys hiking along the Kentucky river, flying kites, and reading Dickens. Rich hopes to have some free time some day.

**Ken Coar** is a director and vice president of the Apache Software Foundation and a Senior Software Engineer with IBM. He has over two decades of experience with software engineering and system administration. Ken has worked with the Web since 1992 and, in addition to working on Apache and PHP, he is heading the project to develop Internet RFCs for CGI. He is the author of *Apache Server for Dummies*. He currently lives in North Carolina with his wife, Cathy, and four cats. He can be reached at `Ken.Coar@MeepZor.com`.

# Contributing Authors

**Patrik Grip-Jansson** (`patrikj@gnulix.org`) has been working with computers for 15 years and has spent the last 5 years specializing in Web, Internet, and intranet issues. He is currently working as a systems architect for the Swedish National Road Administration. He is also a major contributor to the Gnulix Society's efforts to increase knowledge about open source solutions.

**Slava Kozlov** (`kozlov@banet.net`) has been involved in Internet software development for five years. He is currently a loosely coupled software consultant and developer in New York.

**Didimo Emilio Grimaldo Tuñon** was born in 1963 in Panama City, Panama, and currently lives in Europe. He has more than 10 years of experience in software development from embedded systems for telephony hardware to enterprise class client/server programming. He enjoys reading good books in addition to the usual technical material, writing when inspiration strikes, and travelling as soon as the opportunity arises. He is currently busy setting up his consulting firm, Coralys Technologies, Inc., in Panama City.

**Matthew Marlowe** is a lead consultant for Jalan Network Services. He has broad experience in UNIX systems administration, network management, and object-oriented software development. His prior experience includes building the networking department of an Internet startup and being part of the team that innovated the science software for NASA's X-Ray Timing Explorer satellite, launched in 1995. His key interests include Linux, networking, and technology. He currently lives in Southern California with his fiancee, Anita.

# Dedication

*To my girls.*

*—Rich Bowen*

*I respectfully dedicate my work on this volume to the memory of my grandfather, Dr. Herbert G. Coar—scientist, educator, and Grand Old Man.*

*—Ken Coar*

# Acknowledgments

Although just a few names appear on the cover of this book, many dozens more have made it possible to produce a tome of this size.

First, I want to thank Angela Kozlowski, our acquisitions editor, who encouraged us (mostly in vain) to get our chapters in on schedule and to abide by the various guidelines that govern this series of books.

Thanks also to Don Roche, who got the ball rolling on this project in the first place; to Susan Dunn, our development editor; and to David Pitts for convincing me, against my better judgement, to do this project.

I want to thank my wife for putting up with the long hours and messy office that goes along with a project of this size. (OK, so my office is always messy. It's nice to have something to blame it on.) Thanks for going to Florida when I needed some uninterrupted time to work and coming home when I missed you. And to my sweet little Sarah, for making sure I didn't work all the time but took some time off to play bus.

Finally, a very belated thank you to my friend and teacher, Ken Rietz, for giving me the excellent education that made all my other ventures possible, even though most of them are in completely unrelated fields.

*—Rich Bowen*

I'd like to acknowledge the invaluable assistance of the following: the editors at Macmillan USA (Angela Kozlowski and Susan Dunn in particular) for interpreting my technobabble; my agent, Neil Salkind at Studio B Literary Agency; and Dean Miller at Macmillan USA for his understanding of the importance of metasyntactic variables. My greatest thanks go to my wife, Cathy, who (again!) put up with my idiosyncrasies while writing.

—*Ken Coar*

I would like to thank Angela Kozlowski for her patience in the publishing process, and also R.B. Smith, for his encouragement across the years.

—*Matthew Marlowe*

# Tell Us What You Think!

As the reader of this book, *you* are our most important critic and commentator. We value your opinion and want to know what we're doing right, what we could do better, what areas you'd like to see us publish in, and any other words of wisdom you're willing to pass our way.

As an associate publisher for Sams Publishing, I welcome your comments. You can fax, email, or write me directly to let me know what you did or didn't like about this book—as well as what we can do to make our books stronger.

*Please note that I cannot help you with technical problems related to the topic of this book, and that due to the high volume of mail I receive, I might not be able to reply to every message.*

When you write, please be sure to include this book's title and authors as well as your name and phone or fax number. I will carefully review your comments and share them with the authors and editors who worked on the book.

| | |
|---|---|
| Fax: | 317-581-4770 |
| Email: | michael.stephens@macmillanusa.com |
| Mail: | Michael Stephens |
| | Associate Publisher |
| | Sams Publishing |
| | 201 West 103rd Street |
| | Indianapolis, IN 46290 USA |

# Introduction

I've been fascinated with the Internet since before there was an Internet.

My first encounter with the Internet was in a computer lab at Florida State University when I was in high school in Tallahassee. I was using *talk* to chat with someone who I assumed was elsewhere in that lab or at least somewhere else on campus. When he told me that he was in Houston, Texas, I was utterly amazed. How could my keystrokes be sent all the way to Texas for us to be conducting this conversation? Clearly this was magic.

That was 1983, and the network we were using was called Plato. It was one of the many parts that eventually became the Internet. I didn't know anything about networking until years later. My fascination has always been with the capability of technology to allow people to communicate, regardless of geographic boundaries.

Although it's a lot of fun to reminisce with fellow geeks about the old days of using Archie to try to find the stuff you wanted, and the days when the Great Internet Search was actually a challenge, the good old days really left a lot to be desired. The arrival of the World Wide Web was, at least for me, a renewal of that feeling that I got in that computer lab at FSU.

I think it was early in 1992 that I first encountered the Web. I was a student at Asbury College, which wasn't yet connected to the Internet. Someone that I knew at the University of Kentucky let me use his SLIP account, and I got online at a blazing 2400 baud. That there was almost nothing of genuine interest on the Web yet was of secondary importance. By tapping a few keys (remember, this is pre-graphical browsers), I could move from a Web site in Switzerland to one at MIT to one at UC-Berkeley. This was truly deep magic.

When I started developing my own Web sites, the magic was on a new plane. I was putting information on this magical web, and people from faraway places could read that information at any hour of the day or night. That my Web site got three or four visitors every day was pretty neat. That these people were located in Australia, Germany, England, and South Africa was mind boggling. The first site that I ever started is still running today, at `http://www.rcbowen.com/kenya/`, and gets a modest 10,000 visitors daily. And although I've come a long way in my understanding of the underlying technologies, I've not yet lost that feeling that this is all magic.

It's sometimes really hard to believe that the World Wide Web is only eight years old. In that time, it has gone from being an experiment to being a critical part of thousands of businesses. In 1996, I was teaching a class about the Internet at Lexington Community College, and most of my students had not heard of the Web and didn't have an email address. They were taking the class, in most cases, because their employer had heard that this Internet thing might amount to something. A year later, it was clearly still a geek phenomenon, but most people had heard of the Web, although they might not really know what it was. Today, a company is as likely to be without a Web site as without a phone.

This rapid growth can be attributed in part to the Web being an idea whose time had come. I read somewhere that the average American is exposed to more raw information in a day than the average nineteenth century American was exposed to in his lifetime. That nineteenth century American could have told you where he read that information, because he probably wouldn't have read all that many things. But between radio, television, billboards, magazines, newspapers, and the backs of cereal boxes, I can't remember where that information came from. (But I could probably find it on the Web! A few minutes at AltaVista gave me a dozen unattributed references to this same statistic.) Hypertext gave us a revolutionary new way to organize information to make it immediately usable. Well-written Web sites could get you exactly the information you need, without subjecting you to all the fluff that you're really not interested in.

# What's So Cool About Apache?

Apache was in the right place at the right time because, quite simply, nothing else was. The people putting up Web sites needed certain features and needed bugs fixed, so Apache was born—software by the users, for the users. The Open Source model was ideal for this project because, especially in the Web's early days, things were moving much more quickly than any company could keep up with, and people couldn't afford to wait for an engineering manager somewhere to decide that a product could ship. They needed a feature immediately, if not sooner, and so had to do it themselves.

Today, Netcraft (`http://www.netcraft.com/Survey/`) reports that 4,078,326 Web sites are running Apache. That's 55.33 percent of all Web sites they surveyed. The nearest competition is Microsoft IIS, at a paltry 22.08 percent.

Apache is running on more Web sites than all other servers combined, because it's just better software. Sure, some folks prefer Apache over other servers because it's free. But even at organizations for whom price is not an issue, such as IBM and the British royal family (`http://www.royal.gov.uk/`), Apache is the server of choice.

There's an old saying in the software industry: "Good, fast, cheap—pick any two." The Apache Project has somehow managed to produce a product that's good, fast, and cheap.

## So What's This Book For?

*Apache Server Unleashed* is our attempt to provide a comprehensive reference manual and how-to guide for anyone running an Apache server. We cover everything from obtaining and installing the software through administering your Web site and writing your own extensions to the product.

## And Who Is This Book For?

This book is aimed at anyone who is using, or thinking of using, Apache to run his Web site, on either a Unix-like operating system or on Microsoft Windows. This might be the system administrator in charge of installing or configuring the server, or it might be a user who has been given permission to have Web content in his home directory.

This book is also for those people who are comparing their various options for Web server software, to get an idea of what the comparative features are. Although we don't compare different servers directly, you should be able to get an idea of what Apache offers so that you can intelligently compare it to another product.

## How This Book Is Organized

This book is divided into the following parts:

- The chapters in Part I, "Introducing Apache," discuss how Apache came to be and how to acquire Apache and get it running on your computer. There's also a chapter about the underlying protocol (HTTP) on which Apache relies and on which the whole World Wide Web is built. By the end of Part I, you should be able to get a barebones server installed and running. Part I consists of Chapters 1 through 4.

- Chapters 5 through 10 in Part II, "Configuring Apache," help you customize and configure your server exactly the way that you want it. One great strength of Apache is the capability to configure every detail of its operation. The chapters in Part II talk about the main configuration files, configuring things on a per-directory basis with .htaccess files, and setting up virtual hosts. You also will see some discussion of MIME types and be introduced to Comanche, a powerful GUI application for configuring Apache. At the end of Part II, your Apache server should be set up exactly the way you need it to be. Chapter 5, "Server Configuration Files," is also a great reference chapter, to which you will refer again and again as you make small changes to your server.

- Chapters 11 through 14 in Part III, "Dynamic Content," will make your Web site more than just an online version of your marketing pamphlets. CGI, SSI, cookies, and handlers all give you ways of making the site respond to user input, give visitors exactly what they came to get, and give them a way to give you feedback about what they are seeing and what they want.

- Your Web site is a way for you to communicate with the world. But there are people out in the world who will attempt to break into your network and do some damage. Chapters 15 through 18 in Part IV, "Setting Up Security and Auditing," talk about the various ways you can protect yourself from such intrusions and watch your server to see what activity your server is seeing. Chapter 15, "Security," teaches you how to make sure that nobody can get more access to your server than you really want them to. Chapter 18, "Logging," gives you insight into your log files, which give you a detailed picture of who is accessing your site and what they are doing there.

- The major portion of Part V, "Development," talks about the modules available for Apache that extend its functionality. These chapters also teach you how you can write your own modules, as well as contribute modules, additional features, and bug fixes to the Apache Project. Chapters 19 through 25 make up Part V.

- The four appendixes in Part VI offer some of the gory details that were left out of various chapters in the interest of space. Perhaps most important is Appendix D, "Where to Get More Information," which lists various resources where you can find more information online, in print, and via email lists and Usenet.

## Conventions Used in This Book

The following typographic conventions are used in this book:

- Code lines, commands, statements, variables, and any text you type or see onscreen appear in a monospaced typeface. **Bold monospace** typeface is often used to represent user input.

- Placeholders in syntax descriptions appear in an *italic monospace* typeface. Replace the placeholder with the actual filename, parameter, or whatever element it represents.

- *Italic* highlights technical terms when they're being defined.

- The ➡ symbol is used before a line of code that's really a continuation of the preceding line. Sometimes a line of code is too long to fit as a single line on the page. If you see ➡ before a line of code, remember that it's part of the line immediately above it.

The book also contains Notes, Tips, and Cautions to help you spot important or useful information more quickly. Some of these are shortcuts to help you work more efficiently.

# Enjoy the Book!

You can contact the authors and find errata for the book (`http://www.ApacheUnleashed.com/`) shortly after this book is available in stores. Thanks for buying this book, and please let us know what you think, since, after all, it is for you.

# Introducing Apache

## IN THIS PART

# CHAPTER 1

# Apache's History and Lore

According to Netcraft (`http://www.netcraft.com/`), the Apache Web server is used more than all other Web servers combined. Of the approximately 7 million Web sites on the World Wide Web, about 4 million of them (55 percent) are running Apache. If you also count server software based on the Apache code, this figure is closer to 60 percent. In this chapter, you'll see how Apache came to be and why it has become so popular.

---

**Note**

Netcraft has been surveying the Web since July 1995, when it registered 18,957 sites on the Web. The company updates its survey monthly, showing the growth or decline of each major player, and offers commentary on these trends. You can see the survey at `http://www.netcraft.net/survey/`. Netcraft is an Internet research company, offering surveys like this one, as well as security consultancy and various Web and Internet services.

---

Figure 1.1 shows a graph of the most popular Web servers and how many Web sites are using those servers.

**FIGURE 1.1**

*Distribution of Web servers in use.*

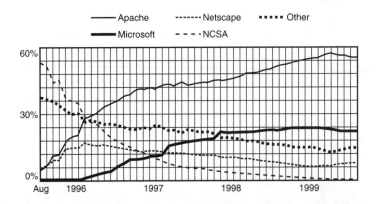

---

**Note**

If you're really interested in hunting down the origins of the World Wide Web, you may want to find a copy of the paper titled "As We May Think," by Vannevar Bush. This paper, written in 1945 (no, that's not a typo), talks about ways to organize information. His ideas look a lot like hypertext. You can read this article online at `http://www.theatlantic.com/unbound/flashbks/computer/bushf.htm`.

---

# In the Beginning

The Web is still a very young phenomenon. Tim Berners-Lee invented the Web in late 1990 while working at CERN, the European Laboratory for Particle Physics. He developed it so that physicists working at various universities around the world could have instantaneous access to information, to enable their collaboration on a variety of projects.

Tim defined URLs, HTTP, and HTML and, with Robert Cailliau, wrote the first Web server and the first Web client software, which was later dubbed a *browser*.

Just a few years ago, it would have been necessary to explain what these concepts meant to all but the most technically aware audience. Now, there are few people (at least in developed nations) who are unaware of the WWW.

Shortly after Tim's initial work, a group at the National Center for Supercomputing Activities (NCSA) at the University of Illinois at Urbana-Champaign (UIUC) developed the NCSA HTTPd Web server and the NCSA Mosaic graphical Web browser. Mosaic wasn't the first graphical Web browser, although it's almost universally remembered as such. That honor rightfully belongs to Viola, written by Pei Wei and available before Mosaic. But Mosaic quickly stole the spotlight—and most users—becoming the most widely used Web browser sometime in 1992.

NCSA HTTPd was the server most used on the Web for the first several years of its existence. However, in 1994, Rob McCool, who had developed NCSA HTTPd, left NCSA, and the project fizzled. There was no longer any central organization collecting fixes, developing new features, and distributing a functional product.

Since the source code of the server was publicly available, many people using it had developed their own bug fixes and additional features that they needed for their own sites. These patches were shared rather haphazardly via Usenet, but there wasn't a centralized mechanism for collecting and distributing these patches.

Thus, Apache—like the World Wide Web—was put together largely by volunteers. Although the demise of the NCSA HTTPd project left developers with a product that didn't work very well at the time and no one to complain to, a far superior product resulted in the long run.

# Who's Responsible?

In February 1995, Brian Behlendorf and Cliff Skolnick put together a mailing list, got some space on a machine, and got bandwidth donated by HotWired. Brian set up a CVS (Concurrent Versioning System) tree, so that anyone who wanted to could contribute new features and bug fixes. This way, a group of developers could collect their code modifications in one place and produce a combined product. Starting with NCSA HTTPd 1.3, they started applying these patches. The first release of this product—named Apache, because it was "a patchy" server—was version 0.6.2, released in April 1995.

The eight original core members of the Apache Group were Behlendorf, Skolnick, Roy T. Fielding, Rob Hartill, David Robinson, Randy Terbush, Robert S. Thau, and Andrew Wilson.

Shortly after the initial release, Thau designed a completely new architecture. Starting with version 0.8.8 in August 1995, Apache was switched to this new code base.

Netcraft shows Apache passing NCSA as the leading HTTP server sometime in early 1996.

> **Note**
>
> NCSA's HTTPd project started and stopped a few times over the years and is currently stopped. As a student-run project, it was really at the mercy of which current students were interested, and whether there was funding. While it was active, the NCSA HTTPd project traded expertise and code with the Apache Group, and there was never really a feeling that they were in competition. They were just colleagues working toward a common goal.
>
> You can learn more about the NCSA HTTPd project at `http://hoohoo.ncsa.uiuc.edu/`. Although much of the documentation there hasn't been updated in several years, it still has some of the best available tutorials on such subjects as CGI and HTML forms.

# Recent Happenings

Suddenly, organizations such as *The Wall Street Journal* and *Forbes* are using the term *open source* in front-page articles.

This seems a little strange to folks who have been familiar with the concept for a few decades and are used to it being ignored, or actively snubbed, by people in the commercial software industry.

In May 1997, Eric Raymond gave a talk, "The Cathedral and the Bazaar," at the Linux Kongress in Würzburg, Germany (see `http://www.linux-kongress.de/1997/`). This started a chain of events, not the least of which was Netscape's decision to release the source code for its Web browser. The software world was no longer able to ignore the "free software" movement, which renamed itself Open Source to shed some of the negative associations surrounding the movement. Eric was already well known in the free software movement and had produced a substantial number of important software products, including GNU Emacs, NetHack, ncurses, and fetchmail. He wrote fetchmail, at least in part, as research into the mystery of why the Open Source software development model worked at all, when traditional capitalistic common sense says that it should not. You can find the full text of his Linux Kongress talk and subsequent talks on his Web site at `http://www.tuxedo.org/~esr/writings/cathedral-bazaar/`.

In June 1998, the Apache Group announced that it was entering an agreement with IBM for continued development of the Apache server so that IBM could include that code in its WebSphere product. This was one of the first examples of a major software company endorsing an existing Open Source project and was one of the linchpins in making the Open Source movement appear viable to the rest of the software world. The endorsement and financial support of the world's largest software company told other companies that the Open Source movement was not just a bunch of long-haired rebels intent on undermining the commercial software industry, but that it was a proven method of producing quality products.

Before the IBM deal, there had been a number of attempts to make Apache work on Windows, but there were some substantial technical difficulties and very few skilled Windows programmers interested in the project. With the funding and resources that came with the IBM agreement, they could make Apache run on Windows and do it well.

Apache on Windows is a great alternative to IIS, particularly for those people already familiar with Unix but who have to use Windows. The modular approach taken by Apache is a welcome relief when compared to IIS, which installs an enormous monolithic application that does everything, including a wide variety of things that you probably are not interested in it doing.

Apache is lightweight, but any feature you want can be added by loading another module. Apache is easy to configure and manage and allows you to configure settings that IIS doesn't even let you think about. And if you just have to have a graphical configuration utility, Commanche provides this without taking away any of your power as a server administrator.

> **Note**
>
> The Apache Group warns that Apache on Windows shouldn't be considered as reliable as Apache on Unix and Unix-like platforms (such as Linux), but improvements are being made. Having a solid, reliable server for Windows is one of the primary goals for the Apache 2.0 release, expected some time in 2000.

# Why Apache Works So Well

Apache is just a fantastic product. It does everything you want it to do, and none of the stuff that you don't want it to do. It's fast, reliable, and inexpensive. What more could you want from a piece of software?

Apache can be all these things because it is *open source*. That means that everyone that uses the product has access to the source code. If you have an idea of something that would be useful, you can write and submit the code for that feature to the Apache Group for possible inclusion in the product. This means that features that make it into Apache are features that real people are actually using on real Web sites, not features that some-one suggested in a marketing meeting after conducting a focus group.

Also, when bugs are found, the many people who have access to the code can determine what's breaking and suggest fixes for the problem. (Or, to quote Eric Raymond, "Given enough eyeballs, all bugs are shallow.") Hence, bug fixes usually follow closely on the heels of bug discoveries. Contrast this to closed-source software products where, if you report a bug, you are at the mercy of someone else's schedule for a bug fix—if, in fact, you ever get one at all.

> **Tip**
>
> You can read Apache's official history on the Apache Web site at
> http://www.apache.org/ABOUT_APACHE.html.

# Summary

Apache was developed by actual users who needed to fix problems with, and add fea-tures to, the Web server software available in the World Wide Web's early days. As such, it's a server that does things that real Web sites need. Apache and its derivatives are used on about 60 percent of the Web sites today—more than all other Web servers combined.

# HTTP

# CHAPTER 2

HTTP—the Hypertext Transfer Protocol—is the language that Web browsers and Web servers use to speak to one another. This chapter discusses the component parts of that language, and what a typical HTTP conversation looks like.

Most of this conversation occurs completely outside your notice most of the time. But, it's very useful to know what's going on behind the scenes so that you have more insight into what's happening when something goes wrong.

The HTTP specification defines the underlying framework on which all Web traffic sits. URLs, HTML, and other components of using the Web are defined in separate specifications. They are kept apart so that they can evolve more freely than if they were tied together in one specification.

You can see all the related Web specifications at the W3C (World Wide Web Consortium) Web site at `http://w3.org/`.

# HTTP Headers

Much of the information exchanged between the client and the server is in the form of HTTP headers. An HTTP header is of the form:

`HeaderName: Data`

When the client connects to the server, it sends several HTTP headers across the wire, telling the server who it is and what it wants. The server will send back a number of response headers, describing the data that's being returned or explaining why no data is being returned.

Although users are most interested in the body of the message—the actual Web page or other resource that they wanted to see—this is the least interesting part of the HTTP conversation.

The HTTP specification defines a large number of headers that can be used. Section 14 of the HTTP/1.1 specification, Header Field Definitions, is 50 pages long. In addition to these headers, the client and server can make up their own headers if they like.

**Note**

You can get a copy of the HTTP/1.1 specification at `http://www.ietf.org/rfc/rfc2616.txt`. There's also a copy of this document on the CD-ROM that accompanies this book.

Table 2.1 shows general HTTP headers, which can be used by either the server or the client. Headers specific to the client request or to the server response are listed in related sections below.

**TABLE 2.1**    General HTTP Headers

| *Header Syntax* | *Meaning* |
| --- | --- |
| Cache-Control: *directives* | Different directives are available, depending on whether this header is being sent by the server or by the client. See Table 2.3 for directives that can be used by the client (request) with this header. See Table 2.5 for directives that can be used by the server (response) with this header. |
| Connection: *type* | Specifies the type of connection, such as Keep-Alive or Close. |
| [1]Content-Language: *language* | Used by either the client or the server to indicate what (human) language the resource is in. These are the standard two-letter codes to indicate various languages. For example, English is represented as en, German as de, French as fr, and so on. These codes are used in content negotiation, if a client requires a document in a particular language. Example: Content-Language: en |
| Content-Length: *number_of_bytes* | When data is being sent by either the client or the server, this header indicates the size in bytes of that data. |
| Content-Location: *URI* | Provides a URI (uniform resource identifier) where the content is available if it's different from the requested URI. |
| Content-MD5: *MD5 digest* | Contains the MD5 digest of the request or response body. |
| Content-Range *range/content_length* | In a request, this indicates that only part of the content is being requested. In a response, it indicates that only part of the content is being returned. Example: Content-Range 0-300/2402 |

*continues*

---

[1]*The following Content-\* headers would be used by the client when POSTing or PUTting data to the server. They would be used by the server when returning a document to the client.*

**TABLE 2.1**    continued

| Header Syntax | Meaning |
|---|---|
| `Content-Type` *type*/*subtype* | Indicates the MIME type of the data being passed in the message body. Example: `Content-Type: text/html` |
| `Date:` *date* | The date and time on which the transaction occurred. Example: `Date: Thu, 23 Sep 1999, 22:58:27 EDT` |
| `Expires:` *date* | Indicates when the data in the body should be considered stale. Example: `Expires: Wed, 03 Dec 2016 22:13:00 GMT` |
| `Last-Modified:` *date* | Indicates when the data in the body was last modified. |
| `Pragma:` *directive* | Can be used to include implementation directives. Example: `Pragma: no-cache` |
| `Transfer-Encoding:` *encoding_type* | Indicates what encoding was performed to transfer the message across the HTTP connection. |
| `Upgrade:` *protocol*/*version* | Lets the sender of the message suggest to the recipient that communication would be better handled in some other protocol. This allows communication to be initiated in an older protocol, but for the client and server to negotiate a newer protocol. Example: `Upgrade: HTTP/2.0` |
| `Via:` *server* | One or more `Via` headers can be put on a message to show that it got to its destination through one or more proxy servers. Example: `Via: 1.1 proxy.com (Apache 1.3.7)` |
| `Warning:` *warning-code message* | Conveys additional information about the request or response. The defined warning messages are as follows: <br>• `110 Response is stale` indicates that the response is stale. <br>• `111 Revalidation failed` indicates that an attempt to revalidate failed. <br>• `112 Disconnected operation` indicates that the information, which will be cache was disconnected from the network intentionally. <br>• `113 Heuristic expiration` indicates that the response's age is greater than 24 hours. <br>• `199 Miscellaneous warning` may include arbitrary information, which will be passed to the user. |

| *Header Syntax* | *Meaning* |
|---|---|
| | • `214 Transformation applied` indicates that the cache or proxy applied some change to the content-encoding. |
| | • 299 Miscellaneous persistent warning may include arbitrary information, which will be passed to the user. |

2

HTTP

**Note**

The following `Content-*` headers would be used by the client when `POST`ing or `PUT`ting data to the server. They would be used by the server when returning a document to the client.

**Note**

MIME (multipart Internet mail extensions) is a way of indicating the type of a document. A MIME type consists of the type and the subtype. The type indicates, in very broad terms, what type the document is. This can be something like `text`, `audio`, or `application`. The subtype is much more specific and indicates exactly what file format the data is encoded with. Subtypes might be something like `html`, `wav`, or `ms-word`. Put together, the type and the subtype very specifically define the file type, such as `text/html`, `audio/wav`, or `application/ms-word`.

The MIME type tells the Web client (browser) what to do with the document that it's receiving. A browser knows, for example, that when it receives a document of type `text/html`, it should format it and display it in the browser window. When it receives a document of type `audio/mp3`, however, it may launch an external program to play the audio content. See Chapter 7, "MIME Types," for more information.

# The HTTP Conversation

Each HTTP transaction is handled as a separate conversation, without memory of previous conversations. For this reason, we say that HTTP is *stateless*—it doesn't remember the state that it was in at the end of the last conversation.

The HTTP conversation consists of several parts, each of which is covered in a separate section of this chapter. The structure of the conversation is as follows:

- **Client request** The client (usually a Web browser) initiates the conversation by connecting to the server and requesting a URI.

> **Note**
>
> Throughout this book, you may see *URI* and *URL* used somewhat interchangeably. Although this practice is a little sloppy, it's pretty common. URL (uniform resource locator) is a subset of URI (uniform resource identifier). However, at this time, it's the only subset, so the terms really are fairly interchangeable.

- **Request headers** In addition to the request, the client will send some additional headers.
- **Request body** The request body can contain additional data.
- **Server status** As the first part of the response, the server returns a status code, indicating whether the request was successful and, if not, what went wrong.
- **Response headers** The server can then return any number of response headers.
- **Requested data** If the request was successful, the requested data will then be returned to the client.
- **Disconnect** The conversation is now over, so the server will disconnect from the client and wait for another request. A possible exception to this is if `Keep-Alive` is enabled, in which case the connection will stay open for the next request from the same client.

# Client Request

The client (Web browser or other HTTP client) initiates the connection to the server and makes a request. This request consists of three parts: the method, the resource being requested, and the HTTP version number. The method is usually `GET`, `POST`, or `HEAD`. Although other methods are permitted by the HTTP specification most are seldom used. The HTTP/1.1 specification defines the request methods in Table 2.2.

**TABLE 2.2**  HTTP Request Methods

| Method | Meaning |
| --- | --- |
| OPTIONS | A request for information about the communication options available for the specified URI. |

| Method | Meaning |
|--------|---------|
| GET | Requests a document from the server. |
| HEAD | Like GET, except only the headers are returned. |
| POST | Sends data to some handler indicated by the URI. |
| PUT | Requests that the data in the body section be stored at the specified URI. |
| DELETE | Requests that the specified resource be deleted. |
| TRACE | For debugging purposes; lets the client see what's being received on the other end. |
| CONNECT | Reserved for future use. |

The following sections cover just the three most commonly used methods. For more information on the other methods, consult the HTTP specification in RFC2616, which you can obtain from the W3C Web site at http://w3.org/. The document is also located at http://www.ietf.org/rfc/rfc2616.txt, and is on the CD-ROM that accompanies this book.

## GET

The GET method requests a particular URI from the server. That URI can be a document, such as an HTML document, a GIF image, or a MP3 audio file, or it can be process, such as a CGI program, that produces output to be displayed by the client.

A GET request will look something like this:

```
GET /fish/salmon.html HTTP/1.0
```

The actual file location of the URI is determined by the server. This determination can be made in several ways. The server checks for Alias directives that match the requested URI. It will check the location obtained by appending the URI to the server's DocumentRoot. Other HTTP servers have other methods of determining what's to be returned to the client. The resource isn't necessarily a file but might be a dynamically generated document. If the URI refers to an executable program and the server is configured to consider it a CGI program, it will execute it and return the results to the client.

### Note

Apache can be configured with other handlers for different types of URIs. See Chapter 14, "Handlers," for more information.

A GET request can be made conditional with any of the If-* request headers listed later in Table 2.3. Table 2.3 also describes the Range request header, which you can use to make a partial GET request.

## HEAD

A HEAD request is similar to a GET request, except that the server should return only the headers that it would have returned for a GET request but not return the data portion. Using HEAD requests is useful for determining if the document has been modified since the last time it was requested. If not, the client can conserve time and bandwidth by using a local cached copy.

## POST

For a POST request, the data contained in the body of the request should be sent to the specified URI. The URI should refer to a handler that can process the data in some fashion. This might be a CGI program.

# Request Headers

After the request, the client can send additional headers to the server, providing additional information about itself or about the request. For example, a typical HTTP request, with the additional request headers, might look something like the following:

```
GET /index.html HTTP/1.0
Connection: Keep-Alive
User-Agent: Mozilla/4.5    (WinNT; U)
Host: www.rcbowen.com
Accept: image/gif, image/x-xbitmap, image/jpeg, image/pjpeg, image/png, */*
```

Apache can limit the number of headers to be accepted from the client with the LimitRequestFields configuration directive. By default, this is set to 100. See Chapter 5, "Server Configuration Files," for more information on LimitRequestFields.

The HTTP specification at http://www.ietf.org/rfc/rfc2616.txt lists the various headers and their meanings. Table 2.3 lists the defined headers that can be sent with a request, in addition to the general headers listed in Table 2.1.

**TABLE 2.3**    Request Headers

| *Header/Syntax* | *Meaning* |
| --- | --- |
| `Accept:` *`type`*`/`*`subtype`*`,` *`type`*`/`*`subtype`* | Lists the document types that the client prefers to receive. |
| `Accept-Charset:` *`charset`* | Indicates the acceptable character set(s) in a response. Example: `Accept-Charset: iso-8859-5` |
| `Accept-Encoding:` *`encoding-type`* | Indicates the acceptable encoding type(s) in a response. Example: `Accept-Encoding: gzip` |
| `Accept-Language:` *`language`* | Indicates the acceptable language(s) in a response. Example: `Accept-Language: en, de` |
| `Authorization:` *`credentials`* | Permits the client to pass authentication credentials to the server, in order to enter a protected area. See Chapter 16, "Authentication," for more details. |
| `Cache-Control:` *`directives`* | Different directives are available according to whether this header is being sent by the server or by the client. See Table 2.5 for directives that can be used by the server (response) with this header. The directives that can be used in the request are as follows: |

- `no-cache`—Don't cache the response.

- `no-store`—The cache must not store any part of the response. Useful for protecting sensitive data.

- `max-age = ` *`seconds`*—The client isn't willing to accept a response that's older than the specified number of seconds.

- `max-stale = ` *`seconds`*—The client is willing to accept a cached response that has exceeded its expiration date by a maximum of the specified number of seconds. If no number of seconds is specified, the client is willing to accept a stale response of any age.

- `min-fresh = ` *`seconds`*—The client will accept a response that will  be fresh the specified number of seconds into the future. That is, the data's expiration date is later than the current time plus the specified number of seconds.

*continues*

**2**

**HTTP**

**TABLE 2.3**    continued

| Header/Syntax | Meaning |
| --- | --- |
| | • `no-transform`—Some proxy servers, in order to save space or for whatever other reason, occasionally convert data from one format to another. For example, they might convert PCX image files to the less wasteful JPEG format to save cache space. This directive indicates that the client isn't willing to accept data that has been converted to another format and is willing to accept it only in its original form. |
| | • `only-if-cached`—The client is willing to accept data only if it comes from a cache. This may be used for reasons of poor network connectivity, for example. |
| `Expect:` *expectation* | Indicates that the client is expecting a particular behavior by the server. Example: `Expect: 100-continue` |
| `From:` *email_address* | Indicates the email address of the user operating the browser. This isn't sent without the user's approval, and so is almost never actually sent in practice. Example: `From: rbowen@rcbowen.com` |
| `Host:` *hostname:port* | The hostname and (optionally) the port number of the host from which the URI is being requested. This is the header that allows name-based virtual hosts to work, because it lets a server know to which virtual host the request was directed. Example: `Host: www.mk.net:80` |
| `If-Match:` *search_string(s)* | Makes the request conditional. The server should return the requested document only if the search string matches the value of the `ETag` response header field. |
| `If-Modified-Since:` *date* | Makes a request conditional. The server should return a `304` (`not modified`) status if the document hasn't been modified since the specified date. Example: `If-Modified-Since: Thu, 23 Sep 1999, 22:58:27 EDT` |

| | |
|---|---|
| `If-None-Match: search_string(s)` | Makes the request conditional. The server should return the requested document only if the search string doesn't match the value of the `ETag` response header field. |
| `If-Range: date` | Combines an `If-Modified-Since` and a `Range` command. It means that if the document hasn't been changed since the specified date, send the missing parts. |
| `If-Unmodified-Since: date` | Makes the request conditional. The server should return the document if it hasn't been modified since the specified date. Example: `If-Unmodified-Since: Thu, 23 Sep 1999, 22:58:27 EDT` |
| `Max-Forwards: number` | Limits the number of times the request will be forwarded. The proxy server should decrement the number before forwarding the request and, if the number reaches 0, it must respond as the final recipient. Example: `Max-Forwards: 5` |
| `Proxy-Authorization: credentials` | Allows the client to pass authentication credentials to a proxy that requires them. |
| `Range: -range` | Allows the client to request just a portion of the document. Example: `Range: 0-500` |
| `Referer: URL` | Indicates the URL of the document from which the link to the current document was taken. That document is called the *referrer*. The header, however, is spelled `Referer`. Example: `Referer: http://www.mk.net/index.html` |
| `TE: transfer_codings` | Indicates what transfer codings the client is willing to receive. |
| `User-Agent: agent_name/version` | Indicates what user agent (browser or Web client) software is requesting the document. Example: `User-Agent: Mozilla/4.5   (WinNT; U)` |

# Request Body

In addition to the request itself and the request headers, the client might send additional data to the server in the request body. This is generally used for sending data to a CGI process with a `POST` request, but it might be used for a number of other purposes, such as publishing a document to the server with a `PUT` request.

The end of the headers is indicated by a single blank line; everything after this blank line is considered to be the body of the request.

When there is data in the body, the client must send information about that content in the headers, with such headers as `Content-Type` and `Content-Length`, as described earlier. This content is passed on to the handling process over standard input (`STDIN`).

# Server Status Codes

Having received the full request from the client, the server will first return a status code and response headers before sending the actual response.

The messages are in five groups, each representing a different type of status condition:

- 100-series messages are informational.
- 200-series messages indicate that a client request was completed successfully.
- 300-series messages indicate that the request was redirected for some reason.
- 400-series messages indicate that there was an error on the client end.
- 500-series messages indicate that there was an error on the server end.

**Table 2.4**    Server Status Codes

| Code Message | Meaning |
| --- | --- |
| `100 Continue` | The client may continue with its request. |
| `101 Switching Protocols` | The server is switching to another protocol, as requested by the client by way of an `Upgrade` header. |
| `200 OK` | The client request was successful, and the server returned the requested information. |
| `201 Created` | A new URI was created. A `Location` header will be returned by the server, indicating the location of that new URI. |
| `202 Accepted` | The request was accepted but not actually acted on. The server may or may not act on the request at a later time, and the body of the response may contain additional information. |
| `203 Non-authorative Information` | The information isn't from the original server but from a local cache or a third-party copy. |

| Code Message | Meaning |
| --- | --- |
| `204 No Content` | The response body contains no content. The browser shouldn't attempt to repaint its page view. This response can be returned from a CGI process that doesn't want to have the client move off the current page, for example. |
| `205 Reset Content` | The browser should clear all content from the HTML form contained on the page. |
| `206 Partial Content` | The server is returning a partial response. This can be used in response to a `Range` header, which requests only a portion of the page. |
| `300 Multiple Choices` | The requested URI might be ambiguous and could refer to any one of several pages. This may be used, for example, if a page is available in several different languages. |
| `301 Moved Permanently` | The URI is no longer available on this server. The new location for the document is provided in a `Location` header. All future requests should be made to the new location. |
| `302 Moved Temporarily` | The document has moved. The new location is indicated with a `Location` header. However, future requests should still be made to the old URI. |
| `303 See Other` | The requested URI can be found at another URI, which is indicated by the `Location` header. |
| `304 Not modified` | This will be passed only if the client passed an `If-Modified-Since` header, if the document hasn't been modified since that time. The client should use whatever copy it has cached locally. This can be used by a proxy to determine whether to serve a cached copy or get the copy from the server. |
| `305 Use Proxy` | The requested document should be accessed through a proxy. The location of the proxy is returned in a `Location` header. |
| `306 Unused` | The 306 code was used in a previous version of the specification but is no longer used. |
| `307 Temporary Redirect` | The requested document is temporarily under a different URI used for a request other than a `GET` or a `HEAD`, and the user must confirm the redirect. |

*continues*

**TABLE 2.4** continued

| Code Message | Meaning |
| --- | --- |
| 400 Bad Request | There was a syntax error in the client request. |
| 401 Unauthorized | The client didn't provide the correct authentication to access the requested document. This response code triggers the password dialog on most browsers. |
| 402 Payment Required | This status code shows that the authors of HTTP were either thinking ahead or had a sense of humor. This code isn't actually used by any servers at this time. |
| 403 Forbidden | The client isn't permitted to have the URI that it requested. |
| 404 Not Found | Perhaps the most common error status code that you will encounter on the Web. It indicates that the document requested isn't available. Either it has moved or the client simply requested a document that doesn't exist. |
| 405 Method Not Allowed | The method used by the client isn't permitted for that particular URI. |
| 406 Not Acceptable | The URI exists but isn't available in the format requested by the client. This usually occurs when the client asks for a document in a particular language or encoding method. |
| 407 Proxy Authentication Required | This message is returned by a proxy server, indicating that it needs to authorize the request before passing it on to the destination server. |
| 408 Request Time-out | The client didn't complete the request within a specified time, and the server is terminating the connection. |
| 409 Conflict | The request conflicts in some way with the server configuration or with another request. |
| 410 Gone | The URL has been permanently removed and has left no forwarding address. |
| 411 Length Required | The request didn't provide a Content-Length header, and one is needed. |

| *Code Message* | *Meaning* |
|---|---|
| 412 Precondition Failed | A condition specified in one of the If-* headers was false. |
| 413 Request Entity Too Large | The body of the request was larger than the server was configured to permit. |
| 414 Request-URI Too Long | The request URI was longer than the server is configured to permit. |
| 415 Unsupported Media Type | The body of the request was of a media type that the server doesn't know how to handle. |
| 416 Request Range Not Satisfiable | The range requested is out of range for the resource requested. For example, the range started after the end of the file being requested. |
| 417 Expectation Failed | An expectation given in the Expect header wasn't met. |
| 500 Internal Server Error | This catch-all error message indicates that something on the server (usually, a CGI program) has failed. |
| 501 Not Implemented | The requested action can't be performed. |
| 502 Bad Gateway | The server, while trying to act as a gateway or proxy, received an invalid response from another server further up the chain. |
| 503 Service Unavailable | The server isn't available, due to overloading or maintenance. The server may indicate the expected length of the delay in a Retry-After response header. |
| 504 Gateway Timeout | The server, acting as a proxy, didn't receive a response from the next server up the chain before the timeout period expired. |
| 505 HTTP Version Not Supported | The HTTP version number specified by the client isn't supported by the server. |

**2**

HTTP

# Response Headers

Following the status code comes one or more response headers. Table 2.5 shows the possible response headers that can be used, in addition to the headers listed in Table 2.1.

**TABLE 2.5**    Server Response Headers

| Header Syntax | Meaning |
|---|---|
| `Accept-Ranges:` *bytes_or_none* | Informs the client whether the server is willing to send partial document ranges. |
| `Age:` *seconds* | Indicates the age, in seconds, of the response. This implies that the response isn't being served firsthand but is being served from cache. |
| `Cache-Control:` *directives* | Different directives are available, depending on whether this header is being sent by the server or by the client. See Table 2.3 for directives that can be used by the client (request) with this header. The server (response) directives are as follows: |

- `public`—The information is public and so may be stored in any cache.

- `private`—The information is intended for a single user and may not be cached. This specifies  only where the content may be cached and doesn't guarantee any kind of data privacy.

- `no-cache`—Don't cache this response.

- `no-store`—Don't store any part of this response. This is meant to protect sensitive material but shouldn't be considered a guarantee of data security.

- `no-transform`—Instructs the client not to perform any content-encoding transformations on the data being sent.

- client must revalidate before getting the content.

- `proxy-revalidate`—Similar to the `must-revalidate` directive but refers to public caches.

- `max-age`—The maximum age that this data should be allowed to attain before it's removed from the cache.

- `s-maxage`—Similar to the `max-age` directive but applicable to a shared public cache.

| Header Syntax | Meaning |
|---|---|
| ETag: *etag value* | Provides the current value of the entity tag of the requested variant. |
| Location: *URI* | Redirects the client to a new location. Example: Location: http://www.mk.net/ |
| Proxy-Authenticate: *challenge* | Included as part of a 407 (Proxy Authentication Required) response. |
| Retry-After: *date or seconds* | Can be used with a 503 (Service Unavailable) response to indicate when the service will again be available. |
| Server: *software version comment* | Indicates the server software that's serving the request, the version number, and any other comment about that software. Example: Apache/1.3.9 (Unix) mod_perl/1.21 |
| WWW-Authenticate: *challenge* | Must be included with a 401 (Unauthorized) response. See Chapter 16 for more details. |

# Requested Data

The end of the response headers is indicated by a single blank line. Everything following this is the response body.

The returned data can be the contents of a file or the response from a CGI process. Although this is what the user is actually interested in, this is the least interesting part of the entire transaction.

# Disconnect or Keep-Alive

At this point, the HTTP conversation is complete. The data has been sent to the user. The server will either terminate the connection or, if it's a Keep-Alive connection, it will hold it open until it receives another request over the connection or until the connection times out, whichever happens first.

# An Example HTTP Conversation

To see what an HTTP conversation looks like, it is useful to try it yourself. You don't have to have a Web browser to connect to a Web server—a simple Telnet client will do.

At your command prompt, (shell or DOS, as appropriate) enter

```
telnet www.apacheunleashed.com 80
```

If you're using Windows, you'll probably have a new window launched. If on a Unix machine, you'll see something like

```
Trying 204.146.167.214...
Connected to www.rcbowen.com.
Escape character is '^]'.
```

In either case, you'll see nothing more—just a cursor waiting for input. You've connected to a Web server as an ordinary Web client. The server is waiting for a request. At the prompt, you can type a HTTP request.

```
GET /index.html
```

> **Note**
>
> Remember that case matters—GET must be uppercase.

Once you press Enter or Return, you'll see some HTML scroll past. This is either the page you requested or a page telling you that something was wrong with your request. In either case, you have completed the simplest HTTP conversation with an Apache Web server. Experiment with different requests and headers to see what sort of responses you get.

# Summary

HTTP, the Hypertext Transfer Protocol, is the language that the client and server use to communicate with one another and is the basis for traffic on the Web. The HTTP conversation consists of a request, headers, and possibly a body being sent from the client, and a status, headers, and a body being returned by the server.

For more details about HTTP, see `http://www.ietf.org/rfc/rfc2616.txt`. A copy of this document is also provided on the CD-ROM that accompanies this book.

# Compiling and Installing Apache

Apache is available in binary form for several platforms but is mostly available as source code. This means that you need to have a C compiler and compile and install Apache yourself. A discussion of the relative merits of doing things this way, as compared to having an InstallShield installation program, isn't particularly beneficial. Windows users, who are probably the ones most familiar with having a friendly graphical installation program, will be pleased to know that such a program is available for Windows.

This chapter walks you through installing Apache, from obtaining the source code to installing all the files in the right places.

> **Note**
>
> If you will be using Apache on Windows, it's unlikely that you will be interested in the first part of this chapter, and you should skip down a few pages. The last few sections of this chapter deal with installing Apache on Windows.

# System Requirements

The system requirements for running Apache are very slim. You need at least 12MB of temporary space on your hard drive for the installation process. After installation, Apache takes up about 3MB, plus whatever space you use for the actual Web content.

You need an ANSI-C compiler. The GNU C Compiler, known as GCC, is the recommended compiler to use, but other compilers will work fine if they are ANSI-C compliant.

Perl (version 5.003 or better) is required for some of the optional support scripts. Support for Dynamic Shared Objects (DSO) is recommended, but not required.

# Obtaining Apache

The Apache Server software is available from the Apache Group's Web site and from dozens of mirror sites around the world. Try to find a mirror site that is geographically close to you, particularly if you are outside the United States. Of course, geographic proximity doesn't necessarily mean that a site is close to you in terms of network connectivity, but it's a good start.

The relevant URLs are as follows:

- The Apache Software Foundation at `http://www.apache.org/`. There's more than one project under the ASF's umbrella, although Apache Server is the best known.

- Apache HTTP Server Project at `http://www.apache.org/httpd.html`. This site is the source for the most accurate and current information about the Apache Server. All server documentation is available online, as well as the bugs database, news archives, historical information, and various other Apache-related resources. Figure 3.1 shows the Apache Server Web site.

**FIGURE 3.1**

*The Apache Server Web site.*

- Download Apache at `http://www.apache.org/dist/`. This is the primary location for obtaining the Apache source code.

- Apache project mirrors at `http://www.apache.org/mirrors/`. This site lists, by country code, the official Apache mirror sites.

Apache is available for download in several versions, in both binary and source code forms, on the Apache download page and on the various mirrors. Some people prefer to use an older version of any product so that they can be assured that the software they're using has been well tested. Using the latest version of any product isn't for everyone and makes some system administrators nervous, particularly when their business—or their job—is at stake.

As of this writing, the latest version of Apache is 1.3.9. Also available for download is version 1.3.6—the next most recent version in the 1.3 series—and 1.2.6, the last release in the 1.2 series.

Downloading the latest version is almost always a safe thing to do because the Apache Group tests the software before it's made available for download. You should, however, read the list of known bugs so that you can be aware of any known issues with the software and avoid a version that you think might contain a problem that will directly affect you. To see the open issues for a particular version, see the bug reporting page at `http://www.apache.org/bug_report.html`.

## Downloading Binaries

Apache is available in binary form for a number of platforms. Before using a binary, make sure that it was built with the options you are interested in using. If you want a fairly generic build with none of the optional modules, you're probably safe using one of these. Make sure also that it was built with a configuration that matches yours closely so that you don't encounter compatibility issues. You're almost always better off building Apache yourself from the source code, if that's an option.

## Downloading Source

If you're going to build Apache for yourself from the source (good choice!), download the `.tar.gz` file corresponding to the version that you've decided to use. For example, the latest version as of this writing is Apache 1.3.9, so the file you would want to download is called `apache_1.3.9.tar.gz`.

### Verifying the File's Authenticity

If you have Pretty Good Privacy (PGP) installed, you can verify that the file you've downloaded is the genuine article. This is particularly important if you download the file from a mirror site, rather than from the main Apache Web site.

You will see another file in the download directory with the same name as the file you just downloaded but with an additional `.asc` file extension. This is the PGP signature that goes with the file you've downloaded. You can use this file to verify the file's authenticity. The PGP keys of the various Apache developers are contained in the file called KEYS, which is available in that same directory.

Figure 3.2 shows PGP telling you that you do indeed have a valid copy of the file.

> **Note**
>
> PGP is a software package that allows users to encrypt data and to "sign" it with a digital signature, verifying its authenticity.

**FIGURE 3.2**

*Verifying the PGP signature on the downloaded file.*

## Extracting the File's Contents

To unpack this file, use the following command:

```
tar -zxf apache_1.3.9.tar.gz
```

If the version of `tar` that you're using doesn't support the `-z` option, you can unzip the file in a separate operation:

```
gunzip apache_1.3.9.tar.gz
tar -xf apache_1.3.9.tar
```

Either way you unpack the file, you end up with a directory named after the version of Apache that you're using. For example, the 1.3.9 version creates a directory called `apache_1.3.9`.

3

COMPILING AND
INSTALLING
APACHE

### Keeping Current on Apache Developments

It's a good idea to get on the Apache Week mailing list and the Apache-Announce mailing list so that you will always be kept up-to-date on the latest developments in Apache, be informed when a new version is available, and see what bugs are now being worked on.

To subscribe to the Apache Week mailing list, send email to `majordomo@apacheweek.com`. If you want to receive Apache Week in a text format, put the text `subscribe apacheweek` in the body of your message. If you want to receive Apache Week in HTML format, put the text `subscribe apache-week-html` in the body of your message. You can find out more about Apache Week at `http://www.apacheweek.com/`.

To subscribe to the Apache-Announce mailing list, send a blank email message to `announce-subscribe@apache.org`.

# Installation for Impatient People

If you're impatient and just want to get this thing installed and move on, here's what you need to do. You will need to be logged in as root to run the following commands successfully:

```
cd apache_1.3.9
./configure --prefix=/usr/local/apache
make
make install
/usr/local/apache/bin/apachectl start
```

You can change the prefix to something else if you want it installed somewhere other than /usr/local/apache. That's the default location to install Apache.

You are now done and can skip the rest of this chapter if you like. The rest of this chapter is for more patient people who want to control every detail of the installation process, or for Microsoft Windows users.

# Configuring Apache

There are two ways to configure your Apache build. The newer way, called APACI, allows you to specify command-line options. The old-fashioned way involves editing a configuration file and selecting the options that you want.

## Configuring with APACI

APACI, the Apache Autoconf-style interface, is new with version 1.3 and gives you a configuration interface that might be more familiar to people who have worked with the GNU Autoconf package. APACI allows you to provide configuration options on the command line, and it will build your Makefile appropriately.

To run APACI, run the script configure from the command line with your list of arguments. The preceding instructions for impatient people run this same script but with just one argument, thus causing Apache to be configured with all the defaults except for that one value.

### --help

Running configure with the --help option gives you a summary of the available options (see Listing 3.1).

**LISTING 3.1**    Getting the Available configure Options

```
bug> ./configure --help
[hang on a moment, generating help]

Usage: configure [options]
Options: [defaults in brackets after descriptions]
General options:
--quiet, --silent     do not print messages
```

```
--verbose, -v          print even more messages
--shadow[=DIR]         switch to a shadow tree (under DIR) for building

Stand-alone options:
--help, -h             print this message
--show-layout          print installation path layout (check and debug)

Installation layout options:
--with-layout=[F:]ID   use installation path layout ID (from file F)
--target=TARGET        install name-associated files using basename TARGET
--prefix=PREFIX        install architecture-independent files in PREFIX
--exec-prefix=EPREFIX  install architecture-dependent files in EPREFIX
--bindir=DIR           install user     executables in DIR
--sbindir=DIR          install sysadmin executables in DIR
--libexecdir=DIR       install program  executables in DIR
--mandir=DIR           install manual pages in DIR
--sysconfdir=DIR       install configuration files in DIR
--datadir=DIR          install read-only  data files in DIR
--includedir=DIR       install includes files in DIR
--localstatedir=DIR    install modifiable data files in DIR
--runtimedir=DIR       install runtime data in DIR
--logfiledir=DIR       install logfile data in DIR
--proxycachedir=DIR    install proxy cache data in DIR

Configuration options:
--enable-rule=NAME     enable  a particular Rule named 'NAME'
--disable-rule=NAME    disable a particular Rule named 'NAME'
                       [DEV_RANDOM=default EXPAT=default    IRIXN32=yes ]
                       [IRIXNIS=no        PARANOID=no       SHARED_CHAIN=de]
                       [SHARED_CORE=default SOCKS4=no        SOCKS5=no   ]
                       [WANTHSREGEX=default                              ]
--add-module=FILE      on-the-fly copy & activate a 3rd-party Module
--activate-module=FILE on-the-fly activate existing 3rd-party Module
--permute-module=N1:N2 on-the-fly permute module 'N1' with module 'N2'
--enable-module=NAME   enable  a particular Module named 'NAME'
--disable-module=NAME  disable a particular Module named 'NAME'
                       [access=yes       actions=yes      alias=yes      ]
                       [asis=yes         auth=yes         auth_anon=no   ]
                       [auth_db=no       auth_dbm=no      auth_digest=no ]
                       [autoindex=yes    cern_meta=no     cgi=yes        ]
                       [digest=no        dir=yes          env=yes        ]
                       [example=no       expires=no       headers=no     ]
                       [imap=yes         include=yes      info=no        ]
                       [log_agent=no     log_config=yes   log_referer=no ]
                       [mime=yes         mime_magic=no    mmap_static=no ]
                       [negotiation=yes  proxy=no         rewrite=no     ]
                       [setenvif=yes     so=no            speling=no     ]
                       [status=yes       unique_id=no     userdir=yes    ]
                       [usertrack=no     vhost_alias=no                  ]
```

*continues*

**3**

COMPILING AND
INSTALLING
APACHE

**LISTING 3.1**    continued

```
--enable-shared=NAME  enable  build of Module named 'NAME' as a DSO
--disable-shared=NAME disable build of Module named 'NAME' as a DSO
--with-perl=FILE      path to the optional Perl interpreter
--without-support     disable the build and installation of support tools
--without-confadjust  disable the user/situation adjustments in config
--without-execstrip   disable the stripping of executables on installation

suEXEC options:
--enable-suexec       enable the suEXEC feature
--suexec-caller=NAME  set the suEXEC username of the allowed caller [www]
--suexec-docroot=DIR  set the suEXEC root directory [PREFIX/share/htdocs]
--suexec-logfile=FILE set the suEXEC logfile [PREFIX/var/log/suexec_log]
--suexec-userdir=DIR  set the suEXEC user subdirectory [public_html]
--suexec-uidmin=UID   set the suEXEC minimal allowed UID [100]
--suexec-gidmin=GID   set the suEXEC minimal allowed GID [100]
--suexec-safepath=PATH
   ➥set the suEXEC safe PATH [/usr/local/bin:/usr/bin:/bin]

Deprecated options:
--layout              backward compat only: use --show-layout
--compat              backward compat only: use --with-layout=Apache
```

Although most of these options are fairly self-explanatory, a few of them merit some additional discussion, as these are the ones that most people will end up actually using. The other options are described in some detail in the INSTALL file, found in the same directory as the configure script.

## --show-layout

A very useful option, --show-layout shows you where all the files will end up when you run make install at the end of this process (see Listing 3.2).

**LISTING 3.2**    Seeing Where Files Will Be Installed

```
bug> ./configure --show-layout
Configuring for Apache, Version 1.3.9
 + using installation path layout: Apache (config.layout)

Installation paths:
              prefix: /usr/local/apache
         exec_prefix: /usr/local/apache
              bindir: /usr/local/apache/bin
             sbindir: /usr/local/apache/bin
          libexecdir: /usr/local/apache/libexec
              mandir: /usr/local/apache/man
           sysconfdir: /usr/local/apache/conf
             datadir: /usr/local/apache
```

```
           iconsdir: /usr/local/apache/icons
          htdocsdir: /usr/local/apache/htdocs
             cgidir: /usr/local/apache/cgi-bin
         includedir: /usr/local/apache/include
       localstatedir: /usr/local/apache
          runtimedir: /usr/local/apache/logs
          logfiledir: /usr/local/apache/logs
       proxycachedir: /usr/local/apache/proxy

Compilation paths:
          HTTPD_ROOT: /usr/local/apache
     SHARED_CORE_DIR: /usr/local/apache/libexec
      DEFAULT_PIDLOG: logs/httpd.pid
  DEFAULT_SCOREBOARD: logs/httpd.scoreboard
    DEFAULT_LOCKFILE: logs/httpd.lock
     DEFAULT_XFERLOG: logs/access_log
    DEFAULT_ERRORLOG: logs/error_log
   TYPES_CONFIG_FILE: conf/mime.types
  SERVER_CONFIG_FILE: conf/httpd.conf
  ACCESS_CONFIG_FILE: conf/access.conf
RESOURCE_CONFIG_FILE: conf/srm.conf
```

## --prefix

The default location for Apache to be installed is /usr/local/apache. The --prefix
option lets you change that to some other location. Earlier versions of Apache kept files
in /usr/local/etc/httpd, and you may want to put files there for compatibility. Here's
an example:

```
./configure --prefix=/usr/local/etc/httpd
```

## --enable-module

The --enable-module option and its associated --disable-module option let you enable
or disable particular modules. If your particular operating system supports DSO
(dynamic shared objects), you will probably use --enable-module with the
--enable-shared option to compile that module as a DSO. In the output of the --help
option (refer to Listing 3.1), you can see the default state of each module. A yes indicates that it's compiled in by default.

To add the mod_speling module, for example, you would use the following command
line:

```
./configure --enable-module=speling --enable-shared=speling
```

# Configuring Manually

Before version 1.3, the only way to configure Apache was by manually editing the configuration files. Thus, people who have been using Apache for a while might find that this is the more familiar and comfortable way to do things. Some prefer this method because you can see all the configurations in one place and are less likely to forget about one when you have to look through a file containing all the options. On the other hand, if you know exactly what you want to modify, APACI lets you make those changes quickly with just a command-line switch. It's really just a matter of preference.

To edit the configuration manually, change to the `src` directory. Copy `Configuration.tmpl` to `Configuration` and then open `Configuration` in your favorite editor:

```
cd src
cp -f Configuration.tmpl Configuration
vi Configuration
```

> **Tip**
>
> Don't change `Configuration.tmpl`. It will give you something to fall back on if you mess up.

Five types of lines are in the file, as noted in the comment near the top of the file. Any line beginning with a # is a comment.

`Makefile` configurations, the first major section, are instructions to your C compiler.

Lines beginning with `Rule` are rules. These tell `configure` how to make the `Makefile`.

`AddModule` lines enable the building of Apache modules. Many of these are commented out, indicating that that particular module isn't compiled in by default. Uncommenting those lines will cause those modules to be built into your version of Apache. Alternatively, you can comment out any modules that you don't want installed. If a module is built into Apache by default and you don't know what it does, you probably shouldn't disable it.

Lines starting with `%Module` indicate that the specified module should be built into Apache but not enabled. You can use the `AddModule` directive in your server configuration file to enable these modules. This option is useful if you're building a binary for distribution to multiple machines, which will have different modules enabled. You can build in all the modules that will be needed on any machine, and just enable the necessary ones on each machine. The disadvantage is that this generates a larger-than-necessary binary file. None of these lines are in the default `Configuration` file.

After you look through the entire file and select those options that you want, generate your Makefiles by running configure at the command line:

`./configure`

# Compiling

Compiling is the easiest part of the whole process. When you are done with the configuration stage, whichever method you chose, just type **make** to start the build process. This may take several minutes.

> **Note**
>
> In the unlikely case that something fails during this stage, you will see various error messages that should point you to the source of the problem. If you don't know what these error messages mean, your best source of help will probably be the comp.infosystems.www.servers.unix Usenet newsgroup or the bug database on Apache's Web site.

# Installing

Installing is almost as easy as compiling. You have to type two words: **make install**. You will need to be logged in as root to execute this command, because the installation is putting files into directories where most users don't have write access.

# Installing and Compiling Apache Under Windows

Most Microsoft Windows users will want to install from the binaries. The Windows binaries are built so that all the available modules are compiled in and can be enabled by using the AddModule directive.

> **Note**
>
> The Apache Group warns repeatedly that Apache on Windows should be considered beta quality, at best. The code hasn't been optimized for Windows NT, and most of the Apache developers aren't Windows programmers. Although the Windows version has come a long way in the last year or so, it's not recommended that you run production Apache sites on Windows NT.

# Installing Apache on Windows

Download the installation file from the Apache download site at
`http://www.apache.org/dist/`. The filename will be `apache_version_win32.exe`,
where *version* is the particular version number you're getting. As of this writing, the file
that you want to download is `apache_1_3_9_win32.exe`.

The installation is the expected Windows installation process. You click Next a few
times, and it's installed.

> **Tip**
>
> The default location for installing Apache on Windows is `C:\Program Files\Apache Group\Apache`. This works, but spaces in file paths can lead to some problems with configuration. For example, file paths with spaces must appear in quotes in your configuration file. Forgetting those quotes is a very common mistake. You can avoid this and related problems by changing the installation to `C:\httpd`, `c:\Apache`, or some other path that makes sense to you.

# Installing as a Windows NT Service

If you plan to have Apache running all the time on your Windows NT machine—for
example, one that will be a production server—you will want to have Apache installed as
a Windows NT service. These services are, as the name implies, a feature of Windows
NT and aren't available on Windows 9*x*.

If you are unfamiliar with Windows NT services, here's a brief overview. Windows NT
services ensure that an application starts when your system restarts. Applications that
aren't installed as services can be made to start up when you log in, or can be started
manually. But if your server is restarted for any reason, those applications won't be
restarted. (See Chapter 4, "Starting, Stopping, and Restarting the Server," for more information on starting and stopping Apache as a Windows NT service.)

When you install Apache on Windows NT, it's not installed as a service by default.
However, it's very simple to make it a service. From the Start menu, choose Programs,
Apache Web Server, Install Apache As Service (NT only). Figure 3.3 shows where this
will be in your Start menu.

**FIGURE 3.3**

*Installing Apache
as a Windows NT
service.*

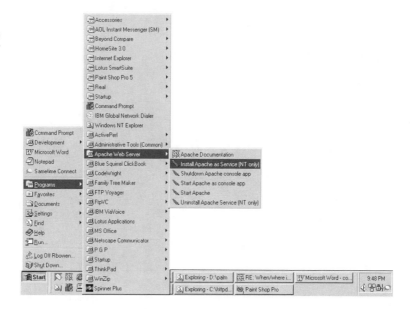

When you select this item from the Start menu, a DOS window will pop up briefly, and
then disappear. This menu item is a shortcut to the command

```
C:\httpd\Apache.exe -d C:\httpd -i
```

Or, if you have Apache installed elsewhere, such as the default `C:\Program
Files\Apache`, that path will appear in the command instead. The Windows-specific `-i`
command switch causes Apache to be installed as a Windows NT service. The `-d` switch
tells Apache what `ServerRoot` directory it should be starting in.

## Compiling Apache for Windows

Complete instructions are included in the documentation that comes with Apache.
The online version of these instructions can be seen at `http://www.apache.org/docs/
windows.html#comp`. Most users won't need to build Apache themselves on Windows,
and so this is left as an exercise for the reader. If you have a genuine need to build from
source code on Windows, you probably already know more than this book can teach you.

# Summary

On most platforms, you will need to build Apache yourself from source code. Binaries
are available for a large number of platforms, but in most cases you are better off obtaining the source code and compiling it yourself. A notable exception to this is Windows,
where you are encouraged to obtain the binary installation file and install that.

# Starting, Stopping, and Restarting the Server

**CHAPTER 4**

Depending on whether you are running Apache on Unix or Windows, there are different ways to start, stop, and restart the server. Apache can be started manually from the command line or as part of the server startup process. On Unix, the `apachectl` shell script gives you the ability to start, stop, and restart Apache from the command line without having to remember a lot of arcane switches.

# Starting Your Server

After you configure and install your server, it would be nice to be able to start it up. In most cases, you start the server by simply running its executable from the command line.

Under Unix and Unix-like operating systems, Apache is typically started when the machine boots, and then continues to run for as long as the machine is up. Startup can be done either manually from the command line or from a startup script.

Under Windows NT, Apache is usually run as a Windows NT service; in other versions of Windows, it's run as a console application.

## Starting Apache Under Unix

Under Unix, you can start Apache from the command line. You may also want to have Apache start automatically when your system boots.

### Starting at the Command Line Under Unix

You can start Apache from the command line on a Unix machine by simply typing the name of the `httpd` executable, with whatever command-line options you want. The Apache server process starts up, switches to running as the user specified in the `User` directive (see Chapter 5, "Server Configuration Files"), launches as many child processes as specified by the `StartServers` directive (also covered in Chapter 5), and returns control to the command line.

You invoke command-line options by simply including them after the `httpd` executable on the command line. For example, you would invoke the `-l` option by typing `httpd -l`. The following command-line options are available for Apache 1.3.9:

- `-d` *path* sets the initial value for the `ServerRoot` to *path*. This doesn't override the `ServerRoot` directive in your configuration file, because it's loaded after the command-line switches. The default location is /usr/local/apache on Unix, /apache on Windows, and /os2httpd on OS/2. Here's an example:

```
httpd -d /home/httpd/
```

- -D *name* sets a variable *name* to be used in <IfDefine> sections. See Chapter 5 for a more complete treatment of <IfDefine>. Here's an example:

  **httpd -D Qook**

  Then, in your httpd.conf file, you might have

  ```
  <IfDefine Qook>
  LogLevel info
  </IfDefine>
  ```

- -f *config* loads the configuration directives from the file *config*, instead of the default configuration file, which is conf/httpd.conf. *config* is assumed to be a path relative to the ServerRoot unless it starts with a leading slash (/). Here's an example:

  **httpd -f /home/httpd/conf/config.file**

- -C "*directive*" executes the given Apache directive before reading in the configuration files. Here's an example:

  **httpd -C "LoadModule status_module modules/mod_status.so"**

- -c "*directive*" is like -C, except that *directive* is processed *after* the configuration files are loaded. This is useful for overriding a directive in the configuration file. Here's an example:

  **httpd -c "TransferLog /tmp/test.log"**

- -X runs httpd in single-process mode, which means that Apache doesn't launch any additional children, but runs as just one process in the console window. This should be used for testing purposes only, never on a production machine. Here's an example:

  **httpd -X**

- -v prints the version of httpd and its build date, and then exits. Here's an example:

  ```
  httpd -v
  Server version: Apache/1.3.9 (Unix)
  Server built:   Aug 31 1999 21:07:00
  ```

- -V prints the base version of httpd, its build date, and a list of compile-time settings (such as -D USE_MMAP_FILES) that influence the Apache server's behavior and performance, and then exits. Here's an example:

  ```
  httpd -V
  Server version: Apache/1.3.9 (Unix)
  Server built:   Aug 31 1999 21:07:00
  Server's Module Magic Number: 19990320:6
  Server compiled with....
   -D HAVE_MMAP
   -D HAVE_SHMGET
   ...
  ```

4

STARTING,
STOPPING, AND
RESTARTING

```
-D ACCESS_CONFIG_FILE="conf/access.conf"
-D RESOURCE_CONFIG_FILE="conf/srm.conf"
```

- -L lists all configuration directives permitted with the modules you've installed.
  It also lists where these directives are permitted (that is, in the configuration files,
  in the .htaccess file, in <Directory> sections, and so on). This is very useful for
  generating a list of permitted directives customized for your particular setup.

- -l lists all modules compiled into the server, and then exits. Here's an example:

```
httpd -l
Compiled-in modules:
  http_core.c
  mod_env.c
  mod_log_config.c
...
  mod_setenvif.c
  mod_perl.c
```

- -h displays a list of available command line options—for example:

```
httpd -h
Usage: httpd [-D name] [-d directory] [-f file]
             [-C "directive"] [-c "directive"]
             [-v] [-V] [-h] [-l] [-L] [-S] [-t] [-T]
Options:
-D name        : define a name for use in <IfDefine name> directives
-d directory   : specify an alternate initial ServerRoot
-f file        : specify an alternate ServerConfigFile
-C "directive" : process directive before reading config files
-c "directive" : process directive after  reading config files
-v             : show version number
-V             : show compile settings
-h             : list available command line options (this page)
-l             : list compiled-in modules
-L             : list available configuration directives
-S             : show parsed settings (currently only vhost settings)
-t             : run syntax check for config files (with docroot check)
-T             : run syntax check for config files (without docroot check)
```

- -S shows the virtual host configuration from the configuration files. Each line of
  the report indicates in which line of the configuration file the particular virtual host
  entry is created. See the following example:

```
httpd -S
VirtualHost configuration:
192.101.204.10:80     is a NameVirtualHost
default server www.databeam.com (/home/www/apache/conf/httpd.conf:931)
port 80 namevhost www.databeam.com (/home/www/apache/conf/httpd.conf:931)
port 80 namevhost www2.databeam.com (/home/www/apache/conf/httpd.conf:965)
port 80 namevhost w3.databeam.com (/home/www/apache/conf/httpd.conf:982)
```

- `-t` tests the configuration files for correct syntax and checks to make sure that all `DocumentRoot` entries actually exist. If there are errors in the files, you will be informed what those errors are; otherwise, you will get a `Syntax OK` message. Here's an example:

```
httpd -t
Syntax error on line 65 of /usr/local/apache/conf/httpd.conf:
Invalid command 'ServeRooot', perhaps mis-spelled or defined by a
module not included in the server configuration
```

- `-T` is like `-t`, except that the validity of `DocumentRoot` directories isn't checked. As a result, this option runs much more quickly, particularly for sites with a lot of virtual hosts.

## Starting Automatically at Boot Time

All flavors of Unix provide some mechanism for automatically starting processes when your system boots. This will vary from one flavor of Unix to another, and you should consult your documentation or your local Unix guru for instructions on how to do this on your particular system. The `apachectl` script can be very useful in providing this functionality because it accepts `start` and `stop` as arguments, which is expected by `/etc/rc.d` scripts on flavors of Unix that support that mechanism. (See the section on `apachectl` near the end of this chapter.)

# Starting Apache Under Windows

On Windows, there are two main ways to start the Apache server: as a Windows NT service or as a console application.

## Running Apache as a Windows NT Service

If you are using the Windows NT version of Apache, you are probably already familiar with the concept of Windows NT services. They are essentially a way of running programs in the background as soon as Windows NT boots up, and keeping them running as long as Windows NT is up. They are similar in concept to daemons on Unix.

The primary benefit of running Apache as a Windows NT service is that you don't have to log in to the machine to restart the service when you restart the machine—it just starts automatically. This way, when you have to reboot Windows NT, you can be assured that Apache will restart when the machine comes back up.

When run as a service, Apache runs in the background—that is, there's no window or taskbar icon, but Apache shows up in the Task Manager's process list.

> **Note**
>
> See Chapter 3, "Compiling and Installing Apache," for instructions for installing Apache as a Windows NT service.

You can start a Windows NT service in several ways. Again, if you are running Windows NT, you are probably already somewhat familiar with Windows services. If not, here are some ways to start a Windows NT service.

## Starting Automatically on Reboot

The most recommended method is that you install Apache as a service set to start automatically on reboot. This is how the service is configured if you installed it from the Start menu shortcut.

To make sure that your service is set to start automatically, open the Services dialog from the Windows Control Panel. Figure 4.1 shows the Services dialog, with Apache set to start automatically.

**FIGURE 4.1**

*The Windows NT Services dialog with Apache set to start automatically.*

If you don't see the word Automatic in the column labeled Startup next to Apache in your Services dialog, select Apache and click the Startup button to see additional options for the service (see Figure 4.2). Select Automatic, so that Apache will start automatically when the system is rebooted.

**FIGURE 4.2**

*Apache service startup options.*

## Starting the Service Manually

If you don't want to have Apache running all the time, you may want to configure the Apache service to be started manually. This is done as explained previously, except that you select Manual as the preferred startup type.

You can then start the service in one of two ways:

- In the Services dialog (refer to Figure 4.1), select Apache and click the Start button. A dialog will appear telling you that the service is starting, and, if startup is successful, the Status indicator will change to Started. Figure 4.3 shows the Apache service being started in this way.

**FIGURE 4.3**

*Starting the Apache service manually.*

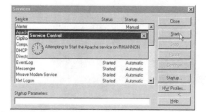

- You can start any service from the Run dialog or from a DOS command line with the command net start *service*, where *service* is the name of the service to be started. So, in the case of the Apache service, you would type **net start apache**.

### Note

There's one more way to start the Apache service. You can start services directly from the Win32 API via either the C interface, or any of the other interfaces available, such as Visual Basic or Perl. That's a little out of the scope of this book, however.

## Running Apache as a Console Application

The other way to run Apache on Windows systems is as a console application. This means that a DOS window will open and remain open for the duration of the Apache process. At this time, this is the only way that you can run Apache on Windows 95 and Windows 98 (hereafter collectively called *Win9x*) systems.

4

STARTING,
STOPPING, AND
RESTARTING

When you installed Apache, an icon labeled Start Apache as Console App was put in your Start menu. This shortcut runs the following command:

```
C:\apache\Apache.exe -d C:\httpd -s
```

Apache on Windows has mostly the same command-line switches as on Unix. So the `-d` switch, as described in the Unix discussion, specifies the `ServerRoot` with which the server should start. The `-s` flag is a Windows-specific flag indicating that Apache should run as a console application. Figure 4.4 shows Apache running as a console application.

**FIGURE 4.4**

*Apache running as a console application under Windows.*

> **Note**
>
> Because Win9*x* operating systems don't have a concept of services or daemons, you have to run Apache as a console application. This is probably okay because you're not likely to run a production Web site on a Win9*x* machine anyway.

# Stopping or Restarting Your Server

If, for some reason, you want to stop your Apache server, again there are different ways of doing this depending on whether you're using Unix or Windows. The most common reason for restarting your server is to reload configuration files if they have been changed.

## Stopping or Restarting Under Unix

On Unix and Unix-like operating systems (such as Linux), you usually stop your server with the `kill` command. The `kill` command is the Unix way of sending termination signals to a process and can be sent in a number of different ways.

Before you send the termination signals, however, you have to know who to send them to. If you look in the process list on your Unix machine, you will see more than one httpd process running. On my Linux machine, the process list looks something like this:

```
ps ax
 PID TTY STAT TIME COMMAND
...
 1599  ?  S    0:00 /usr/sbin/dhcpd
 1740  ?  S    0:04 /usr/sbin/named
 4278  ?  S    0:00 smbd -D
 4287  ?  S    0:14 nmbd -D
13634  ?  S    0:00 /usr/local/apache/bin/httpd
16614  ?  S    0:00 /usr/local/apache/bin/httpd
16615  ?  S    0:00 /usr/local/apache/bin/httpd
16616  ?  S    0:00 /usr/local/apache/bin/httpd
16617  ?  S    0:00 /usr/local/apache/bin/httpd
16618  ?  S    0:00 /usr/local/apache/bin/httpd
16620  ?  S    0:00 /usr/local/apache/bin/httpd
16621  ?  S    0:00 /usr/local/apache/bin/httpd
16629  ?  S    0:00 /usr/local/apache/bin/httpd
16630  ?  S    0:00 /usr/local/apache/bin/httpd
16631  ?  S    0:00 /usr/local/apache/bin/httpd
11630  ?  S    0:02 ./msql2d
13866  1  S    0:00 sh /usr/X11R6/bin/startx
26529 p0  S    0:00 -tcsh
26541 p0  R    0:00 ps ax
```

My machine shows 11 httpd processes running. One is the parent process and the rest are the child processes. If I terminate any of the child processes, the parent process will just respawn the child (like the heads of the hydra), and I will have accomplished nothing.

> **Note**
>
> Of course, in this case, I could make a reasonable guess that the process with the lower PID (process ID) is the parent, and the rest are the children. In this case, I was actually right, but in general, you can't be sure.

**4**

STARTING, STOPPING, AND RESTARTING

The way to be sure that you are terminating the right process is to look in the PidFile for the PID of the parent process. The PidFile file is, by default, located in the logs directory and is called httpd.pid. You can change this location with the PidFile directive in your configuration file. See Chapter 5 for more information on the PidFile directive.

The PidFile contains just one line, with the PID of the parent httpd process.

## Stopping Apache

To stop Apache immediately, issue the `kill -TERM` command to the process ID listed in the `httpd.pid` file. For example, you would type the following command at the command line:

```
kill -TERM `cat /usr/local/apache/logs/httpd.pid`
```

This might take a few seconds, as the parent process will attempt to kill off each of its children, and then will kill itself.

## Restarting Apache

There are two ways to restart your Apache server, depending on how quickly you want the restart to happen:

- To restart immediately, use a `HUP` signal. For example, you would type the following command:

  ```
  kill -HUP `cat /usr/local/apache/logs/httpd.pid`
  ```

  The `HUP` signal causes the parent to kill off all its children immediately. Any requests being served by these children are simply dropped. It then rereads the configuration files and reopens the log files. Then it respawns a new set of children, which immediately start serving requests.

- To restart gracefully, use the `USR1` signal. For example, you would type the following command:

  ```
  kill -USR1 `cat /usr/local/apache/logs/httpd.pid`
  ```

  The `USR1` signal tells the parent to send a termination request to each child. Each child will finish serving the request that it's currently serving, and then exit. If it's idle, it will exit immediately. The parent reloads the configuration files and reopens the log files. As the children exit, they are replaced by a new generation of children with the new configuration settings.

The graceful method is probably preferable for a production server, as it won't cause existing connections to be dropped unceremoniously, but will complete any transactions active at the time of the restart.

## Stopping and Restarting Under Windows

How you stop and restart the Apache server under Windows depends on how you are running the server—as a service or as a console application.

## Stopping and Restarting the Apache Service

With Apache installed as a Windows NT service, there are two ways to stop the service.

The first way is to stop the service from the Services dialog, which you can access from the Control Panel. Select the Apache service and click the Stop button. You will see a timer as you did when starting the service, and the service will be shut down.

Unlike Unix, which spawns multiple child processes, on Windows NT, there's just the main parent process, and one child process that serves all the requests. This is because on Windows NT, Apache is multithreaded, so the one child process can handle multiple requests at the same time.

When you stop the service, the parent kills off the child process, and then exits.

The other way to stop the Apache service is by typing **net stop apache** in the Run dialog or from a DOS command line.

> **Note**
>
> As with starting the service, you can also stop the service directly from the Win32 API. That is beyond the scope of this book.

There's no single-step method for restarting a Windows NT service. Follow the instructions for stopping the service, and then follow the instructions for starting the service.

## Stopping the Windows Console Application

If you have Apache running as a console application, as described earlier, you can stop the server in a few different ways.

When Apache was installed, an icon was placed in your Start menu to shut down the Apache console app. Selecting this menu item will stop Apache if it's running as a console application. (This won't stop Apache if it's running as a Windows NT service.) The icon on the Start menu is a shortcut to the following command:

```
C:\httpd\Apache.exe -d C:\httpd -k shutdown
```

The -k command-line option is a Windows-only option and can take one of two arguments: shutdown or restart. These arguments are the equivalent of the -TERM and -USR1 signals under Unix.

# The apachectl Script

On a Unix installation of Apache, you have a shell script called `apachectl`, which will relieve you from having to remember the myriad ways of starting, restarting, and stopping your server. `apachectl` should be included in the `/src/support` directory of your Apache distribution; after you build Apache, it will contain the correct paths for everything on your system.

## Using apachectl

Using `apachectl` is very straightforward. Simply running `apachectl` from the command line (or with the `help` argument) shows you all the available options:

```
apachectl
usage: /usr/bin/apachectl (start|stop|restart|fullstatus|
➥status|graceful|configtest|help)

start      - start httpd
stop       - stop httpd
restart    - restart httpd if running by sending a SIGHUP or start if
             not running
fullstatus - dump a full status screen; requires lynx and mod_status
             enabled
status     - dump a short status screen; requires lynx and mod_status
             enabled
graceful   - do a graceful restart by sending a SIGUSR1 or start if
             not running
configtest - do a configuration syntax test
help       - this screen
```

`apachectl` is simply a `/bin/sh` script containing some command-line options and `kill` functions already discussed in this chapter. There's nothing complicated going on, but it puts it all in one convenient place so that there's nothing to remember.

## Configuring apachectl

`apachectl` contains four variables that you may need to configure for your system:

- `PIDFILE` lists the location of your process ID file. This is usually located in the `logs` directory with the other log files, but can be configured with the `PidFile` directive. If you change this for some reason, you will need to change it in your `apachectl` script also. See the following example:

  `PIDFILE=/usr/local/apache/logs/httpd.pid`

- `HTTPD` is the path to your `httpd` binary file. Here's an example:

  `HTTPD=/usr/local/apache/bin/httpd`

- LYNX is the command line for running Lynx on your system. This is for displaying status screens when using the status and fullstatus arguments. This is necessary only if you have mod_status enabled. See the chapters in Part V, "Development," for more information on mod_status. Here's an example:

  LYNX="lynx -dump"

- STATUSURL is the URL for the status page on your server, if you have mod_status enabled. This is for the status and fullstatus arguments. Here's an example:

  STATUSURL="http://localhost/server-status"

Listing 4.1 shows the apachectl shell script with the default values for these variables.

**LISTING 4.1**    Default apachectl Values

```
#!/bin/sh
#
# Apache control script designed to allow an easy command line interface
# to controlling Apache. Written by Marc Slemko, 1997/08/23
#
# The exit codes returned are:
#       0 - operation completed successfully
#       1 -
#       2 - usage error
#       3 - httpd could not be started
#       4 - httpd could not be stopped
#       5 - httpd could not be started during a restart
#       6 - httpd could not be restarted during a restart
#       7 - httpd could not be restarted during a graceful restart
#       8 - configuration syntax error
#
# When multiple arguments are given, only the error from the _last_
# one is reported.  Run "apachectl help" for usage info
#
#
# |||||||||||||||||||||| START CONFIGURATION SECTION  ||||||||||||||||||||||
# --------------------                        --------------------
#
# the path to your PID file
PIDFILE=/usr/local/apache/logs/httpd.pid
#
# the path to your httpd binary, including options if necessary
HTTPD=/usr/local/apache/bin/httpd
#
# a command that outputs a formatted text version of the HTML at the
# url given on the command line. Designed for lynx, however other
# programs may work.
LYNX="lynx -dump"
#
```

*continues*

**LISTING 4.1**    continued

```
# the URL to your server's mod_status status page. If you do not
# have one, then status and fullstatus will not work.
STATUSURL="http://localhost/server-status"
#
# --------------------                        --------------------
# |||||||||||||||||||||    END CONFIGURATION SECTION    |||||||||||||||||||||

ERROR=0
ARGV="$@"
if [ "x$ARGV" = "x" ] ; then
    ARGS="help"
fi

for ARG in $@ $ARGS
do
    # check for pidfile
    if [ -f $PIDFILE ] ; then
        PID=`cat $PIDFILE`
        if [ "x$PID" != "x" ] && kill -0 $PID 2>/dev/null ; then
            STATUS="httpd (pid $PID) running"
            RUNNING=1
        else
            STATUS="httpd (pid $PID?) not running"
            RUNNING=0
        fi
    else
        STATUS="httpd (no pid file) not running"
        RUNNING=0
    fi

    case $ARG in
    start)
        if [ $RUNNING -eq 1 ]; then
            echo "$0 $ARG: httpd (pid $PID) already running"
            continue
        fi
        if $HTTPD ; then
            echo "$0 $ARG: httpd started"
        else
            echo "$0 $ARG: httpd could not be started"
            ERROR=3
        fi
        ;;
    stop)
        if [ $RUNNING -eq 0 ]; then
            echo "$0 $ARG: $STATUS"
            continue
        fi
        if kill $PID ; then
```

```
            echo "$0 $ARG: httpd stopped"
        else
            echo "$0 $ARG: httpd could not be stopped"
            ERROR=4
        fi
        ;;
restart)
    if [ $RUNNING -eq 0 ]; then
        echo "$0 $ARG: httpd not running, trying to start"
        if $HTTPD ; then
            echo "$0 $ARG: httpd started"
        else
            echo "$0 $ARG: httpd could not be started"
            ERROR=5
        fi
    else
        if $HTTPD -t >/dev/null 2>&1; then
            if kill -HUP $PID ; then
                echo "$0 $ARG: httpd restarted"
            else
                echo "$0 $ARG: httpd could not be restarted"
                ERROR=6
            fi
        else
            echo "$0 $ARG: configuration broken, ignoring restart"
            echo "$0 $ARG: (run 'apachectl configtest' for details)"
            ERROR=6
        fi
    fi
    ;;
graceful)
    if [ $RUNNING -eq 0 ]; then
        echo "$0 $ARG: httpd not running, trying to start"
        if $HTTPD ; then
            echo "$0 $ARG: httpd started"
        else
            echo "$0 $ARG: httpd could not be started"
            ERROR=5
        fi
    else
        if $HTTPD -t >/dev/null 2>&1; then
            if kill -USR1 $PID ; then
        echo "$0 $ARG: httpd gracefully restarted"
    else
        echo "$0 $ARG: httpd could not be restarted"
        ERROR=7
    fi
    else
        echo "$0 $ARG: configuration broken, ignoring restart"
```

*continues*

**4**

**STARTING, STOPPING, AND RESTARTING**

**LISTING 4.1**    continued

```
            echo "$0 $ARG: (run 'apachectl configtest' for details)"
            ERROR=7
            fi
    fi
    ;;
    status)
    $LYNX $STATUSURL | awk ' /process$/ { print; exit } { print } '
    ;;
    fullstatus)
    $LYNX $STATUSURL
    ;;
    configtest)
    if $HTTPD -t; then
        :
    else
        ERROR=8
    fi
    ;;
    *)
    echo "usage: $0
      ➥(start|stop|restart|fullstatus|status|graceful|configtest|help)"
    cat <<EOF

start      - start httpd
stop       - stop httpd
restart    - restart httpd if running by sending a SIGHUP or start if
             not running
fullstatus - dump a full status screen; requires lynx and mod_status enabled
status     - dump a short status screen; requires lynx and mod_status enabled
graceful   - do a graceful restart by sending a SIGUSR1 or start if not running
configtest - do a configuration syntax test
help       - this screen

EOF
    ERROR=2
    ;;

    esac

done

exit $ERROR

# ====================================================================
# Copyright (c)1995-1999 The Apache Group.  All rights reserved.
#
# Redistribution and use in source and binary forms, with or without
# modification, are permitted provided that the following conditions
# are met:
```

```
#
# 1. Redistributions of source code must retain the above copyright
#    notice, this list of conditions and the following disclaimer.
#
# 2. Redistributions in binary form must reproduce the above copyright
#    notice, this list of conditions and the following disclaimer in
#    the documentation and/or other materials provided with the
#    distribution.
#
# 3. All advertising materials mentioning features or use of this
#    software must display the following acknowledgment:
#    "This product includes software developed by the Apache Group
#    for use in the Apache HTTP server project (http://www.apache.org/)."
#
# 4. The names "Apache Server" and "Apache Group" must not be used to
#    endorse or promote products derived from this software without
#    prior written permission. For written permission, please contact
#    apache@apache.org.
#
# 5. Products derived from this software may not be called "Apache"
#    nor may "Apache" appear in their names without prior written
#    permission of the Apache Group.
#
# 6. Redistributions of any form whatsoever must retain the following
#    acknowledgment:
#    "This product includes software developed by the Apache Group
#    for use in the Apache HTTP server project (http://www.apache.org/)."
#
# THIS SOFTWARE IS PROVIDED BY THE APACHE GROUP ``AS IS'' AND ANY
# EXPRESSED OR IMPLIED WARRANTIES, INCLUDING, BUT NOT LIMITED TO, THE
# IMPLIED WARRANTIES OF MERCHANTABILITY AND FITNESS FOR A PARTICULAR
# PURPOSE ARE DISCLAIMED.  IN NO EVENT SHALL THE APACHE GROUP OR
# ITS CONTRIBUTORS BE LIABLE FOR ANY DIRECT, INDIRECT, INCIDENTAL,
# SPECIAL, EXEMPLARY, OR CONSEQUENTIAL DAMAGES (INCLUDING, BUT
# NOT LIMITED TO, PROCUREMENT OF SUBSTITUTE GOODS OR SERVICES;
# LOSS OF USE, DATA, OR PROFITS; OR BUSINESS INTERRUPTION)
# HOWEVER CAUSED AND ON ANY THEORY OF LIABILITY, WHETHER IN CONTRACT,
# STRICT LIABILITY, OR TORT (INCLUDING NEGLIGENCE OR OTHERWISE)
# ARISING IN ANY WAY OUT OF THE USE OF THIS SOFTWARE, EVEN IF ADVISED
# OF THE POSSIBILITY OF SUCH DAMAGE.
# ====================================================================
#
# This software consists of voluntary contributions made by many
# individuals on behalf of the Apache Group and was originally based
# on public domain software written at the National Center for
# Supercomputing Applications, University of Illinois, Urbana-Champaign.
# For more information on the Apache Group and the Apache HTTP server
# project, please see <http://www.apache.org/>.
#
```

4

STARTING,
STOPPING, AND
RESTARTING

# Summary

Depending on what operating system you are running, you can start, stop, and restart your Apache server in various ways. Windows NT services provide a way for Apache to run in the background like a Unix daemon. The `apachectl` script provides a nice easy front end to many of the options for Apache on Unix systems.

# Configuring Apache

# PART

# II

## IN THIS PART

# Server Configuration Files

The behavior of the Apache server is defined in the server configuration file `httpd.conf`. This chapter covers all the directives that can go into that configuration file and what they do to the server.

# One File Versus Three

Traditionally (since the NCSA days), Apache configuration was split into three configurations files: `httpd.conf`, `access.conf`, and `srm.conf`. Over time, the distinction of what went into one file or another became increasingly blurred and so, as of Apache version 1.3.4, the three files are merged into one configuration file. You can still use three files if you really want to, but there's not much point unless you are upgrading from an existing installation and just want to keep your configuration files.

> **Note**
>
> Using your old configuration files typically isn't such a great idea, because you might either miss out on a feature addition between versions or use syntax for a directive that has been changed for the new version.

In the former way of doing things, `httpd.conf` was the main server configuration file, `access.conf` was the file defining access permissions, and `srm.conf` defined server resources, such as directory mappings and icons. Older server documentation refers to these files, so it's nice to know what they were for.

But even if you have an older version of Apache and, for some reason, don't want to upgrade, you can still use the one-file configuration by concatenating the three files into `httpd.conf` and keeping `srm.conf` and `access.conf` as empty files in the `conf` directory.

> **Tip**
>
> See `http://www.apache.org/info/three-config-files.html` for more discussion of this topic.

# Core and Base Configuration Directives

Apache 1.3's documentation lists 193 Apache directives. Most of these aren't used in the default configuration files, so if you use just the defaults, you will miss out on many of the cool features available.

**Note**

Directive names are not case sensitive. Although the convention is to have initial capitals, such as BrowserMatchNoCase, this doesn't really matter.

The following sections describe the available configuration directives classified as *core* or *base*. In other words, these directives are available to you if you have a standard Apache installation and haven't included any non-standard modules. This brings the list down to about 140.

**Note**

This notation is the same as that used in the Apache documentation, for the sake of consistency.

For each directive, the following will be defined:

- **Syntax:** The directive's format as it should appear in the configuration file.
- **Default:** The default value of the setting, if any.
- **Context:** Which configuration file the directive can appear in. Four possible locations can be listed here, or some combination of these locations, if they are permitted in more than one location.

**Caution**

If you put a directive where it's not permitted, the server won't function correctly and may not even start.

The four possible locations are as follows:

| | |
|---|---|
| Server config | The directive may appear in the server configuration files, but not within <VirtualHost> or <Directory> sections. |
| Virtual host | The directive may appear in <VirtualHost> sections. |
| Directory | The directive may appear in <Directory> sections. |
| .htaccess | The directive may appear in .htaccess files. Depending on the override settings in effect for the relevant directory, the directive may or may not actually be honored. |

- **Override:** Indicates which override must be in effect for the directive to be honored in a `.htaccess` file. This is, of course, relevant only for directives permitted in `.htaccess` files. See the `AllowOverride` directive for more details.

- **Status:** Indicates whether this directive is part of the core Apache code or part of an add-on module. Possible values are as follows:

| | |
|---|---|
| Core | Indicates that the directive is part of the core Apache code and so is always available. |
| Base | Indicates that the directive is part of one of the modules usually compiled into the server by default and so is usually available unless you intentionally removed it. |
| Extension | Indicates that the directive is part of one of the modules available with Apache but isn't compiled in by default, so it won't be available unless you intentionally add that module. |
| Experimental | Indicates that the directive is available with Apache, but it's not really recommended that you use it on a production server, since it's not really supported. |

This chapter will focus on only those directives classified as core and base. For other directives, see the chapters relating to the modules in which those directives are defined. For a full list of available directives, see the file `mod/directives.html` in the HTML documentation that came with your Apache installation.

- **Module:** Indicates which module defines the directive.

- **Compatibility:** Indicates which versions of Apache can be expected to support this directive.

---

**Caution**

Keep backup copies of your configuration files before you experiment!

---

## AccessConfig

**Syntax:** `AccessConfig` *filename*

**Default:** `AccessConfig conf/access.conf`

**Context:** Server config, virtual host

**Status:** Core

This directive indicates the location of the access configuration file. The filename is assumed to be relative to `ServerRoot` (see `ServerRoot`) unless an absolute path is specified. The `AccessConfig` file is read and parsed after the `ResourceConfig` file (see `ResourceConfig`).

If you want to disable this feature, use the following:

```
AccessConfig /dev/null
```

or, for Apache on Windows NT

```
AccessConfig nul
```

The default configuration is to have the file actually exist but contain nothing but a comment explaining that it's there just as a placeholder.

Historically, `access.conf` contained `<Directory>` sections that set server configurations per directory, but it can actually contain any directives that are valid in any server configuration file.

## AccessFileName

**Syntax:** `AccessFileName` *filename filename* ...

**Default:** `AccessFileName .htaccess`

**Context:** Server config, virtual host

**Status:** Core

**Compatibility:** Listing multiple filenames works only in Apache 1.3 and later.

When serving any document, the server looks for this file in the directory containing the document being served and in every directory in the path leading up to the file, if access control files are permitted for that directory. For this reason, it is much more efficient to have these settings in the main server configuration files, rather than in these access control files.

For example, if you have the directive

```
AccessFileName .control
```

and are serving the file `/docs/modules/core/index.html`, the server will look for directives in the files `/.control`, `/docs/.control`, `/docs/modules/.control`, and `/docs/modules/core/.control` before serving the file. Directives are overridden by directives in subdirectories.

To disallow the use of access control files, use

```
<Directory />
AllowOverride None
</Directory>
```

Or, you can disallow their use for only a particular portion of your site with

```
<Directory /docs>
AllowOverride None
</Directory>
```

You might want to set this directive to something other than the default value if you are using Apache on Windows NT; some Windows NT applications have some difficulty with the filename .htaccess. A good alternative is htaccess (without the leading .). Depending on what application you're using to edit your configuration files, this may not matter.

> **Tip**
>
> To make editing .htaccess files easier on Windows NT, you can define .htaccess as a file type and set a certain application (such as Notepad) to always open it. You won't be able to name the file .htaccess in Windows Explorer, so open a DOS window and rename the file by hand (ren htaccess .htaccess). Then, open Windows Explorer, navigate to the directory, and Shift+right-click the file. Choose Open With from the pop-up menu; you will see a list of programs you can use to open the file. Select the program you want, and then check the Always Use This Program to Open This Type of File check box. From now on, you can double-click .htaccess to open it in that application.

## Action

**Syntax:** Action *action-type cgi-script*

**Context:** Server config, virtual host, directory, .htaccess

**Override:** FileInfo

**Status:** Base

**Module:** mod_actions

**Compatibility:** Apache 1.1 and later

The Action directive allows you to specify a CGI program to be invoked whenever a file of a particular type is requested. This could be used to process files in a particular way for display. For example, if you had company press releases that had to be displayed in a particular template, you could simply store the text of the press release in a .release file and then call a formatting CGI program whenever one of these files was requested. To do this, you might put the following directives in your .htaccess file:

```
AddType text/press-release .release
Action text/press-release /cgi-bin/press_releases/formatter.pl
```

Each time a .release file is requested, the specified CGI program is called. The particular file requested can be determined by the PATH_INFO or PATH_TRANSLATED variable.

## AddAlt

**Syntax:** AddAlt *string file file...*

**Context:** Server config, virtual host, directory, .htaccess

**Override:** Indexes

**Status:** Base

**Module:** mod_autoindex

When FancyIndexing is turned on, this directive specifies the alternative text to display in place of an icon for an automatically generated index of filenames. The *file* parameter here is a file extension, a partial filename, a wild-card expression, or an actual filename for which this text is to be displayed. This text is displayed for clients that can't display images or have image loading disabled.

```
AddAlt "Perl program" .pl
```

See the discussion of the mod_autoindex module in Chapter 20, "Using Standard Apache Modules," for more information on auto-indexing.

## AddAltByEncoding

**Syntax:** AddAltByEncoding *string MIME-encoding MIME-encoding...*

**Context:** Server config, virtual host, directory, .htaccess

**Override:** Indexes

**Status:** Base

**Module:** mod_autoindex

Much like `AddAlt`, `AddAltByEncoding` specifies text to display in place of an icon in automatically generated file listings when `FancyIndexing` is turned on. The *MIME-encoding* parameter is any valid MIME content encoding, such as `x-texinfo` or `x-realaudio`. This text is displayed for clients that can't display images or have image loading disabled.

`AddAltByEncoding "Macintosh compressed file" x-stuffit`

## AddAltByType

**Syntax:** `AddAltByType` *string MIME-type MIME-type ...*

**Context:** Server config, virtual host, directory, `.htaccess`

**Override:** `Indexes`

**Status:** Base

**Module:** `mod_autoindex`

`AddAltByType` sets the alternative text to display in place of an icon in an automatically generated file index. *MIME-type* is any valid content type, such as `image/png` or `text/html`. This text is displayed for clients that can't display images or have image loading disabled.

`AddAltByType "Chess portable game notation file" application/x-chess-pgn`

## AddDescription

**Syntax:** `AddDescription` *string file file...*

**Context:** Server config, virtual host, directory, `.htaccess`

**Override:** `Indexes`

**Status:** Base

**Module:** `mod_autoindex`

`AddDescription` provides a description for individual files in indexes generated by `FancyIndexing`. The *file* parameter can be a file extension, a wild card, a partial filename, or a whole filename:

`AddDescription "My ugly mug" /images/photos/rich.jpg`

The description parameter can be no longer than 23 characters because `FancyIndexing` generates fixed-width columns to display the index information. This number can be increased by an additional 7 characters if `IndexOptions SuppressSize` is turned on, and another 19 characters if `IndexOptions SuppressLastModified` is on, for a maximum total of 49 characters.

## AddEncoding

**Syntax:** AddEncoding *MIME-enc extension extension...*

**Context:** Server config, virtual host, directory, .htaccess

**Override:** FileInfo

**Status:** Base

**Module:** mod_mime

This directive maps the specified file extensions to the specified MIME encoding. That is, files with these extensions will be marked as being encoded using that encoding.

The following example marks files with the gz extension as having x-gzip encoding:

```
AddEncoding x-gzip gz
```

## AddHandler

**Syntax:** AddHandler *handler-name extension extension...*

**Context:** Server config, virtual host, directory, .htaccess

**Override:** FileInfo

**Status:** Base

**Module:** mod_mime

**Compatibility:** Apache 1.1 and later

This directive adds a handler to files with a particular extension.

The following example adds the handler cgi-script to all files with the extension .pl, which means that all files with that extension are treated as CGI programs, regardless of the directory they are in.

```
AddHandler cgi-script pl
```

Other handlers include server-status, for generating server status reports, imap-file, for server-side imagemaps, and server-parsed, for documents containing SSI directives. See Chapter 14, "Handlers," for more information.

**5**

**SERVER CONFIGURATION FILES**

## AddIcon

**Syntax:** AddIcon *icon name name* ...

**Context:** Server config, virtual host, directory, .htaccess

**Override:** Indexes

**Status:** Base

**Module:** mod_autoindex

AddIcon sets a particular icon to be displayed in automatically generated directory indexes, when the FancyIndexing directive is in effect. *icon* should be either a relative URL for the icon or the format (*alttext,url*), where *alttext* is the alternative text that is to appear for clients that don't display graphics.

*name* is either a file extension, a wildcard expression, a partial filename, or a complete filename. It can also be ^^DIRECTORY^^ for directories or ^^BLANKICON^^ for blank lines.

The following examples are from the default httpd.conf:

```
AddIcon /icons/bomb.gif core
AddIcon /icons/folder.gif ^^DIRECTORY^^
AddIcon /icons/compressed.gif .Z .z .tgz .gz .zip
```

## AddIconByEncoding

**Syntax:** AddIconByEncoding *icon MIME-encoding MIME-encoding*

**Context:** Server config, virtual host, directory, .htaccess

**Override:** Indexes

**Status:** Base

**Module:** mod_autoindex

This directive sets the icon to be displayed in automatically generated directory listings, when FancyIndexing is in effect. Unlike AddIcon, which sets icons based on filename, AddIconByEncoding adds icons based on the MIME encoding of the files. This directive should be used instead of AddIcon whenever possible.

```
AddIconByEncoding /icons/compress.xbm x-compress
```

## AddIconByType

**Syntax:** AddIconByType *icon MIME-type* [*MIME-type* ...]

**Context:** Server config, virtual host, directory, .htaccess

**Override:** `Indexes`

**Status:** Base

**Module:** `mod_autoindex`

This sets the icon to display for files of a particular MIME-type, when `FancyIndexing` is in effect. As with `AddIcon`, *icon* is either a relative URL to the icon to be displayed or the format (*alttext,url*), where *alttext* is the alternative text to be displayed in browsers that can't display graphics.

```
AddIconByType (SND,/icons/sound2.gif) audio/*
```

## AddLanguage

**Syntax:** `AddLanguage` *MIME-lang extension extension...*

**Context:** Server config, virtual host, directory, `.htaccess`

**Override:** `FileInfo`

**Status:** Base

**Module:** `mod_mime`

`AddLanguage` maps the given file extensions to a particular language. This directive is used most commonly for content negotiation, where the server returns the document that most closely matched the preferences set by the client—in this case, the client's preferred language.

```
AddLanguage en .en
AddLanguage fr .fr
```

This language is set in addition to any encoding set for the file, so that files with multiple file extensions end up doing the right thing. For example, with the following directives, the file `myfile.gz.es` will be seen by the server as a `gzip`'ed Spanish file, and so will the file `myfile.es.gz`:

```
AddEncoding AddEncoding x-gzip gz
AddLanguage es .es
```

For more on content negotiation, see the discussion on `mod_negotiation` in Chapter 20.

---

**Tip**

For multilingual sites, you might put several versions of the same file in a directory, distinguishing them with these file extensions. Content negotiation will cause the correct file to be served to the client, based on the language preference set on the client.

---

## AddModule

**Syntax:** AddModule *module module* ...

**Context:** Server config

**Status:** Core

**Compatibility:** Apache 1.2 and later

AddModule activates a module. Some modules are compiled into the server but aren't necessarily loaded.

## AddType

**Syntax:** AddType *MIME-type extension extension...*

**Context:** Server config, virtual host, directory, .htaccess

**Override:** FileInfo

**Status:** Base

**Module:** mod_mime

This directive sets files with particular extensions to the specified *MIME-type*. This overrides any settings already in effect. Rather than edit the mime.types file, use the AddType directive.

AddType file/download .dnl

## Alias

**Syntax:** Alias *url-path directory-filename*

**Context:** Server config, virtual host

**Status:** Base

**Module:** mod_alias

The Alias directive allows you to place Web content in a directory outside the ordinary DocumentRoot directory. URLs beginning with the specified *url-path* will be served from the specified *directory*.

Alias /perldocs /usr/docs/perl/html

> **Note**
>
> For CGI directories, you need to use `ScriptAlias`.

## AliasMatch

**Syntax:** AliasMatch *regex directory-filename*

**Context:** Server config, virtual host

**Status:** Base

**Module:** mod_alias

**Compatibility:** Apache 1.3 and later

This directive is roughly equivalent to `Alias` except that, instead of a specific URL path, you can redirect anything that matches a given regular expression. This allows for aliasing several possible spellings (or misspellings) of a URL. The following example provides an alias for `/pix`, `/pics`, `/pictures`, and several other combinations that I might not have anticipated, as long as they begin with `pix` or `pic`:

```
AliasMatch ^/pi(c|x)(.*) /home/ftp/pub/images
```

## allow

**Syntax:** allow from *host host* ...

**Context:** Directory, .htaccess

**Override:** Limit

**Status:** Base

**Module:** mod_access

This directive limits which hosts can request content from a particular directory. *host* can be one of the following:

- `all`   All hosts are permitted:

  `allow from all`

- A domain name   All hosts that match or end in the given string are permitted. This compares the whole name, so that `bowen.com` doesn't match `rcbowen.com`.

  `allow from .mk.net`

- An IP address   A host with that exact IP address is permitted:

  `allow from 192.101.203.72`

- A partial IP address    The first 1 to 3 bytes of an IP address can be used. All hosts in that subnet are permitted access.

  `allow from 192.101.203`

- A network and a netmask    Hosts on the included subnets are permitted.

  `allow from 192.101.0.0/255.255.0.0`

  A network and a netmask in terms of number of high-order bits are also allowed:

  `allow from 192.101.0.0/16`

See also deny.

> **Note**
>
> allow, deny, and require are the only Apache directives that begin with a lowercase letter. This is a holdover from the NCSA days and doesn't have any real significance. Directives aren't case sensitive.

> **Note**
>
> There are two forms of the allow directive—allow and allow from env=—that provide two different (although similar) functions.

## allow from env=

**Syntax:** `allow from env=variablename`

**Context:** Directory, `.htaccess`

**Override:** `Limit`

**Status:** Base

**Module:** `mod_access`

**Compatibility:** Apache 1.2 and later

Similar to `allow`, this directive permits hosts with a certain environment variable set. This is usually used with `BrowserMatch` or `SetEnvIf` to allow access to directories based on certain inobvious requirements. The following example denies access to a directory for all clients except those with a `UserAgent` string containing `MSIE`:

```
BrowserMatch MSIE ie
    <Directory /docroot>
        order deny,allow
```

```
        deny from all
        allow from env=ie
</Directory>
```

See also deny, BrowserMatch, order, and <Directory>.

## AllowOverride

**Syntax:** AllowOverride *override override* ...

**Default:** AllowOverride All

**Context:** Directory

**Status:** Core

AllowOverride specifies what parts of the configuration can be overridden in .htaccess files. This can be set to All, in which case all settings in .htaccess files are honored; None, in which case the file isn't even read; or any combination of the following.

- AuthConfig allows use of authorization directives—that is, any directive specifying who can get access to a directory.
- FileInfo allows use of directives setting document types.
- Indexes allows use of directives controlling automatically generated directory indexes.
- Limit allows use of directives controlling host access (allow, deny, and order).
- Options allows use of directives controlling specific directory features (Options and XBitHack).

If you intend to make all configuration settings for the whole server in the configuration files, set AllowOverride none. However, if you will have anyone else providing Web site content, being able to change directory settings without having access to the configuration files is very convenient for them. It also allows you make configuration changes per directory without restarting the server.

## AuthAuthoritative

**Syntax:** AuthAuthoritative on|off

**Context:** Directory, .htaccess

**Default:** AuthAuthoritative on

**Override:** AuthConfig

**Status:** Base

**Module:** mod_auth

This directive specifies whether the standard authentication rules are authoritative, or if control should be passed to one of the lower lever authentication modules such as mod_auth_db, mod_auth_msql, mod_auth_anon, or mod_auth_dbm.

Don't set AuthAuthoritative to off unless you are sure that you know what you are doing, as it circumvents the normal methods of protecting Web site content.
See Chapter 16, "Authentication."

## AuthDigestFile

**Syntax:** AuthDigestFile *filename*

**Context:** Directory, .htaccess

**Override:** AuthConfig

**Status:** Base

**Module:** mod_digest

AuthDigestFile sets the location of the file containing the user IDs and encrypted passwords for authentication using MD5 Digest authentication (see Chapter 16). Place this file outside the document root so that someone can't download the file to crack at his leisure.

```
AuthDigestFile /home/httpd/passwd/.htdigest
```

## AuthGroupFile

**Syntax:** AuthGroupFile *filename*

**Context:** Directory, .htaccess

**Override:** AuthConfig

**Status:** Base

**Module:** mod_auth

This directive sets the location of the file containing group definitions for user authentication. In that file, groups are specified by the group name, followed by a colon and the list of users, separated by spaces:

```
authgroup: rich tim eddie carol
```

Each username should correspond to a user in the password file specified by
AuthUserFile or AuthDigestFile.

AuthGroupFile /home/httpd/passwd/.htgroup

> **Note**
>
> For very large groups, consider using the more efficient AuthDBMGroupFile.
> See Chapter 16.

## AuthType

**Syntax:** AuthType *type*

**Context:** Directory, .htaccess

**Override:** AuthConfig

**Status:** Core

AuthType specifies the *type* of authentication to be used: Basic or Digest. Since Digest
isn't supported by most available browsers, it's recommended that you use Basic for
public Internet sites.

## AuthUserFile

**Syntax:** AuthUserFile *filename*

**Context:** Directory, .htaccess

**Override:** AuthConfig

**Status:** Base

**Module:** mod_auth

This directive sets the location of the file containing the user IDs and encrypted passwords of users allowed access to this directory. For very large sets of users, use
AuthDBMUserFile. See Chapter 16.

> **Note**
>
> Make sure that the user file is placed outside DocumentRoot; otherwise, some-
> one could download the file to crack at his leisure.

## BindAddress

**Syntax:** BindAddress *address*

**Default:** BindAddress *

**Context:** Server config

**Status:** Core

BindAddress specifies which IP address the server should watch for connections. By default, if the machine has multiple IP addresses, the server will listen on all of them for HTTP requests. *address* can be either * (to listen to all addresses), an IP address, or a fully qualified domain name:

BindAddress www.mk.net

See also Listen.

## BrowserMatch

**Syntax:** BrowserMatch *regex envar[=value]* [...]

**Context:** Server config

**Status:** Base

**Module:** mod_setenvif (in Apache 1.2: mod_browser, now obsolete)

**Compatibility:** Apache 1.2 and later

BrowserMatch defines one or more environment variables based on text found in the User-Agent HTTP header. This is useful for directives such as allow if env= and deny if env= and can also be used in CGI programs.

The same effect can be attained with the SetEnvIf directive.

BrowserMatch MSIE InternetExplorer=yes

### Note

The regular expression matching for BrowserMatch is case sensitive. For case-insensitive matching, see BrowserMatchNoCase.

## BrowserMatchNoCase

**Syntax:** `BrowserMatchNoCase` *regex envar[=value]* `[...]`

**Context:** Server config

**Status:** Base

**Module:** `mod_setenvif` (in Apache 1.2: `mod_browser`, now obsolete)

**Compatibility:** Apache 1.2 and later

This is the same as the `BrowserMatch` directive except that the regular expression is matched with case-insensitive matching.

```
BrowserMatchNoCase compatible Mozilla=spoof
```

# The Cache... Directives

For `CacheDefaultExpire`, `CacheDirLength`, `CacheDirLevels`, `CacheForceCompletion`, `CacheGcInterval`, `CacheLastModifiedFactor`, `CacheMaxExpire`, `CacheRoot`, `CacheSize`, and `NoCache`, see Chapter 10, "Proxy and Caching."

## CheckSpelling

**Syntax:** `CheckSpelling on|off`

**Default:** `CheckSpelling off`

**Context:** Server config, virtual host, directory, `.htaccess`

**Override:** `Options`

**Status:** Base

**Module:** `mod_speling`

**Compatibility:** `CheckSpelling` was available as a separately available module for Apache 1.1 but was limited to miscapitalizations. As of Apache 1.3, it is part of the Apache distribution. Before Apache 1.3.2, this directive was available only in the server and virtual host contexts.

When set to `on`, `CheckSpelling` tries to correct spelling errors and redirects to the correct URL. For example, mistyping a URL such as `http://www.mk.net/palns.html` would redirect to the correct URL `http://www.mk.net/plans.html`. `CheckSpelling` also corrects miscapitalization.

This correction is accomplished by scanning the current directory for files with similar spelling and picking the one that best matches the URL requested. With that in mind, don't enable this directive for directories containing confidential files that might accidentally be matched and served to the user.

If two or more files are possible matches, a menu of options is presented to the user. Figure 5.1 shows an example of such a menu, when a user mistyped a URL.

**FIGURE 5.1**

*Menu of options provided by the* CheckSpelling *directive.*

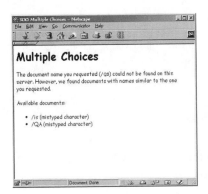

## ClearModuleList

**Syntax:** ClearModuleList

**Context:** Server config

**Status:** Core

**Compatibility:** Apache 1.2 and later

This directive clears the list of currently loaded modules. You should then load a new list of modules by using the AddModule directive.

## CoreDumpDirectory

**Syntax:** CoreDumpDirectory *directory*

**Default:** The same location as ServerRoot

**Context:** Server config

**Status:** Core

CoreDumpDirectory sets the location where the server will attempt to put a core dump. The default location is the ServerRoot, so a core dump ordinarily won't get written, since that directory usually isn't writable by the user the server runs as.

CoreDumpDirectory /tmp

## CustomLog

**Syntax:** CustomLog *file-pipe format-or-nickname*

**Context:** Server config, virtual host

**Status:** Base

**Compatibility:** Nickname available only in Apache 1.3 or later

**Module:** mod_log_config

CustomLog defines a log file. See Chapter 18, "Logging."

## DefaultIcon

**Syntax:** DefaultIcon *url*

**Context:** Server config, virtual host, directory, .htaccess

**Override:** Indexes

**Status:** Base

**Module:** mod_autoindex

For use with FancyIndexing, this directive sets the icon to be displayed in automatically generated indexes for files of unknown type. *url* is the URL of the icon file.

DefaultIcon /icons/default.gif

## DefaultLanguage

**Syntax:** DefaultLanguage *MIME-lang*

**Context:** Server config, virtual host, directory, .htaccess

**Override:** FileInfo

**Status:** Base

**Module:** mod_mime

This directive indicates that documents not explicitly marked with a language extension are to be considered this language type. This might permit you to designate a particular portion of your site for a particular language without having to add the filename extension (such as .en or .fr) to each file. See the AddLanguage directive's discussion earlier in this chapter.

## DefaultType

**Syntax:** DefaultType *MIME-type*

**Default:** DefaultType text/html

**Context:** Server config, virtual host, directory, .htaccess

**Override:** FileInfo

**Status:** Core

DefaultType sets the MIME type to be used for files whose type can't be determined by the filename. For example, if you have a directory full of PostScript files that don't have filename extensions, you might use the following for that directory:

DefaultType application/postscript

## deny

**Syntax:** deny from *host host* ...

**Context:** Directory, .htaccess

**Override:** Limit

**Status:** Base

**Module:** mod_access

See allow and order. This directive denies access to a particular directory based on the host's address, where *host* can be one of the following:

- all   All hosts are denied access.

  deny from all

- A domain name   All hosts that match or end in the given string are denied access. This compares the whole name, so bowen.com doesn't match rcbowen.com.

  deny from .microsoft.com

- An IP address   A host with that exact IP address is denied access:

  deny from 192.101.203.76

- A partial IP address   If you specify the first 1 to 3 bytes of an IP address, all hosts in that subnet are denied access:

  deny from 192.101.210

- A network and a netmask   Hosts on the included subnets are denied access:

  deny from 192.101.0.0/255.255.0.0

A network and a netmask in terms of number of high-order bits also are denied access:

```
deny from 192.101.0.0/16
```

## <Directory>

**Syntax:** <Directory *directory*> ... </Directory>

**Context:** Server config, virtual host

**Status:** Core

The <Directory> section encloses one or more directives that are applied only to the specified directory and subdirectories. If this chapter indicates that a directive is permitted in directory context, it is permitted in one of these directory containers. *directory* can be one of the following:

- A directory name    The absolute path to a particular directory:
  ```
  <Directory /usr/local/httpd/htdocs/images>
  DefaultType image/gif
  </Directory>
  ```

- A wild-card string    With the use of various characters, you can indicate several directories that might match the wild card:

  ?        Matches any single character

  *        Matches any sequence of characters

  []        In Apache 1.3 or later, encloses a character range

> **Note**
>
> No wild card characters match the / character.

The following example forbids the use of .htaccess files in user directories:
```
<Directory /home/*/public_html/>
AllowOverride None
</Directory>
```

- A regular expression    With Apache version 1.2 and later, you can use regular expression matching to indicate which directories get the directives. You need to add the ~ character to the directive to indicate that you are using this feature. The following example matches all directories that contain the string "pressrelease" and applies a set of directives to those directories:

```
<Directory ~ "pressrelease">
  directives
</Directory>
```

## `<DirectoryMatch>`

**Syntax:** `<DirectoryMatch` *regex`>` ... `</DirectoryMatch>`

**Context:** Server config, virtual host

**Status:** Core

**Compatibility:** Apache 1.3 and later

`<DirectoryMatch>` works similar to `<Directory>`, except that it takes a regular expression as the argument rather than a directory.

## `DirectoryIndex`

**Syntax:** `DirectoryIndex` *url url* ...

**Default:** `DirectoryIndex index.html`

**Context:** Server config, virtual host, directory, `.htaccess`

**Override:** `Indexes`

**Status:** Base

**Module:** `mod_dir`

`DirectoryIndex` sets the default document to be displayed when a URL requests a directory. For example, if the URL `http://www.rcbowen.com/imho/` is requested, the server will consult the `DirectoryIndex` directive for that directory and serve that file out of that directory. If `DirectoryIndex` is set to `index.html`, this request would be equivalent to `http://www.rcbowen.com/imho/index.html`.

*url* must be a URL on the local server, but it doesn't need to be a file in the current directory—that is, it can be a relative URL to elsewhere on the site.

Several *url*s can be provided; the server will use the first one that it actually can locate. For example, with

`DirectoryIndex index.html index.shtml /errors/no_index.html`

the server will first attempt to serve the file `index.html`. If that file isn't found in the directory, it will then try to serve the file `index.shtml`. Finally, if that file isn't found, it will serve the URL `/errors/no_index.html`. If none of the files listed in this directive are found, what is to be served will fall through to the automatic indexing directives. If none of those are set, the server will display an error message, indicating that access to that directory is forbidden.

## DocumentRoot

**Syntax:** DocumentRoot *directory-filename*

**Default:** DocumentRoot /usr/local/apache/htdocs

**Context:** Server config, virtual host

**Status:** Core

This directive sets the directory from which your HTML files will be served. Other directories containing HTML files can be set with the Alias directive.

The following example is the default setting if you installed from the Red Hat RPM:

```
DocumentRoot /home/httpd/html
```

## ErrorDocument

**Syntax:** ErrorDocument *error-code document*

**Context:** Server config, virtual host, directory, .htaccess

**Status:** Core

**Override:** FileInfo

**Compatibility:** The directory and .htaccess contexts are available only in Apache 1.1 and later.

ErrorDocument provides for customizable error messages when something goes wrong on the server. By default, users are presented with unfriendly, cryptic messages that leave them thinking that they did something wrong. With ErrorDocument, you can explain what happened, what they can do about it, and who to contact about the problem. Or you can redirect to a CGI program that logs the problem or notifies someone about it.

*error-code* is the 4xx or 5xx error status returned by the server. *document* is one of the following:

- A text message   The text message is simply returned to the user:
  ```
  ErrorDocument 404 "That document does not exist, or has been moved.
  ```

- A local or external URL   These can be HTML pages or CGI programs that handle the error in some way:
  ```
  ErrorDocument 404 http://cgi.databeam.com/cgi-bin/not_found.pl
  ErrorDocument 401 /createaccount.html
  ErrorDocument 500 /cgi-bin/report_error.pl
  ```

When an ErrorDocument directive redirects to a local URL, a special set of environment variables are sent with the redirect so that a CGI program can try to find out more about the error. These environment variables consist of all the environment variables available prior to the redirect, with REDIRECT_ prepended. For example, REQUEST_METHOD would become REDIRECT_ REQUEST_METHOD. In addition to these variables, two new variables are created: REDIRECT_URL, containing the originally requested URL, and REDIRECT_STATUS, containing the error status code that caused the redirect.

When redirecting to external URLs, these special environment variables aren't available. Be careful—*external* means any URL that begins with http://, even if it actually points to the local server.

## ErrorLog

**Syntax:** ErrorLog *filename* | syslog[:*facility*]

**Default:** ErrorLog logs/error_log (Unix)
ErrorLog logs/error.log (Windows and OS/2)

**Context:** Server config, virtual host

**Status:** Core

This directive sets the location of the error log. (See Chapter 18 and the LogLevel directive's discussion later in this chapter.)

*filename* can be an actual filename or, if it begins with a pipe ( | ), a command that will be launched to process error log entries. Unless the filename begins with a /, it's appended to the value of ServerRoot.

As of Apache 1.3, you can log to *syslog*, for those systems that support this:

ErrorLog /var/log/httpd/error_log

## ExtendedStatus

**Syntax:** ExtendedStatus On | Off

**Default:** ExtendedStatus Off

**Context:** Server config

**Status:** Base

**Module:** mod_status

**Compatibility:** Apache 1.3.2 and later

`ExtendedStatus` turns on extended information tracking for each server request. `mod_status` isn't turned on by default; you must turn it on to use this directive.

## FancyIndexing

**Syntax:** `FancyIndexing On|Off`

**Default:** `FancyIndexing On`

**Context:** Server config, virtual host, directory, `.htaccess`

**Override:** `Indexes`

**Status:** Base

**Module:** `mod_autoindex`

Figures 5.2 and 5.3 show the difference between `on` and `off`. Figure 5.2 shows a file listing generated with `FancyIndexing` turned on, whereas Figure 5.3 shows the same directory listing with `FancyIndexing` turned off.

**FIGURE 5.2**

*Directory index generated with* `FancyIndexing` *turned on.*

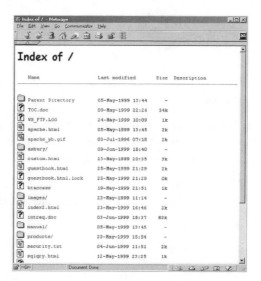

It's recommended that, rather than use the `FancyIndexing` directive, you use `IndexOptions FancyIndexing`. The `IndexOptions` directive implements all the other qualities of automatically generated indexes. It makes sense to keep all your configuration in one place, rather than use `IndexOptions` for most of it and `FancyIndexing` for this one other part. Also, prior to Apache 1.3.2, these two directives will override each other, and you have to be careful about ordering. Better to just use `IndexOptions` for everything and remove the confusion.

**FIGURE 5.3**

*Directory index generated with* FancyIndexing *turned off.*

## <Files>

**Syntax:** <Files *filename*> ... </Files>

**Context:** Server config, virtual host, .htaccess

**Status:** Core

**Compatibility:** Apache 1.2 and later

The <Files> section allows configuration directives to be applied based on filenames. This is analogous to the <Directory> section, except that <Files> can be used in .htaccess files. This is a great way for users to specify options in their directories file by file.

As with the <Directory> section, you can use wild cards or extended regular expressions to specify a group of files.

## Wild Cards

The wild cards available are as follows:

| | |
|---|---|
| ? | Matches any single character |
| * | Matches any sequence of characters |
| [] | In Apache 1.3 or later, encloses a character range |

The following example will restrict access to files with names that look like Jan, followed by two characters, followed by .htm, optionally followed by anything else. These files will be viewable only by clients from hosts on the mk.net network. All other clients will get an "access denied" error message.

```
<Files Jan??.htm*>
    order deny,allow
    deny from all
    allow from mk.net
</Files>
```

## Regular Expressions

By prepending the ~ character, you enable matching via regular expressions. This gives a little more flexibility than the wild-card approach. This functionality is also available in the `<FilesMatch>` directive, which is preferred over `<Files>`.

The following example will apply the directives to files with names such as `Jan.htm`, `january.html`, `jan1999.htm`, and so on:

```
<Files ~ "[jJ]an.*\.htm.*">
...
</Files>
```

For a more complete treatment of regular expressions, see Jeffrey Friedl's excellent book *Mastering Regular Expressions*.

## `<FilesMatch>`

**Syntax:** `<FilesMatch regex> ... </FilesMatch>`

**Context:** Server config, virtual host, `.htaccess`

**Status:** Core

**Compatibility:** Apache 1.3 and later

The `<FilesMatch>` section supercedes the ~ regular expression functionality of the `<Files>` section. It permits the application of directives to files matching arbitrary regular expressions.

The following example will apply the directives to files with names such as `Jan.htm`, `january.html`, `jan1999.htm`, and so on:

```
<FilesMatch "[jJ]an.*\.htm.*">
...
</Files>
```

## `ForceType`

**Syntax:** `ForceType MIME-type`

**Context:** Directory, `.htaccess`

**Status:** Base

**Module:** mod_mime

**Compatibility:** Apache 1.1 and later

This directive forces all files in a particular directory to be served with the specified MIME type. This is similar to the DefaultType directive in that it causes files with an unknown file extension to be served with the specified MIME type. However, it also overrides files with an extension that would otherwise determine the file type.

The following example will cause all files in a directory to be served with the application/unknown MIME type. This is very useful if you have a directory of files that you want people to be able to download, as it will ask the users if they want to save the file, rather than display it in the browser window.

```
ForceType application/unknown
```

## Group

**Syntax:** Group *unix-group*

**Default:** Group #-1

**Context:** Server config, virtual host

**Status:** Core

This directive sets the group under which the server process will execute. This is meaningful only on Unix systems. This is used with the User directive to specify the permissions with which the server runs. It's recommended that this group (and the user) have limited permissions. See Chapter 15, "Security," for further discussion of security issues.

## HeaderName

**Syntax:** HeaderName *filename*

**Context:** Server config, virtual host, directory, .htaccess

**Override:** Indexes

**Status:** Base

**Module:** mod_autoindex

This directive is used with automatically generated indexes. It specifies a file that will be displayed at the top of the directory listing. This is useful for providing informational messages or a description of the directory contents.

The server first looks for *filename*.html and, if that is not found, it will look for *filename*. The following directive, for example, will cause the file info.html to be displayed at the top of directory listings, if it exists, or the file info to be displayed otherwise. If neither file exists, nothing is displayed.

```
HeaderName info
```

See also the ReadmeName directive, which displays something at the bottom of the directory listing.

## HostNameLookups

**Syntax:** HostNameLookups on|off|double (double available only in Apache 1.3 and later)

**Default:** HostNameLookups off (HostNameLookups on before Apache 1.3)

**Context:** Server config, virtual host, directory

**Status:** Core

HostNameLookups turns name lookups on or off. When set to off, client names will appear in the logs and be passed to CGI in the REMOTE_HOST environment variable as just an IP address. When set to on, the server will do a DNS lookup on every client access to get the hostname. Since this requires one DNS lookup for every document that the client requests, this can significantly slow things down. Don't turn HostNameLookups on unless you actually have a good reason for doing so.

The double setting causes the server to perform double-reverse lookups, which means that after a name lookup is performed, a lookup is then performed on that name, and the resulting IP address must match the original client address. This is sometimes done for security reasons.

## IdentityCheck

**Syntax:** IdentityCheck on|off

**Default:** IdentityCheck off

**Context:** Server config, virtual host, directory

**Status:** Core

When IdentityCheck is turned on, the server can log the remote user's username. This username is obtained from the client machine via identd or another similar method. Long ago, when the Web was young, many browsers would pass the user's email address for this value. This feature was quickly abused by shameless marketing types and has been removed from every major browser.

The information obtained from this directive isn't reliable, so it's seldom worthwhile to turn this directive on. This might possibly be useful on an intranet, but on the Internet, the latency introduced by having this directive turned on would far outweigh any benefits.

## `<IfDefine>`

**Syntax:** `<IfDefine [!]parameter-name> ... </IfDefine>`

**Context:** Server config, virtual host, directory, `.htaccess`

**Status:** Core

**Compatibility:** Apache 1.3.1 and later

This section encloses a directive, or set of directives, that will be processed only if the parameter was specified when the server was started up. If the ! is used, the enclosed directive(s) is processed only if the parameter isn't specified.

A parameter is specified on the command line, when the server is started, with `-Dparameter-name`. For example, `dolookups` might be specified by starting the server with the following command line:

```
httpd -Ddolookups
```

You might then turn on the `HostNameLookups` directive, only if that parameter was specified, with the following directives:

```
<IfDefine dolookups>
    HostNameLookups on
</IfDefine>
```

This allows you to define custom server configurations within the same configuration file and turn various features on and off via the startup command.

> **Tip**
>
> You can nest `<IfDefine>` sections to test more than one condition.

## `<IfModule>`

**Syntax:** `<IfModule [!]module-name> ... </IfModule>`

**Context:** Server config, virtual host, directory, `.htaccess`

**Status:** Core

**Compatibility:** Apache 1.2 and later

The <IfModule> section encloses a directive, or set of directives, that will be processed only if the named module is compiled into Apache. If the ! is used, the enclosed directive(s) is processed only if the module isn't compiled into Apache.

The following directive will turn on the spelling correction feature of mod_speling, if that module is compiled in:

```
<IfModule mod_speling.c>
    CheckSpelling on
</IfModule>
```

## Include

**Syntax:** Include *filename*

**Context:** Server config

**Status:** Core

**Compatibility:** Apache 1.3 and later

This directive includes another file into the configuration file. This could be useful for keeping several different server configuration files and switching between them. The desired configuration directives might be loaded with an <IfDefine> directive and enabled with a command-line parameter:

```
<IfDefine config1>
include config1.conf
</IfDefine>
```

## IndexIgnore

**Syntax:** IndexIgnore *file file ...*

**Context:** Server config, virtual host, directory, .htaccess

**Override:** Indexes

**Status:** Base

**Module:** mod_autoindex

This directive, used with automatically generated directory listings, specifies the list of files to ignore when building those listings:

```
IndexIgnore README .htaccess *.stub *.cfm
```

## IndexOptions

**Syntax:** IndexOptions [+|-]*option* [+|-]*option*

**Context:** Server config, virtual host, directory, .htaccess

**Override:** Indexes

**Status:** Base

**Module:** mod_autoindex

IndexOptions is used to configure the options available with the automatic indexing functions of the mod_autoindex module. *option* can be any of the following:

- FancyIndexing turns on "fancy" indexing of directories. If FancyIndexing isn't turned on, the directory listing is simply a bulleted list of filenames, and none of the rest of these options make any difference. This should be used in preference to the FancyIndexing directive, so that you can have all your indexing option configurations in one place.

- IconHeight[=*pixels*] tells the server to use the HEIGHT attribute in the HTML <IMG> tag when displaying the file icon for items in the index listing. If you don't specify a value for the *pixels* option, Apache uses the standard height of the icons that ship with Apache (22 pixels high).

- IconsAreLinks turns the file icons into a link to the file. By default, icons aren't links.

- IconWidth[=*pixels*] tells the server to use the WIDTH attribute in the HTML <IMG> tag when displaying the file icon for items in the index listing. If you don't specify a value for the *pixels* option, Apache uses the standard width of the icons that ship with Apache (20 pixels wide).

- NameWidth=[*n*|*] specifies how many characters wide the filename column will be. If the filename is longer than the number specified, the name will be truncated at *n*-3 characters, and the last three characters will be displayed as ..> to indicate that the name has been truncated. If the value is set to *, the column is set to the length of the longest filename.

- ScanHTMLTitles scans each HTML file and uses the contents of the HTML <TITLE> tag in the description column, if that file doesn't have a description given by an AddDescription directive. As you can imagine, this slows things down considerably, as Apache has to open and read every HTML file individually.

- SuppressColumnSorting turns off the default behavior of FancyIndexing, which is to make each column header a link that you can click to sort by that column.

- SuppressDescription turns off the displaying of the description column in directory listings.

- SuppressHTMLPreamble specifies whether to skip the HTML "preamble." Apache usually begins automatically generated index pages with this preamble, which resembles the following:

```
<!DOCTYPE HTML PUBLIC "-//W3C//DTD HTML 3.2 Final//EN">
<HTML>
 <HEAD>
  <TITLE>Index of /products</TITLE>
 </HEAD>
 <BODY>
```

If the directory contains a file specified by the HeaderName directive, the contents of that file are then displayed here. If no such file exists, Apache inserts a header indicating the name of the directory that is being indexed, such as the following:

```
<H1>Index of /products</H1>
```

With the SuppressHTMLPreamble option turned on, this preamble will be skipped, and the page generated will start with the contents of the file specified by the HeaderName directive. If there is no such file, the preamble will be generated as usual.

- SuppressLastModified turns off the display of the file's last modification date.
- SuppressSize turns off the display of the file's size.

## KeepAlive

**Syntax:** KeepAlive on | off

**Default:** KeepAlive on

**Context:** Server config

**Status:** Core

**Compatibility:** Apache 1.1 and later

KeepAlive turns on (or off) the ability to serve more than one request on the same connection. This speeds up response, since the client doesn't need to open a new connection for every request. For example, if a Web page contains 5 images, that's 6 requests: one for the page, and then one for each image. See also the MaxKeepAliveRequests directive.

## KeepAliveTimeout

**Syntax:** KeepAliveTimeout *seconds*

**Default:** KeepAliveTimeout 15

**Context:** Server config

**5**

**SERVER CONFIGURATION FILES**

**Status:** Core

**Compatibility:** Apache 1.1 and later

`KeepAliveTimeout` specifies the number of seconds to wait for another request before closing the connection.

## LanguagePriority

**Syntax:** `LanguagePriority` *MIME-lang MIME-lang...*

**Context:** Server config, virtual host, directory, `.htaccess`

**Override:** `FileInfo`

**Status:** Base

**Module:** `mod_negotiation`

This directive lists, in decreasing order, the language preference for negotiated documents. See the discussion on `mod_negotiation` in Chapter 20.

```
LanguagePriority en fr de
```

## <Limit>

**Syntax:** `<Limit` *method method* `... > ... </Limit>`

**Context:** Server config, virtual host, directory, `.htaccess`

**Status:** Core

Directives included in a `<Limit>` container apply only to the HTTP methods specified. Valid HTTP methods are `GET`, `POST`, `PUT`, `DELETE`, `CONNECT`, and `OPTIONS`, and they are case sensitive. `HEAD` requests are included in `GET` requests. The following example requires a valid username and password for `POST` and `PUT` requests but will allow `GET` requests through unauthenticated:

```
<Limit POST PUT>
require valid-user
</Limit>
```

## <LimitExcept>

**Syntax:** `<LimitExcept` *method method* `... > ... </LimitExcept>`

**Context:** Server config, virtual host, directory, `.htaccess`

**Status:** Core

**Compatibility:** Apache 1.3.5 and later

This is the opposite of the `<Limit>` directive. Directives appearing inside a `<LimitExcept>` container apply to all methods except those specified. See `<Limit>` for more information.

## LimitRequestBody

**Syntax:** LimitRequestBody *number*

**Default:** LimitRequestBody 0

**Context:** Server config, virtual host, directory, `.htaccess`

**Status:** Core

**Compatibility:** Apache 1.3.2 and later

LimitRequestBody specifies the maximum size of a client request body. The body of the request is used to send the contents of HTML forms, or for file uploads using a PUT request. The number specified can be anywhere from 0 (meaning unlimited size) to 2147483647 (2GB). This is a convenient way to restrict the size of files that can be uploaded to a server, or to avoid denial-of-service attacks where the client attempts to overwhelm the server with an enormous request body.

## LimitRequestFields

**Syntax:** LimitRequestFields *number*

**Default:** LimitRequestFields 100

**Context:** Server config

**Status:** Core

**Compatibility:** Apache 1.3.2 and later

LimitRequestFields specifies the maximum number of HTTP header fields that will be accepted from a client. *number* can be anywhere from 0, meaning unlimited, to 32767. This might be useful in avoiding denial-of-service attacks where the client attempts to overwhelm the server by sending an enormous amount of data in the form of HTTP headers.

## LimitRequestFieldsize

**Syntax:** LimitRequestFieldsize *number*

**Default:** LimitRequestFieldsize 8190

**5**

**SERVER CONFIGURATION FILES**

**Context:** Server config

**Status:** Core

**Compatibility:** Apache 1.3.2 and later

`LimitRequestFieldsize` limits the size of any individual HTTP header. This should usually not be changed from the default setting. The default value gives a reasonable upper limit on the size of this header while protecting you from possible denial of service attacks.

## LimitRequestLine

**Syntax:** `LimitRequestLine` *number*

**Default:** `LimitRequestLine 8190`

**Context:** Server config

**Status:** Core

**Compatibility:** Apache 1.3.2 and later

This directive limits the length of an HTTP request. This needs to be long enough that any possible URL on your server can fit into this many characters, including any data that might come in as part of a `GET` request.

This limit might prevent certain kinds of denial-of-service attacks where the client attempts to overwhelm the server with an enormous request line.

This should usually not be changed from the default setting. The default value puts a reasonable upper limit on URL length while protecting you from possible denial of service attacks.

## Listen

**Syntax:** `Listen [`*IP_address:*`]`*port_number*

**Context:** Server config

**Status:** Core

**Compatibility:** Apache 1.1 and later

This directive tells the server to listen for requests on more than one IP address and/or TCP/IP port. By default, Apache listens on all network interfaces, but only on the one port specified by the `Port` directive.

If a port number is specified without an IP address, as in the following example, Apache listens on that port on all interfaces:

```
listen 80
listen 8081
listen 1352
```

If an IP address is specified as well as a port, as in the following example, Apache listens on just that specific IP address/port combination:

```
listen 192.168.1.1:80
listen 9.95.147.22:999
```

> **Note**
>
> Try to avoid using ports that might already be in use for other purposes, since this will cause the server to fail to start up, as it will be unable to bind to the port.

## ListenBacklog

**Syntax:** ListenBacklog *backlog*

**Default:** ListenBacklog 511

**Context:** Server config

**Status:** Core

**Compatibility:** Apache versions after 1.2.0

ListenBacklog sets the maximum number of requests to keep in the queue to be serviced. This will be relevant only on extremely busy sites; in most cases, this number doesn't need to be changed.

## LoadFile

**Syntax:** LoadFile *filename filename* ...

**Context:** Server config

**Status:** Base

**Module:** mod_so

This directive links in the named object files or libraries when the server is started. *filename* is either an absolute path or a path relative to ServerRoot.

## LoadModule

**Syntax:** LoadModule *module filename*

**Context:** Server config

**Status:** Base

**Module:** mod_so

This directive loads the named *module* contained in the named *filename*. This will look different on Windows and Unix systems, as show in the following examples:

- On Unix:

  LoadModule speling_module modules/mod_speling.so

- On Windows:

  LoadModule speling_module modules/ApacheModuleSpeling.dll

## <Location>

**Syntax:** <Location *url*> ... </Location>

**Context:** Server config, virtual host

**Status:** Core

**Compatibility:** Apache 1.1 and later

The <Location> container defines directives based on *url*. It's very similar in syntax and behavior to the <Directory> section but doesn't necessarily have anything to do with directories.

You can use wild cards in the URL. ? matches any single character, and * matches any sequence of characters.

As with the <Directory> section, by adding the ~ character, you can use regular expressions to match various URLs. The following example would match URLs that contain the string /products/hypercal or /download/hypercal:

<Location ~ "/(products|download)/hypercal">

You can also achieve this behavior with the <LocationMatch> container.

The <Location> section is used in the default configuration file in an example involving the SetHandler directive. In this example, a URL is created that maps to a handler, rather than to a directory and files. The following example provides for clients from hosts only on the mk.net network to access the URL /status to view server status reports:

```
<Location /status>
SetHandler server-status
order deny,allow
deny from all
allow from .mk.net
</Location>
```

## <LocationMatch>

**Syntax:** <LocationMatch *regex*> ... </LocationMatch>

**Context:** Server config, virtual host

**Status:** Core

**Compatibility:** Apache 1.3 and later

<LocationMatch> provides similar functionality as the <Location> section, with a regular expression matching instead of just a string for the URL. This section should be used instead of the ~ option with <Location>.

## LockFile

**Syntax:** LockFile *filename*

**Default:** LockFile logs/accept.lock

**Context:** Server config

**Status:** Core

This directive specifies the location of the lockfile used by Apache if it's compiled with USE_FCNTL_SERIALIZED_ACCEPT or USE_FLOCK_SERIALIZED_ACCEPT. This file must be stored on a local drive.

## LogFormat

**Syntax:** LogFormat *format* [*nickname*]

**Default:** LogFormat "%h %l %u %t \"%r\" %s %b"

**Context:** Server config, virtual host

**Status:** Base

**Compatibility:** Nickname available only in Apache 1.3 or later

**Module:** `mod_log_config`

This directive defines a logging format and a nickname by which that format can be called. See Chapter 18 for more information on this directive.

## LogLevel

**Syntax:** LogLevel *level*

**Default:** `LogLevel error`

**Context:** Server config, virtual host

**Status:** Core

**Compatibility:** Apache 1.3 or later

`LogLevel` sets the level of error messages that are to appear in the error log, from `debug`, which gets all messages, to `emerg`, which gets only the most dire messages. Setting this directive to somewhere in the middle makes the most sense. Table 5.1 lists the possible values for this directive.

**TABLE 5.1**   LogLevel Values

| Level | Description |
|-------|-------------|
| emerg | Emergencies; system is unusable. Example: `Child cannot open lock file. Exiting` |
| alert | Action must be taken immediately. Example: `getpwuid: couldn't determine user name from uid` |
| crit | Critical conditions. Example: `socket: Failed to get a socket, exiting child` |
| error | Error conditions. Example: `Premature end of script headers` |
| warn | Warning conditions. Example: `child process 1234 did not exit, sending another SIGHUP` |
| notice | Normal but significant condition. Example: `httpd: caught SIGBUS, attempting to dump core in ...` |
| info | Informational. Example: `Server seems busy, (you may need to increase StartServers, or Min/MaxSpareServers)...` |
| debug | Debug-level messages. Example: `Opening config file ...` |

See Chapter 18 for more information on this directive.

## MaxClients

**Syntax:** MaxClients *number*

**Default:** MaxClients 256

**Context:** Server config

**Status:** Core

This directive sets the maximum number of simultaneous client requests that will be served. See also the ListenBacklog directive.

## MaxKeepAliveRequests

**Syntax:** MaxKeepAliveRequests *number*

**Default:** MaxKeepAliveRequests 100

**Context:** Server config

**Status:** Core

**Compatibility:** Apache 1.2 and later

This directive sets the maximum number of requests that will be served for one connection, when KeepAlive is enabled (see also the KeepAlive directive discussion earlier in this chapter). Setting MaxKeepAliveRequests to 0 makes it unlimited.

## MaxRequestsPerChild

**Syntax:** MaxRequestsPerChild *number*

**Default:** MaxRequestsPerChild 0

**Context:** Server config

**Status:** Core

MaxRequestsPerChild sets the number of requests that will be served by a single child process before the child process will exit. When set to 0, child processes never exit.

This directive doesn't affect the Win32 server, which handles additional requests with threads within one child process, rather than with forks of additional child processes. See the ThreadsPerChild directive for the equivalent directive for Windows.

**5**

**SERVER CONFIGURATION FILES**

## MaxSpareServers

**Syntax:** MaxSpareServers *number*

**Default:** MaxSpareServers 10

**Context:** Server config

**Status:** Core

This directive sets the maximum number of permitted idle child processes. If more processes than this go idle, they are killed off. This directive does not affect the Win32 server.

## MetaDir

**Syntax:** MetaDir *directory_name*

**Default:** MetaDir .web

**Context:** .htaccess

**Status:** Base

**Module:** mod_cern_meta

**Compatibility:** Apache 1.1 and later

MetaDir specifies the name of the directory in which Apache can find meta information files. See the section on mod_cern_meta in Chapter 20.

## MetaFiles

**Syntax:** MetaFiles on|off

**Default:** MetaFiles off

**Context:** .htaccess

**Status:** Base

**Module:** mod_cern_meta

**Compatibility:** Apache 1.3 and later

This directive turns on metafile processing on a per-directory basis.

## MetaSuffix

**Syntax:** MetaSuffix *suffix*

**Default:** MetaSuffix .meta

**Context:** .htaccess

**Status:** Base

**Module:** mod_cern_meta

**Compatibility:** Apache 1.1 and later

The MetaSuffix directive sets the filename extension for files containing meta information. The default will cause Apache to look for a file called mine.html.meta when a file called foo.html is served. It will use the contents of that file to generate additional MIME header information for that HTML file.

## MinSpareServers

**Syntax:** MinSpareServers *number*

**Default:** MinSpareServers 5

**Context:** Server config

**Status:** Core

MinSpareServers sets the minimum number of idle child processes that should be running at any time. If there are fewer than this, Apache will create additional child processes to handle future requests. This directive doesn't affect the Win32 server.

## NameVirtualHost

**Syntax:** NameVirtualHost *addr*[:*port*]

**Context:** Server config

**Status:** Core

**Compatibility:** Apache 1.3 and later

NameVirtualHost tells Apache that requests on the specified address should be served documents based on the server name requested. Name-based virtual hosts are used when there is more than one cname on the address specified, and each cname is to be treated as a separate virtual host. See Chapter 9, "Virtual Hosting."

NameVirtualHost 192.101.205.15

## NoCache

**Syntax:** NoCache [*word* | *host* | *domain_list*]

**Context:** Server config, virtual host

**Status:** Base

**Module:** mod_proxy

**Compatibility:** Apache 1.1 and later

Used with the caching proxy server implemented in the mod_proxy module, this directive turns off caching on all files, accessed through the proxy, that match the words in the list. The following example disables caching for any URL containing the substring cgi-bin or the substring cgi.databeam.com. The latter will presumably disable caching from any file fetched from the machine cgi.databeam.com, but more generally, it is for *any* URL containing that substring.

NoCache cgi-bin cgi.databeam.com

> **Note**
>
> NoCache * disables all caching.

## Options

**Syntax:** Options [+ | -]*option* [+ | -]*option* ...

**Default:** Options All

**Context:** Server config, virtual host, directory, .htaccess

**Override:** Options

**Status:** Core

Enables (or disables) server features for a particular directory, and all subdirectories thereof. The options can be any of the following:

- None   Don't allow any of these options in the specified directory.
- All   Allow all options except MultiViews.
- ExecCGI   CGI programs may be executed within this directory. You can also use the ScriptAlias directive to enable this, but using the Options directive to accomplish this is especially useful for user directories, so that the user can enable these options without the server administrator's assistance.

- `FollowSymLinks`   The server will follow symbolic links in this directory. This is generally a bad idea, from a security perspective, since it potentially allows a Web client to "escape" from the Web document directory and explore the entire file system. Consider using the `SymLinksIfOwnerMatch` option instead.

- `Includes`   Server-side includes are permitted. Be careful with this, since includes are a potential security risk. Consider using the `IncludesNOEXEC` option instead if you aren't confident of your users' ability and trustworthiness. See Chapter 12, "SSI: Server-Side Includes."

- `IncludesNOEXEC`   Server-side includes are permitted, but the `#exec` and `#include` commands of CGI scripts are disabled.

- `Indexes`   If a directory is requested and there's no file in that directory matching the `DirectoryIndex` directive, a listing of available files will be presented to the client.

- `MultiViews`   Content-negotiated `MultiViews` are allowed.

- `SymLinksIfOwnerMatch`   Symbolic links may be followed only if the target of the link is owned by the same user as the directory itself. This gets around some of the insecurity intrinsic to `FollowSymLinks`.

> **Note**
>
> The `FollowSymLinks` and `SymLinksIfOwnerMatch` options aren't available on Win32 systems.

If all options specified are preceded by a + or -, they are added to options already in force. In the following example, `FollowSymLinks` is enabled for the directory `/www/htdocs/foobar`, and `FollowSymLinks` and `ExecCGI` are both enabled for the directory `/www/htdocs/foobar/subdir`, because the directives in the original `<Directory>` section apply to all subdirectories.

```
<Directory /www/htdocs/foobar>
Options FollowSymLinks
</Directory>

<Directory /www/htdocs/foobar/subdir>
Options +ExecCGI
</Directory>
```

If options aren't preceded by these characters, the options listed completely override those already in effect. In the following example, the directives in the second `<Directory>` section completely override those in the first, and the directory `/www/htdocs/foobar/subdir` has only the `Includes` option enabled:

```
<Directory /www/htdocs/foobar>
Options FollowSymLinks
</Directory>

<Directory /www/htdocs/foobar/subdir>
Options Includes
</Directory>
```

## order

**Syntax:** order *ordering*

**Default:** order deny,allow

**Context:** Directory, .htaccess

**Override:** Limit

**Status:** Base

**Module:** mod_access

This directive specifies the order in which allow and deny directives are to be processed. With the default order, deny directives are processed first, and then allow directives. This permits overriding a general deny directive with a very specific allow directive. The following example permits only hosts from mk.net to access the specified directory:

```
order deny,allow
deny from all
allow from mk.net
```

### Note

Notice that there's no space between deny and allow, just a comma. Putting a space between the comma and allow will cause a startup error.

If you use

```
order allow,deny
```

allow directives are processed first, and then deny directives. This lets you use a general allow statement and then exclude certain hosts with deny statements. This is a good way to keep certain people out, such as folks whom you know are trying to hack your site. For example

```
order allow,deny
allow from all
deny from dialup3.hacker.net
deny from s.ms.uky.edu
```

## PassEnv

**Syntax:** PassEnv *variable variable* ...

**Context:** Server config, virtual host

**Status:** Base

**Module:** mod_env

**Compatibility:** Apache 1.1 and later

PassEnv specifies environment variables that should be passed to CGI programs, in addition to the standard set of variables.

PassEnv PATH

## PidFile

**Syntax:** PidFile *filename*

**Default:** PidFile logs/httpd.pid

**Context:** Server config

**Status:** Core

This directive specifies the location of the file containing the server PID (process ID) number. This file may not contain meaningful information on Win32 systems.

## Port

**Syntax:** Port *number*

**Default:** Port 80

**Context:** Server config

**Status:** Core

The Port directive tells the server the TCP/IP port to which it should listen for HTTP connections. This should be some number between 0 and 65535.

### Note

Ports numbered less than 1024 are reserved ports; you must start the server as root to be able to bind to these ports. If for some reason you need to start the server as some user other than root, pick a port number higher than 1024; otherwise, Apache will complain that it can't bind to the specified port, and startup will fail.

5

SERVER CONFIGURATION FILES

## ProxyBlock

**Syntax:** ProxyBlock [*word* | *host* | *domain_list*]

**Context:** Server config, virtual host

**Status:** Base

**Module:** mod_proxy

**Compatibility:** Apache 1.2 and later

URLs that contain any of the substrings specified in the word list will be blocked by the proxy. This is an easy way to filter out undesirable sites by using a proxy server. Of course, you have to be using the proxy server for this directive to be meaningful. See Chapter 10.

ProxyBlock undesirable.site.com badword spammersite.com

## ProxyPass

**Syntax:** ProxyPass *path url*

**Context:** Server config, virtual host

**Status:** Base

**Module:** mod_proxy

**Compatibility:** Apache 1.1 and later

ProxyPass causes the server to appear as a mirror of an external site. When a request is received for the specified path, Apache proxies the document from the remote site, but appears to serve it from the local server, so that the server appears to be a mirror of the remote site.

ProxyPass /mirror/CPAN/ http://www.cpan.org/

## ProxyPassReverse

**Syntax:** ProxyPassReverse *path url*

**Context:** Server config, virtual host

**Status:** Base

**Module:** mod_proxy

**Compatibility:** Apache 1.3b6 and later

ProxyPassReverse provides much the same functionality as ProxyPass but also extends to any places where the initial URL may redirect the client.

ProxyPassReverse /mirror/CPAN/ http://www.cpan.org/

## ProxyReceiveBufferSize

**Syntax:** ProxyReceiveBufferSize *bytes*

**Context:** Server config, virtual host

**Status:** Base

**Module:** mod_proxy

**Compatibility:** Apache 1.3 and later

ProxyReceiveBufferSize specifies the network buffer size for outgoing HTTP and FTP connections (see Chapter 10). This size must be larger than 512. A setting of 0 indicates that the system default should be used for the buffer size.

ProxyReceiveBufferSize 1024

## ProxyRemote

**Syntax:** ProxyRemote *match remote-server*

**Context:** Server config, virtual host

**Status:** Base

**Module:** mod_proxy

**Compatibility:** Apache 1.1 and later

This directive indicates another proxy server that should be used. The *match* parameter indicates what URLs should be sent through that proxy server. This can be either a transfer protocol, such as http or ftp, or a partial URL for which requests should be forwarded to another proxy server. Examples include the following:

- ProxyRemote ftp http://socks.mk.net/ forwards all FTP requests through the server socks.mk.net. This might be useful if, for some reason, you had separate FTP and HTTP proxy servers.

- ProxyRemote http://databeam.com/ http://proxy.databeam.com/ forwards all requests for documents on the databeam.com server through the proxy server on proxy.databeam.com. This might be useful for proxying requests to a machine that is outside a firewall.

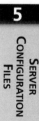

5

SERVER
CONFIGURATION
FILES

- ProxyRemote * http://proxyserver.net/ passes the buck. * indicates that all requests are to be forwarded to the specified proxy server. This might also be useful for a paranoid firewalled environment; users can communicate with the internal proxy server, which, in turn, can communicate with the external firewall server, but nothing else is opened through the firewall.

## ProxyRequests

**Syntax:** ProxyRequests on | off

**Default:** ProxyRequests off

**Context:** Server config, virtual host

**Status:** Base

**Module:** mod_proxy

**Compatibility:** Apache 1.1 and later

ProxyRequests toggles Apache's ability to perform as a proxy server.

## ProxyVia

**Syntax:** ProxyVia [off | on | full | block]

**Default:** ProxyVia off

**Context:** Server config, virtual host

**Status:** Base

**Module:** mod_proxy

**Compatibility:** Apache 1.3.2 and later

The Via: HTTP header defined in RFC2068 (the HTTP/1.1 specification) provides tracking of requests that are passed through a chain of proxy servers. The ProxyVia directive controls Apache's behavior with respect to producing those headers. The possible values for this directive are

- off   Don't add a Via: header to the request.
- on   Add a Via: header to the request, indicating that the request was passed through this proxy server.
- full   Add the Via: header, and also add the Apache version number to that header.
- block   Remove all Via: headers from the request, and don't add a Via: header to the request.

## ReadmeName

**Syntax:** ReadmeName *filename*

**Context:** Server config, virtual host, directory, .htaccess

**Override:** Indexes

**Status:** Base

**Module:** mod_autoindex

This directive specifies the name of the file that should be appended to automatically generated index listings. The server will first look for a file called *filename*.html; if that's not found, it will look for *filename*. If neither file is found, nothing will be appended to the listing.

See also the HeaderName directive, which displays a file at the top of the directory listing.

## Redirect

**Syntax:** Redirect [*status*] *url-path url*

**Context:** Server config, virtual host, directory, .htaccess

**Override:** FileInfo

**Status:** Base

**Module:** mod_alias

**Compatibility:** The directory and .htaccess contexts are available only in versions 1.1 and later. The *status* argument is available only in Apache 1.2 or later.

This directive tells the server to redirect requests for a particular URL to some other location. The optional *status* argument has the server additionally pass a status code to the client. The *status* can be one of the following:

- permanent returns a 301 status code, indicating that the resource has permanently moved.
- temp returns a 302 status code, indicating that the resource has been only temporarily moved. This is the default value if no *status* argument is provided.
- seeother returns a 303 status code, indicating that the resource has been replaced by some other resource.
- gone returns a 410 status code, indicating that the resource is gone—that is, it has been permanently removed. In this case, the redirect URL shouldn't be provided.

You can specify other status codes by using the numerical status code. These should be 3*xx* or 4*xx* status codes. If a 3*xx* status code is used, a URL must be provided for redirection. If a 4*xx* status code is used, the URL must be omitted.

The following example redirects all requests for URLs beginning with /Help to another server, helpdesk.databeam.com:

```
Redirect seeother /Help http://helpdesk.databeam.com/
```

## RedirectMatch

**Syntax:** RedirectMatch [*status*] *regex url*

**Context:** Server config, virtual host

**Override:** FileInfo

**Status:** Base

**Module:** mod_alias

**Compatibility:** Apache 1.3 and later

This directive is similar to the Redirect directive, except that the URL to be directed can be specified as a regular expression. The following example redirects URLs beginning with either /help or /Help to another server, helpdesk.databeam.com:

```
RedirectMatch /[hH]elp http://helpdesk.databeam.com/
```

## RedirectPermanent

**Syntax:** RedirectPermanent *url-path url*

**Context:** Server config, virtual host, directory, .htaccess

**Override:** FileInfo

**Status:** Base

**Module:** mod_alias

**Compatibility:** Apache 1.2 only

This directive redirects a URL and tells the client that the redirect is permanent. This is identical to using the Redirect directive with the permanent status.

## RedirectTemp

**Syntax:** RedirectTemp *url-path url*

**Context:** Server config, virtual host, directory, .htaccess

**Override:** FileInfo

**Status:** Base

**Module:** mod_alias

**Compatibility:** Apache 1.2 only

This directive redirects a URL and tells the client that the redirect is temporary. This is identical to using the Redirect directive with the temp status. In fact, since temp is the default value of the *status* argument for the Redirect directive, this is equivalent to using the Redirect directive with no *status* argument.

## require

**Syntax:** require *entity-name entity entity...*

**Context:** directory, .htaccess

**Override:** AuthConfig

**Status:** Core

The require directive specifies which authenticated users can access the directory. The *entity-name* can be one of the following:

- group indicates that a group of users, defined in a group file somewhere, can access the directory.
- user indicates that only the specified user(s) can access the directory. These users and their passwords should be defined in a user file somewhere.
- valid-users indicates that any user with a valid username and password can access the directory.

This directive is to be used with several other directives that specify the location of the group and user files, what type of authentication is to be used, and what methods are to be restricted. Example

```
AuthType Basic
AuthName admins
AuthUserFile /etc/httpd/passwd/users
AuthGroupFile /etc/httpd/passwd/groups
<Limit GET POST>
require group admins
</Limit>
```

For more details on these directives, see Chapter 16.

**5**

**SERVER CONFIGURATION FILES**

## ResourceConfig

**Syntax:** ResourceConfig *filename*

**Default:** ResourceConfig conf/srm.conf

**Context:** Server config, virtual host

**Status:** Core

ResourceConfig indicates the location of the resource configuration file, which is read for additional configuration options after loading the httpd.conf file. The *filename*, unless it has a leading slash, is assumed to be relative to the ServerRoot. If you want to put all your configuration directives in one file, you can disable the loading of a ResourceConfig file with the following directive:

ResourceConfig /dev/null

The equivalent line on Windows NT is simply the following:

ResourceConfig nul

See also the AccessConfig directive.

## RLimitCPU

**Syntax:** RLimitCPU *number*|max [*number*|max]

**Default:** Unset; uses operating system defaults

**Context:** Server config, virtual host

**Status:** Core

**Compatibility:** Apache 1.2 and later

This directive limits CPU resources used. The first argument is a limit for all processes; the second argument is the maximum resource limit. A value of max indicates that the limit should be set to the maximum allowed by the operating system. You probably shouldn't tinker with this directive unless you really know what you are doing.

## RLimitMEM

**Syntax:** RLimitMEM *number*|max [*number*|max]

**Default:** Unset; uses operating system defaults

**Context:** Server config, virtual host

**Status:** Core

**Compatibility:** Apache 1.2 and later

This directive limits memory used. The first argument is a limit for all processes; the second argument is the maximum resource limit. A value of max indicates that the limit should be set to the maximum allowed by the operating system. Don't alter this value unless you are sure you know what you are doing.

## RLimitNPROC

**Syntax:** RLimitNPROC *number* | max [*number* | max]

**Default:** Unset; uses operating system defaults

**Context:** Server config, virtual host

**Status:** Core

**Compatibility:** Apache 1.2 and later

This directive limits the number of processes used. The first argument is a limit for all processes; the second argument is the maximum resource limit. A value of max indicates that the limit should be set to the maximum allowed by the operating system. Don't alter this value unless you are sure you know what you are doing.

## Satisfy

**Syntax:** Satisfy [any | all]

**Default:** Satisfy all

**Context:** Directory, .htaccess

**Status:** Core

**Compatibility:** Apache 1.2 and later

When more than one criterion is set on access to a directory (for example, username/password and hostname), Satisfy indicates whether all the requirements have to be satisfied or just one of them.

In the following example, the client must come from the databeam.com network or authenticate with the username rbowen, but not necessarily both. If the Satisfy directive is set to all, both criteria must be satisfied for access to be granted.

```
<Limit GET POST>
order deny allow
deny from all
allow from databeam.com
require user rbowen
```

```
Satisfy any
</Limit>
```

## ScoreBoardFile

**Syntax:** ScoreBoardFile *filename*

**Default:** ScoreBoardFile logs/apache_status

**Context:** Server config

**Status:** Core

On some operating systems, this directive is required to create a file that's used to communicate between the parent server process and its children. You can determine if this is required on your platform simply by setting this directive to something and seeing if the file gets created.

## Script

**Syntax:** Script *method cgi-script*

**Context:** Server config, virtual host, directory

**Status:** Base

**Module:** mod_actions

**Compatibility:** Apache 1.1 and later

This directive causes a CGI program to be invoked when a particular HTTP method is used. Valid HTTP methods are GET, POST, PUT, and DELETE. If the method is GET, the CGI program will be called only if there is a QUERY_STRING on the URL—that is, if there is a question mark at the end, followed by one or more arguments.

```
Script GET /cgi-bin/search.pl
```

## ScriptAlias

**Syntax:** ScriptAlias *url-path directory-filename*

**Context:** Server config, virtual host

**Status:** Base

**Module:** mod_alias

See also the Alias directive. ScriptAlias does two things:

- It causes any URLs beginning with the specified *url-path* to be served out of the specified *directory-filename*.
- It causes all files within that directory to be treated as CGI programs.

```
ScriptAlias /cgi-bin/ /home/httpd/cgi-bin/
```

## ScriptAliasMatch

**Syntax:** ScriptAliasMatch *regex directory-filename*

**Context:** Server config, virtual host

**Status:** Base

**Module:** mod_alias

**Compatibility:** Apache 1.3 and later

ScriptAliasMatch is to ScriptAlias as AliasMatch is to Alias. ScriptAliasMatch functions similarly to ScriptAlias except that the URL path is specified as a regular expression.

```
ScriptAliasMatch /(cgi|scripts|progs)/ /www/cgi-bin/
```

## ScriptInterpreterSource

**Syntax:** ScriptInterpreterSource [registry|script]

**Default:** ScriptInterpreterSource script

**Context:** Directory, .htaccess

**Status:** Core (Windows only)

This is a Windows-only directive. Traditionally, the location of the interpreter used to run an interpreted CGI program (script) is contained in the first line of that program, in a #! (often pronounced "she-bang") line, such as #!/usr/bin/perl. When Apache first became available for Windows, this same method was used, but some Windows users, used to file extensions determining file type, found this behavior confusing. When it was suggested that the interpreter would be determined solely on the basis of the file extension, that was met by some resistance from folks who wanted to be able to move code from Windows machines to Unix machines and vice versa.

The ScriptInterpreterSource directive permits the server administrator to determine whether the interpreter will be determined from the file extension or based on a #! line. If this is set to registry, Apache will search the Registry to find out what application is associated with the file extension of the CGI program. If it is set to script, Apache will use the #! line to figure this out.

# ScriptLog

**Syntax:** ScriptLog *filename*

**Context:** Server config

**Module:** mod_cgi

ScriptLog sets the location of a log file used to log error messages from CGI programs. This is intended for debugging purposes only and shouldn't be implemented on an actual production server, since it will degrade performance and may produce a very large log file. The generated file will contain all the request headers and program output of all CGI programs. This is very useful for trying to figure out what went wrong with your CGI program.

See the ScriptLogLength and ScriptLogBuffer directives.

ScriptLog logs/script_log

# ScriptLogBuffer

**Syntax:** ScriptLogBuffer *size*

**Default:** ScriptLogBuffer 1024

**Context:** Server config

**Module:** mod_cgi

This directive limits the rate of growth of the ScriptLog by limiting the size of POST or PUT bodies that are logged to the file. Remember that all the headers and the entire body are posted to the ScriptLog file, and the file could become very large without this directive set at a reasonable value.

See the ScriptLog and ScriptLogLength directives.

# ScriptLogLength

**Syntax:** ScriptLogLength *size*

**Default:** ScriptLogLength 10385760

**Context:** Server config

**Module:** mod_cgi

This directive limits the total size of the ScriptLog file. If the file exceeds this size, data will simply cease to be written to the file.

See the ScriptLog and ScriptLogBuffer directives.

## SendBufferSize

**Syntax:** SendBufferSize *bytes*

**Context:** Server config

**Status:** Core

SendBufferSize sets the TCP buffer size to the number of bytes specified.

```
SendBufferSize 1024
```

## ServerAdmin

**Syntax:** ServerAdmin *email-address*

**Context:** Server config, virtual host

**Status:** Core

This directive specifies the email address of the person responsible for the server. This address is included in the error messages automatically generated by the server.

```
ServerAdmin webmaster@rcbowen.com
```

## ServerAlias

**Syntax:** ServerAlias *host1 host2 ...*

**Context:** Virtual host

**Status:** Core

**Compatibility:** Apache 1.1 and later

When you are using name-based virtual hosts, this directive allows you to specify various alternative names for the server without having to set up a separate virtual host declaration for each name. This is useful, for example, on an intranet, where users might use the server's fully qualified domain name or just the machine name.

```
<VirtualHost 9.95.144.27>
ServerName beamer.databeam.com
ServerAlias beamer
DocumentRoot /home/httpd/html/beamer/
</VirtualHost>
```

## ServerName

**Syntax:** ServerName *fully_qualified_domain_name*

**Context:** Server config, virtual host

**Status:** Core

This directive specifies the name of the server, used when the server is constructing redirect addresses. If this isn't specified, the server will try to figure it out itself, based on DNS lookups. However, this may not return the desired name. For example, the machine that I want the world to think of as `www.rcbowen.com` actually resolves in DNS as `209-249-98-74-virt-ip.mk.net`.

```
ServerName www.rcbowen.com
```

## ServerPath

**Syntax:** `ServerPath` *pathname*

**Context:** Virtual host

**Status:** Core

**Compatibility:** Apache 1.1 and later

`ServerPath` sets a path to access virtual host data on name-based hosts. This is for older browsers that don't send the correct information to tell the server which virtual host they are trying to access and so always get the data from the primary host. See Chapter 9 for more information.

In the following example, clients that can't access the server by the alias—that is, as `http://user2.mk.net/`—can access this host with the primary name of the server with the `ServerPath` appended: `http://www.mk.net/user2/`. It's useful to put a link to this alternative address on the primary site for users who have attempted to access the secondary site with an older browser.

```
<VirtualHost 9.95.144.27>
DocumentRoot /home/user2/html
ServerName user2.mk.net
ServerPath /user2/
</VirtualHost>
```

> **Note**
>
> This directive is seldom used in practice, as most Webmasters assume that users have newer browsers.

## ServerRoot

**Syntax:** ServerRoot *directory-filename*

**Default:** ServerRoot /usr/local/apache

**Context:** Server config

**Status:** Core

ServerRoot sets the directory in which the server's files will be stored. Most directives specifying a path to a file or directory will be assumed to be given relative to this directive, unless they have a leading slash. Directories typically located in this ServerRoot directory are conf/ and logs/. It can also be useful to create symbolic links in this directory to the various other server directories, such as the document and bin directories.

This directive can also be set with the -d command-line option on startup:

httpd -d /home/apache

## ServerSignature

**Syntax:** ServerSignature [Off|On|EMail]

**Default:** ServerSignature Off

**Context:** Server config, virtual host, directory, .htaccess

**Status:** Core

**Compatibility:** Apache 1.3 and later

This directive configures whether Apache will add a "signature" line to automatically generated error message pages. If the directive is set to On, this signature will be appended and will include the server's name and version number. If the directive is set to Email, the server will additionally display a mailto: link for sending email to the ServerAdmin. With this directive set to Off, no signature will be appended.

## ServerTokens

**Syntax:** ServerTokens Minimal|OS|Full

**Default:** ServerTokens Full

**Context:** Server config

**Status:** Core

**Compatibility:** Apache 1.3 and later

`ServerTokens` configures whether the `Server` HTTP response header will contain information about the operating system on which the server is running.

When `ServerTokens` is set to `Minimal`, Apache returns just the version number of the server. (`Minimal` can also be written as `Min`.) For example,

```
ServerTokens Minimal
```

returns

```
Server: Apache/1.3.6
```

When `ServerTokens` is set to `OS`, Apache returns the generic OS type that the server is running on. For example,

```
ServerTokens OS
```

returns

```
Server: Apache/1.3.6 (Win32)
```

When `ServerTokens` is set to `Full`, Apache returns any additional information about add-on packages that the server is running. For example,

```
ServerTokens: Full
```

returns

```
Server: Apache/1.3.6 (Unix) PHP/4.0Beta2
```

## ServerType

**Syntax:** `ServerType [inetd|standalone]`

**Default:** `ServerType standalone`

**Context:** Server config

**Status:** Core

This directive specifies how the server is to run:

- If `ServerType` is set to `inetd`, the server will be run by the `inetd` process, meaning that `inetd` will listen on port 80. Each time there is a request on that port, a new copy of Apache will be fired up to handle that request.

    This is extremely slow and inefficient. Almost the only time you should even consider using this setting is if you are testing configuration file changes. This setting ensures that the newest version of the config files will be used, and they are reloaded each time `inetd` launches the server.

> **Note**
>
> The inetd setting isn't supported on Windows NT, because Windows NT has no inetd process.

- standalone is the more common setting. One parent copy of Apache is launched, and multiple child processes are then spawned to handle requests. This is much faster and more efficient, as you don't have to pay the startup costs each time a request is made to the server.

## SetEnv

**Syntax:** SetEnv *variable value*

**Context:** Server config, virtual host

**Status:** Base

**Module:** mod_env

**Compatibility:** Apache 1.1 and later

SetEnv sets an environment variable that is then passed to CGI programs.

SetEnv PerlVersion 5.005

## SetEnvIf

**Syntax:** SetEnvIf *attribute regex envar*[=*value*] [...]

**Context:** Server config

**Status:** Base

**Module:** mod_setenvif

**Compatibility:** Apache 1.3 and later

This directive sets an environment variable if an attribute of the request matches a certain regular expression. The attribute can be any of the HTTP headers. See Chapter 2, "HTTP," for a listing of available HTTP headers. Some browsers pass HTTP headers that aren't part of the standard list, and any of these can be used also.

The following example sets the Admin environment variable if the authenticated username is either rbowen or tpowell:

SetEnvIf Remote_User "(rbowen)|(tpowell)" Admin

## SetEnvIfNoCase

**Syntax:** `SetEnvIfNoCase` *attribute regex envar[=value]* `[...]`

**Context:** Server config

**Status:** Base

**Module:** `mod_setenvif`

**Compatibility:** Apache 1.3 and later

This directive is similar to the `SetEnvIf` directive except that regular case-insensitive expression matching is performed. This might be useful if you aren't sure if a particular value might be uppercase, lowercase, or some combination.

The following example will set the environment variable `Admin` if the authenticated username is `rbowen`, but will also set it if the username is `Rbowen` or `RBowen`:

```
SetEnvIfNocase Remote_User rbowen Admin
```

## SetHandler

**Syntax:** `SetHandler` *handler-name*

**Context:** Directory, `.htaccess`

**Status:** Base

**Module:** `mod_mime`

**Compatibility:** Apache 1.1 and later

This directive sets a handler that handles requests to a particular directory. See Chapter 14 for more information on some things you can do with handlers.

```
SetHandler cgi-script
```

See also the `AddHandler` directive.

## StartServers

**Syntax:** `StartServers` *number*

**Default:** `StartServers 5`

**Context:** Server config

**Status:** Core

StartServers specifies the number of child processes to start on server startup. The actual number of child processes running at any one time is managed by the server according to the load and is based on the MaxSpareServers and MinSpareServers directives, so there's not much point changing this value.

> **Note**
>
> In Windows, this directive has no effect, as there's always only one child process, and requests are handled by different threads within that child, instead of by forked additional child processes. See the ThreadsPerChild directive for more information.

## ThreadsPerChild

**Syntax:** ThreadsPerChild *number*

**Default:** ThreadsPerChild 50

**Context:** Server config

**Status:** Core (Windows)

**Compatibility:** Apache 1.3 and later with Windows

This directive is valid only on Windows systems, where it takes the place of the MaxRequestsPerChild directive.

## TimeOut

**Syntax:** TimeOut *number*

**Default:** TimeOut 300

**Context:** Server config

**Status:** Core

This directive sets the timeout value for communication with the client. Specifically, it's the time for one of the following events:

- The total time to receive a GET request
- The time between packets on a PUT or POST request
- The amount of time between ACKs on transmission of packets in responses

In the future, these are expected to be three separate configuration options.

## TransferLog

**Syntax:** TransferLog *file-pipe*

**Context:** Server config, virtual host

**Status:** Base

**Module:** mod_log_config

The TransferLog directive tells the server where to write out the log file. *file-pipe* can be a file path or a | followed by a command that the log information is to be piped to. The command will receive this information on standard input.

```
TransferLog logs/access_log
TransferLog | /usr/bin/loghandler.pl
```

> **Note**
>
> The program will run as the user that started the server, which is usually root. Make sure that the program is secure.

You can also use the LogFormat and CustomLog directives to set the location of the transfer log. This is the way it's handled in the default configuration file.

## TypesConfig

**Syntax:** TypesConfig *filename*

**Default:** TypesConfig conf/mime.types

**Context:** Server config

**Status:** Base

**Module:** mod_mime

This directive specifies the location of the mime.types file relative to the ServerRoot. This file contains the MIME-type mappings to filename extensions.

> **Tip**
>
> Don't modify the mime.types file; instead, map all MIME types with the AddTypes directive.

## UnsetEnv

**Syntax:** UnsetEnv *variable variable ...*

**Context:** Server config, virtual host

**Status:** Base

**Module:** mod_env

**Compatibility:** Apache 1.1 and later

UnsetEnv removes environment variables from those sent to CGI programs.

UnsetEnv LD_LIBRARY_PATH

> **Note**
>
> Not all environment variables can be unset. Some of them are required by the CGI specification. See Chapter 11, "CGI Programming," for more details.

## UseCanonicalName

**Syntax:** UseCanonicalName [on|off]

**Default:** UseCanonicalName on

**Context:** Server config, virtual host, directory, .htaccess

**Override:** Options

**Compatibility:** Apache 1.3 and later

If set to on, this directive will cause Apache to use the values of the ServerName and Port directives when it constructs redirect URLs, and for what it passes to CGI programs. If this directive is set to off, the server will continue to use whatever the client passes in.

## User

**Syntax:** User *unix-userid*

**Default:** User #-1

**Context:** Server config, virtual host

**Status:** Core

This directive sets the user the server will run as. Unless you are sure you know what you're doing, this directive should be set to some user with few or no privileges on your system. Although you generally must be `root` to start the server, immediately after starting, the server changes to this user. All child processes will run as this user.

## UserDir

**Syntax:** UserDir [*directory/filename*] [enabled|disabled]

**Default:** UserDir public_html

**Context:** Server config, virtual host

**Status:** Base

**Module:** mod_userdir

**Compatibility:** All forms except the UserDir public_html form are available only in Apache 1.1 or later. Use of the enabled keyword, or disabled with a list of usernames, is available only in Apache 1.3 and later.

In its simplest form, this directive sets the subdirectory of a user's home directory, out of which documents will be served if a request is received for a user. User requests look like http://www.mk.net/~rbowen/—a server URL with a username preceded by a tilde (~).

With the following setting, http://www.mk.net/~rbowen/test.html would be mapped to the file /home/rbowen/htmldocs/test.html:

UserDir htmldocs

UserDir can also be used to redirect to a URL, if your user pages are housed on an entirely different server. You can use an asterisk (*) as a placeholder for the username. With the following setting, a request for http://www.mk.net/~rbowen/test.html would be mapped to the URL http://users.mk.net/rbowen/test.html:

UserDir http://users.mk.net/*/

In addition to these settings, the directive values disabled and enabled can also be used to turn user directory handling on or off, either globally or for particular users. The value disabled turns off all user directory handling, except for users specifically listed with the enabled value:

UserDir disabled

The value disabled, followed by a list of usernames, turns off user directory mapping for those users, even if they are listed as enabled:

```
UserDir disabled tpowell dpitts krietz
```

The value `enabled`, followed by a list of users, turns on username directory mapping for those users, even if a global `disabled` is in effect, but not if those users are listed as `disabled`:

```
UserDir enabled rbowen cbowen sbowen
```

## `<VirtualHost>`

**Syntax:** `<VirtualHost addr[:port] ...> ... </VirtualHost>`

**Context:** Server config

**Status:** Core

**Compatibility:** Non-IP address–based virtual hosting available only in Apache 1.1 and later; multiple address support available only in Apache 1.2 and later.

This directive is used to define a virtual host and what settings will apply to that virtual host:

```
<VirtualHost 9.95.144.27>
ServerName beamer.databeam.com
ServerAlias beamer
DocumentRoot /home/beamer/htmldocs
</VirtualHost>
```

See Chapter 9 for more details.

## `XBitHack`

**Syntax:** `XBitHack [on|off|full]`

**Default:** `XBitHack off`

**Context:** Server config, virtual host, directory, `.htaccess`

**Override:** `Options`

**Status:** Base

**Module:** `mod_include`

`XBitHack` allows the `execute` bit on an HTML file to determine whether that file will be parsed for server-side directives. When `XBitHack` is set to `on`, any file with the user `execute` bit set will be parsed for server-side content. When `XBitHack` is set to `full`, the same will happen, but the `Last-modified` date of the document will also be returned as the last-modified date of the file itself, allowing proxies to cache the resulting page. If `XBitHack` is set to `off`, no processing is done.

See Chapter 12 for more information.

# Summary

In addition to these base and code directives, a number of other directives deal with other extension modules. Part V of this book contains several chapters about Apache modules; those chapters will discuss the directives that go with each module.

Apache gives you, the server administrator, an enormous amount of control over the specifics of how the server will operate, letting you control everything from what error messages look like to the total amount of CPU time that the server is allowed to consume. In most cases, the default values will be adequate, but go ahead and experiment with some of these parameters to see what they do for your site. Although configuration directives are usually stable between releases, if you have a more recent version of Apache than what is discussed in this chapter (1.3.9), check the documentation on the Apache Web site to be sure that the syntax for a particular directive hasn't changed. Make sure that you save a backup copy before you start tinkering.

# Configuring Apache with Comanche

CHAPTER 6

Comanche is a simplified way to configure and administer your Apache server and any other application that relies on a text configuration file.

As you saw in Chapter 5, "Server Configuration Files," Apache has an overwhelming number of configuration directives. Although this means that you have complete control over a large number of things, it also means that there's a lot to know. Configuring your server might mean reading pages and pages of documentation to find just the right directive.

Also, the configuration file itself, although it has a rather simple format, requires that you learn that format before you can make changes. Different directives have different syntax, and certain directives can appear only in certain context. In all, configuring an Apache server can be a little confusing, particularly for beginners or those who are more familiar with products that have GUI (graphical user interface) configuration applications. Particularly for Microsoft Windows users, this is frequently cited as a reason for not using Apache.

To compound this problem, a number of other products have the same problem. Sendmail, DNS, and Samba are just a few examples of great products that are difficult to configure, and each product has its own configuration file format so, for each one, you have to learn a whole new way to configure it.

It's a real shame that when the product is so much better than most of the competition, what prevents people from using it is the method of configuration—something that's done very infrequently.

After looking at the default way of configuring Apache (editing a text file), Daniel Lopez Ridruejo decided to develop an alternative. Aiming for platform independence, he wrote it in Tcl, which runs on all platforms where Apache is available.

In fact, Daniel had a somewhat larger goal in mind than just Apache. He wanted to provide an interface for configuring anything with a text-based configuration file, such as Samba or various aspects of the Linux operating system.

Out of this desire for an easy-to-use configuration interface grew *Comanche* (Configuration Manager for Apache). You can extend Comanche to configure any other applications but, when you install it, it comes ready to configure your Apache and Samba installations.

# How to Get Comanche

You can get Comanche from the Comanche Web site at `http://comanche.com.dtu.dk/comanche/`. A version of Comanche is on the CD that accompanies this book, but you can always obtain the latest version at that URL.

Comanche is distributed as Open Source, much like Apache itself. This means that you can obtain the source code for Comanche and make your own changes if you so desire. Of course, if you make fixes or enhancements, you should tell Daniel about them, so that we can all benefit from your work.

Comanche is also available in binary form for Irix, Solaris, HP, Linux Intel, and Windows 9*x*/NT. An RPM installation is available for Red Hat Linux 5.x. If you are running some other operating system, you can obtain the source code and build it yourself. If you get it working successfully, contact Daniel and tell him that, and offer to send him the binaries that you produced, so that he can offer these in his Web site as well.

# How to Use Comanche

When you have Comanche installed on your system, running it is very straightforward.

> **Tip**
>
> Save a backup copy of your Apache configuration files before you start playing with Comanche. Of course, doing so is always a good idea when you start experimenting with configuration changes, so that you can always get back to a configuration that you know worked.

## Starting Comanche

In Windows, double-click the `comanche.exe` file to start the Comanche application. On Unix, you invoke the Comanche binary from the command line. The GUI looks very similar in either case.

In Windows, Comanche locates your Apache server installation by looking in the Registry. Because you can have more than one installation of Apache running at the same time (on different ports or different IP addresses, for example), Comanche lets you configure more than one Apache installation in the same interface.

On Unix, Comanche will ask where you have Apache installed and work from the location you tell it.

## The User Interface

When you first start Comanche, you will see a two-pane window (see Figure 6.1). In the left pane will be the name of your computer, with a plus sign next to it. Clicking on that plus sign will expand the tree, showing you sections for Apache and Samba. We won't be talking about configuring Samba with Comanche, but the procedure is exactly the same as for Apache.

**FIGURE 6.1**

*Main Comanche screen.*

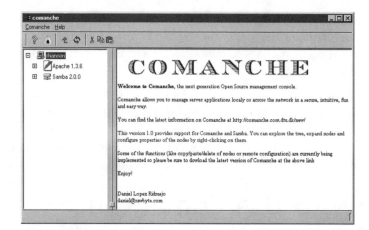

Opening the Apache tree on the left will show you one section for each defined virtual host, as well as for the main server. Under each defined host, you'll see each <Directory> or <Location> section that you've defined in your server configuration file. An additional section is there for Server Management. Figure 6.2 shows Comanche configuring a server with a main server and one virtual host.

**FIGURE 6.2**

*Configuring a server.*

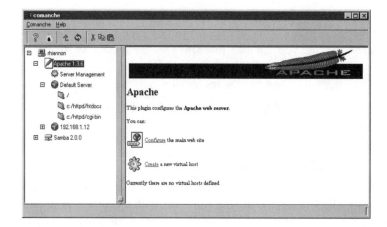

You can navigate to various parts of the configuration file either by clicking the links in the right pane, which works like a Web page, or by right-clicking the various nodes in the left pane, which will bring up a menu of options.

# Configuring Your Server

If you right-click Default Server in the left pane and select Configure from the displayed menu, you will see the dialog box in Figure 6.3. This dialog box lets you configure some of the properties of your server.

**FIGURE 6.3**

*Configuring site properties.*

Each option in the list box represents a logical section of your configuration file. The server properties are divided into five sections:

- *Basic Configuration* contains the name of the server (`ServerName`), the email address of the server administrator (`ServerAdmin`), and the document root directory of the main server (`DocumentRoot`).

- *Listening* contains the TCP/IP port on which the server should listen (`Port`) and the IP address to which the server is to bind (`BindAddress`).

- *Logging* contains the error log file or the syslog facility to which you want to send error messages (`ErrorLog`).

- *Alias* (see Figure 6.4) lets you configure aliases on your server (`Alias`). You can add new aliases and edit or delete existing aliases. As you see in Figure 6.5, you can add regular aliases or pattern-match aliases (`AliasMatch`).

- *CGI* contains the aliases that map to CGI directories (`ScriptAlias`).

**FIGURE 6.4**

*Configuring aliases.*

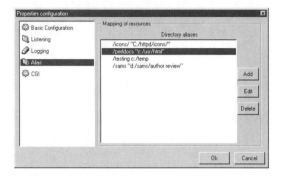

**FIGURE 6.5**

*Adding an alias.*

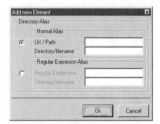

---

**Note**

When entering directory paths, be very careful with any directories that contain spaces. These directories usually are relevant only for Windows users. The real solution is to avoid spaces in your directory names but, if you must have them, be sure to enclose these paths in quotes. Failure to do so will probably result in your Apache server complaining about your configuration file syntax and failing to start.

---

- The *Url Redirection* section allows you to define redirections from one URL to another. This can be redirection either of a simple URL path or of a regular expression, to match more than one possible URL path. Figure 6.6 shows the dialog box for creating a new redirection rule.

  URLs can be redirected with one of several possible status codes:

  ```
  410 Gone
  301 Permanent
  302 Temporary
  303 See Other
  ```

**FIGURE 6.6**

*Creating a new redirection rule.*

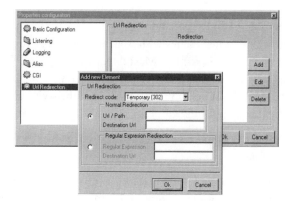

## Sections

Under each server or virtual host, you can add sections, into which you can place additional configuration directives. These sections can be one of three types: directory, location, or file. Each type of section specifies a certain group of resources: <Directory> groups resources by actual directory path, <Location> groups by URL, and <Files> groups by filenames.

To add a new section of any of these types, right-click the server under which the section is to appear and then select Add a New Node. Select the type of section that you are adding and the path, URL, or filename(s) that identifies the section you are adding.

You can also add file sections inside location and directory sections, if you want. You can then configure settings for each of these sections individually.

---

**Tip**

When adding a <Files> section, you can make the file name into a regular expression to match groups of files. To do this, just put a tilde (~) in front of the pattern:

```
~ "\.(gif|jpe?g)$"
```

# Configuring `<Directory>` Sections

In the default configuration file that comes with Apache, notice that very few settings are set in the main server configuration section. Most directives are placed within `<Directory>` sections so that the control can be more fine-grained, with different behaviors for different directories. Most notably, there is different behavior configured for the document directory and for the CGI directory.

Comanche lets you define any number of `<Directory>` sections and set configuration directives for those sections.

As with the main server configuration, directives for a `<Directory>` section are split into several categories. Figure 6.7 shows the layout of the `<Directory>` Properties Configuration dialog box. The dialog box is shown with the Authorisation options.

**FIGURE 6.7**

*Configuring a*
`<Directory>`
*section.*

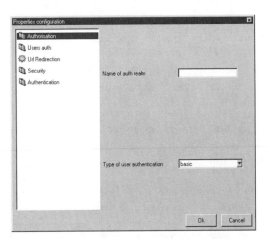

The five types of directives that you can configure are as follows:

- *Authorisation* (as shown in Figure 6.7) configures the authorization realm (`AuthName`) and type (`AuthType`) for protecting access to the directory. See Chapter 16, "Authentication," for more details on these directives.

- *Users auth* allows you to protect a directory for access by only particular users or groups of users. Or, you can decide that any valid user appearing in the password file can have access to this directory. Figure 6.8 shows the dialog box for configuring this option.

**FIGURE 6.8**

*Protecting a directory for only certain users.*

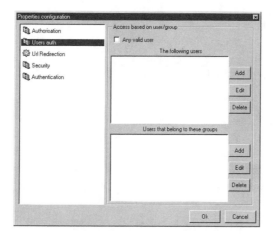

- *Url Redirection*, as in the main server configuration, allows you to create URL redirection rules.

- *Security* configures host access to the directory. The default behavior is to allow access to all hosts, but this can be changed to permit or deny access to any host, with granularity going all the way from a specific IP address or hostname to an entire network (such as `128.*.*.*`) or top level domain (such as `*.mil`). See Chapter 16 for more details on these directives. Comanche lets you configure all these options directly. Figure 6.9 shows you the dialog box listing all the configured options; Figure 6.10 shows the dialog box allowing the addition of new rules.

**FIGURE 6.9**

*Allowing access by host.*

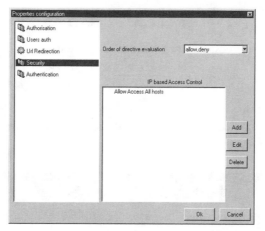

**FIGURE 6.10**

*Adding a new host-based access rule.*

- *Authentication* lets you set the location of the file containing the names and passwords used to authenticate users and the location of the file containing the group names, with the lists of users in those groups.

## Configuring `<Location>` Sections

`<Location>` sections allow for access control based on URL rather than directory path. The URL doesn't need to map to a particular directory at all. Configuring a `<Location>` section with Comanche is the same as configuring a `<Directory>` section. All directives valid in a `<Directory>` section are also valid in a `<Location>` section.

## Configuring `<Files>` Sections

`<Files>` sections allow for access control based on the actual filenames. Under a `<Files>` section, you can configure only security directives. These are exactly the same as the security configuration of a `<Directory>` section.

# Configuring Virtual Hosts

You can create a new virtual host either by right-clicking the icon labeled `Apache 1.3.6` (or whatever your version number is) in the list box or by clicking Create a New Virtual Host on the right.

Figure 6.11 shows the dialog box that lets you add a new virtual host. Although you can enter the FQDN (fully qualified domain name) of the server here, you really should enter the IP address of the virtual server.

> **Note**
>
> At this time, only IP-based virtual hosts are supported. See Chapter 9, "Virtual Hosting," for more information about virtual hosts.

**FIGURE 6.11**

*Adding a new virtual host.*

You can then configure the settings of the virtual host in exactly the same way as for the main server. The only difference is that the Listening section isn't available, because those settings can be configured only for the main server.

# Server Management Tasks

Under the server icon in the main Comanche window is a Server Management section. This section lets you do basic server management, such as starting, stopping, restarting, and gracefully restarting your server. Also, if you are running Apache on Unix and have mod_status compiled in and enabled, you can get the current status of the server as provided by mod_status.

For each option, a button will appear on the right, labeled as appropriate.

> **Note**
>
> As described in Chapter 5, the difference between *restarting* and *gracefully restarting* is that a graceful restart allows all requests being served at the time of the restart to be completed before the child process exits and a new one starts. A regular restart unceremoniously dumps current connections, and the child processes exit immediately.

# Extending Comanche

You can extend Comanche to configure any application with a text configuration file. Comanche comes with modules for Apache and Samba, as well as a sample module for setting your hostname. A Comanche module consists of some Tcl code to define what the user interface will look like and XML files that define the directives that can appear in the configuration file.

For a full treatment of making your own modules, you should see the documentation that comes with Comanche. However, the best way to learn how to make a module is to read through the files that define the standard modules and try to hack together one of your own. The hostname module is intentionally simple so that it can be used as an example on which to build your module.

# Limitations

Although Comanche is a very cool application and greatly simplifies the configuration of Apache, you should be aware of some small limitations.

## You Must Be at the Console

You must be physically at the machine being configured or use some remote console program to view the console of the machine being configured. At this time, Comanche doesn't support the ability to configure services on remote machines, although this will be in future versions of the product.

This is perhaps not as much of a limitation as you might think, because several free remote-console applications are available. The best one out there (in my opinion) is VNC, which you can obtain at http://www.uk.research.att.com/vnc/. It is free and distributed under the GPL. It runs on Windows and Unix (and various other platforms, including PalmOS) and allows you to control a remote machine as though you were sitting in front of it. You can do this via a full client application or via a Java applet in a Web browser. VNC removes the requirement of having to be physically present to configure a machine, particularly when dealing with Microsoft Windows, which requires you to be at the console to perform many administrative tasks.

## You Need to Know Tcl to Extend Comanche

In the current version of Comanche, you need to know Tcl to extend Comanche to configure other applications. In future versions, you will be able to write these modules in any language you want.

However, Tcl is fairly simple syntactically, and examples in the Comanche documentation walk you through creating example modules. Because many configuration files have similar syntax (although not exactly the same), converting an existing module into your own customized module shouldn't be terribly difficult. And once people start creating extension modules to configure various applications, many of these modules will be available for download from the Internet.

## You Need to Know Something About the Configuration Files

Although the graphical user interface (GUI) frees you from working directly with the configuration files, you still need to know something about those files to use this tool. Much of the terminology used in the Comanche interface assumes familiarity with the

files and the directives. Words such as `allow`, `deny`, and `location` are used, with the assumption that you understand what they mean in the context of configuring an Apache server. Although this assumption is reasonable for Apache's current target audience, in the future this will probably be somewhat limiting as more people start using Comanche to configure their servers, having never edited the configuration files directly.

Of course, because this wording can be modified very easily, it's reasonable to assume that in future versions things will be worded so that even a complete beginner with Apache would be able to use Comanche to configure all the settings on his server.

## Summary

Comanche is a powerful way to configure your Apache Web server and any other application that has a text configuration file. It's a great way to get over the initial learning curve in setting up an Apache server, particularly for those of you who are used to a GUI configuration interface.

# MIME Types

**CHAPTER 7**

As mentioned in Chapter 2, "HTTP," MIME types (also called *Internet Media Types* or *IMT*s) are a central pillar of the Hypertext Transfer Protocol (HTTP). They tell the client (browser) what type of document it's receiving, and thus help it decide what it will do with that file. The Apache Web server uses a list of MIME types stored in one of its configuration files, `mime.types`, as well as one-at-a-time definitions found in the other configuration files. The list of publicly known and used MIME types is maintained at a central location on the Internet, as described later.

This chapter discusses what MIME types are, how they're used, and how you can configure your server to associate certain MIME types with certain files or kinds of files.

> **Note**
>
> Documents generated in real time in response to a client request (such as the server status report from the `mod_status` module) also need MIME types, but the mechanism that's generating the content needs to specify the type appropriately. In each case, the means of doing this is specific to the generating mechanism, and is thus beyond the scope of this chapter. Because the vast majority of Web documents are actually based on files on disk, this chapter focuses on that aspect of configuration.

# What Is MIME?

Chapter 2 briefly addressed MIME, but so that you don't have to thumb through the pages to find that note, here are the basics again. MIME (Multipart Internet Mail Extensions) is a way of indicating the type of a particular document or resource, which might or might not be an actual file on the server.

MIME types are composed of a main type, such as `image` or `text`, and a subtype, such as `gif` or `rtf`. A MIME type is written as follows:

```
image/gif
```

This MIME type indicates that a file is an image and is of the specific file format `gif`. This helps the client determine what it needs to do with the bit-stream that it's receiving.

The registry of media types is managed by the Internet Assigned Numbers Authority (IANA), and the complete and up-to-date list of the current registered types can be found on the Web at `ftp://ftp.isi.edu/in-notes/iana/assignments/media-types/media-types`. This Web page also identifies the registrant for each type.

The Content-type field in the response header, which is sent back to the client with the actual response content itself, can contain more than just the media type, however; it can also include information such as the character set in which the document is encoded, as in

```
Content-type: text/plain; charset=ISO-8859-4
```

Although this additional information isn't actually part of the MIME type itself, the same Apache mechanisms that allow you to manipulate the medium type also let you control these factors.

# Why MIME Types Matter

A MIME type is sent as an HTTP Content-type header field in the response from the HTTP server. For example, the MIME type identification for a simple HTML document would look like this:

```
Content-type: text/html
```

This might be one of several HTTP header fields sent with the response. The HTTP header is terminated by a blank line (for more information, see Chapter 2).

MIME types are discussed in RFCs 2045, 2046, 2047, 2048, and 2077, among others. Registering MIME types is important so that two different content types don't end up with the same MIME label, generating confusion as to what type of document is actually signified. (Companies or individuals with a new kind of content can register a MIME type by contacting the IANA.) The special prefix x- on the MIME subtype is reserved for experimental types, such as audio/x-aiff; this is frequently used when a media type has been deployed but has not yet completed the registration process.

If the client is told what sort of data is being sent, it can take appropriate action on receipt. For instance, in the case of a Web browser with an actual person sitting in front of it, the browser can tell whether the document is something it can render and display (such as text/html, text/plain, or image/gif), something for which it needs to activate a plug-in (such as Adobe Acrobat for application/pdf), something that requires a co-processing handler (like Microsoft Word for an application/msword document), or whether it needs to ask the user for instructions if it doesn't already have some that cover the media type.

A document's media type can also be important when the server has multiple versions of a particular document (called *variants*; see the section on mod negotiation in Chapter 21, "Using the Perl Module") and needs to choose which one to send the client. The client might, for instance, have expressed a preference for HTML text over plain text, or GIF images over JPEG.

# Default MIME Types

Apache has a number of directives that control how it figures out the correct MIME type for a document (see Chapter 5, "Server Configuration Files"). If all else fails, though, it will use the value of the `DefaultType` directive, if it exists in the server config files. As distributed, this appears in the `conf/httpd.conf-dist` file as

`DefaultType text/plain`

This means that if the server can't figure out the correct type for a document, it will assume it's a plain text file and tell the client so. For text-based Web sites, this is probably a reasonable default setting. For a Web site that specializes in download packages or astronomy photographs, though, it might not be appropriate. Remember, the client will act according to what it's told is the type of the document, which means that it may try to display a binary file on the user's screen. For Web sites with more binary content than textual, a better default value to set might be

`DefaultType application/octet-stream`

This simply means "a stream of bytes." For a site containing mostly clip art, perhaps the following would work better:

`DefaultType image/gif`

Typically, if the client doesn't know what to do with the document's data type, it will ask the user for instructions, or possibly simply save it to disk.

If your Apache configuration doesn't include an explicit `DefaultType` directive, Apache defines the default as being `text/plain`, which is just what it is in the standard supplied configuration file. You can specify a default MIME type for all files on your server with names that match a particular pattern. The idea of extensions is crucial here, as they are the primary means Apache uses to determine media types. A file *extension* is simply a portion of the filename that begins with a dot or period. For instance, in the filename `index.html`, the extension is `.html`; in the name `food.txt.en`, both `.txt` and `.en` are extensions.

---

**Note**

When an Apache directive accepts a file extension as an argument, the leading dot (period) is almost always optional. Some people prefer to leave the dot in place to make it clear that an extension is involved. Consider the following two lines, which have the same effect:

```
AddLanguage ca ca
AddLanguage ca .ca
```

Both lines declare that files with an extension of `.ca` are in the Catalan language, but which one conveys that more clearly is a matter of personal opinion.

# Determining the MIME Type from the File Contents

Although most Webmasters have a pretty good idea of the content types of the files on their systems, sometimes pretty good isn't good enough. Sometimes the best (or only) way to figure out what's in a file is by actually looking at it. Recent versions of the Apache server software have included a module named mod_mime_magic designed to do exactly that.

The mod_mime_magic module uses the same techniques the UNIX file(1) command does to figure out what type of information is in a file. It actually reads some of the data from the file and applies a series of tests (such as "Are the first two characters #!?" or "Is the fifth byte 23, the seventeenth 127, and the fortieth 64?") until one succeeds.

In the standard Apache distribution, the list of rules used by mod_mime_magic is contained in the file magic in the conf subdirectory under the Serverroot. You can use the MIMEMagicFile directive to change this and tell the module to use a different file; the syntax of the directive is

```
MIMEMagicFile path/filename
```

If the path isn't absolute (that is, doesn't begin with a / on UNIX or a drive letter on Windows), it's regarded as being relative to the ServerRoot.

The MIMEMagicFile directive defines a server-wide setting and can appear only in the server config files outside and <Directory>, <Files>, and <Location> containers. It can appear in the global server settings or within <VirtualHost> containers. Within a particular server environment, the last MIMEMagicFile directive encountered is the one the server will use.

Although this content-driven typing mechanism is very flexible, extending it to recognize new file types isn't simple and carries a fairly heavy performance penalty. In general, using mod_mime_magic for MIME type determination isn't recommended.

# MIME Types and Filenames

Apache provides a number of ways to configure MIME types based on filenames. It provides a default list of associations (called *mappings*) of MIME types to file extensions, and several directives allow you to augment or change these defaults. These defaults are described in the following sections.

Extensions that map to MIME types are processed left to right, with the rightmost one taking precedence and overriding any earlier extensions encountered. This means that Apache will, by default, regard `food.html.bin` as a binary file but see `food.bin.html` as an HTML text document.

See Chapter 5 for more details about the directives mentioned here, including `AddType`, `ForceType`, `RemoveHandler`, `TypesConfig`, `AddEncoding`, `AddLanguage`, and `DefaultLanguage`.

## The Default Mapping File, `mime.types`

The `mime.types` file provided as part of every Apache installation contains a listing of more than 250 MIME types. This file controls what MIME types are sent to the client for each file extension. In some cases, the definition includes a mapping to one or more file extensions, such as

`application/octet-stream bin dms lha lzh exe class`

However, in many cases the definition identifies only a media type without making any assumptions about what documents of that type will be named. The preceding example instructs Apache to treat as binary any files containing `.bin`, `.dms`, `.lha`, `.lzh`, `.exe`, or `.class` in their names.

Listing 7.1 shows the relevant portions of the `mime.types` file provided as part of the Apache 1.3.9 release.

**LISTING 7.1**  MIME Types Defined by the Apache 1.3.9 `mime.types` File

```
# MIME type                              Extension
application/EDI-Consent
application/EDI-X12
application/EDIFACT
application/activemessage
application/andrew-inset                 ez
application/applefile
application/atomicmail
application/cals-1840
application/commonground
application/cybercash
application/dca-rft
application/dec-dx
application/eshop
application/hyperstudio
application/iges
application/mac-binhex40                 hqx
application/mac-compactpro               cpt
```

```
application/macwriteii
application/marc
application/mathematica
application/msword                            doc
application/news-message-id
application/news-transmission
application/octet-stream                      bin dms lha lzh exe class
application/oda                               oda
application/pdf                               pdf
application/pgp-encrypted
application/pgp-keys
application/pgp-signature
application/pkcs10
application/pkcs7-mime
application/pkcs7-signature
application/postscript                        ai eps ps
application/prs.alvestrand.titrax-sheet
application/prs.cww
application/prs.nprend
application/remote-printing
application/riscos
application/rtf                               rtf
application/set-payment
application/set-payment-initiation
application/set-registration
application/set-registration-initiation
application/sgml
application/sgml-open-catalog
application/slate
application/smil                              smi smil
application/vemmi
application/vnd.3M.Post-it-Notes
application/vnd.FloGraphIt
application/vnd.acucobol
application/vnd.anser-web-certificate-issue-initiation
application/vnd.anser-web-funds-transfer-initiation
application/vnd.audiograph
application/vnd.businessobjects
application/vnd.claymore
application/vnd.comsocaller
application/vnd.dna
application/vnd.dxr
application/vnd.ecdis-update
application/vnd.ecowin.chart
application/vnd.ecowin.filerequest
application/vnd.ecowin.fileupdate
application/vnd.ecowin.series
application/vnd.ecowin.seriesrequest
application/vnd.ecowin.seriesupdate
```

7

**MIME TYPES**

*continues*

**LISTING 7.1**    continued

```
application/vnd.enliven
application/vnd.epson.salt
application/vnd.fdf
application/vnd.ffsns
application/vnd.framemaker
application/vnd.fujitsu.oasys
application/vnd.fujitsu.oasys2
application/vnd.fujitsu.oasys3
application/vnd.fujitsu.oasysgp
application/vnd.fujitsu.oasysprs
application/vnd.fujixerox.docuworks
application/vnd.hp-HPGL
application/vnd.hp-PCL
application/vnd.hp-PCLXL
application/vnd.hp-hps
application/vnd.ibm.MiniPay
application/vnd.ibm.modcap
application/vnd.intercon.formnet
application/vnd.intertrust.digibox
application/vnd.intertrust.nncp
application/vnd.is-xpr
application/vnd.japannet-directory-service
application/vnd.japannet-jpnstore-wakeup
application/vnd.japannet-payment-wakeup
application/vnd.japannet-registration
application/vnd.japannet-registration-wakeup
application/vnd.japannet-setstore-wakeup
application/vnd.japannet-verification
application/vnd.japannet-verification-wakeup
application/vnd.koan
application/vnd.lotus-1-2-3
application/vnd.lotus-approach
application/vnd.lotus-freelance
application/vnd.lotus-organizer
application/vnd.lotus-screencam
application/vnd.lotus-wordpro
application/vnd.meridian-slingshot
application/vnd.mif                              mif
application/vnd.minisoft-hp3000-save
application/vnd.mitsubishi.misty-guard.trustweb
application/vnd.ms-artgalry
application/vnd.ms-asf
application/vnd.ms-excel                         xls
application/vnd.ms-powerpoint                    ppt
application/vnd.ms-project
application/vnd.ms-tnef
application/vnd.ms-works
application/vnd.music-niff
application/vnd.musician
```

```
application/vnd.netfpx
application/vnd.noblenet-directory
application/vnd.noblenet-sealer
application/vnd.noblenet-web
application/vnd.novadigm.EDM
application/vnd.novadigm.EDX
application/vnd.novadigm.EXT
application/vnd.osa.netdeploy
application/vnd.powerbuilder6
application/vnd.powerbuilder6-s
application/vnd.rapid
application/vnd.seemail
application/vnd.shana.informed.formtemplate
application/vnd.shana.informed.interchange
application/vnd.shana.informed.package
application/vnd.street-stream
application/vnd.svd
application/vnd.swiftview-ics
application/vnd.truedoc
application/vnd.visio
application/vnd.webturbo
application/vnd.wrq-hp3000-labelled
application/vnd.wt.stf
application/vnd.xara
application/vnd.yellowriver-custom-menu
application/wita
application/wordperfect5.1
application/x-bcpio                          bcpio
application/x-cdlink                         vcd
application/x-chess-pgn                      pgn
application/x-compress
application/x-cpio                           cpio
application/x-csh                            csh
application/x-director                       dcr dir dxr
application/x-dvi                            dvi
application/x-futuresplash                   spl
application/x-gtar                           gtar
application/x-gzip
application/x-hdf                            hdf
application/x-javascript                     js
application/x-koan                           skp skd skt skm
application/x-latex                          latex
application/x-netcdf                         nc cdf
application/x-sh                             sh
application/x-shar                           shar
application/x-shockwave-flash                swf
application/x-stuffit                        sit
application/x-sv4cpio                        sv4cpio
application/x-sv4crc                         sv4crc
```

7

**MIME TYPES**

*continues*

**LISTING 7.1** continued

| | |
|---|---|
| application/x-tar | tar |
| application/x-tcl | tcl |
| application/x-tex | tex |
| application/x-texinfo | texinfo texi |
| application/x-troff | t tr roff |
| application/x-troff-man | man |
| application/x-troff-me | me |
| application/x-troff-ms | ms |
| application/x-ustar | ustar |
| application/x-wais-source | src |
| application/x400-bp | |
| application/xml | |
| application/zip | zip |
| audio/32kadpcm | |
| audio/basic | au snd |
| audio/midi | mid midi kar |
| audio/mpeg | mpga mp2 mp3 |
| audio/vnd.qcelp | |
| audio/x-aiff | aif aiff aifc |
| audio/x-pn-realaudio | ram rm |
| audio/x-pn-realaudio-plugin | rpm |
| audio/x-realaudio | ra |
| audio/x-wav | wav |
| chemical/x-pdb | pdb xyz |
| image/bmp | bmp |
| image/cgm | |
| image/g3fax | |
| image/gif | gif |
| image/ief | ief |
| image/jpeg | jpeg jpg jpe |
| image/naplps | |
| image/png | png |
| image/prs.btif | |
| image/tiff | tiff tif |
| image/vnd.dwg | |
| image/vnd.dxf | |
| image/vnd.fpx | |
| image/vnd.net-fpx | |
| image/vnd.svf | |
| image/vnd.xiff | |
| image/x-cmu-raster | ras |
| image/x-portable-anymap | pnm |
| image/x-portable-bitmap | pbm |
| image/x-portable-graymap | pgm |
| image/x-portable-pixmap | ppm |
| image/x-rgb | rgb |
| image/x-xbitmap | xbm |
| image/x-xpixmap | xpm |
| image/x-xwindowdump | xwd |

```
message/delivery-status
message/disposition-notification
message/external-body
message/http
message/news
message/partial
message/rfc822
model/iges                              igs iges
model/mesh                              msh mesh silo
model/vnd.dwf
model/vrml                              wrl vrml
multipart/alternative
multipart/appledouble
multipart/byteranges
multipart/digest
multipart/encrypted
multipart/form-data
multipart/header-set
multipart/mixed
multipart/parallel
multipart/related
multipart/report
multipart/signed
multipart/voice-message
text/css                                css
text/directory
text/enriched
text/html                               html htm
text/plain                              asc txt
text/prs.lines.tag
text/rfc822-headers
text/richtext                           rtx
text/rtf                                rtf
text/sgml                               sgml sgm
text/tab-separated-values               tsv
text/uri-list
text/vnd.abc
text/vnd.flatland.3dml
text/vnd.fmi.flexstor
text/vnd.in3d.3dml
text/vnd.in3d.spot
text/vnd.latex-z
text/x-setext                           etx
text/xml                                xml
video/mpeg                              mpeg mpg mpe
video/quicktime                         qt mov
video/vnd.motorola.video
video/vnd.motorola.videop
video/vnd.vivo
```

7

MIME TYPES

*continues*

LISTING 7.1   continued

```
video/x-msvideo                          avi
video/x-sgi-movie                        movie
x-conference/x-cooltalk                  ice
```

---

**Caution**

You can add extra MIME types to the `mime.types` file. One disadvantage to modifying this file, however, is that an upgrade to the Apache software will very likely replace it, thus wiping out your changes. Suddenly your documents won't be labeled with the correct document types, and your visitors will start complaining. This problem can be difficult to debug, particularly if you made the changes to `mime.types` long before the upgrade. If you move the `mime.types` file to a different name or location, you then run the risk of not picking up any changes made to it by the Apache upgrade.

A better solution is to leave the `mime.types` file alone, unmodified from its distributed form, and override it with the `AddType` and related directives in the server or directory configuration files. These methods are described in the following sections and in Chapter 5.

---

# The `TypesConfig` Directive

Because the Apache server software comes with a file containing MIME type mappings, it's an obvious place to make changes specific to your local configuration. The `mime.types` file is typically found in the same directory as the server configuration files; the directory is typically named `conf`. You can override this behavior, and the name of the file itself, with the `TypesConfig` directive (see Chapter 5 for more details on this directive). The syntax of this directive is

```
TypesConfig path/filename
```

The `TypesConfig` directive takes a single parameter: the name of (and path to) the file containing the initial type definitions and mappings (usually called `mime.types`). If the path isn't absolute, it's interpreted as being relative to the `ServerRoot`. In fact, the default configuration files distributed with Apache 1.3.9 contain the line

```
TypesConfig conf/mime.types
```

which means that the server should find it in the `conf` subdirectory under the `ServerRoot`.

The `TypesConfig` directive is allowed only in the server configuration files, and even then not inside any `<Location>` or `<Directory>` containers. You can specify a different `TypesConfig` directive for each `<VirtualHost>` section and the global server environment, but for each server environment only the last one encountered will be used. That is, in the following excerpt

```
TypesConfig conf/mime.types
<VirtualHost 10.0.130.23>
    TypesConfig conf/mime.types-1
    TypesConfig conf/mime.types-2
</VirtualHost>
TypesConfig conf/mime.types-3
```

the global server environment would end up using the values in the file `conf/mime.types-3`, and the `10.0.130.23` virtual host shown would be using the values from the `conf/mime.types-2` file.

## The `AddType` Directive

The primary technique used to augment the `mime.types` file is the `AddType` directive. You use this directive to add a mapping that associates a particular filename extension with a MIME type. This mapping will override any other mapping in effect for the same filename extension, whether obtained from the `mime.types` file or from an earlier `AddType` directive. Although this is ordinarily used to add a mapping for a filename extension that's not already in the `mime.types` file, it can also be used to change an existing mapping, to change the behavior of certain files. A specific example of this is discussed later in the section "Forcing the Client to 'Save As.'"

The syntax of the `AddType` directive is as follows:

```
AddType image/x-oilpainting .oil
```

This directive can be used in your main server configuration files, in `<Directory>` or `<VirtualHost>` directives, or in `.htaccess` files.

## The `ForceType` Directive

Usually, a document's MIME type is determined from the filename extension, or occasionally from its contents, as described earlier in this chapter. In some cases, though, it's simpler or more appropriate to be able to tell Apache to use a particular MIME type for all files in a particular directory, or whose names match a particular pattern. This is called *forcing* the MIME type, and it's done, appropriately enough, with the `ForceType` directive.

`ForceType` takes a single argument: the MIME type to be forced onto documents within its purview. A forced type overrides all file mapping instructions, so it's very powerful and can be very far-reaching in its effects. It can be used in `<Files>` containers in `.htaccess` files and `<Directory>` containers in the server config files; you can even use it to force a particular MIME type onto all file-based documents a server transmits by specifying it in the global server context or within a `<VirtualHost>` container.

> **Note**
>
> `ForceType` applies only to documents that are actually files. It will have no effect on CGI scripts or module-generated content (such as that from `mod_autoindex` or `mod_status`).

Typical uses of `ForceType` are in directories containing files automatically generated at regular intervals. For example, in a directory where the only files are `majordomo` archives for a mailing list named `apache-discuss`, the following might be appropriate:

```
ForceType text/plain
```

If the directory contains other files, such as HTML documents, you can limit the type-forcing to just the archive files with something like this:

```
<Files apache-discuss.*>
    ForceType text/plain
</Files>
```

This would limit the effect to just those files with names beginning with `apache-discuss.` (such as `apache-discuss.199909`, a common naming convention for monthly archives).

Likewise, for a directory containing textual log files named according to the day of the week, something like this might be appropriate:

```
<Files *.*day>
    ForceType text/plain
</Files>
```

This would cause Apache to regard `report.Monday`, `totals.Saturday`, and `statistics.Wednesday` as all being of MIME type `text/plain`.

> **Note**
>
> Even though these last two examples are basing the scope of the `ForceType` directive on the filename, they couldn't be done with the `AddType` directive because the name syntax is more complex. For example, to redo the last two examples with the `AddType` directive, you would wind up with
>
> ```
> AddType text/plain .199901 .199902 .199903 .199904 .199905 .199906
>             ➡.199907 .199908 .199909
> ```
>
> and
>
> ```
> AddType text/plain .sunday .monday .tuesday .wednesday .thursday
>             ➡.friday .saturday
> ```
>
> In a way, the Perl credo ("There's more than one way to do it") applies here. Both directives will work, so choose whichever appeals to you more.

## The `AddEncoding` Directive

Another attribute of a Web document is something called its content encoding. *Content encoding* indicates to the client that the document has been compressed or otherwise encoded in some fashion. Content encoding also indicates what type of encoding is being used. This encoding information is often needed in addition to the MIME type information.

For example, a file with the name `fishing.html.gz` is presumably an HTML file that has been compressed with the gzip compression tool. Because it has the file extension `.html`, it will be served with a MIME type of `text/html` (assuming the default mapping settings), but additional information needs to be sent to indicate that it has been compressed by gzip. The `AddEncoding` directive tells Apache how to figure this out so that it can provide this information.

The following example associates a content encoding of gzip with files with a `.gz` file extension:

```
AddEncoding gzip .gz
```

7

MIME TYPES

> **Note**
>
> Files with multiple file extensions will be served with the information derived from all the extensions, unless multiple extensions provide the same type of information. For example, under normal conditions, the file `fishing.html.gz` will be served with a MIME type of `text/html` because of the `.html` file extension, and with a content encoding of gzip because of the `.gz` file extension. If the file was named `fishing.gz.html`, the effect would be the same because the two extensions provide different types of information.
>
> The two primary content encodings in use are *compress* and *gzip*. Due to deployment and implementation issues across the Internet, the `x-compress` and `x-gzip` content encodings are also common, and they have the same meanings as their unprefixed counterparts.

# Inheritance of MIME Settings

Almost all MIME configuration aspects of Apache are handled by the `mod_mime` module, and the directives follow a straightforward set of inheritance and scoping rules. Simply put, the settings of the closest applicable ancestor of the document involved are the ones that apply. Directives in an `.htaccess` file in the same directory will override those in the parent directory or in the server config files, for instance. See Chapter 8, ".htaccess Files," for more information.

All MIME management directives except `TypesConfig` and `MIMEMagicFile` can appear in `.htaccess` files and anywhere in the server config files. Likewise, the availability in `.htaccess` files of all except `TypesConfig` and `MIMEMagicFile` is controlled by the `FileInfo` override setting. (See Chapter 5's discussion of the `AllowOverride` directive for more information.)

# Managing MIME Types

Assignment of MIME types to documents and resources being sent to clients is very important, so correct identification of the right type for each response is crucial. True to form, the Apache server software gives you tremendous flexibility in making this identification at whatever level of granularity—server-wide, per directory, specific file types, or any combination—you need.

# Managing MIME Types with Configuration Files

You can change the way Apache handles the MIME typing of files by using the various directives (such as AddType) in the server config files. When Apache Server starts, it reads and processes the definitions in the mime.types file and then modifies the results by applying the appropriate AddType directives. Because the server config sites control Apache's overall operation, explicit scoping with <VirtualHost>, <Directory>, and <Files> containers is very important; you don't want your settings to have too broad an impact, which can easily happen because of an error in these files.

The server config files are processed only when the server starts up (or is restarted), which means that changing them can be a matter of some small concern for very busy sites.

# Managing MIME Types in .htaccess Files

To make MIME settings specific to only a particular directory and its subordinate subdirectories, you can put the directives into the directory's .htaccess file. The advantage of this is that there's no way the change can have any effect on other directory trees, and you don't have to worry about <VirtualHost> and <Directory> container blocks. On the other hand, the usual bugaboo of .htaccess file usage remains: It imposes a runtime performance penalty on the server for each and every request made for documents in the directory tree because the entire .htaccess file needs to be processed.

# Managing MIME Types for Just a Single Directory

Unfortunately, due to the scoping model used by Apache, it's not a simple matter to make a change to the MIME typing system for files in just a single directory. By default, the changes will also apply to all subdirectories. If you include a line such as

```
AddType application/x-httpd-php3 .html
```

in a <Directory> container or an .htaccess file for a particular directory, all .html files in directories lower in the tree will be affected as well.

There is one common way to make this behavior not affect any subdirectories lower in the tree, and it involves making an explicit statement about those lower levels. For the sake of this example, assume that the following directives are in your server config files:

```
<Directory /usr/htdocs/php>
 AddType application/x-httpd-php3 .html
</Directory>
```

To override this setting at lower levels of the file system tree, either add a line such as the following to an `.htaccess` file in every single subdirectory under `/usr/htdocs/php`:

```
AddType text/html .html
```

or add a section such as the following to your server config files:

```
<Directory ~ /usr/htdocs/php/.*>
 AddType text/html .html
</Directory>
```

Of course, the latter is seen by many as the better approach because there's only one place in which you need to make the change. It also has a lower performance impact because the server-wide config files are processed only at server startup, whereas `.htaccess` files may be processed every time something in their directory is requested. The negative aspect of making changes to your server config files is that the changes won't take effect until the server is restarted.

# Using MIME Information

The MIME type of a file can be used to alter the server's behavior. This is useful for altering behavior based on the content of the files themselves, rather than on directory paths or other file attributes.

The following directives allow configuration of behavior based on a file's MIME type. These are examples of ways in which the Apache server itself is also a user of the MIME information, in addition to the end user's client.

Most of these uses are made by the `FancyIndexing` index option mode specified in the `mod_autoindex` module; see the section on that module for more information about its capabilities.

> **Note**
>
> All the following directives are associated with the `mod_autoindex` module except `ExpiresByType`, which is associated with `mod_expires`. See Chapter 21's section on the `mod_expires` module for more details about the syntax and usage of `ExpiresByType`.

# The `AddIconByType` Directive

When using automatically generated directory indexes, called *fancy indexing*, you can specify what icons are displayed next to each filename. The determination of the appropriate icon is usually made based on the filename. Instead, you can use the `AddIconByType` directive to add icons to each file based on the MIME type associated with it. The format of the directive is

```
AddIconByType icon MIME-type [MIME-type ...]
```

The `icon` parameter is either a URL to the icon image file or a parenthetical expression identifying the alternate text (see the next section) and the image file URL, for example:

```
AddIconByType /icons/sound2.gif audio/*
AddIconByType (SND,/icons/sound2.gif) audio/*
```

# The `AddAltByType` Directive

In a graphics-capable Web browser, inline images frequently have what's called "alternate text" associated with them. This text is commonly shown by the browser until it finishes loading and rendering the image itself, or if the user has disabled image loading. The `AddAltByType` directive allows you to set the value of the alternate text associated with the icon representing the MIME type of the file.

This directive isn't used very often; usually the combined form of the `AddIconByType` directive (see the previous section) is used. Otherwise, both an `AddAltByType` and an `AddIconByType` directive would be required to have the same effect. That is, the following two segments are equivalent:

```
AddIconByType /icons/quill.gif application/x-scribble
AddAltByType "SCR" application/x-scribble
```

and

```
AddIconByType (SCR,/icons/quill.gif) application/x-scribble
```

# The `AddIconByEncoding` Directive

This directive is similar to the `AddIconByType` directive described earlier, except that it specifies an icon for files with a specific content encoding.

If there's an icon associated with a document's content encoding, it will be used in preference to any icon associated with the document's MIME type or filename. That is, any icon defined for the `x-gzip` content encoding will be used for `fishing.html.gz` regardless of any icons that might be defined for the `text/html` MIME type or the `.html` file extension.

# The `AddAltByEncoding` Directive

This directive is essentially identical to the `AddAltByType` directive described earlier, except that the alternate text is associated with a particular content encoding rather than a MIME type.

# The `ExpiresByType` Directive

It's not uncommon for different types of information to have different virtual life spans. For instance, a newspaper's Web site might typically include a masthead logo, some top-story headlines and photographs, and teasers about the hot news items. Not all of these have the same relation to the time scale. The masthead logo, for instance, is likely to remain the same for months, whereas the "Top News Story of the Hour" teaser and photographs are more likely to be changed frequently.

To improve response time for end user clients, a lot of information transmitted across the Web is *cached*—that is, the browser keeps a copy so that it doesn't have to download the whole thing all over again. One control over how long cached copies are allowed to be kept is the item's expiration date.

For something as volatile as an online news site, most content is probably so topical that it should expire almost immediately. The invariant window dressing (like the masthead logo), though, doesn't need to expire anywhere near as quickly.

The `ExpiresByType` directive allows you to draw such distinctions based on the MIME types of documents. For instance, if you assume that GIF files are usually clip art that doesn't change very often, whereas JPEG files are topical photographs and HTML files are the current content, it might be appropriate to add lines such as the following to the site's config files:

```
ExpiresByType image/gif "accessed plus 1 month"
ExpiresByType image/jpeg "accessed plus 1 week"
ExpiresDefault "modified plus 1 hour"
```

As a result, the masthead would be eligible to stay in the browser's cache for up to a month, photographs for a week, and everything else—such as article text or video clips—for only an hour from the time they were modified on the Web site. The browser can, of course, choose to throw out the cached copies before they've actually expired, which would require fetching new copies the next time the documents were accessed.

# Client Behavior

Web clients, particularly browsers, use the transmitted value of the Content-type header field to determine what to do with the document it accompanies. Typical options include

- Render the document or otherwise display it
- Start up a plug-in to deal with the document (such as Adobe Acrobat Reader)
- Start up a co-processing application to handle the document (such as Microsoft Word)
- Prompt for a file to which the browser will save the document
- Ask the user what to do with the document

Which action the browser takes for a particular MIME type is usually defined through some sort of preference screen.

## Forcing the Client to "Save As"

Sometimes you want the document sent to the client to be designated for saving, regardless of the client's instructions regarding the MIME type. Most browsers provide a means of making a downloaded document go directly to a "Save As" screen (for instance, Internet Explorer and Netscape Communicator do this if you Shift+click a link).

Unfortunately, the only way the Web server can force this sort of behavior is essentially to lie to the client and say the document contains something other than it really does by sending a different MIME type as the value of the Content-type field. The usual value used is application/octet-stream, which simply means, "This is a stream of bytes; I have no idea what they mean." Because the server claims not to know what they mean, the client usually follows suit and asks the user for instructions—typically, where to save a copy of the file.

Consider a directory containing scripts to be downloaded by the client rather than rendered or possibly executed by the server. In the case of a script named food.pl, the .pl extension frequently indicates to Apache that the file is a Perl script and will probably tell the client that the content-type is text/plain. To indicate to the client that it should download and save the file instead, the directory's .htaccess file might contain a line such as

```
AddType application/octet-stream .pl
```

which would cause Apache to tell the client the file was an opaque binary document rather than a file containing textual script commands.

# Summary

From simple cross-linked text files, Web technology has grown to incorporate things such as images, sounds, video clips, self-installing software packages, word processor documents, on-demand real-time soundtracks, interviews, and the list goes on. The key to handling all these different kinds of information is the system of MIME types—and the Apache server software gives you all the tools you need to be able to deal with all of them.

# .htaccess Files

.htaccess files (pronounced "dot H T access") allow users who don't have permission to modify the main server configuration files to still have some control over how their portion of the Web server behaves. These directives are simply put in a file called .htaccess and placed in the directory that they are to affect. This chapter discusses the sorts of things that you can do with .htaccess files and how you, as the system administrator, can prevent users from doing things that you might not want them to do.

> **Note**
>
> You can set the actual name of the access file by using the AccessFileName directive. The default value is .htaccess on Unix and htaccess on Windows NT. For this chapter, I will refer to the file as a .htaccess file for simplicity, but you can change the name to anything that makes sense to you.

# Why You Might Want to Use .htaccess Files

Any directive that can be put in a .htaccess file could also have been put in a <Directory> section in the configuration file, to put that same restriction, or add that same feature, to the directory in question. This is, in fact, the desired method because this means that the directives are loaded into memory when the server is started, and the server won't have to open .htaccess files when documents are served.

Frequently, however, the site content developers aren't the server administrators, and so don't have access to the main server configuration files. This might be the case on a server that has multiple virtual hosts, or on sites where the UserDir directive permits individual users to have their own Web space inside their home directory. In either case, it may be very desirable for the content developers to be able to make configuration changes to the server without having to involve you.

Also, it's often very desirable to be able to make local configuration changes without affecting the whole server, and especially without having to restart the server. For example, if the Webmaster on one of the virtual hosts wanted to insert a redirect from an old URL to a new URL, she might simply put a Redirect directive in a .htaccess file at the base of her directory tree. This would take just a few seconds and would be effective immediately. The alternative is to ask the main server administrator to make the change in the configuration files, and then restart the server. This would involve waiting for the admin to get the message, find time to do it, and determine that it was okay to restart the server.

> **Note**
>
> In most cases, end users won't notice a server restart. However, if you have a lot of virtual hosts or very large configuration files or if you're doing anything else time-consuming at server startup (preloading Perl code using `mod_perl`, for example), you might want to wait for a time when the server isn't under a large load, so that there's no service outage.

## When Not to Use `.htaccess` Files

If the entire site is managed by one administrator, it's preferable to put all the directives directly into the main server configuration files, rather than scatter them across multiple `.htaccess` files. In this case, you may also want to disable access files altogether with the `AllowOverride None` directive.

When a client requests a file from your server, and you have the server set to permit per-directory configurations with `.htaccess` files, Apache will search for such a file, not only in the directory from which it is serving the file, but in every directory in the path leading to that file. Assume that your `DirectoryRoot` is set to `/home/www/docs`. If a client asks for the file `http://your.server.com/files/morefiles/myfile.html`, Apache will open and read in the files `/home/www/docs/.htaccess`, `/home/www/docs/files/.htaccess`, and `/home/www/docs/files/morefiles/.htaccess`. If those files don't exist, it will keep on going, but if it finds any of those files, it will parse the file contents, looking for and applying configuration directives before serving the file requested.

For files that are very deep in your directory structure, it might involve a lot of time to open all those files. Putting these directives in the main server configuration file will cause the directives to be loaded at server startup, and no time will be spent loading secondary configuration files.

Directives are applied in the order seen, so you can change the value of a directive from the value assigned for a higher directory by just setting it to something else in a deeper directory.

# What You Can Do with `.htaccess` Files

The Apache documentation (and Chapter 5, "Server Configuration Files") will indicate for each directive whether it's permitted in your `.htaccess` file.

A general rule of thumb is that directives are permitted in `.htaccess` files unless they are configuring some server-wide setting, such as `ServerRoot`, `HostNameLookups`, or `MaxClients`. Don't rely on this rule, however; check the documentation (or Chapter 5) before using a directive in your `.htaccess` files.

More specifically, the permitted directives are those that fall into the following categories: `AuthConfig`, `FileInfo`, `Indexes`, `Limit`, and `Options`. `AuthConfig` directives deal with authentication. `FileInfo` directives control document types. `Indexes` are all those directives that control the automatic generation of directory indexes. `Limit` directives control which hosts can access a directory. `Options` includes the `Options` and `XBitHack` directives.

Directives from these categories of directives can be allowed, or denied, by using the `AllowOverrides` directive. (See the later section "Limiting What's Permitted.")

Using a directive in a `.htaccess` file that's not permitted will result in a server error, which will be displayed to the client browser.

The following section gives examples of what you might want to do with `.htaccess` files. These examples are certainly not exhaustive, but are very common things for which to use per-directory configuration.

## Authentication

One common use of `.htaccess` files is authentication. One frequently asked question on the various Usenet groups and mailing lists that deal with Apache server is usually, "How do I password-protect my Web site?" or something similar.

Authentication is implemented by the `Auth*` directives. These are usually put in `.htaccess` files because they apply only to the directory in which they are placed (and subdirectories thereof).

> **Note**
>
> You can put authentication directives in the main server configuration file by using a `<Directory>` section.

A sample configuration for adding password protection to a directory might look like the following:

```
AuthType Basic
AuthName GoodGuys
AuthUserFile /home/www/passwords/users
```

```
AuthGroupFile /home/www/passwords/groups
<Limit GET POST>
require group goodguys
</Limit>
```

This subject is covered in more detail in Chapter 16, "Authentication."

## Permitting CGI

It might sometimes be desirable, if not recommended, to put CGI programs in a directory that's not a ScriptAliased directory. This is somewhat common on servers where users are permitted to serve Web content out of their home directories. These users may want to be able to run CGI programs on their site, but aren't permitted access to the main server cgi-bin directory.

By using the Options directive, you can turn on the ExecCGI option for a particular directory and permit CGI execution for just that directory. This is shown as follows:

```
Options ExecCGI
```

### Caution

Be cautious in giving this ability to users because it is a potential security problem.

# Limiting What's Permitted

The AllowOverrides directive determines what directives will be honored in .htaccess files. The syntax of AllowOverrides is as follows:

```
AllowOverrides override1 override2
```

where the overrides are one or more of AuthConfig, FileInfo, Indexes, Limit, and Options. These overrides indicate which categories of directives are permitted, as described earlier in the section "What You Can Do with .htaccess Files." The default value is All, indicating that any legal directives may be included.

### Note

The full explanation of the AllowOverrides directive is in Chapter 5.

8

.htaccess FILES

# Security Concerns

The security concern in using .htaccess files is, put simply, that you lose control of what's done in the individual directories on your server. It is, in effect, equivalent to giving all users access to the configuration files. As server administrator, you try to put settings in the configuration file that make sense on your server and protect you from things that users might do to compromise your server. .htaccess files potentially give those users a chance to override your configuration settings.

Most directives that you should be concerned about fall under the Options directive. If your AllowOverrides directive is set to permit Options, be aware of what that allows to happen on a per-directory basis. AllowOverrides Options permits the use of the two directives Overrides and XBitHack.

## Options

The Options directive, although it is just one directive, wields a lot of power. You may want to override some of that power by default, and then give it out as warranted.

Options adds and removes certain options from a directory. These options are one or more of the following:

```
ExecCGI
FollowSymLinks
Includes
IncludesNOEXEC
Indexes
MultiViews
SymLinksIfOwnerMatch
```

These options are described in the following sections.

### ExecCGI

The ExecCGI option allows CGI programs to be executed in this directory, even though it's not a ScriptAliased CGI directory. With AllowOverrides Options enabled, anyone can put a .htaccess file containing the directive Options ExecCGI in any directory, and execute CGI programs there. This has potentially undesirable effects. It means that anyone with access to document directories on your server now has permission to write and execute arbitrary code on your server. These programs will be executed with the user permissions indicated with the User directory, which is supposed to be an unprivileged user, but that user still usually has access to much of the content in the document directories. Also, because CGI programs can now be spread over several directories, instead of in one place, auditing and verifying your CGI programs for secure operations is more difficult. You can't know what CGI programs are being executed on your server.

This also has non-security-related consequences. If some configuration changes on your server, or if you need to move content to a different server, you may have to go to any number of directories to make changes to CGI programs that break because of the changes.

## FollowSymLinks

One thing that makes a Web server secure is the concept of a `DocumentRoot`. This is the directory that contains all the documents that can be served by the Web server. Any document contained in that directory, or any subdirectory of it, can be downloaded and viewed by any client machine on the network. If the network is the Internet, this means that any of those files are available to anyone in the world. However, any documents outside this directory are secure. Permitting the `FollowSymLinks` directive potentially breaks this model because it allows clients to follow symbolic links, which may link to files that aren't contained in the `DocumentRoot` directory.

The worst possible case of this is if someone enables this option, and then makes a symbolic link to your server's root directory. Clients could then effectively get a directory listing of your entire server and download any file on that server, such as `/etc/passwd`, or similar sensitive files. Although the clients will really be able to download only those files that are world-readable, there are usually files like this on any system, many of which, perhaps, should not be there. Consider using `SymLinksIfOwnerMatch` instead.

> **Note**
>
> The `FollowSymLinks` directive does nothing on Windows.

## Includes

The `Includes` option allows server-side includes (SSI) in the target directory. The primary concern here is SSI with the `exec` attribute. With the `exec` attribute, a Web page author can execute an arbitrary shell command on your server simply by putting that directive in an SSI tag on her HTML page. Again, you are protected somewhat because the server is running as an unprivileged server, but it would still be possible to do substantial damage as that unprivileged user.

This could be a concern particularly if you have some method whereby Web users can create content on your server—a "guestbook" script, for example. Those users could potentially insert an SSI directive into that content which executed some unpleasant command on your system. Consider using `IncludesNOEXEC` instead.

## IncludesNOEXEC

The IncludesNOEXEC attribute works just like the Includes attribute, except that the #exec command is not permitted, and the #include command is not permitted if its target is a CGI program. This overcomes the potential security problems caused by using Includes.

## Indexes

Options Indexes enables you to display a directory listing of files in a directory, if there is no index file (such as index.html) in that directory.

You can consider this a potential security problem. After all, Web users will be able to see files in your directory, even though there is no HTML page containing links to those files. This will permit them to download files that you may not actually want them to download. However, if you don't want people downloading files from your Web site, you shouldn't put those files in your Web directories, where someone could possibly download them by guessing a URL.

## MultiViews

There are no security concerns with using MultiViews.

## SymLinksIfOwnerMatch

Using the SymLinksIfOwnerMatch option, rather than the FollowSymLinks option, removes the possibility that a Web user might "escape" from the Web root directory. With this option set, symbolic links may be followed only if the owner of the symbolic link is the same as the owner of the target of that link. That is, if Joe User makes a symlink to /var in his Web directory and tries to make a URL link to that symbolic link, the server will refuse to serve that document, because /var is owned by root, not by Joe User. This removes the security concerns caused by FollowSymLinks.

> **Note**
>
> Having these various options turned off in the main server configuration won't help you if you use AllowOverrides because Joe User can quite happily turn on these options for his personal Web space with directives in his .htaccess files. Make sure that you trust your users before you allow them to use .htaccess files.

## XBitHack

Although it's a rather different mechanism, the security concerns for using XBitHack are the same as those when permitting Includes. XBitHack is just another way of enabling Includes.

See Chapter 12, "SSI: Server-Side Includes," for more information about the XBitHack directive.

## Damage Control

The primary thing that limits the amount of damage that can be done is the server running as an unprivileged user. This means that nefarious commands hidden in #exec statements can only damage those files that are world-readable.

Make very sure that the User directive is set to a user who does indeed have no privileges on your system. Setting this directive to root, or even any regular user, may cause unpleasant results, such as your file systems being destroyed and similar joys.

See Chapter 15, "Security," for additional tips on running a tight ship.

# Summary

.htaccess files permit per-directory configuration without editing the main server configuration files. This is useful for multiuser systems, where users may need to make configuration changes but don't have access to the configuration files. It's always preferable to make configuration changes in the main server configuration files when possible.

8

.htaccess FILES

# Virtual Hosting

**CHAPTER 9**

The term *virtual hosts* refers to running more than one Web site on the same server. These might be multiple names within the same domain, such as `helpdesk.databeam.com` and `cgi.databeam.com`, or different domain names, such as `www.rcbowen.com` and `www.mk.net`. Apache was the first Web server to have this feature, which it has had since version 1.1.

Apache supports two types of virtual hosting:

- *Name-based* virtual hosting refers to hosting a site on a different CNAME, but on the same IP address.

> **Note**
>
> A *CNAME* (canonical name) is an alias to an existing DNS record. CNAMEs are frequently used to reflect multiple services being run on the same physical machine. For example, `www.databeam.com` is a CNAME for the machine `gw.databeam.com`. Both names refer to the same physical machine and resolve to the same IP address.

- *IP-based* virtual hosting refers to hosting sites on different IP addresses on the same machine.

In this chapter, you learn why you might want to run virtual hosts, when you might want to avoid it, and how to configure your server to run virtual hosts.

# Running Separate Daemons

Sometimes running multiple hosts on the same daemon isn't feasible or desirable. The alternative is to actually run multiple copies of Apache on the same server.

## When You Might Want to Do This

The user specified in the `User` directive (see Chapter 5, "Server Configuration Files") must have permission to read the files being served. Hence, the various users hosting Web sites on the same server will very likely be able to read each other's files. This can be undesirable in some cases—one company might not want another company to have direct access to their files, but to have access to them only through the Web interface, where they may have implemented security measures.

It's in cases like this that it might be desirable to run separate servers, running as different Users, so that file-level permissions can prevent one person from reading another person's files. The servers would also need to have different settings for Group and ServerRoot.

> **Note**
>
> Running multiple HTTP daemons on your machine requires some additional resources. Specifically, it will require more CPU time, more memory, and an additional IP address for each daemon. If you don't have these resources, consider one of the virtual host options instead.

## Configuring Separate Daemons

To run separate instances of Apache on the same server, you need a different IP address for each server. You then need to tell Apache which IP address to listen to with the Listen directive. Listen tells Apache which IP address (and port number) to listen to for HTTP requests. Each instance of the server should be set to listen to a different IP address.

```
Listen 192.101.205.15:80
```

If a server configuration doesn't specify which IP address to listen to, Apache listens to all valid addresses. (That's why, when running several daemons on the same machine, it's important to specify, for each daemon, which address it is to listen to.)

## Starting the Server with a Specific Config File

When you have your server configuration files for each daemon, you can start up the separate copies of Apache with each new configuration file.

It's sufficient to have multiple configuration files, one for each daemon, and to start the same httpd binary, specifying the configuration file as shown below. However, if you need different modules installed for each daemon, you will need to compile a different binary for each instance of the server.

As covered in Chapter 4, "Starting, Stopping, and Restarting the Server," you can start Apache with a particular configuration file by using the -f command-line option. The syntax of this option is as follows:

```
httpd -f /home/company1/config/httpd.conf
httpd -f /home/company2/config/httpd.conf
```

**9**

**VIRTUAL HOSTING**

Make sure that your servers aren't fighting for resources, such as log files. On your secondary server(s), make sure that you are pointing to unique locations for your log files, so that there isn't a conflict when the servers try to start up and open those files. The servers can, however, share other things, such as the `/icons` directory, containing the standard icons, so that these files don't have to be on your server in two places.

# Using IP-Based Virtual Hosts

If you don't have the security concerns mentioned earlier, you can just run a server on each IP address, but do it all on one server. This is much less demanding on the machine because all requests are handled by just one process. This is done with IP-based virtual hosting.

IP-based virtual hosting requires a separate IP address for each virtual host. To add additional IP addresses to your machine, you need to consult the documentation for your particular operating system. You can either add an additional network interface device for each address or, on most operating systems, assign multiple addresses to the same interface device.

## The `<VirtualHost>` Section

The `<VirtualHost>` section in a server configuration file includes those directives that apply to that particular virtual host. These include, at a minimum, the `DocumentRoot`, and can also include other directives such as the `ServerAdmin`, `ErrorLog`, `TransferLog`, and most other directives. In Chapter 5, each directive will specify whether it can be used within a `<VirtualHost>` section.

**Caution**

Use caution when assigning separate log files for virtual hosts, particularly for a machine with large numbers of virtual hosts. Under Unix, there is a limit to the number of open file handles that can be in use by any one process. This is typically 64, although this varies some from one OS to another. Having all your virtual hosts log to one main log file is one way of staying within this limit.

An example of the `<VirtualHost>` section follows. This example defines two IP-based virtual hosts running on the same server. The server has been given two IP addresses: `192.168.1.150` and `192.168.1.151`.

```
<VirtualHost 192.168.1.150>
ServerAdmin webmaster@rcbowen.com
```

```
DocumentRoot /home/rbowen/html
ServerName buglet.rcbowen.com
ErrorLog /var/logs/httpd/error_log
TransferLog /var/logs/httpd/access_log
</VirtualHost>

<VirtualHost 192.168.1.151>
ServerAdmin cbowen@rcbowen.com
DocumentRoot /home/cbowen/public_html
ServerName cbowen.rcbowen.com
ServerAlias cbowen
ErrorLog /home/cbowen/logs/error_log
TransferLog /home/cbowen/logs/access_log
</VirtualHost>
```

See Chapter 5 for a more complete treatment of what configuration directives are permitted within a <VirtualHost> container.

> **Note**
>
> You should use the IP address, rather than the server name, in the <VirtualHost> directive. When the server starts up, it needs the IP address of each virtual host, as well as the server name of that host. If the IP address is not provided, Apache will have to look it up, which might delay server startup, or, if the address can't be found, this particular virtual host won't respond to requests at all. In older versions of Apache, the server itself won't even start up.

Any unspecified directives will default to the values made in the main configuration file, so you need to specify only those settings that you want to be different. For example, if you don't mind sharing your log files among your various virtual hosts, just don't specify those configuration directives in your <VirtualHost> containers.

# Using Name-Based Virtual Hosts

You can use name-based virtual hosts when it's not possible or desirable to give multiple IP addresses to your server machine. In this case, you can simply add a CNAME record in DNS, pointing at the same IP address, and run name-based virtual hosts on these distinct names. Name-based virtual hosts have the additional benefit that you can run an unlimited number of virtual hosts off one IP address.

# How a Named-Based Virtual Host Works

When an HTTP request is sent to a server, part of the request identifies the server to which the request is being made. This feature of the HTTP/1.1 protocol is supported by most browsers, even if they don't fully support the HTTP/1.1 protocol. Apache can then determine, based on this information, from which virtual server the request is to be served, even though they all resolve to the same IP address.

> **Note**
>
> Older browsers might not support this feature and therefore not get content from the correct virtual host. This problem can be partially solved with the `ServerPath` directive (discussed later in this chapter).

## The `NameVirtualHost` Directive

Name-based virtual hosts are configured much the same way as IP-based virtual hosts, with one main difference: The `NameVirtualHost` directive tells the server on which IP address requests for name-based virtual hosts will be received. The `VirtualHost` sections then look the same as when using IP-based virtual hosts, except that they all point to the same IP address.

```
NameVirtualHost 192.168.10.2

<VirtualHost 192.168.10.2>
ServerName buglet.rcbowen.com
DocumentRoot /home/buglet/html
</VirtualHost>

<VirtualHost 192.168.10.2>
ServerName rhiannon.rcbowen.com
DocumentRoot /home/rhiannon/html
</VirtualHost>
```

As with IP-based virtual hosts, most configuration directives can appear in a `<VirtualHost>` section, but some can't. Consult your Apache documentation or Chapter 5 to see whether a particular directive can be used.

## Working Around Old Browsers

As mentioned earlier, some older browsers can't take advantage of name-based virtual hosts because they don't pass the name of the server with the HTTP request. Because the Web server can't determine from which named host the client is requesting the document, it serves the request from the default host, which might or might not be what the client is looking for.

A workaround is available for this, and although it's inelegant, it gets the job done. This workaround is the `ServerPath` directive, which provides an alternative way to get data from the desired virtual host. This directive effectively creates a `<Location>` for serving the files from the virtual host. The following example shows an implementation of the `ServerPath` directive:

```
NameVirtualHost 192.101.204.24

<VirtualHost 192.101.204.24>
ServerName timecards.databeam.com
ServerPath /timecards
DocumentRoot /home/httpd/htdocs/tc
</VirtualHost>
```

This means that clients that can't pass the correct information to get data from the named virtual host can now request documents with the path prefix of `/timecards`. That is, pages served off the `timecards.databeam.com` virtual host can also be accessed with the URL `http://timecards.databeam.com/timecards/`.

Note also that if the server's primary name is `riesling.databeam.com`, these documents can also be accessed with the URL `http://riesling.databeam.com/timecards/`, which can be a little confusing. And, of course, clients that can pass the hostname header can access the documents simply with the URL `http://timecards.databeam.com/`. These multiple ways of accessing the same content make it imperative that you specify links as relative, rather than absolute, everywhere on your server.

Fortunately, most browsers now in use support name-based virtual hosts, so this amount of contortion is seldom necessary.

# Other Configuration Options

You might want to use some other configuration options on your server.

## The _default_ Virtual Host

When you are using virtual hosts, it's nice to have something in place so that if a client requests a document from a name that is a valid CNAME for the machine but for which a virtual host isn't defined, that client gets something reasonable. By default, what they will get is whatever is defined in the main server configuration, before getting to the virtual host directives. Of course, it's a really good idea, if you're going to do virtual hosts at all, to have everything defined in terms of virtual hosts. It just makes things easier to read and maintain.

The all-purpose solution to this is to use the `_default_` keyword in your `<VirtualHost>` declaration, to catch anything that might fall through the cracks. Anything not specifically defined in one of the other sections will be served with the values defined here. An example of a `_default_` virtual host is as follows.

```
<VirtualHost _default_:*>
DocumentRoot /www/default
</VirtualHost>
```

The `:*` on the end is a wildcard indicating that this is good for requests coming in on any port on which Apache is listening. You can also indicate specific ports.

## Port-Based Virtual Hosts

To run servers with different configurations on different ports, you can simply treat the different servers as virtual hosts and put the differing configurations in a `<VirtualHosts>` section. An example of this is as follows:

```
Listen 80
Listen 9000
ServerName www.mk.net
DocumentRoot /home/httpd/html

<VirtualHost 192.101.201.32:9000>
DocumentRoot /home/httpd2/html
... etc ...
</VirtualHost>
```

Although this isn't a virtual host in the traditional meaning of the term, requests are handled similarly, so it's useful to think of them in the same way.

This type of configuration is handy when it's not possible or convenient to assign multiple names to a server—for example, if your system administrator is stingy about modifying DNS. You can also use this sort of setup if you are playing games with `mod_rewrite` to transparently map requests to certain URLs to a secondary server. Of course, in the latter case, it might be desirable to actually be running a secondary server as a separate instance of Apache.

# Checking Your Configuration

When your server is configured and running with your virtual hosting setup, you can check your virtual host configuration by invoking the `httpd` executable with the `-S` command-line option. The `-S` option lists all your virtual host settings and tells you where in your configuration file they are configured.

It's apparent from the documentation that this command-line option was once intended to provide more information than just the virtual host settings, or that it will some day provide more information. But, with the current version (as of this writing), that's all the information it provides.

What follows is sample output using the -S option on a server that's running several virtual hosts. Each line indicates one virtual host, and the configuration file and line number where this virtual host is defined.

```
buglet# ./httpd -S
VirtualHost configuration:
192.168.1.1:80  buglet.rcbowen.com (/usr/local/apache/conf/httpd.conf:951)
192.168.1.1:80  is a NameVirtualHost
                default server buglet.rcbowen.com
(/usr/local/apache/conf/httpd.conf:931)
                port 80 namevhost buglet.rcbowen.com
(/usr/local/apache/conf/httpd.conf:931)
                port 80 namevhost devel.rcbowen.com
(/usr/local/apache/conf/httpd.conf:937)
                port 80 namevhost cgi.rcbowen.com
(/usr/local/apache/conf/httpd.conf:944)
                port 80 namevhost perl.rcbowen.com
(/usr/local/apache/conf/httpd.conf:958)
                port 80 namevhost www2.rcbowen.com
(/usr/local/apache/conf/httpd.conf:965)
                port 80 namevhost w3.rcbowen.com
(/usr/local/apache/conf/httpd.conf:973)
                port 80 namevhost rcbowen.rcbowen.com
(/usr/local/apache/conf/httpd.conf:982)
```

If a particular virtual host doesn't seem to be working, this is a quick way to make sure that it's correctly configured.

# Summary

Virtual hosts are a valuable feature, allowing you to run multiple Web sites on the same physical machine under the same instance of the Apache server. Under certain circumstances, you might actually want to run separate instances of the server, but virtual hosts offer you a lot of flexibility if you can use them.

**9**

**VIRTUAL HOSTING**

# Using Apache as a Proxy and Cache Server

A *proxy server* is a specialized server that acts as an intermediary between clients and other Web servers. Clients will connect to the proxy server and send their requests to it, rather than connect directly to the Web servers they want to reach. The proxy will then attempt to retrieve the resources that each client requests and serve them back to the client. Usually the clients and the proxy server reside on the same local network. The proxy server is used to request material from servers on external nets, such as the Internet.

# Why Use a Proxy?

A proxy server is often used with a firewall. Thanks to the proxy server, there is need for only a single computer to have access to the Internet through the firewall. This could reduce the risk of security breaches that might arise if all clients had direct access to the Internet. The proxy can also be used to hide information about the clients, such as what type of Web browsers they are using, what operating system they are running, and so on. This can further reduce the risk of security breaches that can affect clients.

You can use a proxy server to hide the topology and structure of an internal network from the outside world. Large corporations often use what are called *black IP addresses* for their LANs. These addresses are in ranges reserved for private or special purposes—therefore, they aren't routed on the Internet. An easy way to access Web resources on the Internet from such a LAN configuration would be to set up a proxy server. The proxy server would have to be set up with a *white IP address* (an IP address that's valid on the Internet). All Web clients on the LAN would then be configured to access Web resources through the proxy server. By doing this, as far as external servers are concerned, Web requests from within the LAN would appear to be originating from the proxy server. Since the requests come from a valid IP address, they can be served, even though they actually originate from a client with a black IP address.

Having a single entry point to the Internet enables you to keep a close eye on traffic originating from clients within your intranet. By logging all traffic that comes through the proxy server, you can easily monitor your clients' surfing habits. That way, you can create statistics about bandwidth usage. You also can see which sites are the most visited. Should too much traffic be used for unwanted purposes, you can easily block access to those sites in your proxy. For example, you could use the proxy to block access to banner sites and thereby save bandwidth by blocking unnecessary graphics.

Of course, using a proxy server has its downsides. Conceivably, you are adding a single point of failure for Internet traffic. This problem can be avoided to some extent by adding backup proxies. There will also be a slight reduction in access speed, since there is an extra server that needs to handle each Web request. The speed problem might be reduced if you enable caching on the proxy server.

## What Is a Web Cache?

When a server is acting as a proxy, you can also have it save copies of the pages that are being relayed through it. This is referred to as *caching*. As requests are made to the caching proxy server, it will first check to see if there already are local copies of the requested pages. If there are local copies available, there's no need for the access to go further, and the cached pages are delivered to the client immediately. This cuts down on the use of WAN and Internet bandwidth and speeds up Web access considerably.

In some cases, such as where a company has several LANs connected by a WAN, it might be useful to build up a hierarchy of cache servers. An example of such a hierarchy can be seen in Figure 10.1. In such a scenario, a client would connect to a proxy server on its LAN. If the requested page isn't available on the local proxy server, the proxy will send a new proxy request via the WAN to a proxy server higher in the hierarchy. If the request can't be satisfied by any of the proxies that it passes through in the cache hierarchy, it will be forwarded to the appropriate server on the Internet.

**FIGURE 10.1**

*Example of a cache server hierarchy.*

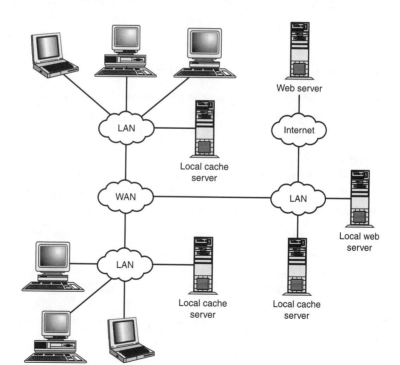

**10**

USING APACHE AS A PROXY AND CACHE SERVER

There's no easy way to predict how much a cache server will reduce your Internet traffic. The hit rate in the cache depends on several factors. For example, how much hard disk space is dedicated to storage of cached material? How long are cached objects retained in the cache before expiring and being deleted? How many users are accessing the cache server? What are the surfing patterns of the local users? And so on....

Knowing only the hit rate is not sufficient information to determine how a cache server can reduce bandwidth. You also need to take into account the size of cached objects. A single hit on a sufficiently large object will outnumber many hits on smaller objects.

A conservative estimate is that you should be reducing Web traffic by about 30 percent if you are using a proxy server. Higher percentages are certainly possible in many situations—especially if your clients have similar surfing patterns and you are using a sufficiently large amount of hard disk for storage of cached material.

Statistics have shown that as much as 50 percent of Internet traffic is generated from Web requests. By using a caching proxy server to access the Internet, it's possible to reduce your traffic flow drastically. Even if you are connected to the Internet via a flat rate service, you will get faster access times for requested material that is already present in the cache. This can give a new lease on life to an old, slow Internet connection. Reducing the amount of Web traffic will also leave more bandwidth for other types of traffic.

## Problems Associated with Proxies and Caches

Several types of Web objects either can't be proxied or proxy very badly. For example, you will most likely find that many streaming video/audio protocols don't proxy very well. Furthermore, they are most likely not cacheable.

A common problem is that some pages might appear to be cacheable but in reality are not. Pages served by content negotiation on the origin server might not be cacheable because their appearance depends on information from the client. Likewise, pages that rely on cookies might not be cacheable. There can be many more reasons.

Caches aren't allowed to cache objects that are subject to authentication. Nor will they cache objects obtained via a secure protocol. That way, secure information can't be found lying about on the cache server for anyone to see. One consequence of this is that you should not serve huge documents or graphics from a secure server, since such Web objects can't be cached. A solution for this might be to serve the graphics for a secure Web page from a separate, open server, although this unfortunately results in a security warning in most Web browsers.

## Apache's Proxy and Caching Capabilities

Apache provides all the basics needed to be used as both a proxy and a cache server. It can be used as a proxy server for CONNECT, FTP, and HTTP/0.9, as well as HTTP/1.0 traffic. It can also be used as a caching proxy server for these protocols. That is apart from CONNECT, since secure traffic should not be cached. Apache can also be used to set up a simple cache hierarchy.

Apache provides all that's needed for a basic proxy server. Since it does not provide the ability to cache HTTP/1.1 requests, however, it can cause problems with many types of Web objects. HTTP/1.1 contains many extensions that enable caching of various types of dynamic materials. These types of Web objects may not cache correctly on Apache.

> **Note**
>
> If you need a proxy or cache server for a large number of users, you will probably want to look at something other than Apache. A very good cache server is the Squid Web Proxy Cache, a robust, high-end caching proxy server constructed for larger sites. Apart from being able to proxy those protocols that Apache supports, it also supports HTTP/1.1. Squid also provides better support for proxy hierarchies by using faster, specialized protocols for the hierarchy communication.
>
> For now, Squid is the most commonly used proxy server on the Internet. And it's being very actively developed and supported.
>
> Those interested in Squid may want to look at its main site at
> `http://squid.nlanr.net`.

# Configuring Apache for Use as a Proxy or Cache Server

Let's start by looking at how Apache is configured as a proxy or cache server, and then examine how clients should be configured to use the proxy server.

## Setting Up Apache as a Proxy Server

The Apache server needs to have the proxy module installed to be used as a proxy server. It's not compiled in by default. You need to recompile the complete Apache server. You also could compile only the proxy module and add it to your server with the `LoadModule` directive.

You can set several directives in Apache's configuration files to manage the proxy's behavior.

## ProxyRequests On|Off

The `ProxyRequest` directive enables or disables the server's proxy capabilities. It can be set to either `On` or `Off`. It is set to `Off` by default.

## ProxyRemote *Match Remote-server*

As discussed earlier in this chapter, it's possible to have a hierarchy of caching proxies. If the cache server doesn't have the requested Web object cached already, it will need to retrieve it. If you have a cache hierarchy, you might want to try to fetch the object from another cache within the hierarchy. By using the `ProxyRemote` command, you can configure how each cache server should communicate with the other proxies within the cache hierarchy.

The *Match* parameter is a partial URL that the server will try to match with each incoming proxy request. If the first part of the requested URL is matched with the content of the *Match* parameter, the request will be forwarded to the proxy specified with the *Remote-server* parameter. Set *Match* to * if you want to forward all requests to a specific proxy server.

The *Remote-server* parameter defines which server the proxy request should be forwarded to. It's also possible to change what type of protocol and which port are to be used for the new request. For example, this might be used to serve incoming FTP requests via HTTP. *Remote-server* is defined by the following syntax: *protocol*://*hostname*[:*port*]. As of Apache 1.3.9, the *protocol* part can be set only to HTTP.

Here are a few examples of how to use `ProxyRemote`:

- This command is triggered once a request arrives at the proxy server, containing a URL addressed to `http://someaddress.com`:

  `ProxyRemote http://someaddress.com/ http://anotherproxy.com:8080`

  The proxy server will try to access the requested page by sending another proxy request through a proxy server named `anotherproxy.com`. That server is listening on port 8080. When the requested resource is returned, it's forwarded to the client that requested it.

- All incoming proxy requests will be forwarded to and served by a server named `anotherproxy.com` that's supplying proxy services on port 8080:

  `ProxyRemote * http://anotherproxy.com:8080`

- The following `ProxyRemote` command will take an incoming FTP request and try to fetch the requested resource from another proxy via the HTTP protocol:

  `ProxyRemote ftp http://anotherproxy.com:8080`

  When the resource is returned to the client that requested it, it is delivered via the FTP protocol.

## ProxyPass *path url*

`ProxyPass` is used to map external Web resources into the name space of the local server. References to the supplied *path* will result in an internal proxy request to a resource located on the server specified by the *url* parameter. Assume that a server named `www.a.org` is configured with a `ProxyPass` directive like this:

`ProxyPass /local/mirror/ http://www.b.org/source/`

This directive will be triggered by requests to resources located within the virtual path of `/local/mirror/`. Once triggered, the server will strip the `http://www.a.org/` `local/mirror/` part from the requested URL. The remaining URL will be appended to `http://www.b.org.source/`. By doing this, subdirectories will also be mirrored. When the new URL has been constructed, the server will issue an internal proxy request to that URL. After the proxy request is completed, the resulting Web object is sent back to the client that requested it. This is transparent to the client, for whom the Web object will appear to have originated from the `www.a.org` server.

The `ProxyPass` directive has numerous uses. For example, it can be used to good effect to fetch a resource from an intranet and deliver it unto the Internet. For all outward appearances, the material is being delivered from your Internet server.

## ProxyPassReverse *path url*

When using internal proxy requests issued from `ProxyPass` or `mod_rewrite`, it's possible that the remote server will issue an HTTP redirect response. This could result in the client being redirected to the server from which you are mirroring material. Most often this isn't a desired result. For this reason, there is a need to be able to change the URL in an HTTP redirect response's `Location` header. This is where `ProxyPassReverse` comes into use.

The *path* parameter is the virtual path used for this resource. The *url* parameter points to the server from which Web material will be mirrored. Both parameters work exactly as they do with the `ProxyPass` directive.

**10**

**USING APACHE AS A PROXY AND CACHE SERVER**

Let's expand the example from the `ProxyPass` section:

```
ProxyPass /local/mirror/ http://www.b.org/source/
ProxyPassReverse /local/mirror http://www.b.org/source/
```

`ProxyPassReverse` is triggered if the `www.b.org` server sends a redirect response to a resource that resides within its `/source/` directory. The `Location` entry in the response header will be rewritten so that it points to the same place in the virtual path of `http://www.a.org/local/mirror/`. For example, a redirect to `http://www.b.org/source/index2.html` would be rewritten as `http://www.a.org/local/mirror/index2.html`.

## ProxyBlock [*word*] [*host*] [*domain*]

`ProxyBlock` blocks certain sites from being accessed. Its parameter is a list that can consist of any combination of words, hosts, and domains. The items in the list should be separated by spaces. Setting the list to * blocks all incoming requests.

If some items in the list appear to be hostnames, Apache will try to determine the IP address of that host. If successful, the IP addresses will also be used when matching against the URL of all incoming requests.

This example of the `ProxyBlock` directive blocks all requests to any host within the `a.org` domain, as well as any requests to the host `server.somewhere.org`:

```
ProxyBlock a.org server.somewhere.nu
```

Since the last item is also a host, Apache will try do determine its IP address. Any request that matches that address will be blocked as well.

## AllowCONNECT *port_list*

The `AllowCONNECT` directive specifies on which ports the proxy `CONNECT` method can be used. The `CONNECT` method is used to proxy HTTPS connections. By default, this directive allows `CONNECT` traffic on ports 443 and 563, the ports defined for HTTPS and snews.

## ProxyReceiveBufferSize *bytes*

The `ProxyReceiveBufferSize` directive specifies the size of the network buffers used for outgoing HTTP and FTP connections. If you set this to `0`, the system's default buffer size will be used. Otherwise, a buffer of the specified size will be used for transfers. You will need to set a size of at least 512 bytes.

## NoProxy *Domain | Subnet | IP_address | Hostname*

Sometimes you will want requests to be served immediately, without being forwarded to servers defined with the `ProxyRemote` directive. Most often this will be the case for requests to servers located on your intranet.

The parameter list can be any mixture of domains, subnets, IP addresses, and hostnames.

The *Domain* is a partially qualified domain name. To be able to distinguish hostnames from domains, the latter must be preceded by a dot, as in `.nu .gnulix.org`.

A *Hostname* is a fully qualified domain name.

Subnets are partially qualified IP addresses. You can also supply a netmask with the IP address. To do this, follow the IP address with a slash, followed by the number of significant bits in the subnet. If you choose to exclude the netmask, Apache will assume that omitted digits or zeroes specify the netmask for the subnet. The following examples will all denote the same subnet: `10.10.0.0`, `10.10`, and `10.10.0.0/16`.

*IP_address* is a fully qualified IP address. In most situations, it's more efficient to specify an IP address rather than a hostname, since there is no need to perform a DNS lookup for the name.

This example of the `NoProxy` directive specifies that there will be no proxy requests for any hosts on the `10.20` subnet, nor any hosts within the `.gnulix.org` domain, `www.a.org`, or the `10.10.10.10` server:

```
NoProxy 10.20 .gnulix.org www.a.org 10.10.10.10
```

## ProxyDomain *Domain*

Users often leave out the domain part of hosts that are part of their intranet. With the `ProxyDomain` directive, you can specify which domain should be appended to hostnames that are not fully qualified. When the server receives a request without a fully qualified domain name, it will try to redirect the request to a host within the specified domain.

For example, assuming a request to the URL `http://www/index.html`, the following directive would tell the server to redirect the request to `http://www.a.org/index.html`:

```
ProxyDomain .a.org
```

## ProxyVia off | on | full

The `via:` HTTP headers are used to control the flow of proxy requests within proxy hierarchies. Table 10.1 shows how the various parameters for this directive affect response headers.

**TABLE 10.1** ProxyVia Parameters

| Parameter | Function |
| --- | --- |
| off | Prevents the processing of via: headers |
| on | Adds a via: header for the current server |
| full | Adds a via: header for the current server and adds the Apache version number to the comment field of the via: header |

# Setting Up Apache as a Cache Server

There are several configuration directives for setting up and tuning Apache for use as a caching proxy server. To use the following parameters, you need to have caching enabled on your server.

## CacheRoot *directory*

This directive sets which directory is to be used to hold cached files. If this directive is set, it will also enable caching for the proxy server. Remember that the directory needs to be readable as well as writable by the server.

## CacheSize *size*

The CacheSize directive specifies how many kilobytes of hard disk space the cache should use. Make sure that plenty of space is left on the device where the cache resides. Disk space is checked only when garbage collection takes place. Therefore, there is a strong probability that disk usage can be significantly larger than the amount specified. When garbage collection begins, old cached files are deleted until the disk space used by the cache is less than the requested size. Therefore, make sure that the *size* parameter is set about 30 percent to 40 percent lower than the available space.

## CacheMaxExpire *time*

This directive specifies the longest time a cached object will reside in the cache without being checked if it is out of date. Some objects have their own expiry date, supplied by their origin server. When CacheMaxExpire *time* has elapsed, such an object will be rechecked even if its expiry date hasn't yet arrived.

The *time* parameter is the number of hours that should pass before objects are rechecked. The parameter is a floating-point number. For example, a value of 1.5 would indicate that all objects should be checked at least every 90 minutes. If you don't set this yourself, it will default to 24 hours.

## CacheLastModifiedFactor *factor*

The *factor* parameter is used to calculate a fake expiry date for those objects that don't supply their own. The fake expiry date is calculated by multiplying *factor* and the amount of time since the last modification value that the origin server supplied. The *factor* parameter is a floating-point number. For example, a *factor* value of 0.1 and a time since last modification of 20 hours would yield a fake expiry date of 2 hours.

## CacheGcInterval *time*

Every now and then the cache has to be checked to see that it hasn't filled more disk space than was configured. If the cache contains too many files, old expired files will be deleted until the cache once again fits the allotted space.

The *time* parameter is a floating-point number that denotes the number of hours that should elapse between garbage collections. Setting a *time* value of 0.25 would result in a check every quarter hour.

The longer the interval between garbage collections, the greater the chance that the cache will be filled and overflow.

> **Caution**
>
> Because this directive has no default parameter, be sure to set this if you enable caching! If you don't define a time interval, there will be no garbage collection, and your cache will continue to grow until it fills all available space.

## CacheDirLength *length*

This directive is used to set the number of characters in the names of subdirectories in the cache. You will most likely never have to change this yourself.

## CacheDirLevels *levels*

Use this directive to specify the number of subdirectory levels in the cache. If this level isn't set, it will default to three levels, meaning that cached data will be saved three directory levels below the root directory of the cache. You will most likely never have to change this directive yourself.

## CacheForceCompletion *percentage*

Even if a transferring request is cancelled, caching it for possible future requests is a good idea. With this directive, you can set how much of a Web object has to be transferred for the request to be complete, even if the client requests a cancellation.

### NoCache [*word*] [*host*] [*domains*]

This directive is used to determine which requests shouldn't be cached on the server. This doesn't affect whether the server proxies objects.

The parameter list can consist of any combination of words, hosts, and domains. The various items in the list should be separated by spaces. Setting the list to * disables caching completely. If some of the list items appear to be hostnames, Apache will try to determine the IP address of that host. If successful, the IP addresses are also used when matching against the URL of incoming requests.

In this example of the NoCache directive, requests to hosts within the a.org domain are not cached, nor are any requests to the host server.somewhere.org cached:

```
NoCache a.org server.somewhere.org
```

Since the last item is also a host, Apache will try to determine its IP address. Any request that matches that address won't be cached, either.

### CacheDefaultExpire *time*

This directive sets a fake expiry time for cached objects that are transferred by protocols that don't support expiry times. The *time* parameter is the floating-point number of hours to use as an expiry time. The default setting is 1 hour.

## Configuration Considerations

Before you begin configuring your server as a caching proxy, make sure that its system time is correct. Otherwise, it won't be able to correctly determine whether requested material has expired. Also, always try to ensure that you have the correct time on your Web server, so that it can give out correct Expires and Last-Modified responses. Otherwise, material from your server might not be cacheable by others.

It's possible for malicious users to abuse proxy servers. If such users make use of your proxy server as an access point when doing their mischief, you might get blamed for whatever they do. Therefore, it's important to be able to control who can access your proxy server. This can be accomplished by using Apache's deny/allow directives. Assume that you want only users from the foobar.net domain to be able to access your proxy. To do this, you would need to add something like this to your configuration file:

```
<Directory proxy:*>
order deny,allow
allow from a.org
</Directory>
```

See the section "Mandatory and Discretionary Access" in Chapter 15, "Security," for more information on how you can set up Apache to control which clients can access your proxy server.

## Putting It All Together

To wrap up the discussion about configuring a proxy server, let's do a couple of example configurations. For all the examples, assume that you are setting up a cache and proxy solution for a small company. It has a server residing in a domain named a.org. All internal servers are using black IP addresses—in this case, in the 10.0.0.0 series. There is a Web server on 10.1.1.1 that is called www.a.org. The company's LAN is protected from the Internet with a firewall, and the only server allowed to access the outside world is proxy.a.org.

First, configure a proxy server for a.org. It will serve as a gateway from the company LAN to the outside world. The server will be named proxy.a.org and will be running on the 10.1.1.2 IP address (of course, if this was a real-world scenario, you would want a white IP address for the proxy so that it can access the Internet). The server will provide the proxy service on port 8080. You want only clients on the company LAN to be able to access the proxy. Since this is supposed to be a gateway, there really is no need to proxy accesses to the LAN. Finally, you want all proxied requests to be logged. The following configuration file would be a good, minimal start to get such a proxy up and running:

```
ServerName proxy.a.org
User nobody
Group nobody
Port 8080
ServerType standalone
ServerRoot /etc/httpd
ProxyRequests On
NoProxy .a.org
ProxyDomain .a.org
LogFormat "%h %l %u %t \"%r\" %>s %b" common
CustomLog logs/proxy_log common
<Location />
 Order Deny,Allow
 Deny from all
</Location>
<Directory proxy:*>
 Order Deny,Allow
 Allow from .a.org 10
</Directory>
```

The following example configures a caching proxy server that will reside on the same LAN as the gateway configured in the previous example. This cache server will provide only caching and will forward all incoming requests to the proxy gateway. The new server will be called `cache.a.org` and will be assigned `10.1.1.2` as its IP address. Use the configuration from `proxy.a.org` as your basis and then flesh it out with the extra directives needed to provide caching services. You don't want clients to be able to access any server that contains the word `xxx` or `porn` in its hostname. The cached material will be placed in the `/var/spool/cache` directory, and the cache should be cleaned out if it becomes larger than 800MB.

```
ServerName cache.a.org
User nobody
Group nobody
Port 8080
ServerType standalone
ServerRoot /etc/httpd
ProxyRequests On
NoProxy .a.org 10
ProxyBlock xxx porn
ProxyDomain .a.org
ProxyRemote * http://proxy.a.org:8080
LogFormat "%h %l %u %t \"%r\" %>s %b" common
CustomLog logs/proxy_log common
CacheRoot /var/spool/cache
CacheSize 809600
CacheGcInterval 2
CacheMaxExpire 12
CacheLastModifiedFactor 0.1
CacheDefaultExpire 1
<Location />
 Order Deny,Allow
 Deny from all
</Location>
```

Assume that the two proxy servers you've configured are located at the company's main office. Now you can configure caching proxy servers for its branch offices that are connected to the main office via WAN links, as shown in the following example. These servers should cache material from the main office's Web server as well as material from the Internet. However, they should not cache material from any Web server that resides on the LAN. Each branch office resides on its own C class IP subnet. Apart from this, each server will be configured more or less like the cache server at the main office.

```
ServerName cache.branch1.a.org
User nobody
Group nobody
Port 8080
ServerType standalone
```

```
ServerRoot /etc/httpd
ProxyRequests On
NoProxy .branch1.a.org 10.1
ProxyDomain .branch1.a.org
ProxyRemote * http://cache.a.org:8080
LogFormat "%h %l %u %t \"%r\" %>s %b" common
CustomLog logs/proxy_log common
CacheRoot /var/spool/cache
CacheSize 809600
CacheGcInterval 2
CacheMaxExpire 12
CacheLastModifiedFactor 0.1
CacheDefaultExpire 1
<Location />
 Order Deny,Allow
 Deny from all
</Location>
```

These examples would create a very basic but efficient proxy hierarchy. It would probably save a considerable amount of Internet and WAN traffic.

# Configuring the Clients

All major Web browsers can be configured to use a proxy. The GUI-based browsers are easily configured via their preference menus, whereas text-only Web browsers such as Lynx usually use environmental variables to set their proxy configuration.

Rather than examine how various browsers are configured, look at an easy way to configure multiple Web browsers from one central configuration file. This can be very useful in a multiuser environment, such as a company or a university.

## Using a Proxy Auto-Config File

Netscape Navigator 2.0 introduced a new way to configure proxy usage for Web browsers. By sending a file containing JavaScript to the browser, it's possible to dynamically define how each request from the client should be handled. This configuration format is also supported by Microsoft Internet Explorer.

To use auto-config files, you need to add an extra MIME type to your Web server: `application/x-ns-proxy-autoconfig`. By associating this MIME type with a file type, the server will tell browsers that it's about to send an auto-config file. The MIME type is usually associated with files that have a `.pac` extension. To get this association, you could add something like this to your `mime.types` file:

`application/x-ns-proxy-autoconfig pac`

It's also possible to add the MIME type by using the `AddType` directive in your Apache configuration file. To do this, you would add the following line to the configuration file:

```
AddType application/x-ns-proxy-autoconfig pac
```

The next step is to create the `.pac` file that will be used to configure how the browser should handle requests. The file will consist of pure JavaScript code and should not be embedded in HTML. The return value from this script code will tell the browser how it should handle each request. Several extra JavaScript functions are available for use in the script.

The entry point in the script will be the mandatory `FindProxyForURL` function. For each request that the Web browser is about to perform, it will call your script in the following manner:

```
ret=FindProxyForURL(url, host);
```

The *url* parameter is the complete URL that the client wants to access. The *host* parameter contains the hostname, as it is entered in the *url* parameter, between `://` and the first `:` or `/` that follows. This parameter is provided only for your convenience and could just as well be retrieved from the *url* parameter.

The return value, *ret*, consists of a single string. The content of this string will tell the browser how the request should be handled. If the string is null, no proxy should be used for the request in question. If the string is not null, it needs to contain one or more of the following strings:

- `DIRECT`   Don't use a proxy for this request.
- `PROXY` *host:port*   The proxy named *host* should be used for the request.
- `SOCKS` *host:port*   The `SOCKS` server named *host* should be used for the request.

It's possible to concatenate more than one of these strings to form the *ret* string. If you include several response strings in the *ret* string, they should be separated by a semi-colon. When the browser interprets a *ret* string that contains multiple options, it will try to use the leftmost option first. If it's not possible to retrieve the requested Web object via this method, the browser will try the next option, and so on. Here is an example of how a valid *ret* string might be defined:

```
PROXY proxy1.gnulix.org:8080; PROXY proxy2.gnulix.org:80; DIRECT
```

For this request, the browser should first try to access the resource via the `proxy1.gnulix.org` proxy, communicating via port 8080. Should this proxy be down, the browser should try `proxy2.gnulix.org`, also on port 8080. Finally, if neither proxy is available, the browser should try to retrieve the resource directly.

Proxies that can't be contacted will automatically be retried after a predefined time. In the case of Netscape Navigator, the first retry will be after 30 minutes, the next after one hour, and so on (adding an extra 30 minutes to wait for each retry).

If all proxies are down and there is no DIRECT option specified, the browser will ask the user if a direct connection should be attempted. This way, users should always have a chance to have their requests served.

> **Note**
>
> A few helper functions are available for use in the `.pac` file. I won't go into these functions here. To learn more about these functions, look at Netscape's specification at `http://home.netscape.com/eng/mozilla/2.0/relnotes/demo/proxy-live.html`.

Look at a brief example of how a `.pac` file might look. Assume that you want to create a `.pac` file for a client that resides on the LAN you used earlier for the examples on how to configure proxies and caches. That Web browser runs on a client that's run on the `a.org` net. It should use `cache.a.org` for all accesses outside the LAN, whereas it should connect directly when trying to access local material. A `.pac` file for this scenario might look something like this:

```
function FindPorxyForURL(url,host)
{
  if(isPlainHostName(host) || dnsDomainIs(host,".a.org")) {
    return "DIRECT";
  } else {
    return "PROXY cache.a.org:8080; DIRECT";
  }
}
```

This example uses two helper functions available in all `.pac` files. The first function, `isPlainHostName()`, returns `true` if the hostname in `host` doesn't contain a domain part. In this example it's assumed that any requests that don't contain a domain part are meant to be served by servers on the LAN. Therefore, these should be served directly. The next helper function, `dnsDomainIs()`, returns `true` if `host` is a server within the `a.org` domain. Should either function return `true`, the request won't be made via the proxy. Otherwise, the Web browser should try to access the resource via the `cache.a.org` proxy server. If that fails, the browser should attempt to fetch the Web object directly.

**10**

USING APACHE AS
A PROXY AND
CACHE SERVER

# Summary

A proxy, especially in combination with caching capabilities, is a very powerful tool. Caching can result in considerable bandwidth savings. Combined with the capability to block access to certain sites, this can give a new lease on life to a slow Internet connection.

By using Apache's capabilities for virtual hosting, it's easy to set up a machine to serve as both a proxy server and a Web server. This can be an inexpensive solution that provides a Web server as well as a proxy for sites on a budget.

# Dynamic Content

## IN THIS PART

# CGI Programming

**CHAPTER 11**

The CGI (common gateway interface) is a specification for communication between your Web server and an application running on the server machine. It defines a method of getting dynamically generated content onto otherwise static Web sites.

This chapter introduces the CGI and shows generally how to write CGI programs. You will also see what can go wrong.

> **Note**
>
> Mind you, this chapter simply introduces CGI; you can find whole books on the subject, such as *Sams Teach Yourself CGI Programming in a Week* by Sams Publishing.

This chapter also discusses some of the alternatives to CGI. When a CGI program is called, a separate process is launched by the server to execute that program. This startup process is notoriously slow and typically takes more time than the execution of the program itself. Other technologies, such as FastCGI and mod_perl, address this by caching the CGI program in the server process itself, improving performance significantly.

# The CGI Specification

The full CGI specification can be found at http://hoohoo.ncsa.uiuc.edu/cgi/. This site also defines how the server and a CGI script are to communicate with one another.

## Environment Variables

CGI defines a set of environment variables for passing around information, much like your operating system environment variables, such as your path and login name. This information consists of things such as the server name, the username of an authenticated user, and the IP address of the client accessing the server. These environment variables are passed to each CGI program invoked by the server. Some variables are required, which means that a server must supply these variables to be considered CGI-compliant; other variables are optional. And finally, the server itself and the client (Web browser) are both at liberty to make up environment variables and pass these on to the CGI program.

## Standard Environment Variables

The variables listed in Table 11.1 will return the same value each time a request is made of the server. The CGI specification calls these *non-request–specific* variables because they don't vary from one request to another.

**TABLE 11.1** Non-Request–Specific Environment Variables

| Variable | Meaning |
| --- | --- |
| SERVER_SOFTWARE | The name and version number of the Web server software that's answering the HTTP request. Example: Apache/1.3.9 (Win32) |
| SERVER_NAME | The hostname or IP address of the server. Example: www.mk.net |
| GATEWAY_INTERFACE | The version of the CGI specification that's implemented on the server. Example: CGI/1.1 |

Other variables will vary from request to request. Table 11.2 lists such variables.

**TABLE 11.2** Request-Specific Environment Variables

| Variable | Meaning |
| --- | --- |
| SERVER_PROTOCOL | The protocol, and version of that protocol, in which the content was sent to the client. Example: HTTP/1.1 |
| SERVER_PORT | The port number on which the client connected to the server to send the request. Example: 80 |
| REQUEST_METHOD | The method with which the request was made. This might be any one of GET, POST, PUT, or HEAD. |
| PATH_INFO | Additional path information can be passed on the end of the URL, following a slash. Example: http://server/ cgi-bin/script.pl/extra/info has PATH_INFO of /extra/info, which is passed to the CGI program. This can be useful for passing additional arguments to CGI programs. |
| PATH_TRANSLATED | This probably doesn't mean what you expect it to mean. PATH_INFO is appended to SERVER_ROOT to produce a full file system path. Example: In the example given for PATH_INFO, PATH_TRANSLATED would be /usr/www/htdocs/extra/info, if your SERVER_ROOT is set to /usr/www/htdocs. A common error is to assume that this variable contains the full path to the CGI program file. |
| SCRIPT_NAME | The virtual path to the CGI script being executed. Example: /cgi-bin/script.pl |
| QUERY_STRING | Any information appearing following a question mark (?) will be removed from the URL and placed into this variable. This is a good way to pass additional information to the CGI script. This can be used with PATH_INFO or by itself. |

*continues*

**TABLE 11.2** continued

| Variable | Meaning |
|---|---|
| REMOTE_ADDR | The IP address of the client accessing the server. Example: 192.101.201.32 |
| REMOTE_HOST | The hostname of the client accessing the server. If the name can't be resolved, or if that function is turned off on the server, this variable should be left unset, and just the IP address will be put in REMOTE_ADDR. Example: webslinger.databeam.com |
| AUTH_TYPE | If the script is password-protected, this will contain the method of authentication that was used. See Chapter 16, "Authentication," for more information. Example: BASIC |
| REMOTE_USER | If the script is password-protected, this is the username with which the user authenticated. |
| REMOTE_IDENT | Almost never used, because very few clients pass anything meaningful in this variable. When set, this variable contains various identification information about the remote user, either from RFC931-type identification, or whatever the client chooses to pass in this variable. Browsers used to pass the user's email address in this field until unscrupulous marketing types started harvesting that information to send out spam. |
| CONTENT_TYPE | If data is being passed with the request, such as with a PUT or POST request, this is the content type of that data. Example: text/plain |
| CONTENT_LENGTH | The size of any data being sent by the client to the server. |

## Other Environment Variables

In addition to the variables in Tables 11.1 and 11.2, any HTTP headers sent by the client to the server will be placed into the environment. This can be things such as the HTTP_USER_AGENT (the browser name and version), or any other information that the browser manufacturer wants to put in its headers.

## The ISINDEX Command Line

For ISINDEX queries, any information following a question mark (?) will be passed directly to the CGI script as command-line arguments, unless that information contains an equal sign (=). Every available browser now supports HTML forms, so the ISINDEX query type is hardly ever used any more.

# STDIN and STDOUT

Any information sent to the server in the HTTP request, either via a POST or a PUT request, will be passed to the CGI program on STDIN (Standard Input). The CGI script sends its output to STDOUT (Standard Output).

## Parsed Headers

The output of a CGI script should begin with an HTTP header (as discussed later in this chapter). These headers are then sent on to the client, unless they are server directives. Three headers are defined as server directives that can be sent by CGI programs.

### Content-type

A Content-type header tells the server the MIME type of the content that you are returning. See the following example:

```
Content-type: text/html
```

### Location

A Location header tells the server that you aren't returning any content, but are asking the server to redirect the client to another location. If this location is a local (relative) path, the server will simply serve the file indicated in the URL. Otherwise, if it's a full URL, the server will send that redirection notice to the client, which will be responsible for following the redirection.

Here's an example of a relative path:

```
Location: /products/index.html
```

Here's an example of a URL redirect:

```
Location: http://www.mk.net
```

### Status

A Status header gives the server an HTTP status line to be sent to the client. This contains the status number and the message string. Here's an example:

```
Status: 404 Not Found
```

## Non-Parsed Headers (nph Scripts)

Some scripts don't want the server to parse their headers. By convention, any script with a filename beginning with nph is allowed to communicate directly with the client, and the headers that it produces won't be parsed by the server before being passed along.

A consequence of this is that data isn't buffered before it's sent to the client, but is sent immediately. With a regular CGI program, nothing is sent to the client until the program has completed execution, and the client will then receive everything at once. With non-parsed headers, for example, you could display a countdown and have the numbers appear on the browser screen one at a time as they are generated.

# Configuring the Server for CGI

One of the most common problems that beginners have with CGI programs is configuring the server to permit execution of CGI programs. The most common symptoms of this problem are either seeing the source code of the CGI script in your browser, or getting a 500-series server error.

Certain settings have to be made in your server configuration files or in `.htaccess` files to execute CGI programs, and usually, you have to put CGI programs in a certain directory. The following sections discuss these settings, which are also covered in Chapter 5, "Server Configuration Files."

## ScriptAlias

The `ScriptAlias` directive defines a mapping between an alias and a directory. It also tells the server that all files in this directory (and its subdirectories) are CGI programs, and should be executed when requested.

The syntax of the `ScriptAlias` directive is as follows:

```
ScriptAlias /cgi/ /usr/local/apache/cgi-files/
```

Files placed in this directory will then be accessed with the URL `http://servername/cgi/filename.cgi`.

> **Note**
>
> Make sure that permissions are set correctly on files in your `ScriptAlias` directory, or you'll get an error message. See the later section "Common Problems" for more information.

**Permitting CGI in Non-ScriptAlias Directories**

If you have `AllowOverride` set to `Options` (or to `All`), users can use `.htaccess` files to execute CGI programs in directories other than the official `cgi-bin` directory. As the server administrator, however, you need to consider the ramifications of this and decide whether you want to permit it.

Consider the security issues of having CGI programs in places that you don't control, and the management issues of having CGI programs scattered all over the place rather than in one centralized location. See Chapter 15, "Security," for some discussion about whether this is a good idea.

To enable CGI execution in a particular directory, place the following directive in a `.htaccess` file or a `<Directory>` section of your main configuration file:

```
Options ExecCGI
```

## AddHandler

An alternative way to have CGI programs execute on your server is to use the `AddHandler` directive to map a particular file extension to the `cgi-script` handler:

```
AddHandler cgi-script pl
```

This will cause any file with a `.pl` extension to be treated as a CGI program and executed when the file is requested.

**Caution**

Exercise caution in using this directive to make server-wide configurations because it may enable CGI execution in places you hadn't intended.

## Options ExecCGI

You can enable execution of CGI programs in a specific directory with the `Options` `ExecCGI` directive. You can also use the `ScriptAlias` directive to enable this, but using `Options ExecCGI` is especially useful for user directories so that users can enable these options without your assistance.

# Writing CGI Programs

Writing CGI programs isn't particularly difficult. You have to keep in mind just a few extra things so that your programs work. The later section "Common Problems" tells you about some of the things that can go wrong. But first, see how to do things right.

# MIME Header

When your CGI program is executed, the server hands control over to your program and gets out of the way. (Okay, that's not entirely true, but it's close enough for this discussion.) One consequence of this is that you are responsible for providing your own MIME type header on your output.

Most of the time, your CGI program will output HTML to display in the client browser. That means that your output will have a MIME type of `text/html`. From Chapter 2, "HTTP," and Chapter 7, "MIME Types," you should remember that your HTTP headers must be followed by a blank line before you start with the body of the HTTP response. With this in mind, nearly every CGI program you write will start with a line that looks like this (in Perl):

```
print "Content-type: text/html\r\n\r\n";
```

Alternatively, if you are writing CGI code in C, this will look like

```
printf "Content-type: text/html\r\n\r\n";
```

`Content-type` is the HTTP header that tells the client what type of data it's receiving so that it knows how to interpret it. `\r\n` is the control sequence representing a carriage return and a line feed (or a line feed and a carriage return, depending on your operating system). You print two of these—one to end the current line, and one to make a blank line, indicating the end of the headers and the beginning of the document body.

> **Note**
>
> Although you are technically required to use both a carriage return and a line feed, many people don't, and browser makers have had to accommodate this error. So, most of the time, you can get away with just one or the other, rather than both.

After this line, you can start outputting your HTML-formatted data.

Of course, if your CGI program outputs something else, such as text, or a GIF image, you need to display the appropriate HTTP header for those content types (`text/plain` and `image/gif`, respectively).

> **Caution**
>
> Failure to print a `Content-type` header will cause a server error. See the later section "Common Problems."

# Getting Input from Users

As explained earlier in this chapter, CGI programs communicate over `STDIN` and `STDOUT`. Under normal circumstances, `STDIN` is the keyboard, and `STDOUT` is your screen. But the CGI program hijacks these handles for its own purposes. `STDIN` now comes in from the browser. The server accepts this input from the browser and passes it on to the CGI process. The output from the CGI process is sent back to the server, which sends it on to the client.

CGI applications can also get information from environment variables, as discussed earlier in this chapter. So, because the CGI program can get data in two ways, the browser can send data to the server in two ways.

The most common ways of actually getting user input are via HTML forms, information sent as additional data on the end of the URL, and cookies.

## HTML Forms

HTML forms are a way for Web page authors to solicit input from users. Text input fields, select lists, check boxes, and radio buttons are presented for users to make selections and type their input.

HTML forms are created with the HTML `<form>` tag and can consist of the following elements:

- `<form></form>` starts the HTML form. Attributes are as follows:
  - `action`    A URL that tells the browser where to send the form data when the submit button is clicked.
  - `method`    Either `GET` or `POST`. Tells the browser what method to use when sending the data to the server.
  - `name`    (Optional) Sets a name for the form. Used primarily for JavaScript.
  - `target`    (Optional) If the form appears on a framed Web page, tells the browser in which frame of the frameset it should display the response from the server.

The following is an example:

```
<form action="/cgi-bin/process.pl" method="POST">
```

* `<input type="text">` displays a single-line text input field. Attributes are as follows:

    * `type="text"`   This attribute is optional because text is the default type when using the `<input>` tag.

    * `name`   The name of the input field. This will be sent to your CGI program for association with the value.

    * `size` (Optional)   The width, in characters, that the input field should be in the browser window. The default will vary depending on which browser you are using.

    * `maxlength`   (Optional) The maximum number of characters permitted in this field. This is a good attribute to set if you are sending data to a database and need to limit values to a certain size.

    * `value`   (Optional) The default value that should   appear in the field when the page is loaded.

The following is an example:

```
<input type="text" name="fname" value="Rich" size="15" maxlength="255">
```

* `<input type="password">` displays a single-line text input field in which all typed text is displayed as asterisks (*) or otherwise obscured. Attributes are identical to `type="text"`.

---

**Caution**

Using `<input type="password">` is purely cosmetic security. The password is still passed over the network in plain text form. Don't use this for any serious security.

---

* `<input type="radio">` displays a radio button. These are usually in a set of several and have the "select only one" behavior. Attributes are as follows:

    * `name`   The name of the input field. This will be sent to your CGI program for association with the value. To create a set of several radio buttons, just give multiple radio buttons the same name.

    * `value`   The value to be passed to your CGI program if this particular button is selected.

    * `checked`   The button that will be selected by default.

In the following example, the AM button is selected by default:

```
<input type="radio" name="ampm" value="am" checked>
```

PM is the other button in the group:

```
<input type="radio" name="ampm" value="pm">
```

- `<input type="checkbox">` indicates a box that's either checked or not checked. Attributes are as follows:

    - `name`    The name of the input field. This will be sent to your CGI program for association with the value.

    - `value`    A value that will be passed to your CGI program if this check box is checked.

    - `checked`    Indicates that the box will be checked by default.

The following is an example:

```
<input type="checkbox" name="paid" value="yes" checked>
```

- `<select></select>` specifies a list containing one or more elements from which users can select one or more items. Items are enclosed in `<option>` tags that appear inside the set of `<select>` tags. Attributes are as follows:

    - `name`    The name of the select list. Any item(s) selected will be associated with this name.

    - `multiple`    Indicates that more than one item can be selected from the list. If more than one item is selected, multiple name/value pairs are sent to your CGI program, with the same name.

    - `size`    A particularly useful attribute if you have a multiple-item select list. It indicates how many items in the list are to be displayed in the select list. By default, only one is shown, in a drop-down list format.

For an example, see `<option>`.

- `<option>` defines a single option in a select list. This tag is followed by the text that's to appear in the list. It has only one optional attribute:

    - `value`    The value that's to be passed to the CGI process as the value for this select variable. If there's no value attribute, the text appearing after the `<option>` tag is passed as the value.

The following is an example:

```
<select name="month>
<option value="01">January
<option value="02">February
<option value="03">March
```

```
<option value="99">etc.
</select>
```

- `<textarea></textarea>` can contain multiple lines of text. Text appearing between the tags is the default text that will appear in the text area on the page. The attributes are as follows:
    - `name`   The name of the input field. This will be sent to your CGI program for association with the value.
    - `cols`   How many columns wide the text area should be.
    - `rows`   How many rows high the text area should be.
    - `wrap`   What wrapping behavior the text area should display. The options are off (the default), virtual, and physical. The latter two options provide different types of text wrapping within the text area. In most implementations, however, both provide simple wrapping, and there's no difference between the two.

    The following is an example:

    ```
    <textarea name="bio" rows=3 cols=40 wrap="virtual">
    I was born, I lived, and then I died</textarea>
    ```

- `<input type="hidden">` lets you pass a form variable that doesn't display on the page as something that users can change.

---

**Caution**

As with `<input type="password">`, `<input type="hidden">` provides only cosmetic security. You can't rely on the idea that the values will be what you set them to be in hidden fields. A user with a clue can download your page, edit the value of that hidden variable on his local copy, and post it back to your server with the altered values.

---

The available attributes are as follows:

- `name`   The name of the input field. This will be sent to your CGI program for association with the value.
- `value`   The value that will be passed with the name. This is optional, but it's a little silly to have a hidden form element with no value.

- `<input type="submit">` indicates a button that, when clicked, sends the form contents to the `action` location defined in the `<form>` tag. When users click a submit button, that data is encoded and sent to the server either via a GET or POST HTTP request (as discussed in the following section). Attributes are as follows:

- name    The name of the input field. This will be sent to your CGI program for association with the value. In some cases, this is useful for a form—for example, when you have multiple submit buttons.

- value    The caption that will appear on the button. By default, it's Submit.

- `<input type="reset">`indicates a button that, when clicked, resets the contents of the form to the default values. There are no attributes other than the type.

## GET

GET requests are the simpler of the two types (GET and POST) to explain. Although the two end up looking very similar in the long run, it's easier to see GET in action when you are using it because all the form arguments end up on the URL.

Form names and values are *URL-encoded*, meaning that certain characters—mostly those that aren't alphanumeric—are converted to entities that can be safely passed in a string. Spaces are converted to plus signs (+), and other characters are converted to their ASCII representation in hexadecimal, preceded by a percent sign (%). The names and values are then combined into name-value pairs, with an equal sign (=) between the name and the value. Finally, these pairs are then joined together with ampersands (&).

In a GET request, the resulting string is prepended with a question mark (?) and tacked onto the end of the URL specified in the action attribute of your `<form>` tag. So, if your action attribute specified that the form contents were to be sent to /cgi-bin/ process.pl, a typical URL generated by a GET form might look like the following:

```
http://your.server/cgi-bin/process.pl?name=Rich%20Bowen&occupation=author
```

When this request reaches the server, everything after the question mark is placed into the environment variable QUERY_STRING, which is passed to the CGI program with the rest of the environment variables.

One main advantage of GET forms is that they are *hackable*. That is, users could modify items in the URL to change the behavior of the CGI program, without having to fill out the form again. For example, I can enter the following directly into the location field of my browser to do an AltaVista search for the term *Apache*:

```
http://www.altavista.com/cgi-bin/query?pg=q&what=web&kl=XX&q=apache
```

By directly changing the string at the end of this URL, you can search for anything you like without having to fill out the search form.

> **Tip**
>
> It's easy to bookmark the results of GET forms because all the information is contained in the URL.

There are also some disadvantages, such as the limits to a URL's length. The LimitRequestLine directive sets the maximum length of a URL. By default, it's set to 8190, which gives you a lot of room. However, other servers, and some browsers, limit the length more.

Because all parameters are passed on the URL line, items that were in password or hidden fields will also be displayed in the URL. Of course, neither method should be used for real security measures and should be considered cosmetic security at best.

> **Note**
>
> I use the term *cosmetic security* to refer to things that make information one step harder to get to but don't offer any real encryption or security. An example might be writing your ATM card PIN number on your card, but writing it backward. You have somewhat obscured the information from the casual glance, but anyone willing to spend more than five minutes on it would be able to figure it out. However, whereas the person using your ATM card only gets three or four tries, someone trying to get into your Web site can try as many times as they like.

### POST

POST forms are handled similarly to GET forms, except that the data itself is sent to the server in the body of the HTTP request, rather than on the request line. It's then passed to the CGI program over STDIN. The length of this data is put into the environment variable CONTENT_LENGTH. You can get this data by reading CONTENT_LENGTH bytes from STDIN.

Because the data is encoded exactly the same way for POST forms as for GET forms, the rest of the decoding process will be exactly the same.

## Decoding Form Data

Decoding form data is just a matter of reversing what's done in the form encoding process. Listing 11.1 shows Perl code for decoding form data. If you want to use this code in your Perl CGI program, you can get a reference to a hash of all the data from a form with the following line:

```
$form = FormParse();
```

**LISTING 11.1**   Perl Code for Decoding Form Data

```perl
sub FormParse  {
#  Parse HTML form, POST or GET.  Returns pointer to hash of name,value
    my ($buffer,@pairs,$pair,$name,$value,$form);

    if ($ENV{REQUEST_METHOD} eq "POST")     {
        read (STDIN, $buffer, $ENV{'CONTENT_LENGTH'});
    } else {
        $buffer = $ENV{QUERY_STRING};
    }

    # Split the name-value pairs
    @pairs = split(/&/, $buffer);

    foreach $pair (@pairs)
    {
        ($name, $value) = split(/=/, $pair);
        $value =~ tr/+/ /;
        $value =~ s/%([a-fA-F0-9][a-fA-F0-9])/pack("C", hex($1))/eg;
        $value =~ s/~!/ ~!/g;
        # Is this part of a multi-valued select?
        if ($form->{$name})     {
            $form->{$name} .= "\0$value"
        } else {
            $form->{$name} = $value;
        }
    }     # End of foreach

    return $form;
}     # End of sub
```

This code undoes the steps described earlier in the section on GET forms. First pairs are split up on ampersands, and then names and values are split on equal signs. Plus signs are converted to spaces. Finally, the bulk of the work is done in that strange-looking line in the middle:

```perl
$value =~ s/%([a-fA-F0-9][a-fA-F0-9])/pack("C", hex($1))/eg;
```

(If this doesn't look strange to you, you probably skipped this section anyway.) What this line does is replace any percent sign (%), followed by two hexadecimal characters (that is, either a letter a through f, or a number 0 through 9) with the associated ASCII character.

For the C version, you might want to look at Tom Boutell's cgi-lib.c, available from http://www.boutell.com/. Alternatively, you can use any of the CGI libraries/modules available for either C++, Perl, Java, or any other language that you want to use. Using an existing library or module, instead of writing your own routines, ensures that the code is thoroughly tested, so it should be free of bugs and security holes.

For Perl, the most popular module for this purpose is Lincoln Stein's `CGI.pm` module. It contains code for parsing forms, generating HTML pages, maintaining variable state from page to page, and various other functions that you might need when writing CGI programs. `CGI.pm` is available from any CPAN site, such as `http://www.cpan.org/`.

## Maintaining State

HTTP is a *stateless* protocol. What this means is that with each HTTP request, nothing is remembered from the previous request. There is no continuity for a particular client from one page load to the next. Consequently, if a CGI program requires some memory of a user's previous choices and input, this will have to be done by the CGI code itself, storing information either in hidden form fields or in cookies on the client. (See Chapter 13, "Using Cookies," for a discussion of maintaining state with cookies.)

# An Example of a CGI Program

Listing 11.2 shows a simple CGI program written in Perl. It doesn't do anything particularly useful, but it should be sufficient to determine whether you have CGI correctly configured on your system. The program prints an HTTP content-type header and a single line of HTML to be displayed in the browser window. Save this file as `example.pl`, put it in your `cgi-bin` directory (as discussed earlier in the section "Configuring Your Server for CGI"), and direct your browser to `http://your.server/cgi-bin/example.pl`.

**LISTING 11.2**    A Simple CGI Program in Perl

```perl
#!/usr/bin/perl
print "Content-type: text/html\r\n\r\n";
print "<h2>This is just a test</h2>";
```

As with regular shell programming, Apache looks at the first line of a CGI program—the "shebang" line—for the location of the interpreter that will run this program. A CGI program can also be a binary executable file, such as a compiled C program.

# CGI Programs Under Windows

Under Windows, the `ScriptInterpreterSource` directive tells Apache whether it should determine how to execute a CGI program from the program itself or should search the Registry for a mapping between the file extension and some executable. For example, you might have a mapping in the Registry between a `.pl` file extension and the program `c:\perl\bin\perl.exe`. The syntax of the directive is

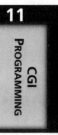

```
ScriptInterpreterSource [registry|script]
```

and the default value is

```
ScriptInterpreterSource script
```

If you have `ScriptInterpreterSource` set to `script` (or if it doesn't appear in your configuration file at all), the location of the Perl executable (or other script interpreter) should be indicated in the first line of the program code, preceded with `#!`:

```
#!/perl/bin/perl
```

You can use forward slashes or backslashes, and you only have to specify the drive letter if it's other than the drive on which `ServerRoot` is located.

CGI programs can also be binary executable (`.exe`) files, such as compiled C programs.

# Common Problems

When your CGI program doesn't work, you should check several things first.

> **Tip**
>
> When a CGI program fails, always check the error logs. They will very likely contain useful information that will tell you exactly what went wrong.

## Permissions

After you put your CGI program in the correct location, you need to make sure that the file has the correct permissions. Remember that the server runs as some user which, hopefully, has very limited permissions on your server. This arrangement is for security reasons, and is discussed in a number of other places, including Chapter 4, "Starting, Stopping, and Restarting the Server," Chapter 5, "Server Configuration Files," and Chapter 15, "Security."

Because the owner of the CGI program and the user who runs the program aren't the same user, the user as whom the server runs might not have permission to run the CGI programs that you have put on your server. A common symptom of this problem is that users can run the CGI program from the command line, but when they try to run it from a browser, they get an error message, as in Figure 11.1.

**FIGURE 11.1**

*Forbidden message from incorrect file permissions.*

The simplest way to make sure that the server can execute your CGI programs is to change the permissions on the file so that anyone can execute it. You do this with the Unix chmod command:

```
chmod a+x example.pl
```

> **Note**
>
> This discussion of file permissions and ownership is aimed at Unix users. File permissions and ownership are handled rather differently on Windows, and so this usually isn't a problem for Windows users.

Make sure that any file that you are trying to open for reading or writing also has permissions on it so that the server can access them. You can use chmod to give the server permission to read from and/or write to your file. If possible, it's sometimes a better idea to change the ownership of the file to the server user, and then just allow that user to have access to the file. This prevents other users on the same system from tinkering with the file. See Chapter 15 for a more thorough treatment of security issues.

## Syntax Errors

Make sure that your CGI program runs from the command line before you try to run it from a browser. By doing so, you can see whether a lot of cryptic error messages about misconfigurations and internal errors result, and then you can fix any problems. If the program doesn't run from the command line, it probably won't run from a browser unless it specifically relies on some CGI environment variables.

## Invalid Headers

Make sure that you've outputted the necessary HTTP headers and included that blank line after the last header. Without this line, the server thinks that the rest of your output is just a continuation of the headers.

---

### Asking a Newsgroup for Help

If you don't know what else to check and still can't get it working, consider posting your question to a Usenet newsgroup or a mailing list. If you are planning to do this, make life a little easier for the folks who are being generous enough to read your questions and suggest solutions. By following these simple recommendations, you can avoid getting flamed and increase your chance of a useful answer:

- Check the FAQ and the list archives first.
- Mention what server software and version you are running.
- Mention the language that your code is written in and, if applicable, the version number of that language.
- Include the source code of the program that's failing, if at all possible.
- Include any error messages that appear in the browser window, in the error log, or at the command line when you run the program.

One main Usenet newsgroup is dedicated to CGI programming, and this is where you should post any questions that you may have:

`comp.infosystems.www.authoring.cgi`.

---

# Alternatives to CGI

CGI programs are notoriously slow. This is because, with every invocation of a CGI program, the program has to be loaded off the disk and executed. If it is a Perl program, the Perl executable has to be loaded into memory, and the Perl program itself must be loaded, compiled, and executed. This time-consuming process must be repeated every time the program is called.

There are several alternatives to CGI that attempt to overcome this limitation in various ways. This list isn't exhaustive, but is a sample of some of the more popular ones.

## Apache's Perl Module: `mod_perl`

Although it's not exclusively a CGI solution, one of `mod_perl`'s greatest strengths is its ability to dramatically improve the performance of Perl CGI programs. See Chapter 21, "Using the Perl Module."

## FastCGI

FastCGI is a reimplementation of the CGI protocol that reduces the overhead normally associated with CGI scripts. It does this with persistent processes, rather than by launching a new process for every request, as CGI does. You can learn more about FastCGI at `http://www.fastcgi.com/`.

## The PHP Module

PHP offers an alternative to CGI and SSI. You can put code in your HTML pages that's executed when the page is served to the user. See Chapter 22, "Using the PHP Module."

# For More Information

You can find a wealth of information online about the CGI and CGI programming in general. There are also a few good books on the subject. Rather than try to offer a comprehensive list, I'll list a few of the better available resources.

## WWW

The following Web sites contain good, reliable information about CGI programming:

- You can find the CGI specification at NCSA at `http://hoohoo.ncsa.uiuc.edu/cgi/`.

- Some things you might want to check when your Perl CGI programs don't work are explained in *The Idiot's Guide to Solving Perl CGI Problems* at `http://www.perl.com/CPAN/doc/FAQs/cgi/idiots-guide.html`.

- The Perl CGI Programming FAQ is at `http://www.perl.com/CPAN/doc/FAQs/cgi/perl-cgi-faq.html`.

- You can find a good list of CGI resources at the HTML Writers Guild at `http://www.hwg.org/resources/?cid=39`.

# Books

Although a large number of CGI books are available, I'll attempt to just list a few that are excellent.

- *Official Guide to Programming with CGI.pm* by Lincoln Stein. CGI.pm is considered the standard way to write CGI programs in Perl. This book, by the author of CGI.pm, walks you through all the intricacies of CGI.pm and teaches you how to make it sing for you.

- *CGI Programming With Perl* by Shishir Gundavaram. An excellent book covering CGI programming—specifically, CGI programming with Perl.

- *CGI Programming in C & Perl* by Tom Boutell. Although most CGI books cover just Perl, this book provides each example in Perl and C.

# Summary

The Common Gateway Interface (CGI) is a simple way to add functionality to your Web site, making it more interactive. Although various people have been preaching the death of CGI for a number of years, it doesn't yet show any signs of going away. The simplicity of writing CGI programs, the ability to write CGI programs in any language, and the ability to run them on any HTTP server has ensured the continued popularity of CGI programming as a means of delivering dynamic, interactive content from your Web site.

In this chapter, you learned how to configure your Apache server to permit execution of CGI programs, and how to write a basic no-frills CGI program to test your configuration. You can find several CGI programming books on the shelves of your local bookstore to get you started on writing more involved CGI programs.

# CHAPTER 12

# SSI: Server-Side Includes

*Server-side includes* (SSI) are directives written directly into HTML pages that the server parses when the page is served to the Web client. Rather than pass the page directly to the requesting client, the server opens and reads through the document, looking for SSI directives. If it encounters one, it replaces it with whatever content is required by that directive.

In this chapter, you will learn how to enable SSI on your server and how to use the various directives available to you. You might use server-side includes to add a small amount of dynamic information to an otherwise static HTML page.

You can accomplish various things with SSI directives: External text files can be included, CGI programs can be called, and environment variables can be accessed. And, since Apache version 1.2, a simple flow control (if/else) structure is even available, so you can display content based on simple conditions.

The SSI directives are defined in the mod_include module, which is part of the standard batch of modules installed with Apache. Much of this functionality was already in the NCSA code when the Apache project began. Some of it, such as the flow control portions, were added later.

> **Note**
>
> The choice of when to use SSI and when to use CGI programs should be considered carefully, particularly for heavily loaded Web sites, as there are performance considerations either way. You might want to do some actual benchmark testing to see what your best approach would be.
>
> The decision whether to use SSI or CGI to accomplish a particular task isn't always clear cut. Generally, you use CGI when more of the page is dynamic than static, and SSI if there's more static than dynamic.

# Configuring Your Server to Permit SSI

By default, the Apache configuration files don't permit SSI because of the potential security risk. For example, an unwise Web page author could use SSI to display your /etc/passwd file for the whole world to see if FollowSymLinks is enabled. A foolish (or malicious) Web author could embed the command rm -rf / (Windows NT users, think format c: /y /y) in a page and do a great deal of damage, even with the limited permissions given to Web users.

By disabling SSI by default, you are required to give at least a little thought to enabling it. When you enable SSI, I encourage you to consider whether you can enable it for just a portion of your site rather than the whole site, whether you can get away with disallowing exec (more about this later), or even if you can avoid using it all together. There is no substitute for a healthy dollop of paranoia when setting security restrictions on your Web server.

The following sections show three ways to enable a particular document to be parsed for SSI directives. Whichever option you choose, you must also enable the Includes option through the Options directive:

```
Options Includes
```

This may be set in the server configuration file or a .htaccess file and can be configured for your whole server, a directory, or for a virtual host.

# Enabling SSI by File Extension

The most common way to enable SSI processing is to indicate that all files with a certain filename extension (typically .shtml) are to be parsed by the server at the time they are served.

In the configuration file httpd.conf (srm.conf before version 1.3.4), you will find the following lines:

```
# To use server-parsed HTML files
#
#AddType text/html .shtml
#AddHandler server-parsed .shtml
```

To enable all .shtml files for server-side parsing, simply uncomment those lines. They should then look like this:

```
# To use server-parsed HTML files

AddType text/html .shtml
AddHandler server-parsed .shtml
```

The AddType directive tells the server that all files with the file extension .shtml are to be served with a MIME type of text/html. The AddHandler line tells the server to enable the handler server-parsed for those same files. server-parsed is one of the built-in handlers that come with Apache, defined in the mod_include module, and tells the server to parse these files for SSI directives, which is what we were trying to accomplish. (See Chapter 14, "Handlers," for more information.)

There are two reasons not to use this approach of enabling SSI:

- If you want to add SSI capability to an existing site, you would have to change the names of all files to which you wanted to add SSI directives and, consequently, change all links in other pages that referred to these pages. This is clearly a huge hassle.

  Some folks have addressed this hassle by simply SSI-enabling all files with the extension .html, in addition to .shtml files. This isn't recommended but would be accomplished with the additional directive:

  ```
  AddHandler server-parsed .html
  ```

  This idea is particularly bad unless either you have a very small site that nobody ever visits or you actually do have SSI directives in all or most of your .html files. It's a bad idea because of the large amount of additional server overhead involved in opening and parsing every single document as it's being served to the waiting client.

- The other reason for not using this approach is one of philosophy, rather than one of technology. In building a Web site, you should think of your user. One aspect of this is making URLs "guessable." If users are looking for some specific information on your site, they should be able to guess at a URL and get to the information they're looking for. If you have .shtml filenames (or something equally non-intuitive, such as .asp), it makes it less likely that users will correctly guess a URL containing the information they came for.

Fortunately, there is an alternative.

## Using the XBitHack Directive

While the name implies that this directive has somewhat less status than some others, it's in the documentation, and I wholly endorse its use. By turning on XBitHack, you enable server-side parsing for all documents on which the user-execute bit is set.

> **Note**
>
> This feature isn't available for Windows NT, because Windows NT doesn't have the concept of marking a file executable.

The XBitHack directive can appear in the server configuration file (httpd.conf) or a .htaccess file and can be configured for the entire server, a directory, or a virtual host. The directive can be given one of three possible values:

| | |
|---|---|
| on | All files with the user-execute bit set are parsed for server-side includes, regardless of file extension. |

| off | (Default) Executable files aren't treated specially. Use this to turn off the directive for a subdirectory where it's undesirable. Remember that directives specified for a directory also apply to all subdirectories. |
|---|---|
| full | The same as on, except that the group-execute bit is also checked. If it's set, the Last-modified date is set to the last-modified time stamp on the file itself. If the group-execute bit isn't set, no Last-modified date is sent to the client, which allows the page to be cached on the client end or by a proxy server. If it's not clear to you why you might want that to happen, you probably shouldn't use the feature. |

Using XBitHack has two main advantages:

- You don't need to rename a file and change all links to that file simply because you want to add a little dynamic content to that file.

- Users looking at your Web content can't tell by looking at the filename that you are generating a page dynamically, so your wizardry is just that tiny bit more impressive.

## Enabling SSI by MIME Type

This method is provided just for backward compatibility and really shouldn't be used at all. It's mentioned here only for the sake of completeness. *Don't use it.*

Documents with a MIME type of text/x-server-parsed-html or text/x-server-parsed-html3 are parsed for SSI directives. The resulting page will be served with a text/html MIME type. You can indicate that a particular sort of file is to have this MIME type with the AddType directive or by adding it to the mime.types file.

# Using SSI Directives

SSI directives look rather like HTML comment tags. This is nice if you happen to have SSI directives in a page, but have SSI parsing turned off, as these directives then don't display in the client.

The syntax of SSI directives is the following:

```
<!--#element attribute=value attribute=value ... -->
```

## SSI Directives

The *element* can be one of the following.

## config

This lets you set various configuration options regarding how the document parsing is handled. Since the page is parsed from top to bottom, `config` directives should appear at the top of the HTML document, or at least before they are referred to. You could change a configuration option several times in a page, if you wanted to.

Three configurations can be set with this command:

- `errmsg` sets the error message that's returned to the client if something goes wrong while parsing the document. This is usually [an error occurred while processing this directive], but can be set to anything with this directive. For Figure 12.1, the following lines appear in the HTML page:

```
<!--#config errmsg="[It's broken, dude]" -->
<!--#directive ssi="Invalid command" -->
```

**FIGURE 12.1**

*Custom SSI error message.*

- `sizefmt` sets the format used to display file sizes. You can set the value to `bytes` to display the exact file size in bytes, or `abbrev` to display the size in kilobytes or megabytes. For example,

```
<!--#config sizefmt="bytes" -->
<!--#config sizefmt="abbrev" -->
```

See `fsize` for an example of this in action.

- `timefmt` sets the format used to display times. The format of the value is the same as is used in the `strftime` function used by C (and Perl) to display dates, as follows:

```
The Date

%A      weekday name                        `Sunday'..`Saturday'
%a      abbreviated weekday name            `Sun'..`Sat'
```

```
%d      day of the month (leading zero)         01..31
%e      day of the month (leading space)        ` 1'..`31'

%B      month name                              `January'..`December'
%b      abbreviated month name                  `Jan'..`Dec'
%m      month as a decimal number               01..12

%Y      year with century                       1970..2038
%C      century number                          00..99
%y      year without century                    00..99
```

The Time

```
%H      hour (24-hour clock)                    00..23
%I      hour (12-hour clock)                    01..12
%M      minute                                  00..59
%S      second                                  00..61
%Z      Time zone name                          `EST', `EDT', `GMT', etc.

%p      locale's equivalent of either...        `AM' or `PM'
```

Shortcuts

```
%r      The time in AM/PM notation              %I:%M:%S %p
%R      the time in 24-hour notation            %H:%M
%T      The time with seconds in 24-hour notation   %H:%M:%S
%D      the date                                %m/%d/%y
```

Locale-dependent representations

```
%x      locale's appropriate date representation
%X      locale's appropriate time representation
%c      locale's appropriate date and time representation
```

Other

```
%j      day of the year                 001..366
%w      weekday as a decimal number     0..6        0=Sun,6=Sat
%u      weekday as a decimal number     1..7        1=Mon,7=Sun
%U      Week number, counting with the first Sunday as the first day
        of the first week
%V      Week number, counting with the first Monday as the first day
        of the first week

%t      the tab character
%n      the newline character
%%      the percent symbol (%) character
```

See strftime(3) for more information. (Type "man strftime" at the Unix
    shell prompt.)

Example:

```
<!--#config timefmt="%B %e, %Y" -->
```

See `flastmod` for an example of this in action.

## echo

This displays any one of the following Include variables. Times are displayed in the time format specified by `timefmt`. The variable to be displayed is indicated with the `var` attribute. Figure 12.2 shows a page using `echo` to display the date, which has been formatted with the `timefmt` function.

| | |
|---|---|
| DATE_GMT | The current date in Greenwich Mean Time. |
| DATE_LOCAL | The current date in the local time zone. |
| DOCUMENT_NAME | The filename (excluding directories) of the document requested by the user. |
| DOCUMENT_URI | The (%-decoded) URL path of the document requested by the user. Note that in the case of nested include files, this isn't the URL for the current document. |
| LAST_MODIFIED | The last modification date of the document requested by the user. |

**Note**

All defined CGI environment variables are also allowed as include variables.

Example:

```
<!--#config timefmt="%B %e, %Y" -->
Today's date is <!--#echo var="DATE_LOCAL" -->.
```

**FIGURE 12.2**
*Custom time format with SSI.*

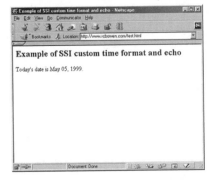

## exec

This directive executes a shell command or a CGI program, depending on the parameters provided. Valid attributes are `cgi` and `cmd`:

- `cgi` specifies the URL of a CGI program to be executed:

```
<!--#exec cgi="/cgi-bin/unread_articles.pl" -->
```

  The URL needs to be a local CGI, not one located on another machine. The CGI program is passed the `QUERY_STRING` and `PATH_INFO` that were originally passed to the requested document, so the URL specified can't contain this information. You should really use `include virtual` instead of this directive.

- `cmd` specifies a shell command to be executed. The results will be displayed on the HTML page. Example:

```
<!--#exec cmd="/usr/bin/ls -la /tmp" -->
```

> **Caution**
>
> In your configuration files (or in `.htaccess`), you can specify `Options IncludesNOEXEC` to disallow the `exec` directive, as this is the most insecure of the SSI directives. Be especially cautious when Web users can create content (like in a guest book or discussion board) and these options are enabled!

## fsize

This directive displays the size of a file specified by either the `file` or `virtual` attribute. Size is displayed as specified with the `sizefmt` directive.

- `file` specifies the file system path to a file, either relative to the root, if the value starts with `/`, or relative to the current directory if not.

- `virtual` specifies the relative URL path to a file.

In Figure 12.3, the following directives appeared in the HTML file:

```
<!--#config sizefmt="bytes" -->
/etc/passwd is <!--#fsize file="/etc/passwd" --> bytes.
```

**FIGURE 12.3**

*Using* fsize *to display the size of a file.*

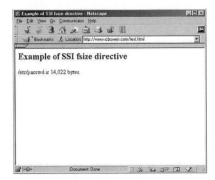

## flastmod

This directive displays the last modified date of a file. The desired file is specified as with the fsize directive. The parameters are the same as with the fsize directive.

In the following example, I display on a Web page when I last received email (see Figure 12.4):

```
<!--#config timefmt="%r" -->
You last received email at
<!--#flastmod file="/var/spool/mail/rbowen" -->.
```

**FIGURE 12.4**

*Using* flastmod *to show when a file was modified.*

## include

This directive includes the contents of the specified file in the Web page. The file is specified with the file and virtual attributes, as with fsize and flastmod. If the file specified is a CGI program and IncludesNOEXEC isn't set, the program will be executed and the results displayed.

Use this directive instead of the `exec` directive. You can pass a `QUERY_STRING` with `include`, but you can't with `exec`.

```
<!--#include file="/etc/aliases" -->
```

### printenv

This directive displays all existing variables (see Figure 12.5). There are no attributes as in the following example:

```
<!--#printenv -->
```

**FIGURE 12.5**

*Output from the* printenv *directive.*

## Variables and Flow Control

The directives described so far allow you to display existing values. Although this is very useful, sometimes you want to define your own variables and do some limited scripting on an HTML page. Various other products offer server-side scripting embedded in HTML pages, and this shouldn't be thought of as rivaling those, since it's very limited. However, it does allow you to do some simple functions without resorting to a third-party product.

There are two aspects to this programming: variables and conditional statements. Variables are provided with the `set` directive and conditionals with the `if/else` flow control statements.

The set directive sets the value of a variable. Attributes are var and value, for example:

```
<!--#set var="animal" value="cow" -->
```

When referenced in other SSI directives, the variable will be distinguished from plain text with the $ character. In this case, $animal can be used in place of any text in any SSI directive.

As shown in the following example, variables can also be references two other ways, depending on the context. Within an echo directive, the var value is understood to be a variable, and the $ isn't required. In a larger string, where the variable might run up against other text, curly brackets are used to delimit the variable from the rest of the string:

```
<!--#set var="basepath" value="/home/rbowen/public_html" -->
Basepath = <!--#echo var="basepath" --><br>
index.html was last modified <!--#flastmod file="${basepath}/index.html" --><br>
<!--#config sizefmt="bytes" -->
test.html is <!--#fsize file="${basepath}/test.html" --> bytes<p>
```

Figure 12.6 shows the results of the above SSI directives.

**FIGURE 12.6**

*Example of using variables.*

Variables could be used, as in the preceding example, to define a string that will be used later in several other directives. This is useful for one-location configuration changes; it also saves you lots of unnecessary typing.

By using the variables set with the set directive and the various environment and include variables, you can use a limited flow-control syntax to generate a certain amount of dynamic content on server-parsed pages.

Conditional flow-control is implemented with the if, elif, else, and endif directives.

The syntax of the if/else function is as follows:

```
<!--#if expr="test_condition" -->
<!--#elif expr="test_condition" -->
<!--#else -->
<!--#endif -->
```

expr can be a string, which is considered true if non-empty, or various comparisons of two strings. Available comparison operators are =, !=, <, <=, >, and >=. If the second string has the format /string/, the strings are compared with regular expressions. Multiple comparisons can be strung together with && (AND) and || (OR). Any text appearing between the if/elif/else directives will be displayed on the resulting page. An example of such a flow structure follows:

```
<!--#set var="agent" value="$HTTP_USER_AGENT" -->
<!--#if expr="$agent = /Mozilla/" -->
Mozilla!
<!--#elif expr="$agent= /MSIE/" -->
Internet Explorer
<!--#else -->
Something else!
<!--#endif -->
```

This code will display Mozilla! if you are using a browser that passes Mozilla as part of its USER_AGENT string, and Something else! otherwise.

> **Note**
>
> The elif portion of this code will very seldom actually be reached, since Internet Explorer passes Mozilla as part of its USER_AGENT string. That is, the elif portion of the code is executed only if the if comparison fails. Of course, not *everyone* uses just IE and Netscape!

# Summary

Server-side includes were extremely popular in the early days of the World Wide Web for things such as hit counters and cute little messages that told you what time it was and where you were visiting from. Fortunately, the appeal has worn off, although you still see them on some beginners' sites. SSI can be used for some genuinely useful things, particularly now that the if/elsif/else flow control directives are available. They provide for dynamic content that can be calculated at runtime, without having to fork off an entirely new CGI process.

**12**

**SSI: SERVER-SIDE INCLUDES**

This chapter covered configuring your server to permit SSI and went through the available SSI directives and their use.

There's a good article about SSI on the Apache Week Web site at `http://www.apacheweek.com/features/ssi`, which covers most of the same material but offers different examples.

# Using Cookies

This chapter examines how a server can save state information about ongoing sessions. The server can then retrieve this information later from the client. This is accomplished using state variables known as *cookies*. These are small pieces of data that are transmitted back and forth between the server and the client. When a session ends, the cookies are stored on the client's hard disk. They remain there until they either expire or until a new session is initiated with the server that originally set the cookies.

Among other things, using these techniques will enable you to save session states. These states can consist of information such as values and selections that a user supplied in a form. This way, personalized information about the client can be saved and reused when the client revisits your Web site later. You also can trace a client's click trail through your site's Web pages. Most importantly, cookies provide you with a simple, efficient mechanism that enables sophisticated inter-application communication.

# What Are Cookies?

When you are developing applications for the Web, you will often be faced with problems that can be solved only if you can retain information between sessions. You will also need to communicate efficiently between different subsystems of your applications. Since the HTTP protocol is stateless (non-persistent), this task can be cumbersome. To alleviate this problem, Netscape defined a way to exchange state objects between the client and the server. Netscape named these state objects "cookies." Today, all major browsers support the use of cookies.

The cookie is a simple method used to pass pieces of information between the server and the client. This is accomplished by using an additional entry in the HTTP response header: `Set-cookie`. This entry is simply an extra piece of text inserted into the rest of the response header. There may be multiple `Set-cookie` entries in each response header.

A cookie entry coming from a server might look something like this:

```
Set-cookie: username=WSB; path=/cgi-bin/; domain=.gnulix.org
```

This would result in the creation of a cookie called `username`. This cookie will be given the string `WSB` as its value. The cookie will be sent back to the server only when the client visits a URL that starts with `/cgi/bin`, and it would be sent out to all Web servers that reside under the `.gnulix.org` domain.

As you can see in the previous example, a cookie header entry can have several attributes. These are used to control the cookie's usage. Among other things, you can tell the client for how long the cookie should be valid. It's also possible to restrain the cookie so that it's valid only in certain parts of your Web site. More attributes will be discussed in depth later in this chapter, in the section "The Anatomy of Cookies."

The only attribute required is the name/value pair that defines the cookie's name and value. All other attributes are optional and, if they aren't present in the header, will be given default values.

When a client returns a cookie to the server, another header entry is used. This entry is aptly enough named `Cookie`. Such an entry can look something like this:

```
Cookie: username=WSB; FavoriteOS=Gnulix
```

In the previous example, two cookies were sent from the client to the server. The first cookie, named `username`, has a value of `WSB`. Of course, the second cookie is called `FavoriteOS` and has a value of `Gnulix`.

For each request that a client sends to a server, all the cookies relevant for the requested URL are included. Including all cookies, whether they are needed or not, is again due to HTTP being a stateless protocol. Once a request has been transmitted, there is no easy way for the server to request further information from the client.

A server can set as many as 20 cookies, and each of these cookies can be up to 4KB in size. This has the potential to create a huge overhead for each request. Therefore, you should strive to keep the cookie data as small as possible and to use a minimum of cookies. Also, be sure to limit in which parts of your Web each cookie is valid. If you follow this advice, you will ensure that communication between server and client isn't bogged down by the transmission of unnecessary data.

The data part of the cookie is often referred to as being *opaque*. Basically, this means that the data has no meaning for anyone but the application that created and sent the cookie. The client that stores the cookies doesn't have to have any knowledge of how to interpret the data. Cookies can contain whatever type of data you see fit, as long as it's text only. If you need to store binary data, you must come up with some method of encoding the data in the form of pure text before sending it to the client.

As you may notice, this protocol isn't very complex or complicated. Using cookies when you are writing an application is just as easy and straightforward as the protocol itself. Even if the language you use for your applications doesn't have direct support for cookies, you should be able to write your own functions for cookie management. However, all the major languages used for writing Web scripts and applications have support for cookies.

# The History of the Cookie

Cookies were first introduced in Netscape Navigator 1.0, which was released in 1994. From the beginning, cookies were an unofficial addition to the HTTP standard. It has since become a *de facto* standard. Even though cookies aren't truly a part of the HTTP standard, their usage is firmly ensconced in the Web community. Now all major browsers support the use of cookies. Many scripting languages for the Web use the cookie as their underlying mechanism for preservation of session states.

According to Netscape's cookie specification, cookies are named as such "for no compelling reason." However, the term *cookie* isn't uncommon in the computer science community. It's usually used when referring to a piece of data held by an intermediary agent for later retrieval. This description fits the use of the term within the Web community. So cookies are aptly named, albeit for a slightly arcane reason.

Cookies have often been accused of being misused. There has been particular criticism against cookies for their potential to divulge private information about a user. For example, companies such as the DoubleClick Network use cookies to track your click trail among all the sites that have DoubleClick's ads on them. By using this information, they can discern what your personal interests are and build a profile about you. They can then make sure that you will be shown personalized ads that adhere to your interests.

Although this type of selective advertising might not be such a big deal, keep in mind that these techniques might be employed by unscrupulous individuals for far more nefarious reasons. The potential for a Big Brother scenario isn't all that farfetched. Assume that a company can collect personal information about you—for example, by having you fill out an innocent-looking subscription form on its site. After you fill out the form, the company could set a cookie with an ID number that it can then use to generate a click trail throughout all sites with its banner ads on them. However, it's not very likely that any company would stoop to such a level; besides, if a user is worried about cookies, all major browsers have the option of disabling them. Whatever you think about cookies, they are here to stay.

> **Note**
>
> An RFC proposal, RFC 2109, for a new type of cookie has been submitted. The author of this new proposal, David M. Kristol, has based his work on Netscape's specification. The proposal tries to address some of the complaints and criticism that surround today's cookie. So far, this proposal hasn't been fully adopted by all major browsers. For this reason we won't cover the proposal in this chapter.

# Cookie Ingredients

You send cookies to the client by using the `Set-cookie` HTTP response header. The header can contain any extra attributes available. These control directives tell the client how the cookie is to be used and stored.

Five different attributes make up a cookie. None of the attribute names are case sensitive. To separate the different attributes from each other in the cookie string, insert a semi-colon between them. Apart from the name/value pair, all the other attributes are optional and, if they aren't present, they are assigned default values.

Let's delve more deeply into the available attributes and their functions. Table 13.1 gives you an overview of the attributes.

**TABLE 13.1** Available Cookie Attributes

| Attribute | Function |
|---|---|
| NAME=VALUE | The name and value of the cookie. |
| Expires=DATE | Marks how long a cookie is valid. |
| Path=PATH | Restricts which URLs a cookie is sent to. |
| Domain=DOMAIN_NAME | Restricts what hosts a cookie is sent to. |
| Secure | Indicates that the cookie should be sent only if the current connection is done over a secure protocol. |

## NAME=VALUE

This must be the first attribute in the Set-Cookie response header, because a cookie name can be the same as the name of any attribute. If you place an attribute before the name/value pair, the browser assumes that the attribute is a cookie name. In this case, you would end up with a misnamed cookie that you probably wouldn't be able to retrieve later.

## Cookie Names

The name part of the cookie can be almost any plain-text string. The restrictions are that the string can't contain semicolons, commas, spaces, or equal signs. Be sure to remember that the length of the name string counts toward the cookie's size restrictions.

> **Note**
>
> You can have several cookies with the same name. If there is more than one cookie with the same name as well as the same value for their respective Path attribute, the most recent of these cookies will be chosen as being the authoritative cookie.

**13**

**USING COOKIES**

# Cookie Values

The value string is text only and, as is the case with the name string, can't contain semicolons, commas, spaces, or any kind of control sequences. Because of this, it might be a good idea to encode your value string before submitting it with the cookie. If your value string contains binary data, you will have to encode it before committing the cookie. Since the data is supposed to be opaque, it's up to the server to encode/decode the data.

# Encoding the Cookie Data

If you are using Perl and the CGI library to write your CGI scripts, you may want to use the library's built-in escape/unescape methods to encode your value strings. The methods encode strings according to the same rules used to encode URLs—that is, all characters not allowed in the string are encoded as %*XX*, where *XX* is the hexadecimal representation of the character's code. The following shows how you can encode a string using the CGI library:

```
#!/usr/bin/perl -w

use CGI;

my %string="a string with white space";
$string=CGI::escape($string);
print "$string\n";
```

When you execute this code, you see the following string:

```
a%20string%20with%20white%20space
```

The %20 part is the hexadecimal representation of the space character.

Decoding a string by using the library is just as easy. You give the string to be decoded as input to the CGI::unescape() method and the return value is the decoded string.

The CGI library has built-in support for cookies in the form of the CGI::Cookie object. If you use this to create and manipulate your cookies, your data will automatically be encoded and decoded for you. As you will see in later examples, it's much easier all around to use this library, rather than cook up your own solutions.

JavaScript has built-in support for encoding strings according to the URL encoding scheme. This is done with the escape() function. To decode the string, you use the corresponding unescape() function. Here is an example of how you could encode a string in JavaScript:

```
encoded=escape(plainstring);
```

Should you choose to encode your cookie data, make sure that you use the proper method to decode the data when retrieving it from the client. Ensuring the correct use of a corresponding encoding/decoding method is especially important if you use multiple languages to write different portions of your Web application.

As long as you do all the hard work of handling the cookies yourself, this shouldn't be a problem. But once you start using function libraries, you must take into account that these might use different coding schemes. If you aren't careful, your cookies won't be interchangeable within the parts of your application that use different libraries. So make sure that you know how the data is encoded beforehand whenever you begin using a new function library.

## Size Considerations

According to Netscape's specification, cookies are restricted in size. A browser should be able to store a cookie that is at least 4,096 bytes (4KB). Some browsers may allow bigger cookies but aren't required to do so, according to the specification. The cookie's size is defined as the combined size of its data string as well as its name string.

Remember to check the cookie's size after you encode its data. No matter which encoding schemes you use, it's possible that the data grows significantly larger after being encoded. If you cross over the 4KB boundary, you may end up with truncated data that can't be interpreted when returned.

## Expires=*DATE*

The Expires attribute specifies how long a cookie should remain valid. Once the time specified in the *DATE* string has come and gone, the cookie expires. It neither remains on the client's hard disk nor is sent back to the server with future requests. Due to this behavior, you will be using the Expires attribute to delete cookies once they are no longer needed.

Even though you mark a cookie with an expiration date that is a long time into the future, you can't be certain that it will be stored on the client for the requested time. The user may remove his cookie file or edit out the portion that defines your cookies. Also, there's a limit on how many cookies a server can send to a client. This limit is defined in the specification as being at least 20 cookies. Once that limit is crossed, the browser will begin removing old cookies and replacing them with newer cookies. When cookies are to be removed to make room for new ones, the old ones are usually removed according to a Least Recently Used (LRU) scheme. This means that there are no guarantees that a cookie will be available for future use. So it's best to make sure that your application handles the absence of a needed cookie as gracefully as possible.

**13**

**USING COOKIES**

The `Expires` attribute is optional. If it's left out, the cookie will expire as soon as the current session ends. The end of a session is usually defined as when the user shuts down his browser. Until the browser closes, cookies are stored in the memory. When the browser is shut down, it iterates through all cookies and determines whether they should be saved for future sessions.

## Date and Time Format

According to Netscape's specification, the format of the date string should be

```
Wdy, DD-Mon-YYYY HH:MM:SS GMT
```

Note that the time must be in the GMT time zone. No other time zones are valid. Make sure that you convert all local times into GMT before creating a date string.

## Deleting Cookies

Setting the date string to a date that has already occurred will delete the cookie from the client. However, most browsers don't update their cookie files until the session ends— that is, when they are shut down. Even though browsers aren't supposed to return cookies that have expired, some do so as long as they have the cookies stored in memory. Therefore, make sure that you set the value of cookies that are about to be deleted to an empty string. That way, you can be sure that even if the cookie is returned, at least it doesn't have a value associated with it.

So if you want to be on the safe side when you are deleting cookies, you may as well employ both attribute changes at the same time. Since the name/value pair is required in a cookie, setting the value to nothing really isn't a big chore.

When a cookie is deleted, both `Path` and its name must be exactly correct. This should be self-explanatory, taking into account that cookies can have the same name but be valid in different paths. Of course, you may delete only cookies valid for your domain. These rules should make sure that you can't delete someone else's cookies by mistake. Vice versa, you can be reasonably sure that no one will delete the cookies that have been set by your application.

To wrap up the discussion about deleting cookies, look at how a reply header might look when you are about to delete a cookie:

```
Set-cookie: username=; Path=/cgi-bin/;Expires=Thu, 01-Jan-1970 00:00:00 GMT
```

This will set the value of the cookie named *username* to an empty string. Furthermore, since the `Expires` time has long since passed, the cookie will be marked as invalid.

If you follow this procedure, you can be sure that your cookies are deleted from the client's cookie file if the browser session ends normally. However, the cookie files usually aren't updated until the browser shuts down. Should the browser session end abnormally—for example, due to a power outage—it's possible that your deletion won't be registered. Keep this caveat in mind if it's very important that a cookie is completely erased. Some browsers update their cookie files on-the-fly and therefore aren't affected by this problem.

### Cookie Bugs

Even though the specification states that years should be supplied as four digits, this causes problems with some older browsers. Therefore, it might be better to set a year by using only two digits. All the major browsers interpret years between 00–50 as though they are actually the years 2000–2050. No matter which numerical representation you choose for years, it will probably work with all browsers that are in use today, since this affects only a few very old browsers. However, it's important to be aware of this bug, since it may cause some obscure problems when you are running your Web applications.

An old version of Netscape Navigator has a bug that's triggered when using the `Expires` attribute. To function properly, the `Path` attribute must also be present and must be set to `/`. If you fail to do this, the cookie won't be stored on the client no matter what the `Expires` attribute is set to. This affects only Netscape Navigator version 1.1 and earlier. Therefore, it might be a good idea to have your scripts check which browser version the client is using and provide a workaround should the need arise.

## Path=*PATH*

A cookie's default behavior is that once you have set it, it's valid only for the document that created the cookie. To enable inter-application communication, it can often be useful to be able to circumvent this default behavior. You will want to be able to set your own restriction about which parts of your Web site a cookie is valid within. This is where the `Path` attribute comes into play.

When a browser checks to see which cookies are to be returned to the server, it will match a cookie's `Path` attribute against the URL that's about to be requested. If the requested URL resides within `Path`, the cookie is sent to the server; otherwise, the cookie is skipped for this request.

The match between the URL and `Path` is done as a substring match. As long as all the `Path` string is included in the beginning of the URL, it's considered to be a match. For example, this means that a `Path` of / matches your whole Web site. Table 13.2 shows more examples of matching.

**TABLE 13.2**    Examples of How Matching Between `Path` and a URL Works

| Path | URL | Match? |
| --- | --- | --- |
| /oreo | /wafer | No |
| /oreo | /oreo/wafer | Yes |
| /oreo | /oreowafer | Yes |
| /oreo/ | /oreo | No |

Some Web pages may have several cookies with the same name, but each with a different path level in its `Path` attribute. In such cases, all the cookies will be sent back to the server. The cookies will be sorted with regard to how specific their paths are. The cookie with the most specific path will be placed first in the `Cookie` header. As a result, be sure to iterate through the `Cookie` header to check for multiple occurrences of a cookie.

## Domain=*DOMAIN_NAME*

The `Domain` attribute works similarly to the `Path` attribute, except that it applies to the hostname of the server rather than the URL. Cookies are usually valid only for the hostname of the server that initially created them. However, there might be situations where a cookie must be valid for a wider range of hosts. For example, a Web farm consisting of multiple machines sharing requests among themselves might host a Web site or Web application. In such a scenario, parts of the application may run on different hosts. To be able to use cookies for inter-application communication in such a scenario, the cookies must be sent to all the servers in the Web farm. To solve such problems, you use the `Domain` attribute.

When sending a cookie, the browser performs a tail match between the parameter of the `Domain` attribute and the fully qualified domain name of the host to which the request is about to be sent. If there is a match, the cookie is included in the request; otherwise, the cookie isn't included.

You can set the `Domain` attribute only to a domain to which your server belongs. Otherwise, a site could easily *spoof* cookies—that is, pretend to be another site and set cookies for that site, which could result in serious security breaches.

The parameter to the Domain attribute has to include at least two or three dot characters. This rule is enforced to prevent Domain parameters such as .COM, which would result in the cookie being sent out to all hosts with a .com address. The following domains require only two dots: COM, EDU, NET, ORG, GOV, MIL, and INT. For all other domains, three dots are required. For example, a cookie with a valid Domain might look like this:

```
Set-cookie: username=; Domain=.gnulix.org
```

Since Domain is an optional attribute, you will usually not need to include it. The default parameter for the Domain attribute is the fully qualified hostname of the server from which the cookie originated. This will suffice in all general usage of cookies.

## Secure

If this attribute is present, it means that the cookie should be sent only if the current connection is done over a secure channel. An absence of this attribute results in the cookie being included in all types of transfers.

The Secure attribute takes no parameters. Therefore, it's not possible to state what type of secure mode should be used. It's up to the browser to decide what is to be considered a secure channel.

Typically, secure transfers use HTTPS (that is, HTTP over SSL). SSL provides strong enough encryption to handle most situations, especially if the data in the transaction is dynamic and of little use a short while after it is transferred (for example, a one-time password). Be sure to use code keys that are as long as possible when dealing with static data that's useful, even if it takes a long time to crack the code—for example, credit card information.

Remember that the cookie is still stored in plain text on the client. So the Secure attribute doesn't ensure that cookies are secure other than during the time when they are being transferred. If you want the cookie to be reasonably safe on the client, you have to encrypt it before sending it and then decrypt it after it's retrieved. But this type of usage is up to the application and isn't a part of the cookie standard.

# Limitations of Cookies

Before looking at the issue of how to send and retrieve cookies, briefly examine some of the most important restrictions and limitations imposed on cookies. None of the limitations are very severe, and there are plenty of workarounds. Generally speaking, it should always be possible to make cookies do what you want them to do—at least within reasonable boundaries.

Most limitations imposed on cookies are due to security reasons and are enforced to protect the client as well as the server. For example, there's a limit on the size of a cookie as well as on the number of cookies a site may set. These limitations are set to ensure that a malicious script can't exploit such weaknesses to create havoc on the client's machine. If the server was allowed to send any number of cookies, this might be used to flood the client with cookies that might result in a denial of service attack.

## Maximum Cookie Size

Cookies can't be used to save arbitrarily large pieces of data. The maximum size of a cookie is limited to 4,096 bytes (4KB). This size limit applies to the combined size of both the cookie's data as well as its name. If you need to save larger amounts of data, you will have to resort to other methods.

To store larger data sets, you could break the data into several chunks and send each off in its own cookie. However, as you will see in the next section, there's also a limit on how many cookies each domain and host may send to the client. Therefore, it might not be such a good idea to break data into chunks. A better way is to store the data on the server, perhaps in a database. Then the server will have to send the client only a cookie containing some sort of receipt that tells the server where to find the data when it's needed again.

If you store user data in a database on the server, be sure to include an expiration date for the data, both in the database and in the cookie. Because cookies can be deleted from the client for a number of reasons, you can never be sure that the receipt that correlates to a database entry will ever be used again. However, if you have set a time limit before which the data has to be accessed again, you are assured that you can perform garbage collection on the database every now and then. Should the client with the correct receipt return to your site within the allotted time, you can just bump the expiration date forward so that the data is valid for a new time span. Using this simple technique should help you avoid storing redundant data on your server.

## Minimum Number of Cookies

Netscape's specification states that a client should be able to store a minimum of 300 cookies. Different browsers have different rules on how many cookies they can store and some can store more than 300 cookies. All browsers that support cookies should be able to meet the minimum requirement. When the limit is reached, old cookies will need to be deleted to make room for new ones. All major browsers delete old cookies automatically.

One server or domain can't send an unlimited number of cookies to a client. It may send no more than 20 cookies before old, unused cookies are deleted on the client. Completely specified hosts and domains are treated as separate entities and, as such, each has its own cookie limit.

When choosing which cookie to delete, the browser uses a Least Recently Used (LRU) scheme. That is, the cookie that hasn't been used in the longest time is deleted. This is done regardless of any parameters set for the cookie. So even if a cookie has an expiration date set way into the future, it will be deleted if it's hasn't been used for the longest time.

# Creating and Sending Cookies

Cookies can be created in a wide variety of ways. The following sections give some examples of how cookies can be set in a couple of different languages.

## HTML

You can set cookies directly from an HTML document by using the HTTP-EQUIV meta tag. The parameter of HTTP-EQUIV is set to Set-cookie and the parameter of the accompanying CONTENT tag is set to the cookie information that should be sent to the client.

Setting cookies this way can be used effectively in several situations. For example, you may send out cookies when the user passes through certain Web pages. Later you can retrieve these cookies and make sure that the user has visited the required pages before proceeding.

Another use for cookies embedded in Web pages could be if you want to see the click trail that a user follows when he visits your site. By setting cookies with different values and creating a custom log that logs cookie activity on your site, you will get as accurate a click trail as is possible. Of course, a true click trail is next to impossible to get, since information might be cached.

To create a log of cookie activity with Apache, you might add something like this to the config file:

```
CustomLog cookie "%{Set-cookie}o %r %t"
```

This will create a log named cookie with entries consisting of the cookie response header, request string, and date. (For more information about how to create your own custom logs, see Chapter 18, "Logging.") An example log entry might look something like this:

```
username=WSB GET /cgi-bin/cookie.cgi HTTP/1.0 [04/Sep/1999:19:11:48 +0200]
```

There also is an Apache module, `mod_usertrack`, that enables you to trace a user's click trail. Using this module will give you all the needed functionality without you having to change any of your Web pages. For more information about this module, see Chapter 23, "Other Well-Known Modules."

An example of how a cookie might be sent with the use of a meta tag is as follows:

```
<HTML>
 <HEAD>
  <META HTTP-EQUIV="Set-Cookie"
   CONTENT="username=WSB;
    expires=Friday, 31-Dec-02 23:59:59 GMT;">
  <TITLE>HTML cookie example</TITLE>
 </HEAD>
 <BODY>
  <P>I've just sent you a cookie!</P>
 </BODY>
</HTML>
```

## JavaScript

Just as you might expect with a language created for Web usage, JavaScript has excellent support for handling cookies. Cookies are handled via the built-in `document.cookie` object.

Here is a short example of how you might use JavaScript to send a cookie:

```
<HTML>
 <HEAD>
  <TITLE>JavaScript cookie example</TITLE>
 </HEAD>
 <SCRIPT LANGUAGE="JavaScript">
  document.cookie="username=WSB;
    expires=Friday, 31-Dec-02 12:34:56 GMT";
 </SCRIPT>
 <BODY>
  <P>I've just sent you a cookie!</P>
 </BODY>
</HTML>
```

## Perl

As always is the case with Perl, there are myriad ways you can do things. Creating cookies is no exception. This section uses two different approaches to creating cookies. By working with these as basic patterns, you should be able to do anything you want to do with cookies.

- The first method is to create all the response headers yourself. By doing this, you get optimal control over how the headers look. It's also a good way to experiment and get a feel for the inner workings of the HTTP protocol function. On the other hand, it's not as easy to maintain the code as if you were to use a function library.

- For the second example, use the CGI function library to help create and send a cookie. This far simpler process is much less error prone. This is an excellent library for working with CGI scripts and is included in the standard Perl distribution.

For the first example, Listing 13.1 creates a cookie that expires 10 minutes after it's sent:

**LISTING 13.1**   Using Perl to Create a Cookie

```perl
#!/usr/bin/perl -w

my @months=(
    "Jan",
    "Feb",
    "Mar",
    "Apr",
    "May",
    "Jun",
    "Jul",
    "Aug",
    "Sep",
    "Oct",
    "Nov",
    "Dec"
);

my @weekdays=(
    "Mon",
    "Tue",
    "Wed",
    "Thu",
    "Fri",
    "Sat",
    "Sun"
);

my $expiretime=time+60*10;

my ($sec,$min,$hour,$mday,$mon,$year,$wday)=
    gmtime($expiretime);

my $datestr=sprintf "%s, %02d-%s-%02d %02d:%02d:%02d GMT",
```

**13**

**USING COOKIES**

*continues*

**LISTING 13.1**   continued

```
    $weekdays[$wday],$mday,$months[$mon],$year,
    $hour,$min,$sec;

my $cookie="username=WSB;expires=$datestr;";

print <<EOF;
set-cookie:$cookie
Content-type: text/html

<!DOCTYPE HTML PUBLIC "-//IETF//DTD HTML//EN">
<HTML>
 <HEAD>
  <TITLE>Perl cookie example</TITLE>
 </HEAD>
 <BODY>
  <P>I've just sent you a cookie!</P>
  <P>It expires: $datestr</P>
 </BODY>
</HTML>
EOF
```

The next example, shown in Listing 13.2, uses the CGI library to do all the work. This example also creates a cookie that expires 10 minutes after it is created.

**LISTING 13.2**   Using Perl's CGI Library to Send a Cookie

```
#!/usr/bin/perl -w

use CGI;

my $q=new CGI;

my $cookie=$q->cookie(-name=>'username', -value=>"WSB",
          expires=>'+10m');

print $q->header(-cookie=>$cookie),
     $q->start_html('Perl cookie example'),
     $q->p, "I've just sent you a cookie!", $q->p,
     $q->end_html;
```

> **Note**
>
> The Expires attribute doesn't have to have a fixed date and time as an argument. The +10m argument is interpreted as 10 minutes after the current time. Thanks to using the library, you need only +10m to get the object to create an appropriate Expires attribute once the cookie is sent.

I think you will agree that the second Perl example is much nicer and should be preferred to the first one. There's no point in reinventing the wheel every time you program something. I am sure that the time used to re-implement the functionality of the CGI library could be used much more creatively.

# Retrieving and Processing Cookies

Now that you know how to send cookies to the client, it's high time to see how you can retrieve the cookies.

## Perl

In Perl, you access cookies via the environment variable `HTTPD_COOKIE`. The variable is a string that contains all the cookies, separated by semicolons. To access a specific cookie, you will have to either search through the string or split the string into separate cookies before accessing them.

The next example, shown in Listing 13.3, uses the latter method to access the cookie. This example retrieves a cookie that was set by one of the test programs from the section about how to set cookies.

**LISTING 13.3**    Using Perl to Retrieve a Cookie

```perl
#!/usr/bin/perl -w

my %cookies=();

foreach (split (/; /,$ENV{"HTTPD_COOKIE"}) {
    my ($name, $data)=split /=/;
    $cookies{$name}=$data;
}

my $cookie=$cookies{"username"};

if ($cookie eq "") {
    $cookie="There was no cookie named username!";
}
else {
    $cookie="Found a cookie named username with a value of " .
            $cookie;
}

print <<EOF;
Content-type: text/html
```

*continues*

**LISTING 13.2**  continued

```
<!DOCTYPE HTML PUBLIC "-//IETF//DTD HTML//EN">
<HTML>
 <HEAD>
  <TITLE>Perl cookie example</TITLE>
 </HEAD>
 <BODY>
  <P>$cookie</P>
 </BODY>
</HTML>
EOF
```

Now try the same thing with the CGI library and let it do the dirty work (see Listing 13.4).

**LISTING 13.4**  Using Perl's CGI Library to Retrieve a Cookie

```
#!/usr/bin/perl -w

use CGI;
use CGI::Cookie;

my %cookies=fetch CGI::Cookie;
my $cookie=$cookies{"username"};

if ($cookie eq "") {
    $cookie="There was no cookie named username!";
}
else {
    $cookie="Found a cookie named username with a value of " .
            $cookie;
}
print $q->header(-cookie=>$cookie),
      $q->start_html('Perl cookie example'),
      $q->p, $cookie, $q->p,
      $q->end_html;
```

> **Note**
>
> The fetch() method tries to decode that cookie data by using the URL escaping method. So if the cookie wasn't created with the CGI library, you could end up with scrambled data. If you aren't sure how the cookie was created, you could use the raw_fetch() method instead. This method doesn't try to interpret and decode the data for you; rather, it just retrieves the data verbatim as it's sent in the query header.

# JavaScript

In JavaScript, as in Perl, cookies are stored as a single string, with each cookie separated by a semicolon. Therefore, it's not quite as easy to retrieve a cookie with JavaScript as it is to set one. The string with the cookies and their values is stored in the built-in document.cookie object. To find the correct cookie, you have to search through the string. This can be an awkward process.

Listing 13.5 is an example of how to parse the document.cookie object and extract a cookie from it.

**LISTING 13.5** Using Java to Extract a Cookie from an Object

```
<HTML>
 <HEAD>
  <TITLE>JavaScript cookie example</TITLE>
 </HEAD>
 <SCRIPT LANGUAGE="JavaScript">
  var cookies=document.cookie;
  var cookie="There was no cookie named username!";
  var searchfor="username=";
  var start=0;
  var end=0;
  if (cookie.length > 0) {
   start=cookies.indexOf(searchfor);
   if(start != -1) {
    start+=searchfor.length;
    end=cookies.indexOf(";",start);
    if (end == -1) {
     end=cookies.length;
    }
    cookie=" Found a cookie named username with a value of "+
           cookies.substring(start,end);
   }
  }
  alert(cookie);
 </SCRIPT>
 <BODY>
  <P>JavaScript example</P>
 </BODY>
</HTML>
```

As you can see, it took quite a lot of code to extract a cookie in JavaScript. Several function libraries are available for managing cookies in JavaScript. If you are serious about using cookies with JavaScript, you will be better off if you acquire such a library before you begin programming.

# Summary

Cookies provide an easy-to-use mechanism for preserving state information. They improve the stateless HTTP protocol so that it can be used for Web applications that require persistent data. By applying the various cookie attributes, you can control the behavior of each cookie to suit your particular needs.

Using cookies programmatically is easy in all languages used to create Web scripts and applications. Function libraries are available for most languages to make cookie management really easy. By using the appropriate language and a good function library, you can easily and quickly create powerful server-side applications.

Using cookies and CGI enables you to create truly dynamic Web sites. Combined, these techniques serve as the foundation for large, real-world Web applications. If you get serious about developing Web applications, you surely will find cookies to be a valuable tool that will come in handy time and time again.

# Handlers

**CHAPTER 14**

The main power of the Apache Web Server is its ability to tailor its actions based on the attributes of the file it's processing. Chapter 7, "MIME Types," describes how the Webmaster can control how the server recognizes the type of information a file contains from looking at its name. This chapter covers how you can control what the server actually *does* with a file, or even with a document that isn't a file.

# Definition of Handler

In Apache parlance, the term *handler* actually has multiple meanings. From the perspective of a software developer, the term refers to a piece of code that the main server will call under certain conditions. From the Webmaster's point of view, however, a handler is simply a type of processing that can be associated with a document—which is only one of the handlers significant to the developer. In Apache hackers' terminology, we're talking specifically about *content handlers* for the most part.

## Phases in Request Processing

Each request received by the server goes through a series of processing phases. At each phase, the modules that are part of the server's configuration have a chance to do something with the request if they choose; the module callbacks the server will invoke are called handlers. As of Apache 1.3.9, here are the different callbacks and the order in which they're called:

```
post_read_request
translate_handler
header_parser
access_checker
check_user_id (authenticate)
auth_checker (authorize)
type_checker
fixer_upper
content_handler
logger
```

An Apache module indicates in which phases it wants to participate by listing a routine in the module structure, as shown by Listing 14.1.

**LISTING 14.1**   Module Structure for the Core Module

```
API_VAR_EXPORT module core_module = {
    STANDARD_MODULE_STUFF,
    NULL,                         /* initializer */
    create_core_dir_config,       /* create per-directory config structure */
    merge_core_dir_configs,       /* merge per-directory config structures */
    create_core_server_config,    /* create per-server config structure */
    merge_core_server_configs,    /* merge per-server config structures */
    core_cmds,                    /* command table */
    core_handlers,                /* handlers */
    core_translate,               /* translate_handler */
    NULL,                         /* check_user_id */
    NULL,                         /* check auth */
    do_nothing,                   /* check access */
    do_nothing,                   /* type_checker */
    NULL,                         /* pre-run fixups */
    NULL,                         /* logger */
    NULL,                         /* header parser */
    NULL,                         /* child_init */
    NULL,                         /* child_exit */
    NULL                          /* post_read_request */
};
```

It's beyond the scope of this chapter to describe the details of all the phases; we focus here on the significance, use, and control of the content-handling phase. By the time the content handler receives control, almost all the other phases have completed their work successfully; otherwise, the content handler wouldn't have been invoked.

## Content-Handling Phase

A content handler has the responsibility of actually processing—or generating—the body of the document being sent back to the client. In Apache 1.3 and earlier versions, content handlers are called as the next-to-last phase of request processing and are the last aspect of the server that has contact with the client. The only phase that follows deals with logging the request information on the server.

The content handler is not only responsible for sending the body of the response to the client, but also for ensuring that the response header is sent. In practice, this means that the handler checks to see that all the header fields with which it is concerned are correctly set in the r->headers_out and r->err_headers_out tables and calling ap_send_http_header(). But only module writers need to worry about that level of detail.

Content handlers, particularly those that can take a significant time to complete their output or emit it piecemeal, need to beware of timeout considerations. If they wait too long between blocks of content sent to the client, either the client or the Apache server itself may decide that something has broken and abort the transaction.

After a content handler finishes sending the body of the resource, it simply returns control to its caller, and the main code of the Apache server will take care of closing the connection and doing other end-of-request cleanup operations.

Apache, even in its simplest form, includes at least one content handler: the default handler. This is described in its own section later in this chapter.

Even though you might think the default handler has a very simple job ("find the file and ship it to the client"), it's actually quite involved. One reason it's so complicated is because it's designed to work with actual files found on disk. A handler that generates its content without any such file system requirement can conceivably be much simpler; Listing 14.2 shows the content handler from the Apache-supplied `mod_example` module. More than half of its 65 lines are comments, and most of the rest of it is structured in a simple manner for clarity rather than efficiency, but it nevertheless serves as a fairly good demonstration of how simple a content handler can be.

**LISTING 14.2**    The Simple `mod_example` Content Handler

```
static int example_handler(request_rec *r)
{

  excfg *dcfg;

  dcfg = our_dconfig(r);
  trace_add(r->server, r, dcfg, "example_handler()");
  /*
   * We're about to start sending content, so we need to force the HTTP
   * headers to be sent at this point. Otherwise, no headers will be sent
   * at all. We can set any we like first, of course. **NOTE** Here's
   * where you set the "Content-type" header, and you do so by putting it
   * in r->content_type, *not* r->headers_out("Content-type"). If you don't
   * set it, it will be filled in with the server's default type (typically
   * "text/plain"). You *must* also ensure that r->content_type is lower-
   * case.
   *
   * We also need to start a timer so the server can know if the connexion
   * is broken.
   */
  r->content_type = "text/html";
  ap_soft_timeout("send example call trace", r);
  ap_send_http_header(r);
```

```
/*
 * If we're only supposed to send header information (HEAD request),
 * we're already there.
 */
if (r->header_only) {
    ap_kill_timeout(r);
    return OK;
}

/*
 * Now send our actual output.  Since we tagged this as being
 * "text/html", we need to embed any HTML.
 */
ap_rputs(DOCTYPE_HTML_3_2, r);
ap_rputs("<HTML>\n", r);
ap_rputs(" <HEAD>\n", r);
ap_rputs("  <TITLE>mod_example Module Content-Handler Output\n", r);
ap_rputs("  </TITLE>\n", r);
ap_rputs(" </HEAD>\n", r);
ap_rputs(" <BODY>\n", r);
ap_rputs("  <H1><SAMP>mod_example</SAMP> "
         "Module Content-Handler Output\n", r);
ap_rputs("  </H1>\n", r);
ap_rputs("  <P>\n", r);
ap_rprintf(r, "  Apache HTTP Server version: \"%s\"\n",
           ap_get_server_version());
ap_rputs("  <BR>\n", r);
ap_rprintf(r, "  Server built: \"%s\"\n", ap_get_server_built());
ap_rputs("  </P>\n", r);;
ap_rputs("  <P>\n", r);
ap_rputs("  The format for the callback trace is:\n", r);
ap_rputs("  </P>\n", r);
ap_rputs("  <DL>\n", r);
ap_rputs("   <DT><EM>n</EM>.<SAMP>&lt;routine-name&gt;", r);
ap_rputs("(&lt;routine-data&gt;)</SAMP>\n", r);
ap_rputs("   </DT>\n", r);
ap_rputs("   <DD><SAMP>[&lt;applies-to&gt;]</SAMP>\n", r);
ap_rputs("   </DD>\n", r);
ap_rputs("  </DL>\n", r);
ap_rputs("  <P>\n", r);
ap_rputs("  The <SAMP>&lt;routine-data&gt;</SAMP> is supplied by\n", r);
ap_rputs("  the routine when it requests the trace,\n", r);
ap_rputs("  and the <SAMP>&lt;applies-to&gt;</SAMP> is extracted\n", r);
ap_rputs("  from the configuration record at the time "
         "of the trace.\n", r);
ap_rputs("  <STRONG>SVR()</STRONG> indicates a server environment\n", r);
ap_rputs("  (blank means the main or default server, otherwise "
         "it's\n", r);
ap_rputs("  the name of the VirtualHost); <STRONG>DIR()</STRONG>\n", r);
```

**14**

HANDLERS

*continues*

**LISTING 14.2**   continued

```
ap_rputs("  indicates a location in the URL or filesystem\n", r);
ap_rputs("  namespace.\n", r);
ap_rputs("  </P>\n", r);
ap_rprintf(r, "  <H2>Static callbacks so far:</H2>\n  <OL>\n%s  </OL>\n",
           trace);
ap_rputs("  <H2>Request-specific callbacks so far:</H2>\n", r);
ap_rprintf(r, "  <OL>\n%s  </OL>\n", ap_table_get(r->notes, TRACE_NOTE));
ap_rputs("  <H2>Environment for <EM>this</EM> call:</H2>\n", r);
ap_rputs("  <UL>\n", r);
ap_rprintf(r, "   <LI>Applies-to: <SAMP>%s</SAMP>\n   </LI>\n",
           dcfg->loc);
ap_rprintf(r, "   <LI>\"Example\" directive declared here: %s\n"
           "   </LI>\n",
           (dcfg->local ? "YES" : "NO"));
ap_rprintf(r, "   <LI>\"Example\" inherited: %s\n   </LI>\n",
           (dcfg->congenital ? "YES" : "NO"));
ap_rputs("  </UL>\n", r);
ap_rputs(" </BODY>\n", r);
ap_rputs("</HTML>\n", r);
/*
 * We're all done, so cancel the timeout we set. Since this is probably
 * the end of the request we *could* assume this would be done during
 * post-processing - but it's possible that another handler might be
 * called and inherit our outstanding timer. Not good; to each its own.
 */
ap_kill_timeout(r);
/*
 * We did what we wanted to do, so tell the rest of the server we
 * succeeded.
 */
return OK;
}
```

# Handlers and MIME Types

Content handlers are frequently associated with the actual content-type of resources—also called their *MIME types*. Usually this association is made indirectly; the server configuration files define certain file extensions as signifying particular MIME types (such as associating files with an .shtml extension with the MIME type text/html) and relate a particular handler name to the extension as well (for example, marking files with the .shtml extension as being handled by the server-parsed handler).

Because of the way Apache deals with the various data structures involved, you can also connect a handler name directly to a MIME type, such as with

```
AddHandler text/x-server-parsed-html .shtml
```

For this to work, the module must recognize the MIME type as one for which it is responsible. The following two sets of directives are equivalent and show how this feature can be used:

```
AddType text/html .shtml
AddHandler server-parsed .shtml
```

```
AddType text/x-httpd-server-parsed-html .shtml
```

`text/x-httpd-server-parsed-html` is what's called a *magic MIME type* in Apache parlance. This is because it has a special significance to an Apache module and almost certainly does *not* reflect the actual content type of the file or the content type that will be attached to the outgoing response.

Taking advantage of magic MIME types like this is a dangerous practice, because the results may be unpredictable unless you are extremely conversant with the source code. The following example, for instance, probably won't result in the desired effect, because none of the standard Apache modules declare a useful handler specifically for the `text/html` MIME type:

```
AddHandler text/html .htm .html
```

> **Note**
>
> Actually, there *is* a handler for the `text/html` MIME type, but it isn't intended to be used this way. That it doesn't work as you might expect merely reinforces the point that you should stick to the "advertised" handler names rather than try to use the magic MIME types that some modules recognize.

To ensure predictable results and for clarity, it's best to use the two-phase approach and treat the MIME type and content handler as two separate and distinct things to associate with documents.

You *can* associate a CGI script with a MIME type, as a content handler, with the `Action` directive, which is described later in this chapter.

# The `AddHandler` Directive

The primary means of connecting a content handler to a document is with the `AddHandler` directive (as covered briefly in the previous section). `AddHandler` is an `ITERATE2` directive, which means it takes its first argument and does its thing with it and each of the subsequent arguments in turn.

In the case of `AddHandler`, the first argument is the name of a content handler, and the second and subsequent arguments are file extensions that should be marked as being processed by that handler. For example

```
AddHandler application/x-httpd-php3 .phtml .php3
```

causes Apache to invoke the `application/x-httpd-php3` handler for each file requested that has an extension of `.phtml` or `.php3`.

> **Note**
>
> This example may seem a bit at odds with the warning in the preceding section that the handler name looks suspiciously like a magic MIME type. Well, that's true, but that's also how the PHP module developers chose to name their handler.

The association between a handler and a file extension remains in effect throughout the scope of the `AddHandler` directive, typically for the entire server or for a particular directory and its subdirectories. An association can be removed with the `RemoveHandler` directive, as described later in this chapter.

# The `SetHandler` Directive

While the `AddHandler` directive allows you to set the content handler on files according to their extensions, the `SetHandler` directive allows you to set it for a broader range of documents, such as an entire directory or Web location. Content handlers set with the `SetHandler` directive take precedence over any `AddHandler` settings.

A common use for the `SetHandler` directive is to associate a handler with a virtual Web location, which doesn't map onto a file system directory. For example, the `mod_status` module generates its responses at runtime and doesn't have anything to do with files on disk. How could you associate its content handler with a real file when it doesn't have anything to do with one? Well, you actually *could* do something like the following:

```
<Directory /usr/local/web/documentroot>
    AddHandler server-status .status
</Directory>
```

The main problem with this, however, is that you'd then need to actually have such a directory, and you'd have to request some file with a .status extension (such as foo.status) to get the report.

More commonly, though, SetHandler is used to make an appropriate association. Instead of the preceding, the following might be used:

```
<Location /status>
    SetHandler server-status
</Location>
```

The effect of this is that *any* request for *anything* in the /status virtual Web location will result in the content handler being invoked. If that container were in effect for a server named WWW.Foo.Com, all of the following would activate the server-status handler and give the same result:

```
http://WWW.Foo.Com/status/
http://WWW.Foo.Com/status/index.html
http://WWW.Foo.Com/status/home.htm
http://WWW.Foo.Com/status/some/bogus/path
```

So SetHandler is generally used to force a particular handler into effect for all documents in a particular location or to enable a content handler that doesn't have anything to do with the file system.

# The RemoveHandler Directive

If you want to undo the association between a file extension and a content handler, you have two ways of doing it:

- Replace it with an explicit association to the default handler:

  ```
  AddHandler default-handler .foo
  ```

- Remove all existing associations with the RemoveHandler directive:

  ```
  RemoveHandler .foo
  ```

Both methods have the same ultimate effect and scope (the directory to which the directive applies and all subdirectories thereof); the RemoveHandler technique probably makes the intent a little more clear.

Despite the names, there's no way (as of Apache 1.3.9) to "push" handler associations and later "pop" them. As an example, you might want to set a default condition of having all .html files handled by the server-parsed handler—but in one particular directory *only*, you want the handler for .html files to be the PHP handler instead—and for subdirectories under there to go back to using the server-parsed handler

14

HANDLERS

again. Each application of the `AddHandler` directive unconditionally sets the handler for the named extensions, and each use of `RemoveHandler` unconditionally removes *all* associations (causing the server to fall through to the default handler).

# The `Action` Directive

The `Action` directive permits you to define a new content handler name and declare the handler itself to be a CGI script. Alternatively, you can declare the script to be the content handler for a specific MIME type. As described earlier in the "Handlers and MIME types" section, Apache may regard a MIME type as a handler name, so in fact the `Action` directive is simply registering a handler name for the script. If the name happens to be the same as a MIME type, the script will be considered the handler for documents with the corresponding content type—if the definition isn't overridden by other settings.

The following are equivalent:

```
AddType application/x-bagatelle .bhtml
Action application/x-bagatelle /cgi-bin/bagatelle-handler

AddHandler bagatelle .bhtml
Action bagatelle /cgi-bin/bagatelle-handler
```

Both sets of directives have the effect of

- Labeling files with an extension of `.bhtml` as being of MIME type `application/x-bagatelle`
- Declaring the CGI script `/cgi-bin/bagatelle-handler` as the content handler for files of that type

Whether you declare a script to be a content handler based on the file extension (with `AddHandler`) or the MIME type (with `AddType`) is entirely up to you and depends on your needs and situation.

# The `Script` Directive

Unlike the `Action` directive, which declares a content handler based on the attributes of the document being requested, the `Script` directive declares a handler according to *how* the document was requested.

Documents are requested by using what are called *methods*. The most common methods are `GET`, `HEAD`, and `POST`, and Apache has built-in handlers for each. However, more and more alternative methods are appearing all the time, each with a special significance, and the `Script` directive allows you to keep up. For instance, as document uploading became common, the PUT method started being used to allow the upload to be done through the Web server itself, rather than through an FTP server or other mechanism. Publishing tools appeared that tried to use PUT to do this, but alas for the user if the Web server hadn't been educated in how to respond. Individual Apache Webmasters can enable PUT handling with the appropriate Script directive and supporting software.

> **Caution**
>
> Because of security concerns, the Apache server doesn't come with a built-in handler for PUT the way it does for GET, HEAD, and POST. Due to the largely anonymous nature of the Web, allowing people on the network to upload files onto your system is something to be approached with caution. In other words, Apache gives you the rope with the Script directive; if you want to hang yourself with it, you need to tie the knot yourself.

As of Apache 1.3.9, you can declare a Script handler only for methods already known to Apache—namely, GET, PUT, POST, DELETE, CONNECT, OPTIONS, PATCH, PROPFIND, PROPPATCH, MKCOL, COPY, MOVE, LOCK, and UNLOCK. The TRACE method is also known to Apache but is not meaningful for a handler to be declared for it, and so it's explicitly disallowed from appearing in a Script directive.

A method-based content handler declared with Script is invoked as a normal CGI script. The URL of the document being requested is passed to the script using the PATH_INFO environment variable.

# Customizing Error Handling with ErrorDocument

The ErrorDocument directive allows you to enable a special type of content handler—one that will be activated when a particular class of error occurs.

The errors in this case are defined by the HTTP protocol specification and are identified with three-digit numbers. You may have seen some of these numbers on error pages when surfing the Web—for example, 500 Internal Server Error, 404 Resource Not Found, or 403 Access Forbidden. If you've seen pages like this, you're probably aware that they look pretty terse and are fairly unattractive. With the ErrorDocument directive, you can customize the appearance of such pages as well as see that additional actions are taken.

You can declare a different `ErrorDocument` handler for any or all of the defined HTTP status codes. (Be warned, though, that Apache will invoke only the ones that make sense.)

> **Note**
>
> You *can* declare an `ErrorDocument 200` handler, but it won't do any good—200 is the status code for OK. Apache doesn't consider an OK status to be an error and won't invoke the error handler for it.

`ErrorDocument` follows the usual scoping rules: It applies to the location in which it's declared and in all subordinate directories or locations unless overridden. There are three formats for `ErrorDocument`:

- One that merely supplies a simple string of text to be used instead of the default error page for the specific status code
- One that specifies a full URL (which might possibly be on a remote server)
- One that specifies a local URI on *your* server

These options are described in more detail in the following sections.

## One-Line Error Text

The syntax for this type of `ErrorDocument` usage is as follows:

```
ErrorDocument code "error text
```

Note that there is no closing quotation mark. This is because the argument to the directive is *not* a quoted string; the initial quotation mark simply identifies what follows as a text message rather than a URL. If you include another quotation mark at the end of the text, it will appear in the error message. Figure 14.1 shows an example error generated from the following directive.

```
ErrorDocument 403 "just a line of text
```

This can be prettied up a bit by embedding HTML in the text string, as shown by the following example and by Figure 14.2, which shows its output.

```
ErrorDocument 403 "<h1>Sorry, not allowed</h1>
```

FIGURE **14.1**

*Plain-text*
ErrorDocument.

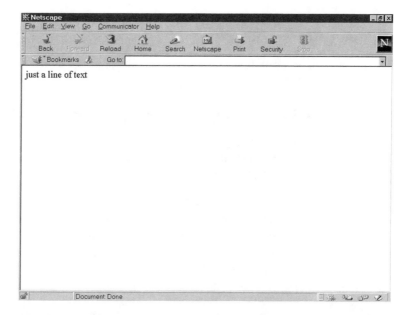

FIGURE **14.2**

*A fancier*
*plain-text*
ErrorDocument.

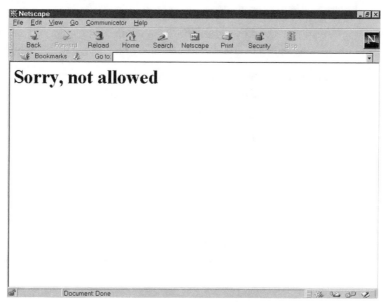

While certainly quick, this means of dealing with errors is generally unsatisfactory.
Among other things, the error page sent to the client is labeled as text/html by default,
even if your text isn't valid HTML. For another, there's no way of acting on the error or

customizing the response page based on any criteria; the text from the ErrorDocument statement gets sent, and that's it.

This mechanism is generally good for debugging the layout of directory structures and not much else.

## Handling Errors with a Local Document

If the second argument you supply to ErrorDocument is a relative rather than an absolute URL (that is, it doesn't include the scheme, hostname, or port portion), Apache will use what's called an *internal redirect* to access the specified URL on the local server.

This is the most powerful, efficient, and flexible way of dealing with ErrorDocument content. Since the request is being handled by the same server where the error occurred, there's no back-and-forth network traffic with the client; the server discovered the error and is dealing with it internally as part of the original request. Also, all the relevant information (such as the referring page, the error status code, the page that was originally requested, and so forth) is available to the local error document if it knows how to use it. This can mean some impressively tailored error messages that deal with the finest details of a transaction error, for instance.

Most information about the original request—and the error—is available to the error handler through environment variables. The standard ones that Apache will always include are

- REDIRECT_ERROR_NOTES (present if Apache has any comments about the error)
- REDIRECT_QUERY_STRING (present and set to the query string from the original request if there was one)
- REDIRECT_REQUEST_METHOD
- REDIRECT_STATUS
- REDIRECT_UNIQUE_ID (present and set to the unique identifier assigned to the original request if you have mod_unique_id configured into your server)
- REDIRECT_URL

The REDIRECT_STATUS environment variable contains the actual status code, so you can use a single error handler to deal with multiple status codes and act appropriately based on the value of this environment variable in each case.

The REDIRECT_URL environment variable contains the local URL of the originally requested document, including any path-info or query string but minus the scheme, hostname, and port information.

In addition, the local document will have access to any environment variables set for the original document as a result of Apache's processing it through the phases until the error occurred. These too are prefixed with REDIRECT; for example, if the original request had an environment variable named FOO set to bar, then the error document will have an environment variable named REDIRECT_FOO set to bar.

This information makes tailoring responses very possible with error content handlers that are "active" documents, such as PHP scripts, mod_include pages, or CGI scripts.

## Using a CGI Script

If you're sticking to using the set of modules included in the base Apache package, a CGI script gives you the most flexibility and power as an error document handler.

Since a CGI script is a fully active document, such as an actual application or program, you have complete control over what actions are taken by the server. You also have the option of propagating the error status to the client, which is quite important—that way, the client will know that its request caused an error and behave appropriately. In other cases, the client just gets a response page back, almost always with a 200 status (which, if you'll recall, means OK), and so won't realize that there was a problem, even if the user does (by reading the actual content of the response).

## Redirecting Errors Off-Site

If you use a full URL, such as http://some.other.host.com/error.html, the Apache server will send a redirect request back to the client, which will (or should) then fetch that page from the other server. Although this allows some centralization, it's generally not as flexible as using a local URI; since what the client ends up seeing came as the result of a successful request made to the other system, it won't be recorded by the browser as being an error (unless that other system did things *exactly* right). The other system also won't have access to all the information that would be available to a local URI, such as the access control information and other attributes of the original request, as described a couple of sections ago.

# Standard Handlers

The following sections describe some of the content handlers that are bundled as part of the base Apache package. As long as you have the appropriate module in your server's configuration, you should be able to use any of these.

14

HANDLERS

# The Default Content Handler

The Apache server has a built-in catchall content handler that it will use if none of the loaded modules can be identified as being responsible. This default handler is found in the `src/main/http_core.c` file.

The default handler's responsibility is quite simple: Assume that the requested object is a file in the file system, locate it, and ship its contents to the client without any special processing. Although that sounds like a pretty simple assignment, if you look at the 1.3.9 source of the handler, shown in Listing 14.3, it becomes clear that there are some complicating concerns.

The default handler is located using the same mechanism as any other content handler. It is marked as the default through the definition of the content types for which it's responsible. Listing 14.4 shows this definition.

As mentioned earlier, handler determination from the content-type progresses from the most specific to the least specific match. The type of `*/*` is as unspecific as you can get, so the default handler should always be found after all other possibilities are exhausted.

> **Note**
>
> A module *could* declare its own handler for the `*/*` content-type, in which case its interactions with the default handler might lead to unpredictable results.

The presence of the default handler means that your Apache server should never be at a loss when it comes to handling a request. The response might be an error (such as if the resource isn't a file, doesn't exist, or is protected), but a handler will *always* be found.

**LISTING 14.3**   The Default Content Handler

```
/*
 * Default handler for MIME types without other handlers.  Only GET
 * and OPTIONS at this point... anyone who wants to write a generic
 * handler for PUT or POST is free to do so, but it seems unwise to provide
 * any defaults yet... So, for now, we assume that this will always be
 * the last handler called and return 405 or 501.
 */

static int default_handler(request_rec *r)
{
    core_dir_config *d =
      (core_dir_config *)ap_get_module_config(r->per_dir_config,
                                              &core_module);
```

```
        int rangestatus, errstatus;
        FILE *f;
#ifdef USE_MMAP_FILES
        caddr_t mm;
#endif
#ifdef CHARSET_EBCDIC
        /* To make serving of "raw ASCII text" files easy (they serve faster
         * since they don't have to be converted from EBCDIC), a new
         * "magic" type prefix was invented: text/x-ascii-{plain,html,...}
         * If we detect one of these content types here, we simply correct
         * the type to the real text/{plain,html,...} type. Otherwise, we
         * set a flag that translation is required later on.
         */
        int convert_flag = ap_checkconv(r);
#endif

        /* This handler has no use for a request body (yet), but we still
         * need to read and discard it if the client sent one.
         */
        if ((errstatus = ap_discard_request_body(r)) != OK) {
            return errstatus;
        }

        r->allowed |= (1 << M_GET) | (1 << M_OPTIONS);

        if (r->method_number == M_INVALID) {
        ap_log_rerror(APLOG_MARK, APLOG_NOERRNO|APLOG_ERR, r,
                "Invalid method in request %s", r->the_request);
        return NOT_IMPLEMENTED;
        }
        if (r->method_number == M_OPTIONS) {
            return ap_send_http_options(r);
        }
        if (r->method_number == M_PUT) {
            return METHOD_NOT_ALLOWED;
        }

        if (r->finfo.st_mode == 0 || (r->path_info && *r->path_info)) {
        ap_log_rerror(APLOG_MARK, APLOG_ERR|APLOG_NOERRNO, r,
                "File does not exist: %s",r->path_info ?
                ap_pstrcat(r->pool, r->filename, r->path_info, NULL)
                : r->filename);
        return HTTP_NOT_FOUND;
        }
        if (r->method_number != M_GET) {
            return METHOD_NOT_ALLOWED;
        }

#if defined(OS2) || defined(WIN32) || defined(NETWARE)
```

*continues*

**Listing 14.3**   continued

```
    /* Need binary mode for OS/2 */
    f = ap_pfopen(r->pool, r->filename, "rb");
#else
    f = ap_pfopen(r->pool, r->filename, "r");
#endif

    if (f == NULL) {
        ap_log_rerror(APLOG_MARK, APLOG_ERR, r,
            "file permissions deny server access: %s", r->filename);
        return FORBIDDEN;
    }

    ap_update_mtime(r, r->finfo.st_mtime);
    ap_set_last_modified(r);
    ap_set_etag(r);
    ap_table_setn(r->headers_out, "Accept-Ranges", "bytes");
    if (((errstatus = ap_meets_conditions(r)) != OK)
     || (errstatus = ap_set_content_length(r, r->finfo.st_size))) {
        return errstatus;
    }

#ifdef USE_MMAP_FILES
    ap_block_alarms();
    if ((r->finfo.st_size >= MMAP_THRESHOLD)
        && (r->finfo.st_size < MMAP_LIMIT)
        && (!r->header_only || (d->content_md5 & 1))) {
        /* we need to protect ourselves in case we die while we've got the
         * file mmapped */
        mm = mmap(NULL, r->finfo.st_size, PROT_READ, MAP_PRIVATE,
                fileno(f), 0);
        if (mm == (caddr_t)-1) {
            ap_log_rerror(APLOG_MARK, APLOG_CRIT, r,
                    "default_handler: mmap failed: %s", r->filename);
        }
    }
    else {
        mm = (caddr_t)-1;
    }

    if (mm == (caddr_t)-1) {
        ap_unblock_alarms();
#endif

#ifdef CHARSET_EBCDIC
    if (d->content_md5 & 1) {
        ap_table_setn(r->headers_out, "Content-MD5",
            ap_md5digest(r->pool, f, convert_flag));
    }
#else
```

```
    if (d->content_md5 & 1) {
        ap_table_setn(r->headers_out, "Content-MD5",
            ap_md5digest(r->pool, f));
    }
#endif /* CHARSET_EBCDIC */

    rangestatus = ap_set_byterange(r);

    ap_send_http_header(r);

    if (!r->header_only) {
        if (!rangestatus) {
        ap_send_fd(f, r);
        }
        else {
        long offset, length;
        while (ap_each_byterange(r, &offset, &length)) {
            /*
             * Non zero returns are more portable than checking
             * for a return of -1.
             */
            if (fseek(f, offset, SEEK_SET)) {
                ap_log_error(APLOG_MARK, APLOG_ERR, r->server,
                    "Failed to fseek for byterange (%ld, %ld)",
                    offset, length);
            }
            else {
                ap_send_fd_length(f, r, length);
                }
        }
        }
    }

#ifdef USE_MMAP_FILES
    }
    else {
        struct mmap_rec *mmd;

        mmd = ap_palloc(r->pool, sizeof(*mmd));
        mmd->mm = mm;
        mmd->length = r->finfo.st_size;
        ap_register_cleanup(r->pool, (void *)mmd, mmap_cleanup,
                            mmap_cleanup);
        ap_unblock_alarms();

        if (d->content_md5 & 1) {
            AP_MD5_CTX context;

            ap_MD5Init(&context);
```

*continues*

**14**

HANDLERS

**LISTING 14.3**   continued

```
        ap_MD5Update(&context, (void *)mm,
                    (unsigned int)r->finfo.st_size);
        ap_table_setn(r->headers_out, "Content-MD5",
                      ap_md5contextTo64(r->pool, &context));
    }

    rangestatus = ap_set_byterange(r);
    ap_send_http_header(r);

    if (!r->header_only) {
        if (!rangestatus) {
            ap_send_mmap(mm, r, 0, r->finfo.st_size);
        }
        else {
            long offset, length;
            while (ap_each_byterange(r, &offset, &length)) {
                ap_send_mmap(mm, r, offset, length);
            }
        }
    }
}
#endif

    ap_pfclose(r->pool, f);
    return OK;
}
```

**LISTING 14.4**   Declaration of the Default Handler

```
static const handler_rec core_handlers[] = {
{ "*/*", default_handler },
{ "default-handler", default_handler },
{ NULL, NULL }
};
```

# cgi-script

The cgi-script handler is declared by the mod_cgi module and has the responsibility of treating the resource as a CGI application, executing it, and sending its output back to the client. Describing the CGI runtime environment is far beyond the scope of this chapter, but CGI scripts are known for two things:

- They're very powerful and flexible.
- They tend to be performance hogs.

To find out more about the CGI environment, see any number of good books on the subject; read Chapter 11, "CGI Programming"; or visit the ongoing specification area on the Web at `http://Golux.Com/coar/cgi/`. To find out more about the `mod_cgi` module itself, see the online documentation page at `http://www.apache.org/docs/mod/mod_cgi.html`.

## server-parsed: Server-Side Includes

The `server-parsed` content handler is how Apache provides support for server-side include (SSI) directives. An SSI directive is embedded in an HTML document as part of its text; when the server receives a request for the document, it first goes through the file and executes (*parses*) the SSI directives.

SSI directives can do things such as include other documents (where the name came from) or conditionally include—or not—portions of the document based on environment variables, or insert things like the last modification date of the file, and so on.

Since Apache provides lots of support for manipulating environment variables, SSI documents provide a convenient means of keeping lots of different alternative text fragments in a single document and sending only the appropriate portions to the client. For example, the following fragment would cause different text to be sent to the client, depending on whether the client was Opera:

```
<!--#if expr="HTTP_USER_AGENT = /Opera/" -->
  Welcome, user of innovative software!  We genuflect before your
  magnificence and open wide our site to you!
<!--#else -->
  Please choose an option from the list below.
<!--#endif -->
```

For more information about server-side includes, see Chapter 12, "SSI: Server-Side Includes," the section in Chapter 20, "Using Standard Apache Modules," on `mod_include`, or the online documentation at `http://www.apache.org/docs/mod/mod_include.html`.

## server-status: How Apache Is Running

The `mod_status` module provides one of those "generate content on-the-fly" content handlers mentioned earlier. It doesn't relate to any files on disk but generates a report on how the Apache server is functioning. The report is generated from scratch every time it's requested. Figure 14.3 show a fragment of sample output from the `server-status` content handler.

**14**

HANDLERS

FIGURE 14.3

*Output from the*
server-status
*handler.*

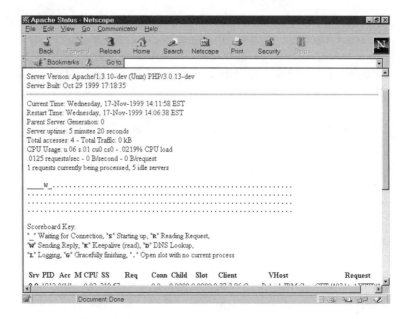

Since this output may contain information that you'd rather keep confidential, it's a good idea to protect whatever location you use for the handler. For example

```
<Location /server-status>
    SetHandler server-status
    AuthType Basic
    AuthUserFile /etc/.htpasswd-status
    Require valid-user
</Location>
```

would restrict the page from being seen by anyone who didn't know an appropriate username and password (as defined in the /etc/.htpasswd-status file).

## ExtendedStatus

To get the most information out of the server-status content handler, you need to enable extra statistic recording capabilities with the ExtendedStatus directive. This directive takes a value of either On or Off; if you select the former, much more detail will be available in the report. The cost of this extended status report is performance; the server is spending more time collecting the information than it would otherwise, so Off is usually a better selection unless you're actively examining your server's capacity and performance.

# server-info

Like the `server-status` handler described in the previous section, the `server-info` handler (supplied in module `mod_info`) generates a page in real time that reports on the Apache server's configuration. Rather than describe the actual operation of the server, though, it displays information about how the server is set up: what modules are loaded, what directives they support, and (under certain circumstances) the actual settings of the directives.

Like the `server-status` handler, though, a lot of the information displayed by this handler (Figure 14.4 shows a sample with sensitive bits blocked out) is probably something you want to keep private, so it's recommended that you protect it similarly, such as with a section like the following:

```
<Location /server-info>
    SetHandler server-info
    AuthType Basic
    AuthUserFile /etc/.htpasswd-info
    Require valid-user
</Location>
```

**FIGURE 14.4**

*Output excerpt from the* server-info *content handler.*

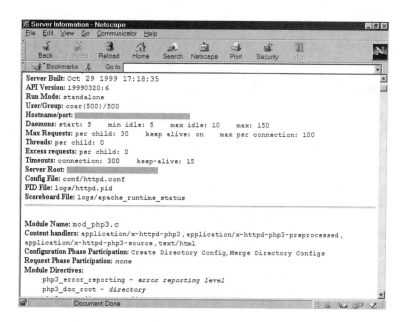

For more information about this handler, see the section in Chapter 20 about the mod_info module, or the online documentation at http://www.apache.org/docs/mod/mod_info.html.

## imap-file

This handler is defined by the mod_imap module and provides server-side active mapping capabilities. An *active map* is an image that's sensitive to being clicked; what happens following a click depends on where on the image the click occurred.

HTML made provision for active mapping even in the very early versions, with the ISMAP attribute to the <IMG> tag. If an image tag includes the ISMAP attribute *and* is the body of an anchor (<A>) tag, a click on the image causes the coordinates of the click point to be sent to the server.

If everything is set up correctly, something on the server side is prepared to translate the coordinates of the click into some sort of action. This is the purpose of the mod_imap module; it performs this translation according to its instructions. (See the section on mod_imap in Chapter 20 for more detailed information.)

Although server-side active map processing is uncommon these days, this is still considered one of the standard modules, and so this handler will generally be available to you should you care to use it.

### Why This Used to Be Cool

Active maps gave Webmasters a way to make a picture really worth a thousand words. By creating, say, a schematic layout of a university campus, the Web visitor could simply click a particular building or parking lot to be taken to a page with more detail. A museum could do something similar, allowing a click on a particular wing to bring up a page of highlighted exhibits currently housed there. The concept of active maps brought the "you are here" mall directory concept onto the user's desktop and made it applicable to situations limited only by the map creator's imagination.

### Why We Don't Use It Anymore

Server-side image mapping has become passé because the HTML tag language has been enhanced to include the mapping instructions, and the most popular clients understand those instructions directly. This means that the client can do the clickpoint-to-URL translation itself, without the back-and-forth communication with the server. This is called *client-side image mapping*, and it's clearly more network friendly and improves response time for Web users.

However, a few old browsers out there still don't know about client-side mapping, so there's a limited place yet for this server-side capability.

# Summary

Apache's use of handlers gives you control over the most basic part of Web-served resources—the content. Handlers that are part of the server itself, such as `mod_include` or `mod_status`, have the most flexibility to manipulate the content. Apache's modular nature allows new modules to be added to an existing server core, so if you're looking for a particular functionality that isn't supplied in the base server package, there's a good chance someone has already written a module to do it (see the Apache module registry at `http://modules.apache.org/`). And if no one has yet, and you're not interested in writing a module yourself (which *can* be a daunting task), most module capabilities are available to CGI script handlers identified with the `Script` and `Action` directives.

14

HANDLERS

# Setting Up Security and Auditing

# PART

# IV

## IN THIS PART

# Security

The World Wide Web is the latest electronic frontier. It has been characteristic of other frontiers that opportunities abound for steady, hard-working, solid citizens—and for those who would prey on them. You don't need to look any further than the closest newspaper to see that this is as true of the Web as it was of the Western territories of the United States in the nineteenth century. Almost daily, stories describe how corporate Web sites have been subverted in some way.

"Security" includes the techniques and actions planned or taken to keep from being victimized in the new frontier. Unfortunately, security is one of those business expenses that show no positive value when successfully applied—just the lack of a negative value. As a consequence, budgeting for the implementation of proper security measures may be less generous than it ought to be. A computer security specialist once developed a novel way of dealing with this. He clipped a particularly obnoxious headline and splash coverage of a high-profile break-in from the newspaper and then waved it in front of his boss, with the question, "How much is it worth to the company to keep our name *out* of headlines like this?"

Regardless of what methods you employ to protect your Web system, you need to beware of at least two threats: unauthorized access to your information through the Web and unauthorized access to your Web system itself.

# Protecting the Files on Your Web Server

In fact, almost all Web documents are based on files on a disk on the Web server itself. Therefore, modifying or damaging the underlying files will modify or damage the pages as seen through the Web. Also, the various operational and security controls of the Web server software itself are represented in terms of disk files, so protecting the files on your server is a very basic precaution at the root of all your security measures.

## Read/Write Versus Read-Only Files

Most files that control your Web server's operation are in the directory tree under `ServerRoot`. There are exceptions, such as `.htaccess` files and possibly authorization databases, but those affect only secondary aspects of the server's behavior.

When the server is running, it's doing so with a set of access rights associated with some user ID on your system, such as `root`, `nobody`, or possibly `httpd` on Unix systems, and usually `LocalSystem` on Windows NT. When I refer to *the server* in the following paragraphs, it means "the identity under which the server runs."

> **Note**
>
> This user ID applies only to multiuser systems such as Windows NT, OpenVMS, or some variant of Unix (such as AIX, FreeBSD, or Linux). Single-user systems such as Windows 95 or MacOS have no concept of user identity; the single user owns and has access to everything on the system. This means that if the Web server is compromised, there are essentially no restrictions on what an intruder can do.

The server generally doesn't need—and shouldn't have—the ability to modify any of its own control files. The obvious exceptions are the error log and access log files, which the server needs in order to record information as events occur. Having files such as the main config file, `http.conf`, writable by the server is a potentially disastrous situation, since it opens the possibility that a misconfiguration could allow an intruder out on the Web to subvert the server and use it to modify its own configuration.

With the exception of the log files (which may not even be under the `ServerRoot` tree, if you've used the `ErrorLog` and `CustomLog` directives to put them somewhere else), none of the files under `ServerRoot` should be modifiable by the server itself—only that person (or persons) responsible for managing the server should be able to alter them.

Likewise, most if not all files in the tree of files to be servers—the `DocumentRoot`— should be read-only as far as the server is concerned. This is less of a hard-and-fast rule, however, since site-specific environments (such as the use of WebDAV to allow remote document management) might dictate that modifiability is a required attribute of some documents.

The basic rule of thumb is this: Do you want a stranger on the Net to be able to alter this file, under *any* circumstances? If the answer is no, the file's permissions and ownership should not permit the server to modify it.

# Symbolic Links

The concept of *symbolic links* seems to occur only on Unix or Unix-like systems. The closest thing on Windows, for instance, is a *shortcut file*, and it really isn't the same at all. If you're not familiar with the term, symbolic links (also called *symlinks*) allow you to make a file look as though it lives in multiple locations, possibly with multiple names. It *really* lives only in one location, and all the other links are just references to that one. So if you modify the real file, all the links look like they've changed, too—which makes sense, since they're all really the same file.

If you try to edit or display a document that's actually a link, you'll be modifying or viewing the contents of the real file to which the link refers. Any user can create a link in her own directory that points to any file elsewhere on the system, even if she can't touch or see the actual file herself.

Symbolic links can be dangerous because they might inadvertently provide access to files through unexpected paths. It's a good idea to periodically check all places where your Web documents live to make sure that any existing links are really supposed to be there. A typical Unix command to do this is

```
find documentroot -type l -print
```

This command will display a list of all files under the *documentroot* directory that are actually symbolic links to other files or directories. Windows shortcut files don't present the same dangers because Apache doesn't recognize their special nature; it treats them as normal files rather than try to locate the resources to which they point.

When it comes to checking access for documents to be served through the Web, Apache provides some directives for controlling whether links should actually be followed; these are `Options FollowSymLinks` and `Options FollowSymLinksIfOwnerMatch`.

The `FollowSymLinks` option tells Apache to actually follow links to the real file or directory to which they point, so the full utility of symbolic linking is enabled. But since there's no restriction on who can create a symbolic link, what's to prevent a malicious user on your Web server system from exposing documents you don't want seen?

This is where the `FollowSymLinksIfOwnerMatch` option comes in. It instructs Apache to follow a link *if and only if* the user ID that owns the link is the same as the one that owns the actual file.

## The `Indexes` Option

When a request is made for a URL that translates into a directory rather than a specific file, Apache can respond in several ways:

- It can look for a special file in the directory and process and return it.
- It can display a list of files in the directory.
- It can return an error page ("access denied").

These possibilities work together. The server will check the first criterion by seeing whether any files in the directory are also listed in a `DirectoryIndex` directive. If so, the first one listed in the directive that also exists in the directory is processed and returned. (This work is done by the `mod_dir` module, which is part of the base Apache package.)

If no `DirectoryIndex`–specified files are found in the directory, Apache next checks the status of the `Indexes` option. If it isn't enabled for the directory in question, the server will return a 403 status code, which means "access denied."

If the `Indexes` option *is* enabled for the directory, the server will generate a list of files and display it in an effort to be helpful. Depending on the value of the `FancyIndexing` setting in the `IndexOptions` directive, this list will look either like that in Figure 15.1 (with `FancyIndexing` turned off) or like that in Figure 15.2 (with `FancyIndexing` enabled). As you can see, the "fancy" part of the index listing reveals quite a lot of information about the files—possibly quite more than you want.

**FIGURE 15.1**

*Normal directory listing.*

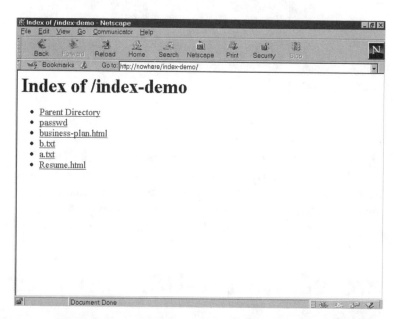

**Note**

The generation of directory listings (indexes) is handled by the `mod_autoindex` module, which is also part of the base Apache package. See Chapter 20, "Using Standard Apache Modules," for more information on this module and the `mod_dir` module mentioned earlier.

**FIGURE 15.2**

*"Fancy Indexed"*
*directory listing.*

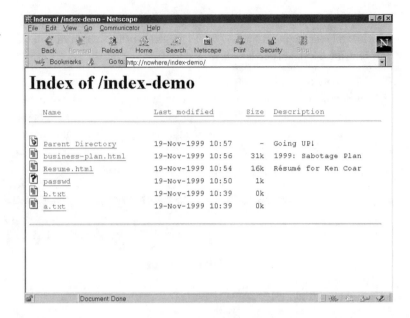

The moral of this lesson is that you should carefully check all the directories accessible through your Web server and make sure that you aren't inadvertently revealing sensitive information (such as the names of files that are there but aren't officially linked to). Add lines such as Options -Indexes in the .htaccess files or <Directory> containers where needed. (Remember, the leading - means "turn this specific option off without affecting any others.")

# Protecting the URLs on Your Web Site

Assuming that the files on your server are adequately protected, what about the actual Web documents that are visible through browsers? Can outsiders see the company's balance sheet? Can anyone outside the Personnel and Payroll departments access employee compensation records?

This issue is different from protecting the files on your system. In some cases, even a file's name can be considered sensitive; if you have it protected so that it can't be accessed, simply that it exists might be too revealing. For example, even knowing the name of the business-plan.html file in the previous section could give an intruder a definite target.

Protecting the URLs involves not even allowing that much information to be divulged, or at least restricting it to only trusted people.

# Mandatory and Discretionary Access

The two basic types of protection mechanism are *mandatory* and *discretionary* access control (abbreviated *MAC* and *DAC*, respectively). Mandatory control mechanisms, also sometimes called *nondiscretionary* controls, limit access based on some attribute over which the attempting accessor has no control. Discretionary controls depend on information supplied by the applicant.

Security theory defines three types of attribute used in access control:

- What you have
- What you know
- What/who you are

These are easily illustrated: You can start an automobile if you *have* the ignition key, log on to your account if you *know* the password, and open an ultra–high-tech lock if your body capacitance, retinal pattern, fingerprint, or DNA *is* what it expects.

The first two kinds of attributes are essentially variations on a theme, with tangibility and quantity usually being the aspects that distinguish them. For instance, when you lend your key to someone, you can no longer unlock things with it—but you could have made a copy. When you share your password with someone else, you still have it; giving it to someone else hasn't deprived you of it.

These types of attributes are often used in combination. You might need a key to open your office door, for instance, as well as your password to use your computer. Or perhaps logging on requires that you use a challenge/response cryptokey, which requires both that you have the device and that you know the PIN to use it.

Discretionary access controls typically use the "what-you-know" type of attribute. For instance, to log on to your system, you need to *know* the right username and password. What you type in response to the prompts is at your discretion, which is where the name comes from; you *could* type in someone else's information or complete garbage.

Mandatory controls tend to use the attributes at the other end of the spectrum. For instance, a common mandatory access control on the Web is to limit access according to the IP address of the requestor. The address isn't something that can be chosen at random; it's assigned to the user's system by a network administrator or perhaps a dial-in access system. After the address is assigned, the user can't change it in midstream and, due to the way the network routing works, neither can he pick arbitrary or random

**15**

SECURITY

addresses and expect them to work. Once on the network, the address is a "what-you-are" type of attribute for the user's system.

## Address-Based Protection

Apache 1.3.9 provides a means of limiting access based on the client's IP address. Defined by the mod_access module, this method allows Webmasters to grant or deny access to Web resources on their systems according to the address the client is using or the network from which it is coming.

Since the address of the client is known as soon as it makes a connection to the server, the decision of whether to let it proceed can be made very quickly.

### Using `allow` and `deny` Directives

The mod_access module permits Webmasters to specify what hosts or IP networks the server will permit requests to come from. The basic rules work by exclusion, such as "allow everyone except *this* network" or "deny everyone except people on *this* system."

In fact, the two primary directives for managing this level of access control are allow and deny. The allow directive specifies criteria for permitting access, and deny quite reasonably indicates rules for disallowing it. There are two forms for these directives:

- `allow|deny from address-expression`
- `allow|deny from env=environment-variable`

The `address-expression` can be one of the following:

- The special keyword `all`, meaning that all possible hosts are affected
- A full or partial host or domain name, such as `hoohoo.ncsa.uiuc.edu` or `.ncsa.uiuc.edu`
- A full IP address, such as `127.0.0.1`
- A partial IP address, such as `10.0.0`
- A network/netmask pair, such as `10.0.0.0/255.255.0.0`
- A CIDR address specification, such as `127.0.0.0/24` (this is the same as `127.0.0.0/255.255.255.0`)

For performance reasons, it's recommended that you use actual addresses rather than domain or host names. When a connection is made to the server, Apache *knows* the IP address of the client—but to verify the hostname, it has to translate the address into a name for comparison purposes.

**Note**

When it comes to security, the Apache software is very paranoid. The resolution of IP addresses to host names is usually controlled by the HostNameLookups directive (discussed in Chapter 5, "Server Configuration Files"). When you use host or domain names in your allow/deny statements, Apache actually forces what's called a *double-reverse lookup*. This means that the server contacts a DNS server to translate the IP address into a hostname—and then translates the name it gets back into one or more IP addresses. If the original IP address isn't in the list from the double-reverse lookup, Apache doesn't trust the host name to be valid.

You can limit access to your pages with combinations of these directives, as with

```
deny from all
allow from 127.0.0.1
```

or

```
allow from all
deny from spamhost.org
```

However, the manner in which these directives is interpreted is controlled by yet another directive, Order (covered in the next section).

The second form of the directives, allow|deny from env=*environment-variable*, allows you to take advantage of some of the other modules included with Apache. Rather than use a network expression as the controlling aspect of the request, such as an address or hostname, the env= format lets you say "allow (or deny) access if this environment variable is set."

Because the access-checking process occurs quite early in request processing, only modules that affect environment variables in earlier phases can affect mod_access's behavior. The most common and flexible module for this purpose is mod_setenvif, which sets environment variables according to the rules you give it. For example

```
BrowserMatch "EmailCollector" SPAMBOT=1
Order allow,deny
allow from all
deny from env=SPAMBOT
```

would result in access being denied from *any* host if the name of the client or browser being used contained the word EmailCollector.

See the documentation for the `mod_setenvif` module, online at `http://www.apache.org/docs/mod/mod_setenvif.html`, for more information about its powerful capabilities.

## Order

Since the `allow` and `deny` directives complement each other and are used together, there needs to be a way to indicate which should be processed first. This is supplied by the `Order` directive, which should precede any `allow` or `deny` directive in a particular scope and can be in one of the following formats:

- `Order allow,deny`
- `Order deny,allow`
- `Order mutual-failure`

> **Note**
>
> Don't use spaces between the keywords on the `Order` directive. `Order allow,deny` is valid, but `Order allow, deny` will cause a syntax error.

The meanings of the first two formats are fairly self-explanatory. `Order allow,deny` instructs Apache to check *all* the `allow` statements first before looking at the `deny` directives, and the opposite for `Order deny,allow`.

The `mutual-failure` keyword needs a little more explanation, though. When it's used, for a request to be allowed through, the host making the request *must* match at least one `allow` condition and not match *any* `deny` ones. This means that `mutual-failure` doesn't work at all in exclusionary configurations using `deny from all`.

What's the default access granted to a client that doesn't match the conditions? For the `allow,deny` order, by default every client starts out being denied; it won't be allowed through unless it meets at least one of the `allow` conditions. For a scope covered by `Order deny,allow`, the initial condition is to allow all access until it's disabled by a `deny` directive match.

The easy way to figure out the initial state is to remember that it matches the final keyword in the order. For `Order allow,deny` it's denied; for `Order deny,allow` it's allowed.

There is no initial state for `mutual-failure` mode. To have access, a client must be allowed and must not be denied.

> **Note**
>
> All `allow` and `deny` directives for the requested document's scope are processed when Apache does its access checking. There is no "short-circuiting" that will stop the process after only a few checks are made.

## User-Supplied Credentials

When a client (typically a browser) tries to access a document protected by discretionary controls, the Apache server will respond with an error status (401, `Authorization Required`). Figure 15.3 shows a typical challenge pop-up window displayed by a browser to get user credentials.

**FIGURE 15.3**

*Authentication challenge for user credentials.*

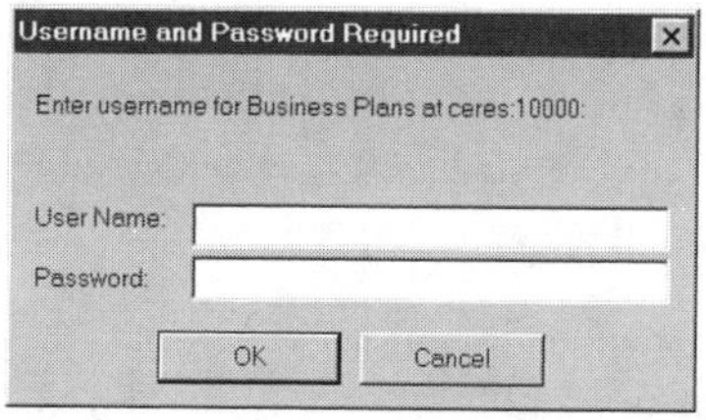

> **Note**
>
> If the client has accessed the protected area previously and still remembers the credentials it used last time, it will send them along as part of the request and therefore won't have to go through the challenge process again. Of course, this is unless the server rejects the credentials, such as if a password has been changed. In that case, the server will reject the credentials, and the client will tell the user so and ask for some new ones.

This is a great example of why this type of access is called *discretionary*. The user is free to enter any username and password she likes; the choice is entirely at her discretion.

## Combining Mandatory and Discretionary Access Control with `Satisfy`

How does Apache figure out what to do if a document is covered by both mandatory (such as `allow` or `deny`) and discretionary (for example, `AuthType` and `Require`) control directives? The answer is controlled by the `Satisfy` directive.

`Satisfy` takes a single keyword argument, which can be either `Any` or `All` (the default is `All`). If the keyword is `All`, for a client to be allowed to access a document, it must pass both the mandatory control check (such as the `allow` or `deny` condition) *and* the discretionary ones (supply a valid username and password).

If the keyword is `Any`, discretionary checks are waived if the mandatory ones were passed. If the `allow` and `deny` directives permitted access to the document, Apache won't bother asking for credentials, even if discretionary controls are in place for the resource.

This applies only to documents that are within the scope of both mandatory and discretionary controls. If a document is in only one or the other, obviously the appropriate checks *must* be passed successfully.

## Authentication, Authorization, and Access

Apache uses three separate module callbacks for the different types and stages of checking for access to a document. The *access* phase refers specifically to the early checking of access based on nondiscretionary attributes such as the network address. The other phases, authentication and authorization, deal with discretionary credentials and are sometimes confused with each other.

*Authentication* refers to requiring proof of identity or credential validity. As an example, verifying that a valid username and matching password have been supplied is part of the authentication process; a client that has proven itself is said to have been *authenticated*.

*Authorization*, on the other hand, refers to the process of verifying that validated credentials grant access to the requested resource. Bob might have provided his correct username and password and been authenticated, but unless he's also on the list of people whom Clarissa is allowing to see her files, his successful authentication won't matter—he needs to be authorized as well.

Apache tends to lump control of authentication and authorization together into a single set of directives.

## Authentication Control

The Apache authentication and authorization control model depends on two different basic pieces of information: Where does the server find the list of authorized users, and which ones are allowed access?

The former is defined by directives such as `AuthUserFile` and the latter by the `Require` directive. These are described in the following sections.

## Scope and Realms

As with many other aspects of Apache, access control is managed according to *scope*. That is, controls can be set on each directory or URL location, and they apply not only to that location but also to any and all subordinate locations (unless explicitly overridden). So if you allow user `Leslie` to have access to the `/home/worker` directory, access is also granted to `/home/worker/bee`, `/home/worker/hourly`, and `/home/worker/bee/honey/clover`. All of those are subordinate to the `/home/worker` directory to which you've applied the controls.

Named authorization scopes are called *realms*. This name, called the *realm name*, together with the URL in question, is used by the server and the client to figure out which credentials are valid. You can see the realm name in the challenge pop-up window shown earlier in Figure 15.3. The declaration for this realm was

```
AuthName "Business Plans"
```

So the pop-up box is said to be asking for credentials for the `Business Plans` realm. Until overridden by a different `AuthName` statement, any subdirectories or sublocations under the one requested are also considered to be in the `Business Plans` realm.

It's possible for different credentials to be valid in different parts of the same realm, as illustrated by the following:

```
<Directory /home/worker>
    AuthName "Drones"
    AuthType Basic
    AuthUserFile /etc/httpd/passwords
    Require valid-user
</Directory>
<Directory /home/worker/bee>
    Require user Sales
</Directory>
```

Both `/home/worker` and `/home/worker/bee` are in the `Drones` realm. However, only username `Sales` is allowed to access the `bee` subdirectory, although any valid user can access the parent directory.

### Limit

The `<Limit>` container directive restricts the scope of the directives within it to only requests made using a particular method or methods. For instance, consider the following:

```
<Directory /foo>
    Options ExecCGI Includes
    <Limit POST>
```

```
        AuthName "Restricted POST"
        AuthType Basic
        AuthUserFile /etc/passwords/pwfile
        Require valid-user
    </Limit>
</Directory>
```

This does *not* create a blanket restriction on access to files in the /foo directory. If documents in the directory are requested by using the GET, HEAD, or PUT method—in fact, any method *except* POST—there's no restriction at all. Only if the request is made using the POST method are authentication and authorization required. If the intent was to create a blanket restriction, the correct solution would be to omit the <Limit> directive altogether, as in

```
<Directory /foo>
    Options ExecCGI Includes
    AuthName "Restricted POST"
    AuthType Basic
    AuthUserFile /etc/passwords/pwfile
    Require valid-user
</Directory>
```

Now the authentication and authorization directives apply to *all* requests, regardless of the method.

> **Caution**
>
> The <Limit> container directive is incredibly misunderstood and the cause of many problems and basic support questions. This is probably because it appeared in a large number of basic configuration examples that have been copied and propagated through all sorts of documentation. To avoid problems, don't use <Limit> unless you really want to restrict access based on how documents are requested.

## AuthName

The AuthName directive is used to declare a realm, despite the possibly confusing directive name. A better name for this directive would probably have been AuthRealm or even just Realm. AuthName is a legacy from older configuration files and is firmly entrenched in the Apache 1.3 series. The directive name may change with the next major release, however.

This directive has gone through some changes in recent (1.3.*) versions of the Apache software. Originally, it was a RAW_ARGS type of directive, which means that everything after the word AuthName was taken to be the argument. This caused a statement such as

```
AuthName Business Plans
```

to declare the realm name to be Business Plans. Unfortunately, this caused problems when people included actual quotation marks in the realm name, so the directive was changed to a more conventional and obvious TAKE1 style. Now (Apache 1.3.9) the preceding statement will result in a configuration error, and the effect must be accomplished this way instead:

```
AuthName "Business Plans"
```

This change of behavior has caused some problems for sites that are upgrading from older versions and use multiple words in their realm names. Quoting the realm names should fix the problem.

## AuthType

The AuthType directive instructs Apache concerning the manner in which authentication is to be performed. The most widespread type of authentication is Basic, so most occurrences of the directive will look like this:

```
AuthType Basic
```

Another well-known and increasingly popular—as well as more secure—type of authentication is called Digest authentication. Other types may become available as Web technology continues to mature.

Although most authentication currently uses the Basic method, there's no default for this directive. You must specify an AuthType directive for every realm.

## Basic Authentication

Basic authentication causes the username and password to be sent across the network encoded in an easy-to-decipher manner. As a consequence, if someone can intercept the credentials (which are sent every time the client accesses a URL in a realm for which it *has* credentials), he can impersonate the original user.

Unfortunately, better authentication mechanisms (such as Digest authentication, described in the next section) aren't very widely accepted or deployed, so in many cases Basic is the only method there is.

**15**

SECURITY

Basic authentication for a realm is chosen by including a directive such as the following in your configuration files:

```
AuthType Basic
```

The keyword is not case sensitive.

## Digest Authentication

It's beyond the scope of this book to describe the Digest authentication mechanism in detail, but the key points are as follows:

- Digest authentication is more secure than Basic and much less susceptible to *replay attacks*.
- More and more clients and browsers are coming to market with the ability to use the Digest authentication method.

You enable Digest authentication for a realm with the following statement:

```
AuthType Digest
```

You should do this only for realms that you know will be accessed by Digest-aware clients. Otherwise, the entire authentication process will fail, and your users will get frustrated at the endless "wrong password" errors when they know they're typing the password correctly. (And in fact they are—it's the failing of the software, not their fingers, that's at the root of the error.)

## Password Encryption

Passwords in transmission—that is, being sent across the network—have a different set of vulnerabilities than those stored in the master authentication databases. Although the Basic authentication system doesn't encrypt passwords as part of the network protocol, that has no impact on how the Apache server deals with the password once it's received.

In fact, Apache stores passwords in most authentication databases in an encrypted form. The encryption algorithms used are called *one-way* or *trapdoor* algorithms, because as soon as the password is run through them, there's no way to get back to the original (called the *plaintext*) form.

If the password can't be recovered, how does Apache check to see if a transmitted password matches what's in the database? The answer is that Apache doesn't actually compare the passwords at all. Instead, it forces the transmitted password through the same algorithm the stored one went through, and then it compares the encrypted result with the encrypted value in the database. If the end results are the same, the assumption is that the starting values were the same, too—in other words, that the right password was transmitted.

> **Note**
>
> Since the encrypted form of a password (called the *cryptotext*) is often shorter than the plaintext password itself, it's possible that multiple plaintext values could be encrypted to create the same cryptotext result. In actuality, though, the encryption algorithms are mathematically designed so that this chance is vanishingly small. Any two plaintext values that result in the same cryptotext won't resemble each other at all; one will be hundreds of bytes long, contain untypable characters, or otherwise be unusable.

This storage of cryptotext means that even if the authentication database is compromised and an intruder gets to see it, he won't automatically have access to all the usernames and passwords in it. Of course, there's nothing preventing him from running all the words in a dictionary through the same encryption algorithm the database uses, so good password-choosing practices are a necessity.

## Unencrypted (Plaintext) Passwords

Encryption is a touchy subject with many governments, and software that can encrypt information isn't automatically available on all operating systems and platforms. Usually, the restriction is on reversible methods, since they allow the information to be recovered. Trapdoor encryption algorithms, which can't be used this way, are usually permitted by even the most protective governments—but some software distributors don't want to take any chances because of potential penalties. As a case in point, the Windows NT 4 system doesn't include the canonical `crypt()` routine. This means that password databases built on other systems using that routine can't be used on Windows—because Apache couldn't run the transmitted password through the same algorithm.

Until the Apache software was enhanced to include its own government-safe encryption algorithm (a modified MD5, if you're interested), the only way it could deal with passwords on Windows was to not encrypt them at all—just store the unencrypted plaintext. This capability was kept even after Apache's encryption algorithm was added, just in case there's some future operating system or platform out there that needs it.

## Standard `crypt()`

Almost all Unix and Unix-like systems include a library routine called `crypt()`. It performs one-way trapdoor encryption of the data given to it and is usually implemented using a modified DES (Data Encryption Standard) algorithm.

**15**

> **Note**
>
> Some operating systems, such as FreeBSD, have the `crypt()` routine but have changed the algorithm. This means that passwords encrypted on those systems can't be used on systems with other implementations of `crypt()`, and that passwords encrypted elsewhere can't be used on the systems with the modified version. Oh, well—there's really no guarantee that encrypted passwords are *supposed* to be interoperable, anyway.

In fact, almost all Unix operating systems use their `crypt()` routine to encrypt user passwords in their own system authentication databases.

## MD5 Password Encryption

Another encryption algorithm is *MD5 hash*, which is described and defined by an Internet RFC document. The FreeBSD operating system uses a modified version for its `crypt()` routine. In the 1.3.*x* release series, Apache added a further modified version of the FreeBSD algorithm to its portfolio of encryption mechanisms it could use and understand.

In fact, since Apache now incorporates its own trapdoor encryption algorithm, it's recommended that it be used instead of the system-defined `crypt()` algorithm. The reason is that the Apache software will be available anywhere Apache is and will encrypt a password to the same value regardless of platform. This means that cryptotext passwords are interoperable—you can build an authentication database on Linux, and the encrypted passwords will work correctly if you use them on Windows, HP/UX, AIX, or even the Macintosh Unix-like environment.

See the htpasswd utility described later for more information about how to use the modified MD5 encryption algorithm.

## The SHA Encryption Method

Netscape servers store passwords encrypted using an algorithm called SHA. In Apache 1.3.9, the server's authentication routines and the htpasswd utility were enhanced to be able to deal with SHA-encrypted passwords, which makes migration much simpler.

# Authentication Databases

If you plan to use discretionary controls to limit access to your documents, you need to store the authentication information somewhere so that Apache—not to mention you—can find it.

The base Apache package supports several different ways of storing authentication information, and there are lots of add-on modules that expand on the built-in methods, so you have lots of flexibility in this area. However, there are a few concerns and considerations that apply to how and where you store the authentication databases.

## Location of Database Files

The basic rule for locating your access control database files is to make sure they're accessible only on a need-to-know basis. In other words, you probably need access so that you can make modifications, and the server needs access (though only read-only) so that it can perform its checks, but no one else does.

Part of ensuring this sort of protection involves locating the files so that they're in appropriately protected directories. Another part is making sure that they can't be accidentally exposed.

A simple rule that's easy to follow is this: Never put your access control files anywhere that a Web browser might be able to reach them. That typically means not putting them under the server's DocumentRoot or in any user's personal Web directory.

## Support Tools for Password Maintenance

Three standalone applications designed to help you manage authentication files are supplied as part of the Apache base package. Two of them deal with normal text files containing one username/password pair per line, and the third allows you to store the same information in a Unix-style DBM or NDBM database file for better performance when the information is actually being looked up by the server.

The location of the tools in your Apache installation depends on your environment, but the tools are typically found in the same directory as the main Apache httpd (Unix) or apache.exe (Windows) server program.

### *htpasswd*

The htpasswd application (called htpasswd.exe on the Windows platform) allows you to maintain usernames and passwords in a text file. You can also modify such files with normal text editors, as long as you don't alter the value of the encrypted passwords. The htpasswd program manages credentials only for use with Basic authentication; for Digest authentication credentials, use htdigest (described in the next section).

The htpasswd tool takes several options, which are passed to it on the command line in the usual manner of Unix applications. The options may be clustered (as in -cmb) or listed separately (as with -c -m -b), but options must always begin with a dash and must always precede the other command arguments. Once htpasswd comes to a word on the command line that doesn't begin with a dash, it stops checking for options. For instance, these two statements are syntactically correct and equivalent:

```
htpasswd -c -m -b .htpasswd myusername mypassword
htpasswd -cmb .htpasswd myusername mypassword
```

But this one isn't:

```
htpasswd -cm .htpasswd myusername -b mypassword
```

Here are the options that htpasswd understands:

- -b means to use the password from the command line; don't prompt for it. This is used on platforms such as Windows where prompting may not be appropriate and in scripts that set up access information automatically without having a human around to answer the prompt.
- -c means to create the authentication database file.
- -m means to encrypt the password using Apache's modified MD5 algorithm.
- -d means to create the password cryptotext using the `crypt()` routine (this works only on those platforms where it's available).
- -p means to not encrypt the password at all, but use the original plaintext. This may or may not work on various platforms but is included for completeness.
- -s means to encrypt the password by using the SHA algorithm used by Netscape servers.

If none of the -m, -d, -p, or -s options are specified, htpasswd will encrypt the password by using its default algorithm for the current platform. If -b isn't specified, the program will prompt for the password (which won't echo onscreen) and then prompt for it again to make sure that you spelled it correctly.

In addition to one or more options, the htpasswd command line also needs to include the name of the text file in which the authentication information is being stored, the username for which the password is being created or modified, and possibly the password itself (if the -b option was specified).

If you specify a username that already exists in the file, htpasswd will change the password for that username. If the username doesn't exist, it will be added.

Because looking up a username in a text file involves looking at each line in turn until either the end of the file is reached or a username is found that matches the one in the credentials, this type of authentication database is generally useful only for a small number of username/password pairs.

> **Note**
>
> The htpasswd program tries very hard not to destroy any information. For instance, if you are changing the password of a username that already exists in the file, nothing will be changed if you fail the password verification test and can't spell the new password right twice in a row. Likewise, if the disk is full, htpasswd won't wipe out the old file when it creates the new one. However, odd circumstances such as disk errors may prevent fully correct operation, so it's a good idea to make a copy of the authentication file for safekeeping, just in case, before making any changes.

## htdigest

As the htpasswd tool described earlier can be used to maintain username/password credentials for use with Basic authentication, the htdigest application is used to do the same for credentials used with the Digest authentication scheme.

The realm is a major difference between Basic and Digest authentication. Basic authentication credentials can be used in any realm, but Digest credentials actually include the realm in the encrypted value. This means that if you try to use the credential file in another realm, you will have to regenerate them, because they'll be referencing the wrong realm.

This tool has been undergoing changes in the Apache 1.3 cycle and will likely be changed even further, so it's recommended that you refer to the online documentation for your Apache installation to get the correct instructions for the version you have. Issue the following command in the `src/support` directory on your Unix system:

```
man ./htdigest.1
```

## dbmmanage

The dbmmanage tool is actually a Perl script, which means that you need to have the Perl interpreter installed on your system to use it. The version of dbmmanage that ships with Apache 1.3.9 can deal with most Unix database formats that Perl can handle, but it can maintain only username/password credentials—it can't create or update user/group associations.

This utility has been changed quite a bit through recent Apache versions, and additional changes are anticipated. As a result, there's an excellent chance that any detailed instructions included here would be out of date very quickly. See the dbmmanage man page for the details of its use on your Apache installation. You can see this on Unix by moving into the `src/support` directory and issuing the following command:

```
man ./dbmmanage.1
```

## Plain Text (`AuthUserFile` and `AuthGroupFile`)

Text authentication files, like those maintained by the htpasswd tool, are made available to Apache's authentication processing through the use of the `AuthUserFile` and `AuthGroupFile` directives. These directives take a single argument—the name of and path to the appropriate text file.

## Database Credential Storage

The dbmmanage and other tools (not supplied as part of the base Apache package) allow you to maintain authentication information in database files rather than plain text files.

On the positive side, database storage of credentials typically improves performance when you have lots of different credentials, since locating a particular username/password pair involves checking an index instead of sequentially searching through the entire file. On the negative side, however, database storage can take up significantly more disk space (not usually a problem unless you have tens of thousands of credentials). The database files themselves also are typically not portable to other platforms and may require tools from vendors other than Apache.

There's also the issue of corruption. If an authentication database becomes damaged somehow, it's quite likely that *all* the credentials stored in it will be unusable, which will lock out all users. With plain text authentication files, such damage can often be corrected with a simple text editor.

Whether you use a database system, from one as simple as DBM or NDBM to as complex and full featured as DB2, is entirely up to you, of course.

## Anonymous FTP–Style Authentication

If you're familiar with the use of FTP on the Internet, you've probably used a facility called *anonymous FTP*. It allows you to log in to an FTP server using a standard username (typically both anonymous and ftp work) with your email address as the password. You don't need to contact the FTP server administrator to set up an account, and he doesn't need to change the password just so you can access the FTP archive.

The base Apache package includes a module, mod_auth_anon, that allows you to do much the same for realms on your Web server. You can specify a set of "standard" usernames, and the module will allow anyone to access the realm with any password as long as he uses one of those usernames. You *can* impose some restrictions on the password—for instance, that it be a valid email address.

Since this sort of authentication provides almost no security at all, its usefulness is extremely limited. See the mod_auth_anon documentation (such as online at http://www.apache.org/docs/mod/mod_auth_anon.html) for more details about using the module and controlling the passwords it will accept.

# Authoritative Authentication

What happens if multiple types of authentication apply to a particular resource? Consider the following hypothetical fragment from an Apache configuration file:

```
<Directory /usr/local/httpd/business>
    AuthName "Private"
    AuthType Basic
    AuthDBMUserFile /usr/local/http/control/bizpw.db
    Require valid-user
</Directory>
<Directory /usr/local/httpd/business/accounting>
    AuthUserFile /usr/local/http/control/acctpw.txt
    Require valid-user
</Directory>
```

Due to the way scoping works, documents in the /usr/local/business/accounting directory are actually within the scope of two different authentication databases. How does Apache figure out which one to use?

The decision is made clear by the use of additional directives, one for each authentication module, that inform Apache if each module's decision is final. If the above fragment is modified as follows (the added line is marked in boldface),

```
<Directory /usr/local/httpd/business>
    AuthName "Private"
    AuthType Basic
    AuthDBMUserFile /usr/local/http/control/bizpw.db
    Require valid-user
</Directory>
<Directory /usr/local/httpd/business/accounting>
    AuthUserFile /usr/local/http/control/acctpw.txt
    AuthAuthoritative On
    Require valid-user
</Directory>
```

the decision made by the mod_auth module (which is what implements the AuthUserFile and AuthAuthoritative directives) is final. If the credentials of a would-be accessor aren't found in the /usr/local/httpd/control/acctpw.txt file, access is denied, even if they *are* found in the /usr/local/httpd/control/bizpw.db file named in the broader scope.

If this directive were set to AuthAuthoritative Off (the default condition), Apache would look in the DBM database if it couldn't find matching credentials in the text-based database.

Most if not all authentication modules have similar directives, such as
AuthDBMAuthoritative, AuthDBAuthoritative, and so on. Each indicates whether the
corresponding module's authentication decision is the ultimate authority in the appropriate scope.

Which authentication module is consulted first is a consequence of the module's priority—that is, the order in which it appears in the server's module list. This is controlled in
the runtime configuration files with the LoadModule and AddModule directives and in the
compile-time src/Configuration file with the AddModule instruction. Module priorities
are in inverse order of their appearance; modules listed last have the highest priority and
are consulted first.

# Authorization Control

Authentication is handled very simply in Apache: Either the credentials submitted by the
client are valid or they aren't. However, authentication and authorization are tied
together. If a resource isn't under any sort of access control (meaning that some authorization needs to be checked), Apache won't force or even check the credentials.

Since mandatory access control uses credentials inherent in the request itself and doesn't
depend on anything the user himself sends, it happens always and automatically in
scopes where the necessary controls are put in place. Discretionary controls, though,
need to be activated (basically, you need to tell the server to "check credentials and
authorization in this realm"). This is done with the Require directive, described in the
next section.

## Require

The Require directive is what enables discretionary access checking. A realm may have
a name (such as AuthName "Business Plan") and an authentication method (such as
AuthType Basic) and even an authentication database defined (as with AuthUserFile
/usr/pwfile.txt)—but if there's no Require directive, none of the others will have any
effect.

The keywords and arguments on a Require directive are entirely arbitrary as far as the
core Apache server is concerned. It just records the information, notes that discretionary
authentication is required for the current scope, and makes the arguments available to
modules when they request it. However, here are the meaningful values for the mod_auth
module included in the base Apache package:

- user *username username* ...   Access is granted if the username portion of the
  credentials submitted by the client matches any of the specified usernames and if
  the username/password pair is authenticated in the AuthUserFile file.

- `valid-user`   Access is granted if the submitted username and password match any of those in the `AuthUserFile` file.

- `group groupname groupname ...`   Access is granted if the username and password are successfully authenticated and the username is listed in the `AuthGroupFile` file as being in one of the specified groups.

The precondition common to all of these is that the username and password submitted by the client as part of the request *must* be valid and appear in the `AuthUserFile` list of credentials.

Since each authentication module interprets the `Require` settings in its own way, some may require that *all* conditions match, and others allow access if only one does. The `mod_auth` module falls into the latter category; the conditions of the first, and *only* the first, `Require` directive in the scope must be met successfully for access to be allowed.

# Controlling Real-Time Activity

The previous sections dealt with placing access controls on your documents and controlling who or what could access them. Other aspects of Apache operation, however, have ramifications relative to your system's security, such as what sort of scripts are allowed to be run and under what circumstances.

## Options and Overrides

Each scope has a list of options that are enabled for it and a list of the types of directives that can appear in `.htaccess` files within the scope. The first list is managed by the `Options` directive, which can take one or more of the following keywords:

- `All` enables all options except `MultiViews` (which must be explicitly turned on, as with `Options All MultiViews`). This is the default setting for a scope if no `Options` directive appears at a higher/broader one.

- `ExecCGI` enables the execution of CGI scripts within the scope.

- `FollowSymLinks`, if enabled, causes the server to follow any symbolic links it finds within the scope. Since a symlink is a file system concept, within a `<Location>` container this option is meaningless and is ignored.

- `Includes` enables server-side include processing by `mod_include` within the scope for files that are candidates for such (see the description of `mod_include` for more information).

- `IncludesNoEXEC` is similar to `Includes` except that it disables `mod_include`'s `#exec` server-side include directive and the use of the `#include` SSI directive to include the output of CGI scripts.

15

SECURITY

- `Indexes` controls whether `mod_autoindex` will be used (if present in the server configuration) to generate default directory listings.

- `MultiViews` enables content negotiation for the scope, permitting the server to infer the correct or best document name from a list of possible choices matching the request criteria.

- `SymLinksIfOwnerMatch` is similar to the `FollowSymLinks` option except that symbolic links are followed only if the owner of the link is the same as the owner of the document to which the link points.

Each of these, if enabled, can result in more or different information than you anticipate being displayed in response to a request. It also could result in the users on your own Web server unintentionally violating security by installing a poorly implemented script or an unintentional link.

The directives appearing in `.htaccess` files are executed only if their use is permitted by what's called the current *overrides* setting—so called because the enabled directives can be used to override a particular kind of activity.

Which activities may be overridden in a scope—in other words, what overrides are allowed—is controlled by the `AllowOverride` directive, which takes a list of one or more of the following keywords:

- `All` allows any directive that may appear in `.htaccess` files to be processed when encountered.

- `AuthConfig`, if included in the `AllowOverride` directive, indicates that directives affecting discretionary access controls (such as `AuthType` or `Require`) will be processed if found in `.htaccess` files in the scope.

- `FileInfo` controls whether directives that affect file processing (for example, `AddType` or `ErrorDocument`) will be processed if encountered in `.htaccess` files.

- `Indexes` (not to be confused with the `Indexes` keyword to the `Options` directive) controls whether the directives that affect indexing (if enabled) are processed. Such directives include `DirectoryIndex`, `AddDescription`, and `IndexOptions`.

- `Limit` controls whether directives dealing with mandatory access control (such as `allow`, `deny`, or `Order`) are processed if found in `.htaccess` files in the scope.

- `None`, as might be expected, completely disables the processing of `.htaccess` files. The server won't even bother looking for them in a scope with this `AllowOverride` keyword.

- `Options` simply informs the server that `Options` directives found in `.htaccess` files within the scope will be processed.

> **Note**
>
> Overrides apply *only* to .htaccess files; directives found in the server-wide configuration files aren't affected.

### Includes, IncludesNoEXEC, and execCGI

Although server-side includes can be very powerful and help your Web documents become more dynamic, their use can incur penalties. For one thing, enabling processing of includes can seriously affect server performance. No longer is Apache simply taking a file and sending it to the client; with SSI processing enabled, it's examining the file first and potentially constructing a modified version to send.

This very flexibility also can be a drawback if you allow their use by those on your Web server whom you don't trust completely. They can be used to execute arbitrary command lines or CGI scripts—and, since the processing will be done by the Web server rather than the user, this can potentially lead to Trojan horses on your system.

The safest approach is to make sure that these options aren't enabled in any scope over which you don't have sole control, with one of the following directives:

```
Options None

Options -Includes -IncludesNoEXEC -execCGI
```

The latter will selectively disable SSI processing without affecting any other options that may be enabled.

> **Caution**
>
> Directories identified as containing scripts by being named in a ScriptAlias directive are automatically marked as permitting script execution. Even more, all files in such a directory and subdirectories under it are automatically considered to be scripts and eligible to be executed if requested (and if file permissions allow). For this reason, be very cautious about what files you put into such directories.

# Summary

Even if you run a Web site that has no secrets, you still are probably going to be concerned about people breaking in and making changes. If you have documents that you don't want to be available to the millions of users on the Net, that's just an additional concern. As any experienced system administrator or Webmaster can tell you, security is something that should be considered up front, because if it isn't designed into the site, it's almost certain that a time will come when you will have to apply it, after the damage is already done. While this isn't necessarily as bad as "closing the barn door after the horse is stolen," it can lead to regrets and recriminations. Save yourself the headaches and heartache, and consider security as part of your Web site's design.

# Authentication

## IN THIS CHAPTER

Occasionally, you will have portions of your Web site that you want to keep most people out of. Authentication gives you a way to protect these parts of your site from prying eyes.

# What Is Authentication?

*Authentication* is the process of ensuring that you are who you say you are. This shows up to the user as a dialog box asking him to enter his username and password. The password serves to confirm the claim made by the username.

HTTP authentication is defined in RFC 2617, which is included on the CD-ROM that accompanies this book. RFC 2617 defines two types of authentication: Basic and Digest. However, most clients implement only Basic authentication.

## Basic Authentication

*Basic authentication* is, true to its name, the simplest form of authentication available. The server asks the client to authenticate itself, and the client passes a username and password to the server. If the server can verify that the username and password are valid, it serves the requested resource.

The server challenge is of the following form:

```
WWW-Authenticate: Basic realm="ProtectedArea"
```

where `ProtectedArea` is a string specified in the configuration of the protected area. `realm` is a portion of your site for which the same authentication rules apply. It doesn't necessarily all need to be in the same place; a collection of several different directories might be part of the same realm if they have the same authentication requirements. For example, perhaps your Sales department needs to get into the `/Sales` directory on your Web site and into the `/CustomerLeads` section. Those two directories might be put into the same realm so that users need to be authenticated only once but can access both areas.

The client browser will cache the username and password you enter and resend them whenever presented with the same `realm` string in a `WWW-Authenticate` header so that you don't have to retype this information each time you request a resource from an authentication portion of a Web site. The browser will also generally assume that resources that are in the same directory as an authenticated resource, or in subdirectories of that directory, are also protected in the same realm and will frequently preemptively send the `Authentication` header for those resources before the server requests it. This saves some time in the HTTP conversation. Most browsers will cache this information just for the duration of the current session.

> **Note**
>
> Remember that HTTP is stateless and doesn't remember who you are from one request to the next. This means that the server must verify your username and password again for each request. On high-traffic sites, this can really slow things down.

The username and password are sent back to the server in the form *username:password*, which is then wrapped in a base64-encoded string in an `Authorization` response header.

A response header from a client requesting access to an authenticated resource, using a username of `scrooge` and password of `marley`, would look like the following:

```
Authorization: Basic c2Nyb29nZTptYXJsZXk=
```

> **Caution**
>
> Basic authentication shouldn't be used to protect sensitive or confidential material. Base64 is an encoding technique, not an encryption method. You are passing your username and password across the network in the clear, and it would be a simple matter to intercept that information and use it to gain unauthorized access to the protected area.
>
> For example, anyone intercepting the `Authorization` header shown earlier (`Authorization: Basic c2Nyb29nZTptYXJsZXk=`) could decode it, returning the original username and password, by using this Perl one-liner:
>
> ```
> perl -MMIME::Base64 -e 'print decode_base64("c2Nyb29nZTptYXJsZXk=")'
> ```
>
> which returns:
>
> ```
> scrooge:marley
> ```
>
> This uses the Perl `MIME::Base64` module, which is freely available on the Internet (see http://www.cpan.org/).

Basic authentication, despite its inherent insecurity, is in wide use on many Web sites. This seems to be because Basic authentication is universally supported by all browsers, and other authentication schemes are less well supported.

# Digest Authentication

*Digest authentication* was proposed as an alternative to Basic authentication in an attempt to solve the security problems inherent to Basic authentication. If you want to read about the gory details of Digest authentication, read section 3 of RFC 2617, which is included on the CD-ROM that accompanies this book.

> **Note**
>
> Although Digest authentication is more secure than Basic authentication, it still doesn't solve all the problems of Basic authentication, just the most glaring one—that Basic authentication sends your username and password across the network in the clear. However, the body of the resource is still sent in the clear, so the same people who could intercept your username and password sent in the clear would also be able to intercept the resource being sent back to the user who authenticated with Digest authentication.

The general idea behind Digest authentication is that your password is never passed across the network to the server, and so nobody can intercept it. What is passed is a *digest*—a value that's calculated based on your username, password, and various other information, such as the resource you are requesting, the server that you are requesting it from, and a special key passed to you by the server, called a *nonce*.

A *nonce* is a value chosen by the server. This value is supposed to be different every time so that someone watching the wire can't simply record your response headers and play them back at a later date. A different nonce will be sent the last time, so the captured data will no longer match the new nonce.

The server performs the same calculation, based on its copy of your username and password, and compares its result to what the client passed. If the two values match, all the various parts must have matched, and the server returns the requested resource.

The calculation is what's known as a *one-way hash*, meaning that it's impossible to undo the calculation. There's no way to determine the password from its hashed value. The only way to verify that a password is correct is to compare the hashed values. By default, the encryption technique used is MD5, although another algorithm can be specified.

At the time of this writing, neither Netscape Navigator nor Microsoft Internet Explorer supports Digest authentication. Although Apache implements Digest authentication, and I'll tell you how to configure it, it's moderately pointless to use it, since nobody will be able to get in. (Spry Mosaic supports Digest authentication, but you don't see many people using that browser anymore.)

# Authentication Configuration Directives

The following are the configuration directives you will need to use to set up authentication on your server. These directives can appear in a `<Directory>` section in your main server configuration file or in a `.htaccess` file in the directory to be protected.

## AuthName

The `AuthName` directive defines the name of the *realm* being protected. A *realm* is a collection of documents and/or resources that are subject to the same authentication requirements. A realm is mostly for the client's benefit so that it knows which username/password pair to send. When a client requests a document from a protected area without providing correct credentials, the server returns a `401 Unauthorized` response header, accompanied by this realm name. If the client has seen that realm before on this server, it sends the same username and password that worked the last time for this same realm. This avoids requiring the user to type in his username and password each time he requests a resource from this realm.

The `AuthName` is simply any string. If the string contains spaces, it should be placed in quotes. Because this string will appear in the username/password dialog, make it somewhat informative.

The syntax of the `AuthName` directive is as follows. Figure 16.1 shows what the password dialog will look like with this setting.

```
AuthName "Floyd's Fresh Fish"
```

**FIGURE 16.1**

*Password dialog for the realm "Floyd's Fresh Fish."*

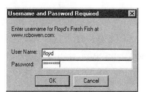

## AuthType

The `AuthType` indicates whether Basic or Digest authentication will be used for this resource. As noted earlier, both are supported by Apache, but most browsers support only Basic.

The syntax of this directive is as follows:

```
AuthType Basic
```

Possible values for this directive are, of course, `Basic` and `Digest`.

## AuthUserFile

The `AuthUserFile` directive specifies the location of the file containing the usernames and encrypted passwords, against which credentials will be validated.

> **Note**
>
> Your `AuthUserFile` file should be located outside your `DocumentRoot`; otherwise, someone could download it and then attempt to crack it at his leisure. Although there's no way to reverse the encryption, the would-be hackers could try all the words in the dictionary or other, perhaps randomly generated, words until something matched. Because they have all the time in the world, their odds are pretty good.

This file is of the form

```
username:encrypted-password
```

with one record per line. See the later section on creating passwords for more information about how this file is generated.

The format of the `AuthUserFile` directive is as follows:

```
AuthUserFile /path/to/userfile
```

If the file path doesn't begin with a slash, it's taken to be relative to the `ServerRoot` directory. Otherwise, it's considered an absolute file system path. On Windows, you can use forward slashes or backslashes, and you don't have to include the drive letter unless it's on a different drive than the `ServerRoot`.

The `AuthUserFile` is often called `.htpasswd`.

## AuthGroupFile

`AuthGroupFile` indicates the location of a file containing listings of user groups and the members of those groups. Creating user groups allows you to specify a larger number of people who are permitted to view a resource, but allows each to have his own username and password.

The syntax for this file is as follows:

```
TM3: cbowen llang bhall
```

As with `AuthUserFile`, the `AuthGroupFile` directive shouldn't be stored inside the document root, where a user could download the file. Knowing which users are permitted access to a particular resource may give a cracker an additional advantage when trying to get into a restricted area.

The format of the `AuthGroupFile` is as follows:

```
AuthGroupFile passwds/groups
```

If the filename doesn't begin with a slash, it's taken to be relative to the `ServerRoot` directory. Otherwise, it's considered an absolute file system path. On Windows, you can use forward slashes or backslashes, and you don't have to include the drive letter unless it's on a different drive than the `ServerRoot`.

If you are using just a user file and don't actually need a group file, you can specify the `AuthGroupFile` as `/dev/null` on UNIX, or `nul` on Windows, to indicate that there is no group file.

The `AuthGroupFile` is often called `.htgroup`.

# `<Limit>`

By default, authentication directives apply to all methods used to access resources in the given directory. A `<Limit>` section specifies methods to which authentication directives will apply. You must know what you're doing when using `<Limit>` because the effect of this directive is to leave all other methods unprotected, and this may not be what you actually wanted.

The syntax of a `<Limit>` section is as follows:

```
<Limit GET POST>
directives here
</Limit>
```

The list of methods in the opening `<Limit>` tag can contain any of the methods defined in Chapter 2, "HTTP," (`OPTIONS`, `GET`, `POST`, `PUT`, `DELETE`, or `TRACE`). Specifying `GET` also protects `HEAD` requests. These methods *are* case sensitive!

# `<LimitExcept>`

A `<LimitExcept>`container works exactly opposite from a `<Limit>` container. Directives contained in one of these sections are applied to all methods except those specified.

```
<LimitExcept GET>
directives
</LimitExcept>
```

Although this may seem like a rather redundant directive, using `<Limit>` often causes people to leave methods unprotected that they hadn't really thought about. Using `<LimitExcept>` forces you to think about what you are leaving unprotected, and so probably ends up being more secure for most people.

## require

The final piece of the puzzle, `require`, actually applies the other authentication directive by saying what users will be permitted to access the specified resources. `require` must be accompanied by `AuthName` and `AuthType` directives, as well as `AuthUserFile` and `AuthGroupFile` directives to define the users and the groups being referred to. If you are using DBM or DB files to contain your users and groups, the appropriate equivalent directives should be used. (More about this later in this chapter.)

`require` can be used in one of three ways: You can specify permitted users, specify permitted groups, or state that all valid users are permitted.

To specify one or more permitted users, use the following syntax:

```
require user rbowen dpitts tpowell
```

The specified users, of course, should appear in the referenced `AuthUserFile`.

To specify one or more groups that are permitted access, use the following syntax:

```
require group TM3
```

Only users listed in that group in your `AuthGroupFile` file will be permitted access.

Finally, to say simply that all valid users are allowed to get in, use the following syntax:

```
require valid-user
```

All users listed in `AuthUserFile` will be permitted to view the resource.

## How This All Works

When a request is received for a resource that's protected with the preceding directives, Apache returns a `401 Unauthorized` response header, as discussed in the earlier section on Basic authentication. The client then asks the user for his username and password and sends a new request with that username and password.

On receiving a request with authentication credentials attached, Apache opens up the specified `AuthUserFile` and `AuthGroupFile` files and searches for the user specified in the credentials. This can take a lot of time and takes progressively more time as the size of these files grows. Also, because HTTP is stateless, Apache doesn't remember the next time around that your username and password were accepted before. The next time the same client requests a document and passes in the same credentials, Apache will have to reopen those files and check for the user.

There are a few ways around this slowdown. The best way is to use DBM files for your authentication, as discussed a little later in this chapter. Another way is to separate your users into more than one file so as to keep your file sizes lower. If you have two distinct user groups that need to authenticate to different parts of your site, keep those groups of usernames and passwords in different files. This will cut down on the time taken to search for a user in `AuthUserFile`.

# order, deny, and allow

In addition to usernames and passwords, a few other criteria might be used to restrict access to resources. Two important examples of this are hosts and environment variables. The `allow` and `deny` directives specify who can get into a directory.

## allow

`allow` can be used two ways.

The first is to specify which Internet hosts can access a resource. The syntax of this directive is

`allow from host`

where *host* can be one of the following:

- `all`   All hosts are permitted access. This might be used along with a `deny` directive, such as

  ```
  allow from all
  deny from rcbowen.com
  ```

- *A domain name or partial domain name*   All hosts that match or end in this string are permitted access. Note also that this compares the entire component—that is, `beam.com` would not match `databeam.com`. Here's an example:

  ```
  allow from mk.net
  ```

- *A full or partial IP address*   In the case of a partial IP address, you are specifying the *first* 1 to 3 octets of the address—to specify an entire subnet, for example:

```
allow from 192.101.203
```

- *A network/netmask pair*   The netmask can be specified either as the number of high-order bits or as `a.b.c.d`. The following examples specify the same range of addresses:

```
allow from 192.168.0.0/255.255.0.0
allow from 192.168.0.0/16
```

The second way to use `allow` is to specify admission based on the presence, or absence, of an environment variable. The syntax of this use of `allow` is as follows:

```
allow from env=variable
```

This can be used with `BrowserMatch`, `SetEnvIf`, and related directives, for example, to control access to resources. The following example permits access to a resource if the client agent name is `Scooter`:

```
BrowserMatch Scooter Permitted
allow from env=Permitted
```

## deny

The syntax and use of the `deny` directive are exactly the same as the `allow` directive, but the meaning is the opposite. All requests that match the specified criteria are denied access. To recap, there are two uses.

To deny access to particular hosts, deny should be used as

```
deny from host
```

where *host* is one of

- `all`
- A full or partial domain name
- A full or partial IP address
- A network/subnet mask combination

To deny access based on the presence or absence of an environment variable, use the syntax

```
deny from env=variable
```

For more details about the syntax of the `deny` directive, see the explanation of the `allow` directive earlier, as the syntax is identical.

## order

Usually, when specifying either `allow` or `deny`, it's useful to also specify the other so that the groups to be allowed or denied can be more clearly defined. When this is done, it's important that these directives get applied in the order that you expect them to be. It also sets the initial state before the `allow` and `deny` directives are evaluated.

There are three possible settings for `order`:

- `order deny,allow`    All deny directives are processed before all `allow` directives. The initial state is set to `OK`, to let everyone in.

- `order allow,deny`    All `allow` directives are processed before all `deny` directives. The initial state is set to `FORBIDDEN`, to deny access to everyone.

> **Note**
>
> Remember from Chapter 15, "Security," that `allow,deny` and `deny,allow` don't contain any spaces.

- `Mutual-failure`    All the `allow` directives *and* all the `deny` directives must be obeyed. That is, only hosts that appear on the `allow` list and don't appear on the `deny` list are permitted access. Because of this, the initial state really doesn't matter.

## Satisfy

In cases where `require` is used and `allow` or `deny` is also used, you may need to use the `Satisfy` directive to specify which ones need to be obeyed. The argument to `Satisfy` can be `all` or `any`. `all`, the default behavior, indicates that both conditions must be fulfilled. `any` indicates that either condition is sufficient for access. This can be used to allow some host to enter a protected area without being prompted for a password but require other hosts to supply one.

# Putting Them Together: Sample Configurations

What follows are several examples of authentication configurations. This should give you an idea of how this is used in practice.

# Permit Only Specific Users

The following configuration will prompt users for a username and password, and will permit access only to the users rbowen and dpitts, assuming that they provide valid passwords as specified in the file passwd/.htpasswd. That file path is understood to be relative to the configured ServerRoot.

```
AuthType Basic
AuthName Administrators
AuthUserFile passwd/.htpasswd
AuthGroupFile /dev/null
require user rbowen dpitts
```

# Allow Only Specific Users to Post

This configuration might be useful if, for example, you want to allow everyone in the world to look at your site, but you only want a particular group of people to be able to post responses to your CGI program:

```
AuthType Basic
AuthName TheEliteFew
AuthUserFile passwd/.htpasswd
AuthGroupFile passwd/.htgroup
<Limit POST>
require group MyBuddies
</Limit>
```

# Permit/Deny Access from a Particular Domain

The following configuration permits access only from hosts on the databeam.com network:

```
order deny,allow
deny from all
allow from databeam.com
```

The following configuration allows access to everyone except users on the evilhackers.com network:

```
order allow,deny
allow from all
deny from evilhackers.com
```

# Protect Just One File

You can use a <Files> section to protect certain files but not others:

```
AuthType Basic
AuthName Admin
AuthUserFile passwd/.htpasswd
AuthGroupFile passwd/.htgroup
```

```
<Files admin.cgi>
require user rbowen
</Files>
```

## Block Internet Explorer

The following example denies access to anyone using Internet Explorer (not that I would recommend this—it's just an example):

```
BrowserMatch MSIE IE
deny from env=IE
```

## Using Satisfy

With the following configuration, users not from a host on the rcbowen.com network will be prompted for a username and password, but users on that network will be let right in:

```
AuthType Basic
AuthName Stats
AuthUserFile passwd/.htpasswd
AuthGroupFile passwd/.htgroup
Satisfy any
allow from rcbowen.com
require group Stats
```

# Managing Password Files

To use password authentication to protect your site, you need to have a password file containing the usernames and passwords of those users who need to get access to the site. The passwords are stored in this file in encrypted form.

On UNIX systems, the encryption technique is the same as that used by the standard UNIX utility crypt, which is also the format used in your /etc/passwd file on UNIX machines. On Windows systems, the encryption technique is MD5. In older releases of the Windows version of Apache, passwords weren't encrypted at all. Although this is no longer true, you will occasionally find documentation that states that it is still the case.

### Note

Some bright individuals have made the observation that because the /etc/passwd file looks a lot like your .htpasswd file, you could use it rather than go to all the trouble of creating a new password file. All you have to do is set AuthUserFile to /etc/passwd, and it just works.

Although this is true, it is a really bad idea. Because usernames and passwords are passed across the network in the clear, this is roughly equivalent to putting your password in your email signature and wearing a "hack me" sign.

Apache comes with a utility for creating password files, or you can do it yourself. Located in the src/support subdirectory of your Apache distribution is a utility called *htpasswd*, which helps you to create and populate your password file. Running htpasswd without arguments gives you a full list of available arguments:

```
bug> htpasswd
Usage:
        htpasswd [-cmdps] passwordfile username
        htpasswd -b[cmdps] passwordfile username password

 -c  Create a new file.
 -m  Force MD5 encryption of the password.
 -d  Force CRYPT encryption of the password (default).
 -p  Do not encrypt the password (plaintext).
 -s  Force SHA encryption of the password.
 -b  Use the password from the command line rather than prompting for it.
On Windows and TPF systems the '-m' flag is used by default.
On all other systems, the '-p' flag will probably not work.
```

> **Note**
>
> Notice that this help text warns that plaintext passwords probably won't work. htpasswd will quite happily create the plaintext password for you, but authentication will fail on some platforms when you provide your username and password to the browser.

In most cases, you will need to know just the following two ways of using htpasswd.

## Create a New Password File

To create a new password file, use the -c switch and the name of the first user you want to add to the file:

```
htpasswd -c .htpasswd rbowen
```

htpasswd will prompt you for the password. You are then asked for confirmation and, if the two passwords match, the file will be created, and the new user will be added to it:

```
bug> htpasswd -c .htpasswd rbowen
New password: ******
Re-type new password: ******
Adding password for user rbowen
```

You can then look in the file to give yourself the satisfaction that it was indeed created. You'll see something like this:

```
rbowen:twUSgw3mmejnc
```

The part after the colon is the encrypted password against which passwords will be compared to verify authenticity.

> **Note**
>
> Make sure that your password file is located outside the document root on your server. Putting it inside the document root might result in someone downloading your password file and being able to crack your passwords at his leisure.

## Add a User to an Existing Password File or Change a Password

To just add a user to your (already existing) password file, or to change the password of an existing user, use the same function without the -c switch.

```
htpasswd .htpasswd tpowell
```

As before, you will be asked for the password and asked to type it again for confirmation.

## Forcing MD5 Encryption

If you use the -d flag to force htpasswd to encrypt in MD5 on a UNIX machine, Apache will do the right thing when you provide your credentials to access a resource. That is, even if you create some passwords with crypt and some with MD5, Apache will correctly authenticate with all of them. (Using the -d flag on Windows is ignored; encryption is always done with MD5.)

## Removing a User from Your Password File

To remove a user from your password file, you need to open the file in a text editor, such as Notepad or vi, and manually delete the line containing the username and password. Go through your password file(s) regularly and remove users that should no longer be there.

See Chapter 15 for more tips on how to keep your Apache server secure.

## Creating Group Files

Creating group files requires just a text editor. The format of the group file, as mentioned earlier, is the name of the group followed by a list of the members of that group:

```
Managers: robert barry jim brian
```

The group file can contain as many groups as you like, and a group can contain as many members as you like. Members can be in more than one group—meaning simply that they have access to more than one restricted area.

# mod_auth_dbm and mod_auth_db

The preceding method of creating password files is easy and convenient, but doesn't scale very well. When you start having hundreds or thousands of users, your password files get large, and it's very slow and inefficient to search them to see if the user requesting access is allowed to get in. And because the username and password have to be validated with every HTTP request, you spend a lot of time waiting.

The best solution to this problem is to move your users and groups out of text files and into DBM (or DB) files. DBM files are a somewhat standard way of storing keys and values in a file so that the data can be accessed very quickly. The file stores an index (often in a second file) so that, if you know the key, you can immediately know where the value is stored. This leads to very rapid data access. Berkeley DB is another implementation of the same idea. On some platforms, such as the various BSD operating systems, DBM automatically maps to DB.

Because access to these files is so much quicker than access to flat-text files, Apache modules have been created to permit using these files for authentication. This is ideal for either very large sets of users or very busy sites. These modules are `mod_auth_dbm` for using DBM files and `mod_auth_db` for using DB files.

## Preparing Apache to Use `mod_auth_db(m)`

`mod_auth_dbm` and `mod_auth_db` aren't compiled into Apache by default. You have to specifically enable the one that you want and rebuild Apache to enable this functionality.

You will need to edit your configuration file and uncomment (delete the leading #) the line that says

```
# Module dbm_auth_module    mod_auth_dbm.o
```

Then rerun `./Configure` and rebuild Apache.

If you can't compile Apache after making this change (you see errors about various `dbm*()` functions not being found), you probably don't have the DBM libraries installed on your system. Contact your system administrator and get him to download and install these libraries where you can get to them.

See Chapter 3, "Compiling and Installing Apache," for more information about installing particular modules.

# Managing Your User Files

With regular password files, you use htpasswd to create and manage your password files. With DBM, you use *dbmmanage*, located in the src/support directory of your Apache distribution.

## Adding a New User

To add a new user to your DBM user file, use the adduser argument.

```
dbmmanage users.dbm adduser rbowen
```

dbmmanage will then prompt you for the password and ask you to confirm it. If you enter the password the same both times, it will be added to the DBM file.

If you already have the password in an encrypted form, you can add the record directly to the DBM file with the add argument:

```
dbmmanage users.dbm add elent xyrHgu26VDIOo
```

To verify that users have been added to your DBM file, you can use the view argument, which dumps the various entries in the file. Using the view argument with a particular username will show just that user's entry:

```
dbmmanage users.dbm view
dbmmanage users.dbm view llang
```

DBM files are binary files, so you can't simply look at the contents of the file in a text editor. (Well, you could, but you might not find it particularly edifying.)

You can also verify that a password is in the file correctly by using the check argument. Enter the following command line:

```
dbmmanage users.dbm check username
```

dbmmanage will ask you for the password, and then return Password ok if you entered it correctly, Password mismatch otherwise.

## Modify a User's Password

An existing user's password can be changed with the update argument:

```
dbmmanage users.dbm update dpitts
```

dbmmanage will ask you for the new password, and then ask you to retype it to confirm. If you enter it the same way twice, the password in the file will be updated to the new value.

## Deleting a User

You can delete a user from the password file with the `delete` argument:

```
dbmmanage users.dbm delete gbenson
```

## Using Configuration Directives

To protect a particular directory by using DBM or DB files, you should use almost exactly the same directives as you saw in the preceding section about flat-text password files. The only difference is that you use the `AuthDBMUserFile` (for DBM files) or `AuthDBUserFile` (for DB files) directive instead of the `AuthUserFile` directive, and the `AuthDBMGroupFile` (for DBM files) or `AuthDBGroupFile` (for DB files) directive instead of the `AuthGroupFile` directive. These directives should point to your user database file.

```
AuthType Basic
AuthName Managers
AuthDBMUserFile passwd/users.dbm
AuthDBMGroupFile passwd/users.dbm
require user barney
```

# Other Security Considerations

You should keep in mind a number of security considerations when setting up authentication on your Apache server. Some of these were covered from one angle or another in Chapter 15, but they bear mentioning again here, in this context.

## Getting Passwords to Users

No level of security on your Web server will do you much good if you distribute passwords to users insecurely. Make sure that the delivery mechanism for getting these passwords to users in the first place isn't the weak link in your chain. Consider using PGP or a similar secure transfer method if you send passwords by email.

## Changing Passwords

If you provide a method for users to change their authentication passwords, be very sure that it's as secure as possible. A security hole in this process might let one user change another user's password and thus gain access to things that he wasn't meant to see.

## File Permission to the Password Files

Make sure that file permissions on your password files are what they should be. Ordinarily, this would mean that only root can write to the files. Obviously, the user as whom Apache runs must be able to read from the file, but normal users shouldn't be able to read from it.

If you have some sort of CGI application to allow users to change their passwords online (convenient, but usually rather insecure), the password files will need to be writable by the user running Apache.

In either case, make sure that the files are as restricted as you can make them and still have things work.

## Don't Use Your Login Password!

Although it's extremely convenient to have one password for everything and not have to remember a dozen different passwords, it's a really bad idea to use a password for HTTP authentication that's also your network login password, email password, UNIX login password, or other important password. As mentioned before in this chapter, your HTTP passwords are (usually) passed in the clear across the network, and someone could quite easily intercept that information and use it to gain access to more than just your Web site.

## Don't Use Basic Authentication if It's Really Sensitive

As emphasized earlier in this chapter, Basic authentication isn't secure. Your username and password are passed in the clear across the network. Don't use Basic authentication to secure truly confidential information. Try to use some other method, such as access by IP address, or, if it's available to you, use SSL or another secure transfer method.

# Summary

HTTP authentication provides the ability to protect a portion of your Web site from prying eyes. Two authentication types are available: Basic and Digest. Neither should be considered a secure transfer method. Digest is more secure than Basic but isn't universally supported by the browsers available at this time.

# Spiders, Robots, and Web Crawlers

When the Web was young—or at least when you were new to the Web—it was interesting to spend hours clicking links and looking at Web pages. Eventually, you got over that, and now you just want the information you want, when you want it, and you no longer want to do the work for yourself. That's where spiders come in.

*Spiders* are programs that walk the Web for you, following links and grabbing information. They're also known as *robots* and *crawlers*. You can find a list of many of the currently available and active spiders online at `http://info.webcrawler.com/mak/projects/robots/active/html/index.html`.

Spiders are very useful, but they can also cause a lot of problems. If you have a Web site on the Internet, you will find that a steady percentage of the visits to your site are from spiders. This is because most of the major search engines use spiders to index the Web, including your Web site, for inclusion in their database.

This chapter discusses what a spider is, how spiders can make your life easier, and how to protect your Web site against spiders that you don't want to let in. You also see how to give spiders the right information about your site when they visit. Finally, you learn briefly about writing your own spider.

# What's a Spider?

The Web Robots FAQ defines a robot as "a program that automatically traverses the Web's hypertext structure by retrieving a document and recursively retrieving all documents that are referenced." (You can find the Web Robots FAQ on the CD that accompanies this book and at `http://info.webcrawler.com/mak/projects/robots/faq.html`.) What this means is that a spider starts with some page and downloads all the pages that page has links to. Then, for each of those pages, it downloads all the pages they are linked to, and so on, *ad infinitum*. This is done automatically by the spider program, which will presumably be collecting this information for some useful purpose.

Spiders may be collecting information for a search engine, collecting email addresses for sending spam, or downloading pages for offline viewing.

Some examples of various common types of robots are as follows:

- *Scooter* is the robot responsible for the AltaVista search engine. Scooter fetches documents from the Web, which are then incorporated into AltaVista's database. You can search that database at `http://www.altavista.com/`. Most major search engines also use some type of spider to index the Web, and you will see many of them in your server logs.

- *EmailSiphon* and various other spiders with similar names rove the Web, retrieving email addresses from Web pages. The people who run EmailSiphon then sell those addresses to various low-lifes, who send unsolicited bulk email (also known as *spam*) to those addresses. See the later section on excluding spiders from your site to learn how to deny access to these robots and protect your mailbox.

- *MOMspider* is one that you can download and use on your own site to validate links and generate statistics. You can run it from your server or from your desktop. There are a large number of similar products for Web site developers to use on their own sites.

# Spiders: The Good Versus the Bad

In general, spiders are good things. They can help you out in a number of ways, such as indexing your site, searching for broken links, and validating the HTML on your pages.

A common use for spiders is collecting documents from the Web for you, so that you can look at them at your leisure when you aren't online. This is called *offline browsing* or *caching*, among other things, and the products that do this are sometimes called *personal agents* or *personal spiders*. One such product, called AvantGo (http://www.avantgo.com), will even download Web content to your palm-top computer so that you can look at your favorite Web pages while on an airplane or bus.

However, spiders also can cause a lot of problems on your Web site, because their traffic patterns are not the sort that you typically plan for.

## Server Overloading

One potential problem is server overload. Whereas a human user is likely to wait at least a few seconds between downloading one page and the next, the spider can start on the next page immediately after receiving the first page. Also, it can fork multiple processes and download several pages at the same time. If your server isn't equipped to handle that many simultaneous connections, or if you don't have the bandwidth to handle the requests, this may cause visitors to have to wait a long time for their pages to load or even cause the server to become overloaded.

## Black Holes

Occasionally, poorly written spiders may get trapped in some infinite portion of your Web site, such as a CGI program that generates pages with links back to itself. The spider may spend hours or days chasing its tail, so to speak. This can cause your log files to grow at an alarming rate, skew any statistical information that you might be collecting, and lead to an overloaded server.

# Recognizing Spiders in Your Log Files

Before you try to keep spiders out of your site, you might want to get a good idea of what spiders are visiting your site and what they're trying to do. You'll notice log entries from spiders in several ways:

- The first thing that will stand out will be the user agent (if you are logging the user agent in your log files). It won't look like an ordinary browser (because it's not) and will tend to have a name such as `harvester`, `black widow`, `Aracnophilia`, and the like. You can see a full listing of the various known spiders in the Web Robots FAQ, discussed earlier in this chapter.

- You might notice that a large number of pages are requested by the same client, often in quick succession.

- The address from which the client is connecting can tell you quite a lot. Connections from the various search engines are frequently spiders indexing your site. For example, a connection from `lobo.yahoo.com` is a good indication that your site is being indexed for the Yahoo! Internet directory.

# Excluding Spiders from Your Server

You can keep spiders off your site—or at least off certain parts of your site—in several different ways. These methods tend to rely on the cooperation of the spider itself. However, you can do a number of things at the server level to deny access.

As mentioned earlier, you will probably want to keep spiders out of your CGI directories. You also will want to keep them out of portions of your site that change with such regularity that indexing would be fruitless. And, of course, there may be parts of your site that you'd just rather not have indexed, for whatever reason.

## `robots.txt`

The Robots Exclusion Protocol, also known as A Standard for Robot Exclusion, is a document drafted in 1994 that outlined a method for telling robots what parts of your site you want them to stay out of. You can find the full text of this document on the WebCrawler Web site at `http://info.webcrawler.com/mak/projects/robots/norobots.html`.

To implement this exclusion on your Web site, you need to create a text file called robots.txt and place it in your server's document root directory. When a spider visits your site, it is supposed to fetch this document before going any further, to find out what rules you have set.

The file contains one or more User-agent lines, each followed by one or more Disallow lines, specifying any directories that particular user agent is not permitted to access. Most commonly, the user agent specified will be *, which should be obeyed by all robots. In the following sample robots.txt file, all user agents (spiders) are requested to stay out of the directories /cgi-bin/ and /datafiles/:

```
User-agent: *
Disallow: /cgi-bin/
Disallow: /datafiles/
```

In the following example, a particular user agent, Scooter, is requested to stay out of the directory /dont-index/:

```
User-agent: Scooter
Disallow: /dont-index/
```

robots.txt files can also contain comments. Anything following a hash character (#), until the end of that line, is a comment and will be ignored.

Unfortunately, it is very easy to write a spider but considerably more difficult to write one that is well behaved. Consequently, many people write spiders that blatantly ignore your robots.txt file. Like many parts of Internet standards, it's just a suggestion, and particular implementations are free to ignore the suggestion.

## The ROBOTS Meta Tag

Another method for requesting that spiders not enter your Web site is the ROBOTS meta tag. This HTML tag can appear in the <HEAD> section of any HTML page. The format of the tag is as follows:

```
<HTML>
<HEAD>
<META NAME="ROBOTS" CONTENT="arguments">
<TITLE>Title here</TITLE>
</HEAD>
<BODY>
...
```

Possible arguments to the CONTENT attribute are as follows:

- FOLLOW tells the spider that it's okay to follow any links that appear on this document.

- INDEX tells the spider that it's okay to index this document. That is, the contents of this document can be cached or added to a search engine database.

- NOFOLLOW tells the spider not to follow any links from this page.

- NOINDEX tells the spider not to index this page.

Any of these arguments can be combined, separated by commas, as shown in the following example:

```
<META NAME="ROBOTS" CONTENT="INDEX,NOFOLLOW">
```

Two other directives also specify a grouping of the preceding arguments. ALL is equivalent to INDEX,FOLLOW, and NONE is equivalent to NOINDEX,NOFOLLOW.

As with the robots.txt file, obeying the rules specified in this tag is optional. Most major search engines follow any requests that you make with this meta tag.

## Contacting the Operator

If a spider appears to be running wild on your site or visiting parts of your site that you really don't want it to, you first should attempt to contact the operator. You have the client's address in the log files. Try to email an administrator at the offending site to get hold of whoever is running the robot. Tell him what his robot is doing to your server and ask him nicely to stop, or at least to obey your robots.txt file.

## Blocking Out a Spider

If you can't get any response or if the operator refuses to pay any attention to you, you can shut out the spider completely with some well-placed deny directives:

```
<Directory /usr/web/docs>
order allow,deny
allow from all
deny from unfriendly.spiderhost.com
</Directory>
```

If all else fails, have the spider's traffic blocked at the router. This has a disadvantage, however, in that it will also block traffic from any legitimate users coming from that system.

# Writing Your Own Spider

Perhaps you want to write your own special-purpose spider to do some work for you. The best advice I can give you is, simply, don't write your own spider. A plethora of spiders is already available online, most of which you can download for free. They do everything from checking links on your site to getting the latest basketball scores to validating your HTML syntax to telling you that your favorite Web site has been updated. It is very unlikely that you have a need so specialized that someone has not already written a spider to do exactly what you need. You can find a spider to suit your needs at `http://info.webcrawler.com/mak/projects/robots/active/html/index.html`.

> **Tip**
>
> It can be difficult to write a spider that correctly implements the Robots Exclusion Protocol (that is, obeys all the suggestions given in the `robots.txt` file and any `ROBOTS` meta tags), so you might as well use one that someone else has already written.

If you really feel that you must write your own spider, the best tool for the job is probably Perl. Perl's main strength is processing large quantities of text and pulling out the information that's of interest to you. Spiders spend most of their time going through Web pages (text files) and pulling out information, as well as links to other Web pages.

There are several Perl modules specifically for processing HTML pages. These modules are available on CPAN (`http://www.cpan.org/`). Of particular interest would be the LWP modules, in CPAN's `modules/by-module/LWP/` directory, and various `HTML::*` modules in CPAN's `modules/by-module/HTML/` directory.

Listing 17.1 shows a very simple spider, implemented in Perl. This subroutine gets a Web page, does something with that page, and then gets all the pages linked from the first page, recursively. The `HTML::LinkExtor` module extracts all links from an HTML document. `HTML::FormatText` formats an HTML page as text, so that you can get to the information without all the HTML markup. And `LWP::Simple` is a simple way to fetch documents from the network.

**LISTING 17.1**  A Simple Spider in Perl

```
use HTML::LinkExtor;
use HTML::FormatText;
use LWP::Simple;

my $p = HTML::LinkExtor->new();
my $Docs = {};
searchpage(0, 'http://www.yoursite.com/', $Docs);

sub searchpage  {
```

*continues*

**LISTING 17.1** continued

```perl
    my ($cur_depth, $url, $Docs) = @_;
    my ($link, @links, $abs);

    print "Looking at $url, at depth $cur_depth\n";
    $Docs->{$url} = 1; # Mark site as visited

    my $content = get($url);
    $p->parse($content);
    $content = HTML::FormatText->new->format(parse_html($content));
    DoSomethingWith($url, $content);
    @links = $p->links;
    for $link (@links)  {
        $abs = url($link->[2], $url)->abs if
            ($link->[0] eq 'a' && $link->[1] eq 'href');
        $abs =~ s/#.*$//;
        $abs =~ s!/$!!;

        # Skip some URLs
        next if $abs=~/^mailto/i; # Email link
        next if $abs=~/(gz|zip|exe|tar|Z)$/; # Binary files
        next if $abs=~/\?\S+?=\S+/; # CGI program

        searchpage($cur_depth+1, $abs, $Docs)
            unless ($Docs->{$abs});
    }
} # End sub searchpage
```

The function call in the middle—DoSomethingWith($url, $content)—is, of course, where you would fill in whatever it is you wanted to do with the content you were collecting from the page.

---

**Caution**

Be careful when using this code, because it can put a heavy load on a server very quickly. It doesn't follow the standard for robot exclusion, as discussed earlier, and it continues to fetch pages forever because the recursion has no exit condition. (A good approach might be to exit from the loop as soon as $cur_depth reaches a certain value.) Test it on your server, not mine.

# Summary

Spiders are very useful tools for doing tedious work that we don't want to do manually. If carelessly written or used, they can also wreak havoc on your Web server. This chapter focused on the various uses for spiders, as well as the ways in which they can be misused. You saw how to block them from your site and even how to write your own spider.

# Logging

When an HTTP client connects to your Apache Web server, a great deal of information is exchanged. Any of this information can be logged by the Apache process. Two default log files are set up by default—`error_log` and `access_log`—but you can create any number of custom log files with the `LogFormat` and `CustomLog` directives. This chapter discusses those directives and gives some examples of how you might use them.

Two log files are defined in the default configuration files that come with the Apache distribution: `access_log` records basic information about the HTTP transaction, and `error_log` records anything that goes wrong. Although you can generate any number of other logs, most people stick to just these two and generate whatever additional reports they need from these logs.

> **Note**
>
> Although I have called these the "standard" log files, Apache doesn't generate `access_log` unless the configuration files tell it to. You have to specifically configure logging directives in your server configuration files. These directives are in the default configuration files that ship with the Apache distribution but, without these directives, no transfer log is generated.

Once you have your log files, a plethora of tools is available for distilling meaningful statistics from them, and we will look at several of those.

Finally, we'll look at some of the other tools available for maintaining archives of your logs and other basic administrative tasks you might want to perform regarding logging.

# The Transfer Log (`access_log`)

The transfer log contains basic information about every HTTP transaction that the server handles. This can be used for generating statistical reports about what sort of usage patterns your Web site sees. You can also generate customized transfer logs to collect any specific information that you might be interested in.

## Contents of `access_log`

An entry from `access_log` looks like the following:

```
192.101.203.72 - - [12/May/1999:23:25:11 -0400] "GET /apache.html
➡HTTP/1.0" 200 108
```

This format, called the *Common Log Format*, is generally the log format assumed by most available log analysis software. It contains seven pieces of information, separated by spaces, except for those fields that are enclosed in quotes or square brackets. The pieces of information logged are as follows:

- *Hostname*  In the preceding example, this is 192.101.203.72, which is the IP address of the client that requested the document from the server. In this particular example, the HostnameLookups directive is set to Off, so only the IP address is logged. If that directive were set to On, the fully qualified domain name (fqdn) of the machine would be logged instead.

> **Note**
>
> Setting HostnameLookups to On causes a lot of additional work. For every HTTP transaction, a query must be made to DNS. Particularly for hosts that aren't already in some local DNS cache, this can cause a substantial slowdown.

- *Remote logname*  If IdentityCheck is enabled and the client machine runs identd, this is the identity information reported by the client. Because having IdentityCheck enabled results in rather serious performance issues and very few client machines are likely to be running identd, in practice a remote logname is almost never used, and this field is almost always in the log as - (what's displayed for undefined values). In the good old days, when people behaved ethically with log information, many browsers passed the email address of the user as the value for this field. This swiftly stopped when people starting generating mailing lists and sending out spam to those lists.

- *Remote user*  This is the name that the remote user typed in response to a user-name/password query. This will be set only in authenticated portions of a site (see Chapter 16, "Authentication"). Also note that if the status is 401, this username is very likely not valid.

- *Time*  This is the date and time that the request was served, including time zone information.

- *Request*  This is the first line of the request that was actually made to the server. This will typically be HEAD, GET, or POST, followed by the URL requested, followed by the HTTP version in which the response is expected.

- *Response code*   This indicates whether the request was successful and, if not, what type of error occurred. The section "Server Status Codes" in Chapter 2, "HTTP," provides for a complete listing of the possible response codes and their meanings.

- *Bytes transferred*   This is the total number of bytes transferred to the client. It doesn't include the HTTP headers.

# Location of `access_log`

The location of the `access_log` file is set one of two ways:

- If you don't intend to modify the log file's format, you can just accept the default value of `LogFormat`, which is the common log format described above, and set the location of your log file with the `TransferLog` directive. The format of the directive is shown in the following example:

  ```
  TransferLog logs/access_log
  ```

  If a relative file path is given, it's taken to be relative to the `ServerRoot` directory. (See Chapter 5, "Server Configuration Files," for more information on this directive.) An absolute path to a file can also be specified.

- If you want to be able to modify the log file's format, use the `LogFormat` directive, described later in this chapter, to define the format of the log files, and a "nickname" for that format. You can then apply the format to a log file and set the location of that file with the `CustomLog` directive. This is the way that the access log's location is specified in the configuration files that ship with Apache.

  ```
  LogFormat "%h %l %u %t \"%r\" %>s %b" common
  CustomLog logs/access_log common
  ```

  As with the `TransferLog` directive, a relative path is assumed to be relative to the `ServerRoot` directory.

Remember that these directives have no default values. If you don't specify where you want the log file, no log file is generated.

> **Note**
>
> In the configuration files that ship with the Windows NT version, `access_log` is called `access.log` because Windows NT wants filename extensions on files. This is certainly not required, but it seems to make Windows NT users more comfortable.

# Generating Custom Log Files

Although the common log format—the default value of the `LogFormat` directive—generates a log file that contains most of the information that you will ever be interested in, sometimes you might want to get some additional information about the clients that visit your site. What Web browsers are they using? Where did they find a link to your site? These sorts of questions can be answered by generating customized log files that contain just this information.

Most available log file analysis tools, such as Wusage from Boutell.com, expect that you will use the common log format. However, the later section "Log Analysis Tools" talks about writing your own simple log file analysis tools in Perl to handle your customized log file format.

The directives that allow you to generate these customized log files are the `LogFormat` and `CustomLog` directives.

## The `LogFormat` Directive

The `LogFormat` directive defines the format of a log file and assigns a nickname to this format, so that later you can apply the format to a particular log file by using just the nickname. The syntax of the directive is as follows:

```
LogFormat format [nickname]
```

Without the optional *nickname* parameter, `LogFormat` sets the default value to be used with the `TransferLog` directive, as discussed earlier in the section "Location of `access_log`."

The *format* parameter defines what fields will be in a line of the log file. It is composed of a sequence of format strings, as follows:

```
LogFormat "%h %l %u %t \"%r\" %s %b" common
```

This example shows the format for the common log format, as discussed earlier in the section "Contents of `access_log`." The following sections list the possible format strings.

## Log Format Variables

A log file format created with the `LogFormat` directive is composed of any of a number of the variables in Table 18.1.

18

LOGGING

**TABLE 18.1** Log File Formatting Variables

| Variable | Description |
| --- | --- |
| %b | Total number of bytes sent to the client. This doesn't include the HTTP headers and should reflect the actual size of the requested file. If the number reported is smaller than the file size, this indicates that the transfer was interrupted. If the file is pulled from a cache local to the client, this may be logged as -. |
| %f | Filename requested by the client. |
| %{variable}e | Contents of the environment variable *variable*. For example, %{REMOTE_PORT}e will log the port on the client used for the data connection to send the document. |
| %h | Address of the client. If HostnameLookups is set to off, this will just be the IP address of the client machine and so the same as %a. If HostnameLookups is turned on, this will be the fqdn of the client machine. As mentioned before, having lookups turned off is a good idea, unless you have a really good reason for having them on. |
| %a | IP address of the client. For default config file settings, this is the same as %h, but if HostnameLookups is turned on, this will still record just the IP address, rather than the fqdn of the client. |
| %{header}i | Contents of the specified HTTP header. For example, %{Referer}i will log the referrer to the requested document—that is, the Web page that had a link to the page that it's now requesting. |
| %l | Remote logname, as described earlier in the section "Location of access_log." This name, supplied by identd on the client machine, is usually blank. |
| %{note}n | Contents of note from another module. |
| %{header}o | Contents of the specified header line in the reply. For example, if you wanted to log the MIME type of the various responses, you could put %{Content-Type}o in your LogFormat directive. |
| %p | Canonical port of the server serving the request. For most sites, this will be the same for every request, but it might be useful if you are running virtual hosts listening to different ports. |
| %P | Process ID of the child that serviced the request. Because Apache threads rather than forks child processes on Windows NT, this doesn't yield meaningful information on Windows NT. |
| %r | First line of request. This will usually be something like GET / HTTP/1.0 and indicates the request that was made to the server. |

| Variable | Description |
|----------|-------------|
| %s | Status. For requests that got internally redirected, this is the status of the original request. (Use %>s for the status of the last request.) See Chapter 2 for a full listing of the meanings of the various status values. |
| %t | Time in common log format time format. |
| %{format}t | Time in the form given by `format`, which is in `strftime(3)` format. See Table 12.1 in Chapter 12, "SSI: Server-Side Includes," to learn how to build these formats. |
| %T | Time taken to serve the request, in seconds. |
| %u | Username entered in response to a username/password challenge. Note that if the status is `401` (`Unauthorized`), this may be invalid. |
| %U | URL path requested. |
| %v | Name of the server serving the request. |

## Conditional Logging

In each format string shown in Table 18.1, you can put a conditional statement in front of the variable that will determine whether the variable is displayed. These conditionals take the form of one or more HTTP status codes. If the request returns one of the specified status codes, the value of the variable is written to the log file. Otherwise, the string - is written instead.

The following example will log the value of the document requested if the HTTP status code is `404` (`Document not found`). Otherwise, it will write the string - to the log.

```
LogFormat "%404f" deadlinks
```

The following example will write the value of the environment variable `REMOTE_USER` to the log file if the return status code isn't `401` (`Unauthorized`). If the return value *is* `401`, the string - will be written to the log.

```
LogFormat "%!401u" unauthorized
```

Defining `LogFormat` doesn't actually apply that value to a log file. To do that, you need to use the `CustomLog` directive.

## The `CustomLog` Directive

After a nickname is defined with the `LogFormat` directive, you can create one or more log files using that format with the `CustomLog` directive. The syntax of the `CustomLog` directive is as follows:

```
CustomLog logs/access_log common
CustomLog logs/referer_log Referer
```

The two arguments to the `CustomLog` directive are the location of the log file and the nickname of the format to be used. The location of the log file is specified relative to `ServerRoot`, unless the path is specified with a leading /.

---

### The Conditional `CustomLog` Directive

Another form of the `CustomLog` directive allows you to write entries to your log file if a certain criterion is satisfied. The syntax for this directive is as follows:

```
CustomLog filelocation nickname env=[!]variable
```

The first two arguments are the same as with the generic `CustomLog` directive. The last argument checks to see whether a particular environment variable is set for a given request. If it is, the data from that request is logged; otherwise, no entry is made.

This is frequently used along with the `SetEnvIf` directive, which allows you to set environment variables on a per-request basis. The syntax of the `SetEnvIf` directive is

```
SetEnvIf attribute regex variable[=value]
```

If, for example, you wanted to log requests from a particular domain and ignore all other domains, you could put the following in your configuration file:

```
SetEnvIf Remote_Host \.databeam\.com$ LocalRequest
CustomLog logs/localrequests_log common env=LocalRequest
```

This example will log only those requests that come from hosts ending in .databeam.com. The $ character indicates that the regular expression match is to appear on the end of the string.

---

# The Error Log (`error_log`)

The `error_log` file records what went wrong. In some cases, each record is rather cryptic, but usually the messages contain enough information to diagnose and fix the problem.

Something will end up in `error_log` if the return status code is any of the 400 or 500 codes. See Table 2.4 in Chapter 2 for a full listing of the possible error codes.

The following example shows up in the error log when a client requests a document that doesn't exist on your server:

```
[Wed May 12 22:03:43 1999] [error] [client 192.101.205.24] File does not
➥exist: /usr/local/apache/htdocs/missing.html
```

# Contents of `error_log`

Each message in `error_log` contains four pieces of information: the time the error occurred, the level of the message, the address of the client that caused the problem, and the actual error message.

## Time of Error

The time that the error occurred is written to the log in the format [*Day Mon dd hh:mm:ss yyyy*]. This format isn't configurable.

## Log Level

The error message level indicates the severity of the error being reported. Table 18.2 lists the possible values for this level.

**TABLE 18.2**   Log Message Levels

| Level | Description |
| --- | --- |
| emerg | Emergencies—system is unusable. Example: `Child cannot open lock file. Exiting` |
| alert | Action must be taken immediately. Example: `getpwuid: couldn't determine user name from uid` |
| crit | Critical conditions. Example: `socket: Failed to get a socket, exiting child` |
| error | Error conditions. Example: `Premature end of script headers` |
| warn | Warning conditions. Example: `child process 1234 did not exit, sending another SIGHUP` |
| notice | Normal but significant condition. Example: `httpd: caught SIGBUS, attempting to dump core in ...` |
| info | Informational. Example: `Server seems busy, (you may need to increase StartServers, or Min/MaxSpareServers)...` |
| debug | Debug-level messages. Example: `Opening config file ...` |

**18**

LOGGING

With the `LogLevel` directive, you can set a lower bound on the error messages that you want to end up in your log. The default value of this directive is `error`, meaning that you will get all messages that are of level `error` and more severe.

Setting `LogLevel` to anything much less than `notice` tends to flood your error log with informational messages that aren't particularly important or meaningful to the average Web site administrator. `debug` is really of interest only to Apache developers, and generated messages will be meaningful only if you happen to be the one who wrote the code.

# Client Address

The client address will be displayed in the error log either as the IP address of the client machine or as the fully qualified domain name (fqdn) of the machine, depending on the value you've set for the HostnameLookups directive. A value of on will give you the fqdn of the machine, if that name can be determined from DNS, and the IP address otherwise. A value of off will give you the IP address.

> **Note**
>
> Don't turn on HostnameLookups just to get the name of clients in the log files. DNS lookups take time and, in the event that the machine name can't be found, you may have to wait for a substantial amount of time (the DNS timeout period is typically 30 seconds) to find out that you can't find the information. This slows down your server considerably, since every client request requires at least one DNS lookup.
>
> The utility logresolve, which ships with Apache, can be used to look up these names after the fact, when you are generating log file statistics. This can take a substantial amount of time but has the benefit that it won't affect your Web server's performance. (The logresolve utility isn't available for Windows NT, but you could write such a tool in Perl or some other language.)

# Error Message

The last part of the error log entry is the actual error message returned by the server. This part is the most useful in trying to determine what went wrong. The message should tell you in plain English what went wrong, in most cases. For example

```
File does not exist: /home/httpd/html/fun/gpf/main.shtml
```

indicates that the client requested a file that isn't on your server. The client address will tell you what client requested this file and, if you are so inclined, you might be able to use this information to track down the user and figure out if he just mistyped the address or if he followed a link from another site that was either incorrect or linked to a file that's no longer available. If the file is no longer available, you might want to use the Redirect directive to redirect clients to the new location of the file.

The following message indicates that the server was started or restarted and reloaded the configuration files:

```
Apache/1.3.6 (Unix) (Red Hat/Linux) configured — resuming normal operations
```

You will see this message (or a similar one, with the appropriate OS information for your platform) every time your server is restarted.

This is the sort of unhelpful error message you will get when a CGI program fails:

```
access to /home/httpd/cgi-bin/program.pl failed for 192.101.203.72, reason:
➥Premature end of script headers
```

Occasionally, the error log will provide additional information if the CGI program itself returned any error messages, but not always. Of course, since the Apache developers didn't write your CGI program, they can't know what went wrong with it, so such an uninformative error message should really be expected. See the following section for some tips on how to get more detailed information about what went wrong with your CGI program. You also can read Chapter 11, "CGI Programming," to see what might go wrong with CGI programs to generate such an error message.

# ScriptLog and Associated Directives

The ScriptLog directive lets you do detailed debugging on failing CGI programs. This is useful when you just can't figure out what's going wrong and want all the information that you can get.

The ScriptLog directive is part of the mod_cgi module and is available by default. It sets the location of the CGI error log file. If this directive isn't specified, no such log file is created, which is the default behavior. The format of the directive is as follows:

```
ScriptLog filename
```

*filename* is either an absolute path to a filename or a relative path, which is interpreted to be relative to ServerRoot.

> **Note**
>
> This log file will be opened and written to as the user specified in the User directive. This means that you have to either specify a location that this user can write to or create the file manually ahead of time and set the permissions on it so that the user can write to the file. It's not recommended that you change permissions on your main log directory so that this user can write to that directory, as this opens up the possibility of security breaches.

Every time a CGI program is run, the server logs the entire request (all headers, all POST or PUT data, all query information) to this file, and all output from the CGI program is also logged. This gives you very detailed information about what went wrong (if something goes wrong) and lets you figure out what you can do to fix it.

However, as you can imagine, this can generate very large log files very quickly, and so you should use this only when you are specifically trying to track down a problem, and then, if possible, only on a test server.

## ScriptLogBuffer

The ScriptLogBuffer directive sets the limit on the amount of POST or PUT data written to the ScriptLog file. If you have a CGI program that handles file uploads, for example, the entire body of the upload (PUT data) could potentially be logged to this log file, which may not be desirable and will certainly cause the log file to grow very rapidly. By setting ScriptLogBuffer to a reasonable value (1KB by default), you can limit the growth rate. If you need to see more of the data, you can set this directive as large as you like.

Example: ScriptLogBuffer 2048

## ScriptLogLength

The ScriptLogLength directive limits the total size of the ScriptLog file, preventing it from running wild and filling up your file system. By default, this is set to 10MB. If this size is reached, Apache simply stops logging to the file.

Example: ScriptLogLength 10385760

# Piped Logs

For any directives that specify the location of log files (CustomLog, TransferLog, or ErrorLog) rather than specify a file location, you can specify that the log data be piped to some process that will handle the data. This is done by using the | (pipe) character, followed by the path to the command that will receive the data. Data is provided to that process on standard input.

Example: ErrorLog |/usr/bin/htttp_error_process.pl

This feature lets you do on-the-fly analysis of your traffic, send data to databases, email notification of server errors, or any variety of other data handling, rather than have to use the built-in logging functions.

There are a number of considerations when using piped logging:

- *Security* The logging process will be started as root or whichever user you are when you start the server. Make sure that the program that will handle logging is secure and can't be hijacked by some nefarious user.

  Also make sure that you specify a full path to the program. If you rely on your environment path to locate the program, you may end up running the wrong program, or someone might put another program that doesn't do what you were expecting earlier in your path.

- *Buffering* Carelessly written programs might try to buffer all their output until the program exits. The logging process will be launched when the server is started and will stay active until the server is stopped. This may be days or even months; if your program buffers its output for all this time, the process will grow very large. Make sure that you don't buffer your output.

- *Virtual hosts* If your virtual hosts inherit their log settings from the main server configuration, there will be just one instance of the log process—that is, the server won't automatically spawn separate copies of the log process for each virtual host. You have to do this yourself if that is what you want to happen.

## A Simple Piped Logging Example

So that you have a general idea of what a logging process might look like, Listing 18.1 shows a very simple example written in Perl. The example takes log data and writes it to a file if it satisfies certain criteria.

> **Note**
>
> This particular example could be better implemented by the CustomLog directive with the conditional parameters discussed earlier, but this is just an example to show you how you might write such a handler.

18

LOGGING

The program will be located at `/usr/bin/loghander.pl`, so the following directive needs to be set in your `httpd.conf` file:

```
CustomLog |/usr/bin/loghandler.pl common
```

The program will receive log data, in common log format, on standard input. If the request came from a host on the `databeam.com` network, it will write the value of the remote host, and the document that it received, to a log file.

**LISTING 18.1**    A Simple Logging Example

```perl
#!/usr/bin/perl
use strict;
my (@fields, $hostname, $doc);
$| = 1; # Turn off buffering!

# Read data from standard input, and process it
while (<>)
{
    # Lines look like
    # rbowen.databeam.com - - [13/Aug/1999:12:09:48 -0400]
    # "GET / HTTP/1.0" 200 1945
    @fields = split (/ /, $_);
    $hostname = $fields[0]; # First field
    if ($hostname =~ /databeam\.com/i)
    {
        # Open the log file for appending data
        open (LOG, ">>/var/log/httpd/customlog");

        $doc = $fields[6];
        print LOG "$hostname got $doc\n";

        close LOG;
    }
} # End of while block
```

This example has some problems. The most glaring of these is the fact that I open and close a file every single time I get a matching log entry, which is very slow. We could fix this by moving the `open` and `close` statements out of the `while` block. And there are some other optimizations that we could make. But hopefully this illustrates how you might go about writing a simple log handler.

## A Somewhat More Complicated Example

A more realistic example might be writing log data to a database. The example in Listing 18.2 does just that, using the Perl DBI module to write to a MySQL database.

> **Note**
>
> For more information on DBI and MySQL, look at the DBI Web site
> (http://www.symbolstone.org/technology/perl/DBI/index.html) and the
> MySQL Web site (http://www.mysql.org/).

**Listing 18.2** A More Realistic Example

```perl
#!/usr/bin/perl
use strict;
use DBI;

my ($dbh, $sth, $hostname, $doc);

# Open connection to database;
$dbh = DBI->connect('DBI:mysql:accesslog', 'username',
        'password') or die "Could not connect to database: $DBI::errstr";

# Get log data
while (<>)
{
    @fields = split (/ /, $_);
    $hostname = $fields[0]; # First field
    if ($hostname =~ /databeam\.com/i)
    {
        $doc = $fields[6];
        $sth = $dbh->prepare("insert into data
                (hostname, document)
                values
                ($hostname, $doc)
                ");
        $sth->execute;
        $sth->finish;
    }  # End if
}  # End while

END { $dbh->disconnect; }
```

> **Note**
>
> When the server is stopped or restarted, Apache will try to have the logging
> process exit gracefully, so the END block should get executed, but it might not.
> Also, as of version 1.3, if Apache determines that the logging process has gone
> away, hung, or just not been reading its input recently, it will attempt to restart
> the logging process.

Here are a few other ideas of how you might use piped logs:

- Send email to the server admin when there is a CGI error. (This could also be accomplished with an `ErrorDocument` directive pointing to a CGI program.)
- Automatically start a new log file at the end of each day.
- Dynamically generate up-to-the-minute statistical graphs.
- Handle hostname resolution in a separate process, rather than in the server process.

# Log Analysis Tools

Now you have all this great data in your log files. It's not a whole lot of good to you unless you can get real information out of it. At the very least, you can count how many lines are in the file and get an idea of how many hits your site has received, but that is a very misleading number, since every HTML page, as well as every image on each page, shows up as an HTTP request, and so that number may have very little connection to how many actual people visited your site.

It's therefore necessary to have some way of crunching all that data into meaningful numbers. How many people looked at my site? What pages are getting the most attention? What pages are people not finding? What CGI programs are breaking? What pages are getting no visits at all?

The following sections look at some of the commercially available tools for parsing your server logs, as well as some of the packages available for writing your own homegrown log analysis tools in Perl, the Practical Extraction and Report Language, which was designed specifically for this type of work.

## Available Log Analysis Packages

Here are some of the tools that you can download or buy. Most of these will generate graphs and reports for you. Some have more features than others—it's really a question of how much information you need from your logs and what sort of information you're looking for.

> **Note**
>
> Most of the available log analysis tools assume (at least in their default configurations) that you're using the Common Log Format or, in some cases, the Extended Log Format. Some of them can be customized to recognize whatever log format you want to use.

For a large list of other log file analysis programs, see
`http://www.uu.se/Software/Analyzers/Access-analyzers.html`.

## Wusage

**Company:** Boutell.com

**Available from:** `http://www.boutell.com/wusage/`

**Runs on:** Linux, Solaris, and many other versions of UNIX, MacOS, and Windows 95/98/NT.

**Cost:** $75

> **Note**
>
> A time-out version of this product is available on the CD-ROM that came with this book.

**Summary:** Wusage is one of the best log analysis tools available, especially for the price. It generates an "executive summary," which lists the total number of visits, the number of distinct addresses seen in the log, and a variety of other information that might be useful for a quick overview of how the site is doing. There are also detailed graphs (as in Figure 18.1) for the whole site and for individual pages within the site.

**FIGURE 18.1**

*Sample output from Wusage.*

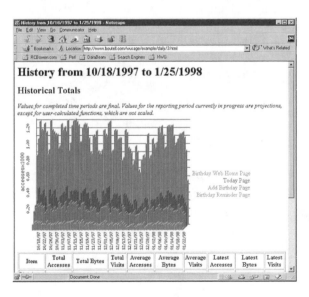

Wusage defines a visit as a particular user coming to the site, looking at one or more pages, and then leaving the site. If more than 5 minutes have elapsed since the last page requested by a particular host, that visit is considered to have ended. If a user requests more documents after that, it's considered to be a new visit. This amount of time is configurable. Wusage allows you to look at the visit "trails" of particular users—what pages they got, in what order, and how long they seem to have spent on each one. This information is particularly useful in determining how people use your site, in order to improve your site navigation.

## wwwstat

**Author:** Roy Fielding, University of California, Irvine

**Available from:** `http://www.ics.uci.edu/pub/websoft/wwwstat/` or on the CD-ROM that accompanies this book.

**Runs on:** Any system with Perl

**Cost:** Free

**Summary:** wwwstat is one of the oldest and most widely used log analysis tools available. There hasn't been a new version released since November 1996, but the Common Log Format (CLF) hasn't changed since then either, so you could argue that there was really no need to release any more versions.

wwwstat generates HTML pages (see Figure 18.2) that summarize the access statistics for your server, including such information as what times of day your server is the busiest, how many files were requested, how many bytes were transferred to clients, and what countries your visitors came from.

**Figure 18.2**

*Sample output from wwwstat.*

A free add-on product called *gr_wwwstat* is available that coverts wwwstat reports into graphs. You can get gr_wwwstat at `http://www.public.iastate.edu/~oz/gr_wwwstat/`. There used to be another product called *gwstat* that did the same thing, and you will find many references to it, but it's no longer available.

> **Note**
>
> gr_wwwstat isn't available on the CD-ROM that came with this book, because explaining how to install it would involve some subjects that are beyond the scope of this book. The gr_wwwstat Web site provides more information.

## WebTrends

**Company:** WebTrends

**Available from:** `http://www.webtrends.com/`

**Runs on:** Windows NT, Solaris, Linux

**Cost:** $399–$15,000

**Summary:** Although WebTrends appears to generate reports very similar to what Wusage generates (see Figure 18.3), it's priced between 5 and 200 times as much, aiming at the corporate market with deep pockets.

**Figure 18.3**

*Sample output from WebTrends.*

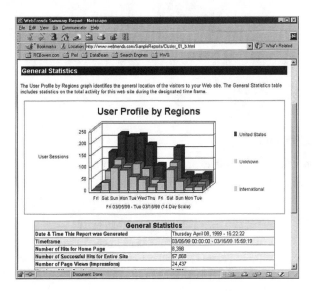

## The Webalizer

**Author:** Bradford L. Barrett

**Available from:** `http://www.mrunix.net/webalizer/`

**Runs on:** A wide selection of UNIX platforms, as well as MacOS, OS/2, and Windows.

**Cost:** Free

**Summary:** The Webalizer produces detailed statistics in various formats (see Figure 18.4) and several languages. Source code is available, so you can build it yourself, but binaries are also available for several versions of UNIX, MacOS, OS/2, and Windows. The Webalizer is released under the GNU General Public License, so it's free, and you are free to modify it and redistribute it as much as you like.

**FIGURE 18.4**

*Sample output from The Webalizer.*

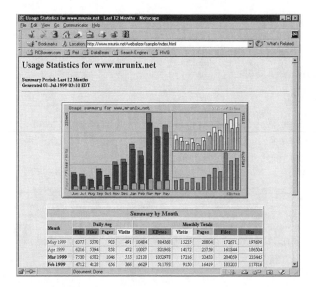

## Do It Yourself

For those of you who have a little experience with Perl and a little time on your hands, you might want to try making your own analysis tool—particularly if you are interested in a very specific piece of information or don't need anything as elaborate as some of the preceding tools.

Perl is particularly well suited to doing this kind of task. A number of tools available for download are written in Perl. The basic method for extracting data from an Apache log file is actually very simple. What you then do with this data is up to you.

The code snippet in Listing 18.3 will read in data from an Apache log file and split it up into its component parts.

**LISTING 18.3**    A Simple Log-Processing Script in Perl

```
open (LOG, '/var/logs/httpd/access_log');
while (<LOG>)      {
    ($host, $logname, $username, $datetime, $zone,
     $method, $URL, $HTTPver, $return, $bytes)
    #  Remove extra characters
    $datetime =~ s/^\[//;
    $zone =~ s/\]$//;
    $method =~ s/^"//;
    $HTTPver =~ s/"$//;
     = split (/ /, $_);
    ... do stuff with these values ...
}  #  End while
```

Remember that one line from the log file looks like:

```
192.101.203.72 - - [12/May/1999:23:25:11 -0400]
➥"GET /apache.html HTTP/1.0" 200 108
```

You will probably want to remove some of the extra characters that aren't part of the actual data, such as the square brackets ([]) around the date and time and the quotes ("") around the HTTP request.

In addition to the method of doing things yourself in Listing 18.3, a Perl module is also available from CPAN that does much of this for you and provides you with a nice object-oriented interface to the data that is much easier to use. The module, called Apache::ParseLog, is available in the /modules/by-module/Apache/ directory on CPAN.

**18**

LOGGING

**Note**

CPAN, the Comprehensive Perl Archive Network, is a network of mirrored FTP sites containing the combined wisdom of the Perl community. You can find modules there to do just about anything that you might ever want to do in Perl, from managing socket connections (the IO::Socket module) to figuring out what gender someone is from a name (the Text::GenderFromName module). You can find one CPAN site at http://www.cpan.org/.

# Rotating Your Log Files

As your server runs, your server logs will grow. Eventually, the file size will start affecting server performance, not to mention filling up your disk space. It's therefore useful to *rotate* your log files occasionally. Rotating log files just means that you remove the old one—usually archiving it—and start with a fresh one. You might want to do this weekly, daily, or even hourly, depending on your server's activity level.

Most flavors of UNIX come with some `logrotate` facility. If yours didn't or if you're running Apache on Windows NT, the concept is simple: You want to move the existing log file to some archive location and probably compress it in some fashion. Then, create a new, empty file in the log directory. Restart the HTTP server, and it will start logging to the new file.

> **Note**
>
> It's important to restart the HTTP server after creating a new log file. On some systems, Apache keeps track of its position in the log file. It will continue to try to write to that location in the file, even after the new file has been put in place. This can cause some strange behavior, as Apache tries to write to a nonexistent location in the file.

# Summary

The Apache server will log data to a file, or a process, to give you information about what clients are accessing your server, what documents they are requesting, and what goes wrong. Various tools are available for analyzing this data, or you can write your own log analyzer or logging process to generate any statistics that interest you.

# Development

# PART
# V

# Introduction to Apache Modules

This chapter attempts to explain what modules are, how they can be used, and which ones you'll likely work with. You'll see how to configure and install modules into Apache and learn about advanced techniques for writing your own modules.

First, you must understand why Apache has "modules." To do that, this chapter will briefly focus on the concept of code modularization in software.

# What Are Apache Modules?

Modules provide the key glue that Web sites of all sizes use when customizing the server for their needs. Without modules, Apache certainly wouldn't be as capable or as popular as it is today. In fact, it would be difficult to put the Apache server into productive use without at least understanding the basics of modules. In the future, Apache modules will play a more significant role.

More than 40 modules are now distributed with Apache 1.3.9. They are listed and described briefly later in this chapter and in more detail in Chapter 20, "Using Standard Apache Modules."

## Code Modularization

*Program modularity* is a key concept. Its advantages are better extensibility (extending the program by adding features), better decomposition (developing and testing features independently of each other), and configuration flexibility (enabling or disabling features as needed).

Software features can be changed when the program is created (compile time) or before execution (dynamic). Some advanced software packages allow for the addition or removal of features while the program is running (runtime). Apache has historically provided compile-time customization but supports dynamic in recent versions.

> **Note**
>
> This text is making a vast simplification to describe modules simply as *add-on features*. Modules are actually sophisticated operating system objects that can be loaded into or shared among other running programs. Modules are also commonplace and can be found as Windows dynamic link libraries and UNIX shared object libraries. They work by replacing elements of the *symbol table*, the table of contents generated when a program is created. For more information, read the section "Shared Libraries," later in this chapter. The Apache Software Foundation also provides online information about modules at
> `http://www.apache.org/docs/dso.html`.

Modularization usually doesn't affect the real availability of features themselves. A program doesn't have to be modularized. However, the trend in software is to modularize all features—which is the path Apache development takes. The Apache Web server is currently distributed with approximately 40 separate modules. Hundreds of additional modules are available from commercial vendors and open source projects.

# A Restaurant Analogy

To properly understand the motivation for modules, you can reasonably compare software with a restaurant. Menu elements are analogous to the features of a software package (see Table 19.1).

Most commercial packages come with a predefined set of features and fixed system requirements. This is the "house special" at a reasonable restaurant or the "value meal," for those of you who are into fast food. This is how most software is sold and used.

**TABLE 19.1**    Software Modules Versus Restaurant Choice Analogy

|  | *Software* | *Food* |
| --- | --- | --- |
| No Modules | The vendor provides a predefined set of features and occasional upgrades to new versions. | *"House Special":* You choose the restaurant but take whatever is offered that day. |
| Compile-Time Modules | You choose and purchase the features you want in the software once. You can't change the features without buying the whole product again. | *Standard Restaurant Menu:* You choose what you want to eat from their list and make an order. |
| Dynamic Modules | Not only can you choose the features you want in the software, but you also can add features any time you want before loading the application. | *World's Greatest Cafeteria:* You can order any dish you want every time you go there, but you can't order anything new after you sit down. |
| Runtime Modules | You choose the features you want and can add features without having to shut the application down. | *Cafeteria with a Waiter:* You order any dish you want anytime during the meal. |

**19**

**INTRODUCTION TO APACHE MODULES**

The advantage of the House Special is that it's usually economical and does what you need it to do. The disadvantage is that your control of the dining process is restricted primarily to which restaurant you choose and the House Specials available.

If you want to replace the Big Mac that comes with your Coke and fries with a salad, you can't do that while paying the value meal price. To get your choices, you need to order items on the menu separately.

Compile-time modularization is the analogy for ordering items on the menu. You tell the cashier what you want, taking into account your desires, budget, and health requirements. You have to do more work, probably pay a little more, but you get exactly what you want. Compile-time modularization allows users to select the features they want and determine the software configuration based on the system requirements they're willing to expend.

Dynamic code modularization is a different type of restaurant. Think of a cafeteria that has ready whatever you might want to order. You take your tray, choose the specific items you want today and pay for the meal prior to eating. A cafeteria approach to software is more feasible than the real-world approach because the replication cost in cyberspace is almost zero. If cafeterias had the same quality as restaurants and nearly the same cost, we'd probably eat at them often.

Obviously, the dynamic approach has all the advantages of the modularization for little extra cost. If Microsoft knew how to make it amazingly easy for users to select or remove features they wanted at startup, we'd all be using a word processor that was perfect for us. We couldn't complain about the system requirements of Microsoft Office if we controlled what it contained. We could build a miniature version for the old family PC and a fully decked out one for the new computer at work.

Obviously, modularization is very important to long-term customer satisfaction with software. Fortunately, Apache is very open to modularization because it has some additional benefits for the development of an open source Web server. New modules can be written, debugged, and rewritten without significant effect on a running server, and modules are typically managed by different developers who are experts in their use.

# Modularization History

The first modular architecture for Apache, released in August 1995, supported compile-time modules. The standard modules were defined and included in Apache 1.0, released in December 1995. Dynamic module loading was defined and implemented in version 1.3.

New modules are now created by using the Apache API, a set of written specifications for programming interfaces. Netscape and Microsoft have their own APIs: NSAPI and ISAPI, respectively.

# Standard Uses

Modules provide a means for extending Apache's functionality at a low level. The core section of a Web server is really just a fileserver responding to HTTP requests. Modules are frequently used for custom security extensions, specific application and programming language interfaces, customized logging, specific server operation and performance modifications, URL parsing, and support for additional types of content. The following sections cover these usage types in detail.

## Authentication

*Authentication* is technospeak for proving one's identity. The Internet is the perfect anonymous medium, where you can visit any site with just a mouse click. Visits merge into one large stream of bytes into and out of networks. However, you and other organizations will eventually want to control or otherwise track access to sensitive online resources. Anonymity can go only so far toward enabling the wired millennium.

Proving one's identity requires that the authenticator and the authenticatee agree on one of the following:

- Something only the authenticatee knows
- Something only the authenticatee has
- Something only the authenticatee can do

A username/password combination is the predominant example of something a visitor might be required to know. Many organizations now require important employees to use electronic devices that display changing passwords (something only the authenticatee has). Finally, access to data may be allowed within an organization's internal network but forbidden to other visitors by a firewall. Accessing the data is something only the authenticatee can do.

Generally, the best security is a combination of something that someone knows and has (your ATM card and PIN, for example). The weakest security usually relies only on something that someone can do. In this case, after an intruder breaches the first line of defense, he can beat any succeeding layer with increasing ease (each layer allows him to pretend to be able to do more).

Apache is bundled with several modules providing standard authentication capabilities. However, additional modules are available on the Web. Table 19.2 lists all readily available authentication modules.

**TABLE 19.2**  Modules Providing Authentication Capabilities

| Module Name | Description |
| --- | --- |
| mod_auth | Authenticate via standard Apache methods (htaccess and htgroup files) |
| mod_auth_db | Modified mod_auth to use the Berkeley DB routines with htaccess and htgroup files |
| mod_auth_dbm | Modified mod_auth to use the GNU DBM routines with htaccess and htgroup files |
| mod_auth_cookie | Authenticate via cookie |
| mod_auth_cookie_file | Authenticate via cookie and password file |
| mod_auth_external | Authenticate via external program |
| mod_auth_system | Authenticate via standard UNIX password file |
| mod_auth_yp | Authenticate via NIS (UNIX-based network authentication service) |
| mod_auth_cookie_msql | Authenticate via cookies and mSQL |
| mod_auth_NDS | Authenticate via NDS (Novell's Network Directory Service) |
| mod_ldap | Authenticate via LDAP (Lightweight Directory Access Protocol) |
| mod_auth_kerb | Authenticate via Kerberos (widely deployed security framework developed at MIT) |
| mod_auth_mysql | Authenticate via MySQL (a common UNIX open source database) |
| mod_auth_pgsql | Authenticate via PostgreSQL (another common UNIX open source database) |
| mod_auth_radius | Authenticate via RADIUS (network authentication service frequently used in ISPs) |
| mod_auth_samba | Authenticate via Samba (UNIX tool to access Windows network authentication and fileservers) |
| PAM Auth | Authenticate via PAM (new UNIX scheme for authentication services interoperability) |
| mod_auth_notes | Authenticate via Lotus Notes |
| mod_auth_nt_module | Authenticate via Windows NT security |
| mod_auth_tacacs | Authenticate via TACACS (network device security framework developed by Cisco Systems and others) |
| mod_auth_anon | Authenticate by using anonymous username/password pair, similar to most public FTP servers |
| mod_auth_digest | Extension to mod_auth to support MD5 digest authentication (experimental) |

If you don't see the authentication mechanism in Table 19.2, that doesn't mean it isn't available. New modules are frequently listed at `http://modules.apache.org/`.

# Authorization

Authentication isn't a complete foundation for Web-based security by itself. There is also authorization and accounting. *Authorization* determines what access someone is allowed to have once he has proven his identity. *Accounting* logs the actions taken by visitors.

The authentication modules in Table 19.2 can also provide authorization or accounting directly or indirectly through the network security frameworks they access. Table 19.3 lists authorization modules available within Apache, elsewhere on the Web, and even on the CD-ROM accompanying this book.

**TABLE 19.3**   Authorization Modules

| Module Name | Description |
|---|---|
| mod_allowdev | Restrict access to filespace more efficiently |
| disallow_id | Disallow serving Web pages based on UNIX uid/gid |
| user/domain access control | Allow or disallow access to user/domain pair |

# Encryption

Encryption allows for the private communication of information on the Internet. Authentication, authorization, and accounting ensure that only selected individuals can access sensitive information on a Web server, but they don't defend against eavesdropping after the information leaves the server or a visitor's desktop. Depending on the virtual distance and routing, others might be able to listen in on traffic and reconstruct content.

Many commercial Web servers, including Apache variants, are sold primarily on the value added by their encryption modules. These *e-commerce servers* usually implement the SSL protocol to transmit credit card numbers securely. Encryption can also be used to generally secure authentication, authorization, and accounting. The following encryption module is freely available:

    `mod_ssl`                Free Apache interface to SSLeay

Detailed coverage of commercial SSL implementations and SSLeay is found in Chapter 23, "Other Well-Known Modules."

# Application and Language Support

Useful Web sites are interactive. Their content may be updated regularly by an external process or created dynamically. Web servers must be able to send user input to and receive HTML pages from Web applications. Numerous modules are available.

The predominant modules are mod_cgi and mod_perl. CGI (common gateway interface) is described in detail in Chapter 11, "CGI Programming"; mod_cgi is covered in Chapter 20. Perl is a scripting language commonly used to create CGI applications; mod_perl is described in detail in Chapter 21, "Using the Perl Module." Industry speculation is that server-side applications written in Java will outpace CGI/Perl in the near future.

Embedded scripting languages and interfaces to application servers have also become popular. The three-layer site architecture, composed of a Web server that communicates with an application server that stores all content on a database server, is being used as the basis for e-commerce ventures. Table 19.4 lists modules included with Apache or readily available on the Web.

**TABLE 19.4**  Widely Used Application and Language Support Modules

| Module Name | Description |
| --- | --- |
| mod_cgi | Common gateway interface |
| Includes | Server-side includes |
| mod_perl | Embed Perl interpreters to avoid CGI overhead and provide a Perl interface to the server API |
| ColdFusion Module | Interface to the ColdFusion application server |
| PyApache (mod_pyapache) | Embedded Python language interpreter |
| mod_php, mod_php3 | Server-side scripting language with extensive database support |
| mod_dtcl | Open source server parsed Tcl for Apache |
| Cold Flame | Alpha version of a module to parse ColdFusion code using MySQL |
| FastCGI | Keeps CGI processes alive to avoid per-hit forks |
| Java Wrapper Module | Enables direct execution of Java applications as CGI |
| mod_cgisock | Socket implementation of CGI |
| mod_ecgi | Embedded (non-forking) CGI |
| mod_javascript | JavaScript module (ECMA-262) |
| mod_jserv | Java servlet interface |
| JRun | Deploy server-side Java applications that use Java servlets and JavaServer pages |
| mod_fjord | Java back-end processor |

# Diagnostics and Counters

Some modules provide information about the Web server itself, including internal statistics and page accesses. The modules in Table 19.5 are included with Apache; you also can find them on the CD-ROM accompanying this book.

**TABLE 19.5**   Diagnostic and Web Counter Modules

| Module Name | Description |
| --- | --- |
| mod_status | Server status display |
| mod_info | Server configuration information |
| mod_cntr | Automatic URL access counter via DBM file |
| WebCounter | Dynamically count Web page access |

# Logging

*Logging* is a critical component of the Apache server functionality. It provides the means to diagnose server problems, alert human operators, document access to the site, and provide data for statistical analysis of visitor traffic.

The names and formats of server log files are configurable. Session and referral data is frequently added. Table 19.6 includes modules included with Apache; you also can find them on the CD-ROM that comes with this book.

**TABLE 19.6**   Customized Logging Modules

| Module Name | Module Description |
| --- | --- |
| mod_log_agent | Logging of user agents |
| mod_log_config | Standard logging in the Common Logfile format |
| mod_log_referer | Logging of document references |
| dir_log_module | Implements per-directory logging |

# Server Operations

Occasionally, developers and system administrators need to change the manner in which the Apache server itself responds to URL requests. These may include rewriting the URL, referring visitors elsewhere, or enacting or limiting server capabilities.

These modules can be very complex to configure. Table 19.7 lists such modules included with Apache; you also can find them on the CD-ROM that accompanies this book.

**19**

**INTRODUCTION TO APACHE MODULES**

**TABLE 19.7**  Modules Affecting Server Operation

| Module Name | Module Description |
| --- | --- |
| rewrite_module | Powerful URI-to-filename mapping using regular expressions |
| mod_vhost_alias | Support for dynamically configured mass virtual hosting |
| mod_headers | Add arbitrary HTTP headers to resources |
| mod_access | Host-based access control |
| mod_speling | Automatically correct minor typos in URLs |
| mod_unique_id | Generate unique request identifier for every request |
| mod_usertrack | User tracking using cookies |
| mod_alias | Aliases and redirects |
| mod_bandwidth | Bandwidth management on a per-connection basis |
| mod_cache | Automatic caching of documents |
| mod_lock | Conditional locking mechanism for document trees |
| mod_session | Session management and tracking via identifiers |
| mod_throttle | Suppress access by individual users |
| UserPath | Provide a different method of mapping user URLs |

# Content Support

Apache serves up much more than HTML. Nearly any content type created can be made to work, if the appropriate handler and identification methods are implemented. This is important because not only must the server be able to process the content type, it must notify the visitor to expect to receive new forms of content and then send the information in an optimized, error-handling manner.

Multimedia types are obvious examples, but even the more mundane document types need to be treated differently. Realizing the importance of this, Microsoft has recently made Web server integration an important part of its Office 2000 support. You can expect operating system/Internet integration to push more content-handling capabilities into the Web server. Historically, content identification has been handled through MIME (multipart Internet mail extensions). Apache handles MIME through standard modules and supports additional types through custom modules. Note that some of the more complex media types are now handled through separate servers.

Languages other than English must be accurately displayed for native visitors. These modules are available, as shown in Table 19.8.

**TABLE 19.8**   Content Support Modules

| Module Name | Module Description |
|---|---|
| mod_mime | Determining document types using file extensions |
| mod_mime_magic | Determining document types using "magic numbers" |
| mod_negotiation | Content negotiation |
| mod_expires | Apply Expires: headers to resources |
| mod_actions | File type/method–based script execution |
| mod_beza | Module and patch converting national characters |
| mod_fontxlate | Configurable national character set translator |
| mod_charset | Smart Russian Codepage Translations |
| Russian Charset Handling Module | Russian document support in various charsets |
| SSI for ISO-2022-JP | SSI handling ISO-2022-JP encoding documents (Japanese language) |

# A Simple Example of Modules in Action: Server Status

This section describes one of the standard Apache modules, mod_status, which provides diagnostic feedback on the Apache server itself. The operation, configuration, and loading of a simple module will be demonstrated.

You need to install and register a module before it can be used within Apache. Modules also might need to be configured. Installing modules is covered in the next section.

After a module is installed, it needs to be loaded into Apache. The simplest way to do that is before Apache is started, by placing AddModule and LoadModule commands into httpd.conf. Otherwise, the apxs and apachectl commands can be used.

For the mod_status module, the relevant lines are as follows:

```
LoadModule status_module    lib/apache/mod_status.so
AddModule mod_status.c
```

The LoadModule command is necessary to make the module available to Apache. The AddModule command specifies the order of execution.

The mod_status module works by creating a virtual link between a user-specified URL and HTTP connection statistics in the Apache server. You can tell Apache to associate a URL with the module by inserting a SetHandler command:

**19**

**INTRODUCTION TO APACHE MODULES**

```
<location /server-status>
SetHandler server-status
</location>
```

> **Note**
>
> It's recommended that all administrative/management URLs be protected from outside access. In this case, you'd want to add the following lines inside the `/server-status` location definition:
>
> ```
> order deny, allow
> allow from your-ip-addr-block
> deny from all
> ```

Recent versions of Apache have also added an option to show extended status information. This can be enabled by setting the `ExtendedStatus` variable to `on`.

At this point, the Apache server needs to be restarted to activate your changes. You can use either `apachectl` or the normal service restarting process on your OS.

> **Note**
>
> The Apache error logs should be checked anytime the server is restarted after significant configuration changes. New module activations are notorious for requiring troubleshooting. Module activations can be confirmed in the Apache startup.

With any luck, if you send your browser to the `/extended-status` URL, you should now see something similar to Figure 19.1.

For more information about the meaning of the fields and modifying the output of `mod_status`, see the module reference material in Chapter 20.

**FIGURE 19.1**

*Apache
server status for
keats.jalan.com.*

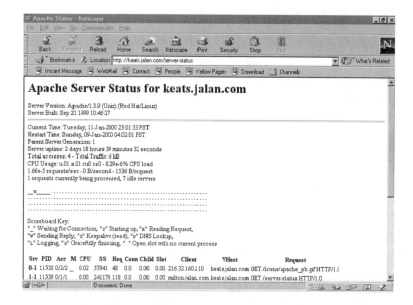

## Installing Modules

Installing modules can be more complicated than configuring them. Before investigating the relevant procedures for standard Apache modules, briefly examine the operating system concepts associated with loading modules.

### Shared Libraries

The preceding section discussed software modularization and why it's done. At a much lower level, programs tend to share the same tasks (open files, write data to the screen, and so on). Programs can do these things because the machine code that tells the computer exactly how to do its tasks is inserted during the final stages of compilation.

In truth, each element of code functionality is given a name, and the start location in memory of its machine instructions is indexed into a table, called the *symbol table*. The symbol table is stored inside the executable and is read on program startup. The code fragment main is looked up and executed first.

Elements referenced inside a symbol table don't need to be part of the executable itself. Some elements naturally belong to the operating system or other functionality. In these cases, the symbol table merely contains a request to the operating system for loading the appropriate section.

*Shared library* is the name given to file system constructs that contain shared code for use by applications or an operating system.

19

INTRODUCTION TO
APACHE MODULES

For example, consider the world-famous program written in the C language and shown in Listing 19.1.

**LISTING 19.1**    helloWorld.c

```
Int main(int argc, char *argv[])
{
    printf("Hello World!");
    exit(0);
}
```

On Linux systems, this program would be compiled with the command

```
gcc -g helloWorld.c -o helloWorld
```

The program simply prints out "Hello World!" and exits. We can inquire into its use of shared libraries by using the ldd command:

```
ldd helloWorld
    libc.so.6 => /lib/libc.so.6 (0x4001b000)
    /lib/ld-linux.so.2 => /lib/ld-linux.so.2 (0x40000000)
```

In this case, the symbol table for helloWorld contains shortcuts to Libc.so.6 and ld-linux.so.2. Both are shared libraries, hence the .so extension. libc contains standard operating system and C constructs, such as printf. ld-linux.so.2 itself is a special case, containing the code for interacting with libraries.

> **Note**
>
> Obviously, the quickest way to disable a UNIX server is to delete or otherwise make unreadable the libc and ld libraries. Indeed, there are many horror stories of OS upgrades gone awry. The only way to recover is to reboot from a rescue media and copy the libraries back into place. Some binaries are compiled explicitly without any reference to shared libraries to help recover from such disasters.

We can also use the nm command to inspect the symbol table of the helloWorld executable itself, as shown in Listing 19.2.

**LISTING 19.2**    Hello World Symbol Table

```
nm helloWorld
08049480 ? _DYNAMIC
08049460 ? _GLOBAL_OFFSET_TABLE_
0804842c R _IO_stdin_used
08049454 ? __CTOR_END__
08049450 ? __CTOR_LIST__
```

```
0804945c ? __DTOR_END__
08049458 ? __DTOR_LIST__
0804944c ? __EH_FRAME_BEGIN__
0804944c ? __FRAME_END__
08049520 A __bss_start
08049440 D __data_start
         U __deregister_frame_info@@GLIBC_2.0
080483e0 t __do_global_ctors_aux
08048350 t __do_global_dtors_aux
         U __gmon_start__
         U __libc_start_main@@GLIBC_2.0
         U __register_frame_info@@GLIBC_2.0
08049520 A _edata
08049538 A _end
0804840c A _etext
0804840c ? _fini
         U _fp_hw
08048298 ? _init
08048320 T _start
08049448 d completed.3
08049440 W data_start
08048398 t fini_dummy
0804944c d force_to_data
0804944c d force_to_data
080483a0 t frame_dummy
08048344 t gcc2_compiled.
08048350 t gcc2_compiled.
080483e0 t gcc2_compiled.
0804840c t gcc2_compiled.
080483c8 t gcc2_compiled.
080483c0 t init_dummy
08048404 t init_dummy
080483c8 T main
08049520 b object.8
08049444 d p.2
         U printf@@GLIBC_2.0
```

For the most part, the symbol table appears to be unreadable magic. It's meant to be read only by the computer, but we can see the references to main, printf, and the startup/closeup code. The format of the table is one line per symbol table entry, showing the start of memory, type of symbol, and symbol name. The nm command can also be used on shared libraries.

The importance of learning these utilities is that Apache modules are sophisticated examples of shared libraries. Returning to our Red Hat Linux system running Apache 1.3.9, note the typical modules found in the modules directory:

```
[root@keats modules]# ls
httpd.exp              mod_bandwidth.so        mod_macro.so
```

| | | |
|---|---|---|
| imap.so | mod_cern_meta.so | mod_mime.so |
| libcache.so | mod_cgi.so | mod_mime_magic.so |
| libperl.so | mod_cvs.so | mod_mmap_static.so |
| libphp3.so | mod_digest.so | mod_negotiation.so |
| libproxy.so | mod_dir.so | mod_peephole.so |
| mod_access.so | mod_disallow_id.so | mod_php.so |
| mod_actions.so | mod_eaccess.so | mod_put.so |
| mod_alias.so | mod_env.so | mod_qs2ssi.so |
| mod_allowdev.so | mod_example.so | mod_rewrite.so |
| mod_asis.so | mod_expires.so | mod_roaming.so |
| mod_auth.so | mod_fastcgi.so | mod_session.so |
| mod_auth_anon.so | mod_headers.so | mod_setenvif.so |
| mod_auth_cookie.so | mod_imap.so | mod_speling.so |
| mod_auth_cookie_file.so | mod_include.so | mod_status.so |
| mod_auth_db.so | mod_info.so | mod_unique_id.so |
| mod_auth_dbm.so | mod_ip_forwarding.so | mod_urlcount.so |
| mod_auth_external.so | mod_lock.so | mod_userdir.so |
| mod_auth_inst.so | mod_log_agent.so | mod_usertrack.so |
| mod_auth_system.so | mod_log_config.so | mod_vhost_alias.so |
| mod_autoindex.so | mod_log_referer.so | pgsql.so |

Notice that all modules have an `.so` extension, the same extension used by shared libraries in UNIX. We can inspect the symbol table of these modules, starting with the status modules described in the previous section. Notice also that the symbol table is different from the simple C application just reviewed (see Listing 19.3).

**LISTING 19.3**    Symbol Table of an Apache Module

```
[root@keats modules]# nm mod_status.so
00000000 A GCC.INTERNAL
0000679c A _DYNAMIC
000066f8 A _GLOBAL_OFFSET_TABLE_
000066ec ? __CTOR_END__
000066e8 ? __CTOR_LIST__
000066f4 ? __DTOR_END__
000066f0 ? __DTOR_LIST__
000066e4 ? __EH_FRAME_BEGIN__
000066e4 ? __FRAME_END__
         U ___brk_addr@@GLIBC_2.0
00006844 A __bss_start
         U __curbrk@@GLIBC_2.0
         U __deregister_frame_info@@GLIBC_2.0
000047a0 t __do_global_ctors_aux
00000be0 t __do_global_dtors_aux
         U __environ@@GLIBC_2.0
         U __gmon_start__
         U __register_frame_info@@GLIBC_2.0
00006844 A _edata
00006868 A _end
```

```
00004800 A _etext
00004800 ? _fini
000009d0 ? _init
         U ap_check_cmd_context
         U ap_escape_html
         U ap_exists_scoreboard_image
         U ap_extended_status
         U ap_get_server_built
         U ap_get_server_name
         U ap_get_server_version
         U ap_hard_timeout
         U ap_ht_time
         U ap_kill_timeout
         U ap_log_rerror
         U ap_my_generation
         U ap_psignature
         U ap_restart_time
         U ap_rprintf
         U ap_rputc
         U ap_rputs
         U ap_rvputs
         U ap_scoreboard_image
         U ap_send_http_header
         U ap_sync_scoreboard_image
         U ap_table_set
         U atexit@@GLIBC_2.0
000065e4 d completed.3
         U difftime@@GLIBC_2.0
00000c3c t fini_dummy
000065e8 d force_to_data
000066e4 d force_to_data
00000d38 t format_byte_out
00000e40 t format_kbyte_out
00000c54 t frame_dummy
00000be0 t gcc2_compiled.
00000be0 t gcc2_compiled.
000047a0 t gcc2_compiled.
00004800 t gcc2_compiled.
00000ca0 t gcc2_compiled.
00000c88 t init_dummy
000047d4 t init_dummy
00006844 b object.8
000065e0 d p.2
00000ca0 t set_extended_status
00000f00 t show_time
0000685c b status_flags
00001170 t status_handler
00006660 d status_handlers
0000472c t status_init
```

19

INTRODUCTION TO
APACHE MODULES

*continues*

**LISTING 19.3**   continued

```
00006680 D status_module
00006600 d status_module_cmds
00006630 d status_options
         U strcasecmp@@GLIBC_2.0
         U strcmp@@GLIBC_2.0
         U strlen@@GLIBC_2.0
         U strstr@@GLIBC_2.0
         U sysconf@@GLIBC_2.0
         U time@@GLIBC_2.0
```

Notice that there are two interesting sets of symbols: those starting with ap and those starting with status.

- The ap symbols refer to routines defined in the Apache API, the library of functions that modules are allowed to call when interfacing with Apache.

- The status symbols refer to routines defined in the status module itself.

It's common for a module to define its own namespace and have init, handler, and option parsing functions. These functions may be sent to Apache for execution on certain conditions/triggers, such as Web server startup. The status module is run whenever the status URL is accessed.

Now that you understand some basic operating system concepts associated with shared libraries and how they are applied to Apache, you can learn more about what makes Apache modules unique.

## Dynamic Shared Objects

Apache 1.3 supports a special type of shared library—the Dynamic Shared Object (DSO). The Apache server can load or unload DSOs as needed. The core Apache program can also be loaded as a DSO, and all the software modules in the standard Apache distribution can be compiled as a DSO. Therefore, it's recommended that you build Apache for maximum flexibility (complete DSO) and reduce the functionality at runtime to only those options needed by the particular installation.

At last report, DSOs were tested on only the following platforms:

FreeBSD versions 2.1.5, 2.2.*x*, 3.*x*, and 4.*x*

OpenBSD 2.*x*

NetBSD 1.3.1

BSDI 3.*x* and 4.*x*

Linux: Debian 1.3.1 and Red Hat 4.2

Solaris 2.4 through 2.7

SunOS 4.1.3

Digital UNIX 4.0

IRIX 5.3 and 6.2

HP/UX 10.20

UnixWare 2.01 and 2.1.2

SCO 5.0.4

AIX 3.2, 4.1.5, 4.2, and 4.3

ReliantUNIX/SINIX 5.43

SVR4

Mac OS X Server 1.0

Mac OS 10.0, preview 1

OpenStep/Mach 4.2

DGUX

Apache 1.3.9 is now also certified to run under Windows NT 4.0 and supports loadable modules. Comments specific to Windows NT can be found at `http://www.apache.org/docs/windows.html`.

# Building Standard Apache Modules

On UNIX platforms, Apache is built using the `configure` and `make` commands. It's assumed that you are already familiar with the generic Apache configuration process described in Chapter 5, "Server Configuration Files." Tables 19.9 and 19.10 describe the options specific to the configuration of modules in the Apache configuration process.

**TABLE 19.9**   Modules Specific Options to Configure

| *Option* | *Description* |
| --- | --- |
| —`enable-module=module_name` | Selects module to be compiled directly into Apache |
| —`enable-shared=module_name` | Selects module to be compiled as a DSO |
| —`add-module=module_name` | Selects module to be compiled directly into Apache (used only for non-standard modules—that is, those not included in the Apache distribution) |
| —`activate-module` | Same as `add-module`, only for more complex cases such as `mod_perl` and `mod_php`, where multiple files are involved |
| —`enable-rule=SHARED_CORE` | Required on some platforms to support DSOs |

**19**

**INTRODUCTION TO APACHE MODULES**

**TABLE 19.10**    List of Standard Modules in Apache 1.3.9

| Module Name | Default | Description |
| --- | --- | --- |
| mod_env | Enabled | Set environment variables for CGI/SSI scripts |
| mod_setenvif | Enabled | Set environment variables based on HTTP headers |
| mod_unique_id | Disabled | Generate unique identifiers for request |
| mod_mime | Enabled | Content type/encoding determination (configured) |
| mod_mime_magic | Disabled | Content type/encoding determination (automatic) |
| mod_negotiation | Enabled | Content selection based on the HTTP Accept* headers |
| mod_alias | Enabled | Simple URL translation and redirection |
| mod_rewrite | Disabled | Advanced URL translation and redirection |
| mod_userdir | Enabled | Selection of resource directories by username |
| mod_speling | Disabled | Correction of misspelled URLs |
| mod_dir | Enabled | Directory and directory default file handling |
| mod_autoindex | Enabled | Automated directory index file generation |
| mod_access | Enabled | Access control (user, host, and network) |
| mod_auth | Enabled | HTTP basic authentication (user and password) |
| mod_auth_dbm | Disabled | HTTP basic authentication via UNIX NDBM files |
| mod_auth_db | Disabled | HTTP basic authentication via Berkeley DB files |
| mod_auth_anon | Disabled | HTTP basic authentication for anonymous-style users |
| mod_digest | Disabled | HTTP digest authentication |
| mod_headers | Disabled | Arbitrary HTTP response headers (configured) |
| mod_cern_meta | Disabled | Arbitrary HTTP response headers (CERN-style files) |
| mod_expires | Disabled | Expires HTTP responses |
| mod_asis | Enabled | Raw HTTP responses |
| mod_include | Enabled | Server-side includes (SSI) support |
| mod_cgi | Enabled | CGI support |
| mod_actions | Enabled | Map CGI scripts to act as internal handlers |
| mod_status | Enabled | Content handler for server runtime status |
| mod_info | Disabled | Content handler for server configuration summary |
| mod_log_config | Enabled | Customizable logging of requests |
| mod_log_agent | Disabled | Specialized HTTP user-agent logging (deprecated) |
| mod_log_referrer | Disabled | Specialized HTTP referrer logging (deprecated) |
| mod_usertrack | Disabled | Logging of user click-trails via HTTP cookies |
| mod_imap | Enabled | Server-side imagemap support |

| Module Name | Default | Description |
|---|---|---|
| mod_proxy | Disabled | Caching proxy module (HTTP, HTTPS, and FTP) |
| mod_so | Disabled | Dynamic Shared Object (DSO) bootstrapping |
| mod_mmap_static | Disabled | Caching of frequently served pages via mmap() |
| mod_example | Disabled | Apache API demonstration (developers only) |

There are also some special module settings that can be used wherever a module name is required. They are frequently used with the -enable-shared and -enable-module options:

- All   Enable/disable all modules.
- Max   Enable/disable all modules except for the bootstrapping.
- Remain   Enable/disable all modules except those already specified.

# Advanced Modules Installation

Although the standard Apache modules should be sufficient for most installations, sometimes additional modules are needed. The apxs and apachectl utilities are helpful for installing additional modules. Source code for modules can be downloaded from http://modules.apache.org/ or other sites.

## Installing Modules with apxs and apachectl

apxs is a tool for building and installing extension modules for the Apache server. It requires DSO support. Table 19.11 lists options to apxs:

**TABLE 19.11**   apxs Options

| Option | Description |
|---|---|
| -n | Explicitly set module name |
| -q | Perform query |
| -s | Change apxs settings |
| -g | Template generation |
| -c | Separate compilation; usually used to generate .so files |
| -o | Specify name of output DSO |
| -D | Pass variables to compilation process |

*continues*

19

INTRODUCTION TO
APACHE MODULES

**TABLE 19.11**   continued

| Option | Description |
|--------|-------------|
| -I | Add additional includes to compilation |
| -L | Add additional library directories to compilation |
| -l | Link with additional libraries during compilation |
| -Wc | Pass additional flags to compilation process |
| -Wl | Pass additional flags to linking process |
| -i | Install one or more DSOs |
| -a | Activate module by adding AddModule directive to httpd.conf |
| -A | Same as -a, but comment out the AddModule directive |

apachectl, a tool for managing the Apache server itself, allows for the restarting of the Apache server and troubleshooting of module issues. Table 19.12 lists the options to apachectl.

**TABLE 19.12**   apachectl Options

| Option | Description |
|--------|-------------|
| start | Starts the server and gives an error if it's already running. |
| stop | Stops the Apache server. |
| restart | Restarts the Apache daemon by sending it a SIGHUP. If the daemon isn't running, it's started. This command automatically checks the configuration files via configtest before initiating the restart to make sure that Apache doesn't die. |
| fullstatus | Displays a full status report from mod_status. |
| status | Displays a brief status report. |
| graceful | Gracefully restarts the Apache daemon by sending it a SIGUSR1. If the daemon isn't running, it's started. This varies from a normal restart in that currently open connections aren't aborted. |
| configtest | Runs a configuration file syntax test. It parses the configuration files and reports either Syntax OK or detailed information about the particular syntax error. |

Simple external modules can be compiled easily with the following combination of apxs and apachectl:

```
$ apxs -i -a -c mod_foo.c
    gcc -fpic -DSHARED_MODULE -I/path/to/apache/include -c mod_foo.c
    ld -Bshareable -o mod_foo.so mod_foo.o
    cp mod_foo.so /path/to/apache/libexec/mod_foo.so
```

```
      chmod 755 /path/to/apache/libexec/mod_foo.so
      [activating module 'foo' in /path/to/apache/etc/httpd.conf]
$ apachectl restart
      /path/to/apache/sbin/apachectl restart: httpd not running, trying to start
      [Tue Mar 31 11:27:55 1998] [debug] mod_so.c(303): loaded module foo_module
      /path/to/apache/sbin/apachectl restart: httpd started
```

# Installing `mod_perl`

Most sites that depend on Perl/CGI end up using `mod_perl` to improve performance and provide greater integration with Apache. Chapter 21 gives a detailed description of how to use `mod_perl`.

There are many ways to install `mod_perl`, but the most straightforward is to unpack the `mod_perl` distribution in the same parent directory as the Apache distribution, run the `mod_perl` configure script, and recompile Apache with the original options and an additional `mod_perl` activation command:

```
perl Makefile.PL \
    APACHE_PREFIX=/path/to/install/of/apache \
    APACHE_SRC=../apache-1.3.X/src \
    DO_HTTPD=1 \
    USE_APACI=1 \
    EVERYTHING=1

Make
Make test
Make install
```

Because the `mod_perl` makefile doesn't always pass along the proper options to the Apache build script, respond No when it asks whether you want it to rebuild Apache. Then switch back to the Apache distribution directory and rerun the Apache commands you used to originally build Apache, except add `-activate-module=perl` to the arguments.

If all goes well, you will see something like the following the next time you start Apache:

```
[Mon Oct 1 00:02:19 1999] [Notice] Apache/1.3.9 (Unix)  (Red Hat/Linux)
➥mod_perl/1.19 configured — resuming normal operations
```

To make `mod_perl` usable, you need to add lines like the following to your `httpd.conf` or `srm.conf` configuration file:

```
Alias /perl/ /home/httpd/perl/
<Location /perl>
SetHandler perl-script
PerlHandler Apache::Registry
```

19

INTRODUCTION TO
APACHE MODULES

```
Options +ExecCGI
</Location>
```

# Installing PHP

PHP is another popular scripting language frequently used to make interactive Web sites. Detailed information on using PHP is available in Chapter 22, "Using the PHP Module." PHP source code and documentation can be downloaded from www.php.net. The latest release is 4.0.

If you will be using PHP with a database server (for example, MySQL or mSQL), you should install the database server first so that the PHP installation can make a reference to the appropriate database library file.

The following commands are sufficient to install PHP:

```
./configure —with-mysql —with-apache=../apache_1.3.x —enable-track-vars
make
make install
cd ../apache_1.3.x
./configure (original options) —activate-module=src/modules/php3/libphp3.a
make
make install
cd ../php-3.0.x
```

You also need to copy and modify the php3.ini file and add the following to the httpd.conf or srm.conf configuration file:

```
AddType application/x-httpd-php3 .php3
```

# Troubleshooting Module Installation

Assuming that a module compiled and was activated by using axps, you first need to run apachectl with the configtest option. This will report any errors during the Apache startup process. You will also want to review the contents of the error logs.

If the solution isn't obvious, make sure that the appropriate AddModule and LoadModule directives are in the httpd.conf file. If these lines are missing or commented out, the module won't load.

If the module doesn't compile, you need to review carefully the error messages and perform the necessary modifications to the source code or makefile. You also might need to download a newer version of the module or search documentation available on the module Web site.

There are newsgroups you can use to get feedback from other Apache users. One of these newsgroups is `news://comp.infosystems.www.servers.unix`.

# Summary

This chapter covered the core concepts behind Apache modules, including how they are implemented at the operating system level, the benefits of code modularization, and the installation process. You also were introduced to the main categories and descriptions of readily available modules. An example of loading and configuring the status modules was included. In Chapter 20, the standard Apache modules are covered in more detail.

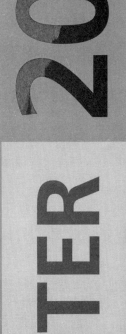

# Using Standard Apache Modules

## IN THIS CHAPTER

This chapter provides detailed coverage of the standard modules included with Apache 1.3.9. The description of each module includes a description, configuration options, and an example. As mentioned in Chapter 19, "Introduction to Apache Modules," in order to use a module you must first register it with Apache. This is done by modifying the `http.conf` file.

# Registration of Standard Modules

When Apache is initially configured, it generates a default `httpd.conf` file based on the modules you specify. The lines in the file related to the loading and unloading of modules are shown in Listing 20.1.

**LISTING 20.1** Module Registration Code in *httpd.conf*

```
# To be able to use the functionality of a module which was built as a DSO
# you have to place corresponding 'LoadModule' lines at this location so
# the directives contained in it are actually available _before_ they are
# used. Please read the file README.DSO in the Apache 1.3 distribution for
# more details about the DSO mechanism and run `httpd -l' for the list of
# already built-in (statically linked and thus always available) modules
# in your httpd binary.
#
# Note: The order in which modules are loaded is important. Don't change
# the order below without expert advice.
#
# Example:
# LoadModule foo_module libexec/mod_foo.so

LoadModule mmap_static_module lib/apache/mod_mmap_static.so
LoadModule vhost_alias_module lib/apache/mod_vhost_alias.so
LoadModule env_module         lib/apache/mod_env.so
LoadModule config_log_module  lib/apache/mod_log_config.so
LoadModule agent_log_module   lib/apache/mod_log_agent.so
LoadModule referer_log_module lib/apache/mod_log_referer.so
LoadModule mime_magic_module  lib/apache/mod_mime_magic.so
LoadModule mime_module        lib/apache/mod_mime.so
LoadModule negotiation_module lib/apache/mod_negotiation.so
LoadModule status_module      lib/apache/mod_status.so
LoadModule info_module        lib/apache/mod_info.so
LoadModule includes_module    lib/apache/mod_include.so
LoadModule autoindex_module   lib/apache/mod_autoindex.so
LoadModule dir_module         lib/apache/mod_dir.so
LoadModule cgi_module         lib/apache/mod_cgi.so
LoadModule asis_module        lib/apache/mod_asis.so
LoadModule imap_module        lib/apache/mod_imap.so
LoadModule action_module      lib/apache/mod_actions.so
LoadModule speling_module     lib/apache/mod_speling.so
```

```
LoadModule userdir_module      lib/apache/mod_userdir.so
LoadModule alias_module        lib/apache/mod_alias.so
LoadModule rewrite_module      lib/apache/mod_rewrite.so
LoadModule access_module       lib/apache/mod_access.so
LoadModule auth_module         lib/apache/mod_auth.so
LoadModule anon_auth_module    lib/apache/mod_auth_anon.so
LoadModule dbm_auth_module     lib/apache/mod_auth_dbm.so
LoadModule db_auth_module      lib/apache/mod_auth_db.so
LoadModule digest_module       lib/apache/mod_digest.so
LoadModule proxy_module        lib/apache/libproxy.so
LoadModule cern_meta_module    lib/apache/mod_cern_meta.so
LoadModule expires_module      lib/apache/mod_expires.so
LoadModule headers_module      lib/apache/mod_headers.so
LoadModule usertrack_module    lib/apache/mod_usertrack.so
LoadModule example_module      lib/apache/mod_example.so
LoadModule unique_id_module    lib/apache/mod_unique_id.so
LoadModule setenvif_module     lib/apache/mod_setenvif.so

LoadModule perl_module  lib/apache/libperl.so

#  Reconstruction of the complete module list from all available modules
#  (static and shared ones) to achieve correct module execution order.
#  [WHENEVER YOU CHANGE THE LOADMODULE SECTION ABOVE UPDATE THIS, TOO]
ClearModuleList
AddModule mod_mmap_static.c
AddModule mod_vhost_alias.c
AddModule mod_env.c
AddModule mod_log_config.c
AddModule mod_log_agent.c
AddModule mod_log_referer.c
AddModule mod_mime_magic.c
AddModule mod_mime.c
AddModule mod_negotiation.c
AddModule mod_status.c
AddModule mod_info.c
AddModule mod_include.c
AddModule mod_autoindex.c
AddModule mod_dir.c
AddModule mod_cgi.c
AddModule mod_asis.c
AddModule mod_imap.c
AddModule mod_actions.c
AddModule mod_speling.c
AddModule mod_userdir.c
AddModule mod_alias.c
AddModule mod_rewrite.c
AddModule mod_access.c
AddModule mod_auth.c
AddModule mod_auth_anon.c
```

*continues*

**20**

**USING STANDARD APACHE MODULES**

**LISTING 20.1**    continued

```
AddModule mod_auth_dbm.c
AddModule mod_auth_db.c
AddModule mod_digest.c
AddModule mod_proxy.c
AddModule mod_cern_meta.c
AddModule mod_expires.c
AddModule mod_headers.c
AddModule mod_usertrack.c
AddModule mod_example.c
AddModule mod_unique_id.c
AddModule mod_so.c
AddModule mod_setenvif.c
```

In this example, notice that each standard module is repeated twice—once with a LoadModule directive and once with an AddModule directive. If you're using DSO, the LoadModule will dynamically load and link the stated module into Apache. The AddModule directive tells Apache to enable the module. If you're not using DSO and have compiled the modules statically into Apache, you do not need these lists.

If you are debugging a module problem, make sure that the right module is being loaded. There is no reason that all the standard modules need to be loaded. To unload a module, comment out the LoadModule and AddModule commands for that particular module.

If you are registering a non-standard module with Apache, you will want to place the AddModule and LoadModule directives at the end of their respective lists. The order is important because modules can depend on each other.

# Standard Module Descriptions

At least 39 standard modules are included with Apache 1.3.9. Further information about each module can be found at http://www.apache.org/docs/mod/index.html.

## The mod_access Module

The mod_access module restricts access to URLs or server functionality based on simple rules involving the visitor's Internet address or hostname. This restriction is extremely important for intranets or site administrative pages where access or changes to information needs to be controlled.

Table 20.1 describes mod_access module configuration directives.

**TABLE 20.1**    mod_access Directives

| *Directive* | *Description* |
| --- | --- |
| allow | Specifies the permissible portion of the access control list and determines which hosts are allowed access. |
| deny | Specifies the blocked portion of the access control lists and determines which hosts are not allowed access. |
| order | Specifies the sequence in which order and deny rules are processed. |

The following is an example using mod_access:

```
<Directory /secretdoc>
        order deny,allow
        deny from all
        allow from .Jalan.com
</Directory>
```

The mod_access module is widely used; the preceding example is similar to what you will find in actual practice. The order directive states that the deny rules are evaluated before the allow statements. The deny statement disallows access from everywhere, whereas the allow statement allows access from only one domain. The practical effect is that only visitors from the Jalan.com domain can access the /secretdoc URL.

An allow or a deny directive will accept aliases, domain names, IP addresses, IP address blocks, or environment variables as arguments. Examples of each of these types of arguments are as follows:

```
Allow from all
Allow from keats.Jalan.com
Allow from .Jalan.com
Allow from 216.32.42.224
Allow from 216.
Allow from 216.32.42.0/255.255.255.0
Allow from 216.32.42.0/24
Allow from env=agrant
```

In the last case, the agrant environment variable needs to be set inside another module's directive, usually the BrowserMatch's. In the .Jalan.com line, any hostname ending with .Jalan.com would be accepted. Similarly, 216. would accept any IP address starting with 216.

**Caution**

IP address- or domain name–based access control is only a very basic form of security. For critical resources, you will also want to require a password or public key encryption.

The order directive permits a special argument: `mutual-failure`. Access is allowed only if the visiting IP address is listed in an `allow` directive and not in a `deny` directive.

All `allow` and `deny` directives are processed.

## The `mod_actions` Module

The `mod_actions` module allows the Apache server to dynamically execute CGI scripts based on the type of HTTP request. It's a method for associating handlers with media types or CGI commands. You use the `AddHandler` and `SetHandler` directives to customize the handlers, as discussed in Chapter 5, "Server Configuration Files."

The `mod_actions` module provides the directives that appear in Table 20.2.

**TABLE 20.2**   `mod_actions` Directives

| Directive | Description |
| --- | --- |
| Action | Associates either a handler or MIME content type with a CGI script. |
| Script | Associates a CGI method with a specific CGI script. |

The following are examples of using `mod_actions`:

```
Action myHandler /cgi-bin/doStuff.cgi
Action application/myMimeType /cgi-bin/playMyMimeType.cgi
Script PUT /cgi-bin/visitorInput.cgi
Script GET /cgi-bin/doSearch.cgi
```

## The `mod_alias` Module

The `mod_alias` module allows you to manage the mapping of file system objects into URLs and to redirect URLs. The `mod_alias` module provides basic services for URL modification. More advanced services are available in the `mod_rewrite` module.

The `mod_alias` module provides eight directives, described in Table 20.3.

**TABLE 20.3**   `mod_alias` Directives

| Directive | Description |
| --- | --- |
| Alias | Allows documents to be stored in the local file system other than under the document root. |
| AliasMatch | Adds regular expression matching to the `Alias` function. |
| Redirect | Maps an old URL into a new one. The new URL is returned to the client, which attempts to fetch it again with the new address. |

| Directive | Description |
|---|---|
| RedirectMatch | Adds regular expression matching to the Redirect function. |
| RedirectTemp | Sets up temporary redirection. |
| RedirectPermanent | Sets up permanent redirection. |
| ScriptAlias | Serves as an Alias directive, with the capability to run CGI scripts in the target directory. |
| ScriptAliasMatch | Serves as a ScriptAlias directive, except with regular expressions matching. |

Examples using these directives include the following:

```
Alias /images /home/httpd/images
Alias /images/ /home/httpd/images/
AliasMatch /(*.)doc /home/httpd/docs/$1.doc
Redirect / http://www.newbox.com/
RedirectMatch /(*.)doc http://www.newbox.com/docs/$1.doc
RedirectTemp / http://www.tempnewbox.com/
RedirectPermanent / http://www.permanentnewbox.com/
ScriptAlias /cgi-bin /home/httpd/cgi-bin
ScriptAliasMatch /cgi-bin/pscript(.*) /home/httpd/pscripts/$1
```

Notice that the first and second examples are slightly different. The second will match only if /images/ is specified in the given URL.

The difference between the Redirect and Alias commands is that aliasing replaces the original URL seamlessly on the server side without informing the browser. A Redirect directive performs no work on the server side but instructs the browser to go to a new location. Therefore, the second argument to the Redirect directive is always a URL instead of a file system path.

## The mod_asis Module

The mod_asis module provides for fine-tuned control of the responses from the Apache Web server. Files with the .asis extension or the httpd/send-as-is MIME type are sent directly to the client without interference from any other module.

The module defines no directives as it is. The following example shows how to use the asis module to send a Redirect command for a moved URL. Create a file with the extension .asis:

```
Status: 301 We've moved
Location: http://www.jalan.com/newurl
Content-type: text/html
```

```
<HTML>
<HEAD>
<TITLE>Notice of URL Move</TITLE>
</HEAD>
<BODY>
<H1>The page you are looking for has moved to
<A HREF="http://www.jalan.com/newurl">http://www.Jalan.com/newurl</A>
</H1>
</BODY>
</HTML>
```

You need to make sure that the asis MIME type is defined via an AddType directive:

```
AddType httpd/send-as-is asis
```

## The mod_auth Module

The mod_auth module provides basic Web-based user and group authentication using password files. It's one of the most common authentication mechanisms because of its similarity to default UNIX authentication: /etc/passwd, /etc/group. The authentication scheme is called Basic Access Authentication.

User and group identification and authentication can be achieved by using mod_auth directives in the httpd.conf file or in the individual AccessFileName files as described in Chapter 16, "Authentication." The mod_auth module attempts to verify username/password combinations by referring to an AuthUserFile or AuthGroupFile. The AuthUserFile is typically named htpasswd, and the AuthGroupFile is called htgroup.

The AuthUserFile file can be created using Apache's htpasswd utility. To create a new htpasswd file, use the -c option. Otherwise, htpasswd always takes the name of the file as its first argument and the user ID to be modified as its second. A typical example using htpasswd would be

```
htpasswd -c /etc/httpd/conf/httpd/htpasswd mmarlowe
```

This command creates an AuthUserFile file with mmarlowe as its first user. The htpasswd utility requires you to specify a password for each user created.

The format of an AuthUserFile file is

```
Username1:Encrypted Password
Username2:Encrypted Password
UsernameN:Encrypted Password
```

Likewise, an AuthGroupFile file is of the form

```
Group1:UsernameofMember,UsernameofMember,...,UsernameofMember
Group2:UsernameofMember,UsernameofMember,...,UsernameofMember
GroupN:UsernameofMember,UsernameofMember,...,UsernameofMember
```

Table 20.4 lists the directives defined by mod_auth.

**TABLE 20.4**  mod_auth Directives

| *Directive* | *Description* |
| --- | --- |
| AuthUserFile | Sets the name of a file containing the list of users and passwords for user authentication. |
| AuthGroupFile | Sets the name of a file containing the list of groups. |
| AuthAuthoritive | Allows another module to extend the username/group checking provided by mod_auth. |

AuthAuthoritive is set to off only when specifically required by vendor-supplied software or other authentication modules. The default setting is on.

## The mod_auth_anon Module

The mod_auth_anon module provides Web-based anonymous authentication similar to anonymous FTP. It defines a "guest" user and can ask for each visitor's email address. This module, a derivative of mod_auth, requires that the AuthAuthoritive directive be set to off.

Table 20.5 lists the directives defined by mod_auth_anon.

**TABLE 20.5**  mod_auth_anon Directives

| *Directive* | *Description* |
| --- | --- |
| Anonymous | This directive lists one or more usernames that guests can use. No password is required. |
| Anonymous_Authoritive | Similar to AuthAuthoritive, this directive specifies whether other modules can extend the username/group checking provided by mod_auth_anon. |
| Anonymous_LogEmail | If set to on, this directive logs all email addresses to the error_log Web server. |
| Anonymous_MustGiveEmail | If set to on, this directive requires an email address for guests to log in. |
| Anonymous_NoUserID | If set to on, this directive allows users to log in as guests without specifying a user ID. |
| Anonymous_VerifyEmail | If set to on, this directive requires the Web server to perform basic sanity checks on email addresses. |

**20**

**USING STANDARD APACHE MODULES**

Consider the following example using mod_auth_anon:

```
Anonymous anonymous, guest, visitor
Anonymous_Authoritive On
Anonymous_LogEmail On
Anonymous_MustGiveEmail On
Anonymous_NoUserID Off
Anonymous_VerifyEmail On
```

In this case, a user identifying himself as anonymous, guest, or visitor is allowed access only if he provides a valid email address as his password, which is also logged. The authentication modules are processed in order of their inclusion in httpd.conf. If the mod_auth module is specified before mod_auth_anon, and AuthAuthoritive is off while Anonymous Authoritative is set to on, user authentication is first checked against mod_auth and then against mod_auth_anon. If mod_auth denies a user access (say, for example, because of a denied IP address), mod_auth_anon will not even get a chance to process an anonymous login.

## The mod_auth_db Module

The mod_auth_db module provides the same services as mod_auth but replaces AuthUserFile and AuthGroupFile with AuthDBUserFile and AuthDBGroupFile, indicating that the files are no longer in text format. Instead, the files are in a binary format created by routines in the Berkeley DB shared library, widely used in BSD UNIX–derived systems. (Information on the Berkeley DB format and its library routines can be found at http://www.sleepycat.com/.)

mod_auth_db defines the directives listed in Table 20.6.

**TABLE 20.6**    mod_auth_db Directives

| Directive | Description |
| --- | --- |
| AuthDBUserFile | Sets the name of a DB file containing the list of users and passwords for user authentication. |
| AuthDBGroupFile | Sets the name of a DB file containing the list of groups. |
| AuthDBAuthoritive | Allows another module to extend the username/group checking provided by mod_auth_db. |

## The mod_auth_dbm Module

The mod_auth_dbm module is slightly different from the mod_auth_db one. It provides the same services but replaces the AuthUserFile and AuthGroupFile directives with the AuthDBMUserFile and AuthDBMGroupFile ones. The name change reflects that the files are no longer in text format. Instead, the files are in a binary format created by routines in the DBM library. This library is used in some UNIX systems.

Table 20.7 lists the directives defined by `mod_auth_dbm`.

**TABLE 20.7**   `mod_auth_dbm` Directives

| Directive | Description |
|---|---|
| AuthDBMUserFile | Sets the name of a DBM file containing the list of users and passwords for user authentication. |
| AuthDBMGroupFile | Sets the name of a DBM file containing the list of groups. |
| AuthDBMAuthoritive | Allows another module to extend the username/group checking provided by `mod_auth_dbm`. |

## The `mod_auth_digest` Module

The `mod_auth_digest` module extends the `mod_auth` module by implementing user authentication via MD5 Digest authentication, as defined in RFC 2617. Digest authentication is more secure than Basic authentication. However, it requires that browsers implement the Digest scheme as well. It is likely that Digest authentication will be standard in future Web browsers.

**Note**

As implemented in Apache 1.3.9, `mod_auth_digest` is experimental, and some directives may not work. For further information on `mod_auth_digest`, visit `http://www.apache.org/docs/mod/mod_auth_digest.html`.

Table 20.8 lists the directives defined by `mod_auth_digest`.

**TABLE 20.8**   `mod_auth_digest` Directives

| Directive | Description |
|---|---|
| AuthDigestFile | Sets the name of a file containing the list of users and encoded passwords for Digest authentication. |
| AuthDigestGroupFile | Sets the name of a file containing the list of groups and their members. |
| AuthDigestQop | Determines the level of Digest authentication to perform. |

*continues*

**20**

**USING STANDARD APACHE MODULES**

**TABLE 20.8**   continued

| Directive | Description |
| --- | --- |
| AuthDigestNonceLifetime | Specifies how long the server Nonce is valid. |
| AuthDigestNonceFormat | Currently under development. Will most likely specify the format of the nonce value passed to the client. |
| AuthDigestNcCheck | Currently under development. Will most likely specify whether the Apache server should verify the nonce count during authentication. |
| AuthDigestAlgorithm | Specifies which Digest algorithm to use. Currently only the MD5 option is supported. |
| AuthDigestDomain | Specifies the base URL secured by Digest authentication. Only one successful authentication is required for the same visitor requesting content at or below the base URL. |

Because the mod_auth_digest module uses the same directives as mod_digest, the two modules cannot be enabled at the same time.

> **Note**
>
> Because of the added features in Digest authentication, the Digest password file cannot be created with htpasswd. A new utility, *htdigest*, must be used instead.

## The mod_autoindex Module

The mod_autoindex module creates a user-friendly interface, similar to FTP, for directly accessing a Web server's file system. HTML-based listings are automatically created while visiting directories.

Table 20.9 lists the directives provided by mod_autoindex.

**TABLE 20.9**   mod_autoindex Directives

| Directive | Description |
| --- | --- |
| AddAlt | Sets the alternative text to display for a file, instead of an icon, for FancyIndexing. A file or regular expression specifying many files is passed as the second argument. |

| Directive | Description |
|---|---|
| AddAltByEncoding | Sets the alternative text to display for a file, instead of an icon, for FancyIndexing. One or more MIME encodings are passed as the second argument. |
| AddAltByType | Sets the alternative text to display for a file, instead of an icon, for FancyIndexing. One or more MIME types are passed as the second argument. |
| AddDescription | Specifies the description to display for a file when FancyIndexing is enabled. |
| AddIcon | Specifies the icon to display for a file when FancyIndexing is enabled. The second argument is a filename, multiple filenames, or a regular expression. |
| AddIconByEncoding | Specifies the icon to display for a file or set of files when FancyIndexing is enabled. One or more MIME encodings are passed as the second argument. |
| AddIconByType | Specifies the icon to display for a file or set of files when FancyIndexing is enabled. One or more MIME types are passed as the second argument. |
| DefaultIcon | Specifies the icon to use to represent a file when no AddIcon directive applies. |
| FancyIndexing | Requests that HTML be dynamically created to represent directory contents. Custom icons represent files. |
| HeaderName | Inserts a file at the top of the directory listing. If the file has the .html extension, the extension is included with the filename. If not, the header filename has no extension and can be found in the directory. Normal behavior is to insert the file's contents after the first content following the <BODY> tag. See option SuppressHTMLPreamble in Table 20.10 to learn how to override this functionality. |
| IndexIgnore | Specifies the files to ignore in directory listings. |
| IndexOptions | Allows fine-grained control of the format of directory. See Table 20.10 for the options. |
| IndexOrderByDefault | Specifies how files need to be ordered in the dynamically created listings. Files can be sorted in ascending or descending direction by name, date, size, or description. |
| ReadmeName | Requests that the Web server display a specific file's contents at the bottom of each directory listing. |

**20**

**USING STANDARD APACHE MODULES**

> **Note**
>
> For these directives, `x-compress` is an example of MIME encoding, and `image/*` is an example of a MIME type. Parentheses must enclose text to be displayed in the `AddAlt` and `AddDescription` directives.

There are many options available for the `IndexOptions` directive. Table 20.10 lists these.

**TABLE 20.10**   `IndexOptions` Options

| Option | Description |
|---|---|
| `IconHeight` | When used with `IconWidth`, causes the server to include `HEIGHT` and `WIDTH` attributes in the `<IMG>` tag for the file icon. |
| `IconsAreLinks` | Makes the icons part of the anchor for the filename, for `FancyIndexing`. |
| `IconWidth` | When used with `IconHeight`, causes the server to include `HEIGHT` and `WIDTH` attributes in the `<IMG>` tag for the file icon. |
| `NameWidth` | Specifies the width of the filename column in bytes. If the value is *, the column is automatically sized to the length of the longest filename in the display. |
| `ScanHTMLTitles` | Enables the extraction of the title from HTML documents for `FancyIndexing`. If the file doesn't have a description given by `AddDescription`, Apache reads the document for the value of the `<TITLE>` tag. |
| `SuppressColumnSorting` | Makes the column headings in a `FancyIndexing` directory listing into links for sorting. |
| `SuppressDescription` | Suppresses the file description in `FancyIndexing` listings. |
| `SuppressHTMLPreamble` | Disables the normal behavior of `HeaderName` by putting the `HeaderName` file's contents directly as the first content of the returned document. The header file must contain appropriate HTML instructions in this case. If there's no header file, the preamble is generated as usual. |
| `SuppressLastModified` | Suppresses the display of the last modification date in `FancyIndexing` listings. |
| `SuppressSize` | Suppresses the file size in `FancyIndexing` listings. |

To learn how to use these directives properly, refer to the `httpd.conf` file generated by your Apache installation. You will no doubt find that a lot of thought went into the default directives.

> **Note**
>
> `mod_dir` provides similar capabilities to `mod_autoindex` but requires Webmasters to create the directory listings by themselves.

## The `mod_cern_meta` Module

The `mod_cern_meta` module provides for CERN HTTPD metafile semantics. It allows for the inclusion of additional low-level HTTPd headers.

The module provides three directives, listed in Table 20.11.

**TABLE 20.11**   `mod_cern_meta` Directives

| Directive | Description |
| --- | --- |
| `MetaFiles` | Enables/disables metafile processing per directory with the options, `on` and `off`, respectively. |
| `MetaDir` | Specifies the name of the subdirectory in which `mod_cern_meta` searches for meta information. |
| `MetaSuffix` | Specifies the filename suffix that `mod_cern_meta` searches for when attempting to access meta information. |

The following is an example using the `mod_cern_meta` directives:

```
MetaFiles On
MetaDir .
MetaSuffix .meta
```

These directives enable CERN metafile semantics per directory, with the Apache server looking for files with a `.meta` extension in each directory containing Web content.

## The `mod_cgi` Module

The CGI module allows for the execution of CGI scripts. It defines the `application/x-httpd-cgi` MIME type. CGI programming is covered extensively in Chapter 11, "CGI Programming."

Three directives are provided to modify logging of CGI error messages, as listed in Table 20.12.

**TABLE 20.12**   mod_cgi Directives

| Directive | Description |
|-----------|-------------|
| ScriptLog | Specifies the name of the CGI error log. It is created or appended in each directory that a CGI script is run in. |
| ScriptLogLength | Specifies the maximum length in bytes that the CGI error log can grow to. |
| ScriptLogBuffer | Specifies the maximum number of bytes that can be sent to the error log during each CGI operation. |

The following is an example using these directives:

```
ScriptLog CGI-error.log
ScriptLogLength 1000000
ScriptLogBuffer 1024
```

## The mod_digest Module

mod_digest is being replaced by mod_auth_digest. The directives for these modules are the same, except for some new ones added by mod_auth_digest, as described earlier in this chapter.

## The mod_dir Module

This module implements the same FTP-like interface that mod_autoindex does, but it expects the Webmaster to provide the HTML-based listings for each directory.

mod_dir uses only one directive:

| Directive | Description |
|-----------|-------------|
| DirectoryIndex | Specifies the default HTML file to look for when a directory URL is passed to the Web server. |

The DirectoryIndex directive is likely to be modified if you make significant changes to a Web server installation. The default is index.html but can be changed to enable scripts to be served when a directory is requested. For example, you can change DirectoryIndex to index.php or index.cgi to serve those scripts.

## The mod_env Module

The mod_env module allows environment variables to be passed to CGI or server-side include (SSI) scripts. Table 20.13 describes the three directives.

**TABLE 20.13**   mod_env Directives

| Directive | Description |
| --- | --- |
| PassEnv | Allows Apache to pass the specified environment variable from its operating environment directly to a CGI or SSI script. |
| SetEnv | Specifies an environment variable and value to be passed to CGI or SSI scripts. |
| UnsetEnv | Removes an environment variable specified by a PassEnv or SetEnv directive. |

The following is an example of each mod_env directive:

```
PassEnv PATH
SetEnv PATH /bin:/foo/bin
UnsetEnv PATH
```

## The mod_expires Module

The mod_expires module allows an expiration time to be added to all HTML documents served by appending an Expires header in the HTTP response. This header provides a basic means for instructing a client about a document's validity or persistence. If a document has expired, it isn't cached by the browser.

The mod_expires module provides a mechanism for modifying the expiration value for Apache documents. Values can be specified relative to a document's last modified date or the time of last access.

The module defines three directives (see Table 20.14).

**TABLE 20.14**   mod_expires Directives

| Directive | Description |
| --- | --- |
| ExpiresActive | Activates/deactivates content expiration using the on and off options, respectively. |
| ExpiresByType | Defines the value of the Expires header generated for documents of the specified type. It adds the number of seconds specified in argument 2 to the base expiration time. |
| ExpiresDefault | Sets the default expiration value. |

Examples of using mod_expires and the "Alternative Interval" syntax for specifying more control over expiration values can be found at http://www.apache.org/docs/mod/mod_expires.html.

**20**

**USING STANDARD APACHE MODULES**

## The `mod_headers` Module

The mod_headers module allows for the customization of the HTTP headers of responses. It provides a generic capability for adding, modifying, or removing the header values. See Chapter 2, "HTTP," for a discussion of HTTP headers.

There is one directive:

| Directive | Description |
|-----------|-------------|
| Header | Modifies the HTTP headers of the response. The form of the directive is<br><br>`"header option" "header name" "header value"` |

There are four options for the Header directive:

set—The HTTP header is set with a given value for a given name, replacing the previous header value.

append—The given value is put into the list of values for the given value.

add—A new header name/value is created. The append option is preferred to add.

unset—The HTTP header for the given name is deleted.

Header directives are processed in the following order:

1. Core Server
2. VirtualHost Declarations
3. Per Directory Sections
4. `<Location>`Directives
5. `<Files>` Directives

## The `mod_imap` Module

The mod_imap module provides for the server handling of imagemap files. Table 20.15 lists the three directives provided by mod_imap.

**TABLE 20.15** mod_imap Directives

| Directive | Description |
|-----------|-------------|
| ImapMenu | Determines which actions the server takes if it's called without valid coordinates for the imagemap. |
| ImapDefault | Specifies the default action to be taken by imagemap files. |
| ImapBase | Defines a URL that is used as the base of URL selections created in the imagemap menus. Its value can be overridden by the imagemap file. |

Table 20.16 lists the options for the ImapMenu directive.

**TABLE 20.16**   ImapMenu Options

| Option | Description |
|--------|-------------|
| None | If ImapMenu is set to None, no menu is generated, and the default action is performed. |
| Formatted | A formatted menu is the simplest menu. Comments in the imagemap file are ignored. A level one header is printed, then an HTML horizontal rule, then the links, each on a separate line. The menu has a consistent, plain look close to that of a directory listing. |
| Semiformatted | On a semiformatted menu, comments are printed where they occur in the imagemap file. Blank lines are turned into HTML breaks. No header or HTML horizontal rule is printed, but otherwise the menu is the same as a formatted menu. |
| Unformatted | Comments are printed, and blank lines are ignored. Nothing is printed that doesn't appear in the imagemap file. All breaks and headers must be included as comments in the imagemap file. This gives you the most flexibility over menu appearance but requires you to treat your map files as HTML instead of plain text. |

More information on the imap module, including details about the imagemap file format, can be found at http://www.apache.org/docs/mod/mod_imap.html.

## The mod_include Module

The mod_include module allows for server-parsed documents, normally referred to as server-side includes (SSI). SSI was one of the first mechanisms for creating dynamic pages. It has largely been replaced by PHP, Perl, application servers, and other languages and software.

Most Web servers create a handler for .shtml files, which are forwarded to mod_include for processing. The XBitHack directive is also frequently enabled to allow for execution of SSI files based on file permissions.

Enabling and using SSI documents are described in Chapter 12, "SSI: Server-Side Includes."

The include module has only one directive relating to XBitHack. In most cases, you will want XBitHack set to on.

More information on mod_include can be found at http://www.apache.org/docs/mod/mod_include.html.

## The `mod_info` Module

The `mod_info` module is used for server diagnostic purposes. It provides a comprehensive overview of the server configuration, including all installed modules and directives in the configuration files.

It has only one directive:

| Directive | Description |
| --- | --- |
| AddModuleInfo | Provides additional information (in HTML format) for the specified module to the listing generated by `mod_info`. |

To use `mod_info`, register a handler and restrict access to its URL. The listing may not fully reflect the server's configuration, as its contents are created only when the server restarts or reloads.

## The `mod_isapi` Module

The `mod_isapi` module allows Apache to support Microsoft's Server Extension API under Windows. Modules and applications created for IIS are therefore compatible with Apache.

Add the following directive to your `httpd.conf` file to activate the module:

```
AddHandler isapi-isa dll
```

## The `mod_log_agent` Module

The `mod_log_agent` module provides a mechanism to log the contents of the `UserAgent` header contained within HTTP requests. The module provides one directive:

| Directive | Description |
| --- | --- |
| AgentLog | Specifies a filename or program into which agent information is sent. |

## The `mod_log_config` Module

The `mod_log_config` module is the standard module for defining and customizing server logging. You can use the common logging format or define your own. By default, hits are recorded in common logging format and sent to the `TransferLog` file at the base of the Apache installation. Information necessary to defining your own custom log format can be found at `http://www.apache.org/docs/mod/mod_log_config.html`.

Logs can be defined per virtual host.

Table 20.17 lists the directives defined by `mod_log_config`.

**TABLE 20.17**   `mod_log_config` Directives

| Directive | Description |
| --- | --- |
| CookieLog | Sets the filename for logging cookies. |
| CustomLog | Associates log files with user-defined formats. It can also use environment variables to perform selective logging. |
| LogFormat | Defines formatting that can be assigned later to individual log files by using the `CustomLog` directive. |
| TransferLog | Specifies the filename of the default server log file. |

## The `mod_log_referer` Module

The `mod_log_referer` module enables the Apache server to log the referrer URL—the URL from which users have linked to this one. Note that the most common spelling of *referrer* is with a double "r", while this module and its directives spell it with just one, that is, "referer." The module is deprecated because the `CustomLog` directive of the `mod_log_config` module accomplishes the same tasks as this module and is more flexible.

Table 20.18 lists the two directives defined by this module.

**TABLE 20.18**   `mod_log_referer` Directives

| Directive | Description |
| --- | --- |
| RefererIgnore | Adds to the list of strings to ignore in `Referer` headers. |
| RefererLog | Sets the name of the file to which the server will log the `Referer` header of incoming requests. |

## The `mod_mime` Module

There are two MIME modules, `mod_mime` and `mod_mime_magic`. The first, `mod_mime`, determines a file's type by its name. The MIME standard and its use with Apache are the focus of Chapter 7, "MIME Types."

Determining a file's content type is important, because different types of content require different handling. If file types couldn't be determined, nearly all Web content would have to be displayed as text files rather than as forms, CGI programs, and graphics.

Table 20.19 lists the nine directives defined by `mod_mime`.

**Table 20.19**  *mod_mime* Directives

| Directive | Description |
| --- | --- |
| AddEncoding | Maps the given filename extensions to the specified encoding type. |
| AddHandler | Maps a filename extension to a handler. |
| AddLanguage | Maps the given filename extensions to the specified content language. |
| AddType | Maps the given filename extensions to the specified content type. |
| DefaultLanguage | Tells Apache that all files in the directive's scope that don't have an explicit language extension should be considered to be in the specified language. |
| ForceType | Forces all matching files in a specified location to be treated as a specified content type. |
| RemoveHandler | Removes any handler associations for files with the given extensions. |
| SetHandler | Forces all matching files in a specified location to be parsed through a specific handler. |
| TypesConfig | Sets the location of the MIME types configuration file. |

## The mod_mime_magic Module

As mentioned in the preceding section, Apache has two standard MIME modules. The second module, mod_mime_magic, determines a file's type by inspecting portions of its content.

There is one directive created by mod_mime_magic.

| Directive | Description |
| --- | --- |
| MimeMagicFile | Enables the mod_mime_magic file by specifying the location of the magic file. |

For more information on the magic file, you can view the UNIX manual page for the file command. mod_mime_magic can use the same configuration file as that provided for the file command with the UNIX distribution.

## The mod_mmap_static Module

The mod_mmap_static module is provided to reduce Web server latency of unchanging files on heavily loaded systems. As the name hints, the module uses the mmap() function to cache files into common system memory. The library is available only with some UNIX systems.

> **Caution**
>
> This module is experimental and should be used with caution.

This module keeps a list of user-supplied pages in memory and avoids file system access. To be useful, this requires Webmasters to have a thorough understanding of the performance characteristics and bottlenecks of their sites.

Because the files' content is cached in system memory using the `mmap()` function, the server will need to be restarted whenever the site contents change.

There is one directive:

| Directive | Description |
| --- | --- |
| MMapFile | Caches one or more files (given as whitespace-separated arguments) into system memory. |

## The `mod_negotiation` Module

The `mod_negotiation` module provides for content negotiation—the selection from several available documents of the document that best matches the client's capabilities. (For more information on content negotiation, see `http://www.apache.org/docs/mod/mod_negotiation.html`.)

The `mod_negotiation` module uses two directives (see Table 20.20).

**TABLE 20.20**   `mod_negotiation` Directives

| Directive | Description |
| --- | --- |
| CacheNegotiatedDocs | Allows content-negotiated documents to be cached by proxy servers. This could mean that clients behind those proxies could retrieve versions of the documents that aren't the best matches for their abilities, but it makes caching more efficient. |
| LanguagePriority | Sets the precedence of language variants for which the client doesn't express a preference when handling a `MultiViews` request. The languages are in order of decreasing preference. |

## The `mod_proxy` Module

The `mod_proxy` module implements a caching proxy for Apache. It implements proxying capability for FTP, CONNECT (for SSL), HTTP/0.9, and HTTP/1.0. The module can be configured to connect to other proxy modules for these and other protocols.

**20**

**USING STANDARD APACHE MODULES**

The proxy module is complex and implements more than 20 directives. Chapter 10, "Using Apache as a Proxy and Cache Server," discusses the module and several of its directives in a little more detail. You can also get information on the module at `http://www.apache.org/docs/mod/mod_proxy.html`.

## The `mod_rewrite` Module

The `mod_rewrite` module provides a mechanism to translate URLs. This translation mechanism is similar to using the `Alias` directive but is much more powerful since it uses regular expressions to allow far more translating options.

Thorough documentation on the module is provided at `http://www.apache.org/docs/mod/mod_rewrite.html` and in the module author's guide at `http://www.engelschall.com/pw/apache/rewriteguide/`.

## The `mod_setenvif` Module

The `mod_setenvif` module provides the capability to set environment variables based on request attributes. The directives are considered in the order they appear in the configuration files and use regular expressions.

There are five directives (see Table 20.21).

**TABLE 20.21**   `mod_setenvif` Directives

| Directive | Description |
| --- | --- |
| BrowserMatch | Defines environment variables based on the User-Agent HTTP request header field. The first argument is a POSIX.2 extended regular expression. The rest of the arguments give the names of variables to set and (optionally) the values to which they are set. |
| BrowserMatchNoCase | Serves as a case-insensitive BrowserMatch. |
| SetEnvIf | Defines environment variables based on request attributes. |
| SetEnvIfNoCase | Serves as a case-insensitive SetEnvIf. |

## The `mod_so` Module

The `mod_so` module provides the functionality to load and run DSO modules. (The `LoadFile` and `LoadModule` directives were described in Chapter 19 and at the beginning of this chapter.) The `mod_so` module itself can't be a DSO module, but it's possible to compile all other modules as DSO. This is the recommended method for configuring Apache.

# The `mod_speling` Module

The `mod_speling` module attempts to correct misspellings of URLs that users might have entered by ignoring capitalization and allowing up to one misspelling.

Its only directive, `CheckSpelling`, has two options, `on` and `off`, which enable and disable URL spell checking, respectively.

# The `mod_status` Module

The `mod_status` module, described at length in Chapter 19, shows internal information about the currently running Apache server. It has only one directive, `ExtendedStatus`, which enables additional diagnostics when set to `on`.

# The `mod_unique_id` Module

The `mod_unique_id` module provides a token for each request, which is guaranteed to be unique across all requests in your site. For a site served from a single machine, no extra steps are needed to take advantage of this directive. For sites that are clustered on multiple machines, please see `http://www.apache.org/docs/mod/mod_unique_id.html`. There are no directives—the module works automatically. The token's value is put in the environmental variable `UNIQUE_ID`. This module is currently only available on UNIX servers.

# The `mod_userdir` Module

The `mod_userdir` module allows multiuser server operating systems, such as UNIX, to have sites associated with their system users by making a subdirectory of each system user's home directory a document root.

The only directive is `UserDir`, which does three things. With a subdirectory name, it sets the home directory's subdirectory to be used for serving URLs. With the `enable` option and a list of users, it will allow the server to serve URLs out of those users' home directories. With the `disable` option and a list of users, it will disallow the server to serve URLs out of those users' home directories.

For example, to set `public_html` as the subdirectory that will be used, enter

```
UserDir public_html
```

To enable the subdirectory for a list of users, enter

```
UserDir enable user1 user2 ... usern
```

Similarly, to disable the subdirectory of a list of users, enter

```
UserDir disable user1 user2 ... usern
```

**20**

**USING STANDARD APACHE MODULES**

Notice that each user is separated by a space.

If the list of users for `enable` or `disable` is empty, all users are affected.

## The `mod_usertrack` Module

The `mod_usertrack` module generates a cookie for user tracking. In order to log the cookie, you need to add a logging configuration using the `CustomLog` directive. For example

```
CustomLog logs/clickstream "%{cookie}n %r %t"
```

will log the cookies in the `logs/clickstream` file in the Apache base using the given format. See the `mod_log_config` module for more information about the `CustomLog` directive.

It has three directives, as shown in Table 20.22.

**TABLE 20.22**    `mod_usertrack` Directives

| Directive | Description |
| --- | --- |
| CookieExpires | Sets the expiration time of the cookie. The value given is either in seconds or in quoted English such as "3 weeks 4 days 7 seconds". The allowed time terms are: years, months, weeks, hours, minutes, and seconds. |
| CookieName | Sets the name of the cookie. By default, the cookie is named Apache. |
| CookieTracking | Enables/disables user tracking with the on and off options, respectively. |

## The `mod_vhost_alias` Module

The `mod_vhost_alias` module provides support for dynamically configured mass virtual hosting. It's one of the most useful improvements in Apache 1.3.9. The central concept behind mass virtual hosting is described at `http://www.apache.org/docs/vhosts/mass.html`. Together with the `mod_rewrite` module, the `mod_vhost_alias` module can be used to administer effectively a large number of virtual hosts served by a single system, as is the case for ISPs.

There are four new directives (see Table 20.23).

**TABLE 20.23**    `mod_vhost_alias` Directives

| Directive | Description |
| --- | --- |
| VirtualDocumentRoot | Determines where Apache will find your documents, based on the value of the server name. |

| Directive | Description |
|-----------|-------------|
| `VirtualDocumentRootIP` | Similar to `VirtualDocumentRoot` except that it uses the IP address of the server end of the connection instead of the server name. |
| `VirtualScriptAlias` | Determines where Apache will find CGI scripts, much as `VirtualDocumentRoot` does for other documents. |
| `VirtualScriptAliasIP` | Similar to `VirtualScriptAlias` except that it uses the IP address of the server end of the connection instead of the server name. |

# Summary

This chapter detailed each standard module included with Apache 1.3.9. Standard modules are the bread and butter of Apache, implementing the features considered essential in a Web server. References were provided to allow you to learn more about each of the modules.

# Using the Perl Module

**CHAPTER 21**

mod_perl is a popular Apache module that helps Web developers create sophisticated applications that perform well with the Perl programming language. This chapter provides an overview of mod_perl and its basic configuration and performance tuning. The mod_perl module is very flexible and complex, and a full treatment would run to several hundred pages so, if you want more detailed information, you should refer to the various online Web sites devoted to it, such as http://perl.apache.org/.

# Introducing mod_perl

Perl as a language was first published in 1987. It became amazingly popular, was significantly revised throughout the 1990s, and continues to be developed and improved on an ongoing basis. The language was an exceptional tool for Unix systems administrators accustomed to using sed, awk, or C for creating custom applications that processed textual data. Perl has been extended to provide a high-level interface for networking, database, system utilities, and Web applications. The first version to gain widespread use was version 4 (called Perl4). At the beginning of 2000, the latest stable version is 5.005. Perl5, which provides support for object-oriented programming, is used for mod_perl.

CGI, the common gateway interface pioneered by NCSA, also gained popularity in the mid-1990s as a way to quickly develop Web applications. Perl has benefited enormously from the deployment of CGI (discussed in Chapter 11, "CGI Programming"). Legions of Perl developers arose from the need to train and support CGI applications.

Unfortunately, CGI and Perl-based CGI in particular don't scale well for high-traffic Web applications. Because Perl is an interpreted language, each visit to a Web document implemented as a Perl CGI script results in the interpreter being launched and the Perl script being compiled at runtime. The combination of high memory usage and delayed Web responses frustrates visitors and system administrators alike. Although Perl is an excellent Web development language, it hasn't been well suited for the production environment on its own.

As a result, a large number of hacks and creative solutions were proposed. The most elegant one was to embed the Perl interpreter within Apache and provide a programming environment that expanded the capability of Perl developers while addressing performance issues. The result was mod_perl. Other alternatives exist, such as embedded scripting languages like PHP.

## Concepts of mod_perl

One of the main ideas behind mod_perl is to allow Perl programmers to write modules for the Apache Web server, a capability generally reserved to C programmers. Another basic intention is to provide improved performance and continued compatibility for existing CGI scripts written in Perl.

Writing even simple `mod_perl` scripts is more complicated than writing CGI scripts, though not much. First, because the Perl interpreter isn't being restarted on each use, programmers must be very careful to release memory allocated during runs. Systems can become highly unstable if files or database connections are opened in each instance and not closed. Furthermore, care needs to be taken so that initial values for variables are set correctly, because values from previous script invocations can persist. Finally, some system calls, such as `exit()`, can't be used; calling `exit()` would result in the master Perl instance being terminated.

## Benefits of `mod_perl`

`mod_perl`'s benefits include its flexibility and performance. Developers have wide access to the Apache API and can intervene in any stage of request processing. Perl users can also run their CGI applications with significant performance gains. It's not necessary to restart the Perl interpreter on each request, so the performance improvements over normal Perl CGI script execution can be incredible. Sophisticated Web applications can be created with `mod_perl`.

## Latest Release and Availability

`mod_perl` has its own development project and isn't distributed as part of the basic Apache Web server package. The most current version can be downloaded from `http://perl.apache.org/` or from CPAN (the Comprehensive Perl Archive Network) at `http://www.perl.com/CPAN/`. Documentation can also be found there or at the `http://www.modperl.com/` Web site.

Like all modules, `mod_perl` may need to be rebuilt or reinstalled if Apache is upgraded, depending on how significant the Apache upgrade is. If the Apache API changes, all modules require recompilation to avoid conflicts; if Apache detects a module with an incompatible version, it will display an error message and not even start.

Vendors such as Red Hat distribute `mod_perl` binaries meant to work with their currently supported versions of Apache.

Perl has its own concept of modularity implemented by using Perl modules. Unfortunately, the current organization uses a single Perl namespace, called `Apache`, to lump together not only all Perl-implementation features of the standard Apache API but also any Apache-style modules that happen to be created with Perl.

# Perl Modules Used with `mod_perl`

Table 21.1 lists some of the most popular Perl modules commonly used with `mod_perl`. This list is by no means all-inclusive; there are dozens more, and new modules are being created all the time. Some add unique functionality to the Apache Web server (such as `Apache::ASP`), some provide access to the Apache API (such as `Apache::Connection`) for other Perl modules to use, and still others (such as `Apache::AutoIndex`) replace the capabilities provided by standard Apache modules. For the latest information about what modules exist and are available, visit the `http://perl.apache.org/` Web site.

**TABLE 21.1**  Popular `mod_perl` Modules

| *Module* | *Description* |
|---|---|
| `Apache::ASP` | Processes Active Server Pages using `mod_perl`. |
| `Apache::AuthenDBI` | Uses a database to authenticate. |
| `Apache::DBI` | Maintains persistent database connections. |
| `Apache::DBILogger` | Keeps a log of all DBI-based database connections. |
| `Apache::EmbPerl` | Similar to PHP, except that it embeds Perl code directly into HTML. |
| `Apache::Filter` | Processes and filters request output. |
| `Apache::GzipChain` | Compresses request output. |
| `Apache::PerlRun` | For difficult cases, where you can't get a CGI script to run properly under `Apache::Registry` mode. |
| `Apache::PHlogin` | Uses a PH database to authenticate. |
| `Apache::Registry` | Attempts to process CGI scripts transparently. Perl scripts are cached and reloaded only when changed. The lack of instantiating a separate Perl process for each request results in a tremendous performance gain. |
| `Apache::Sandwich` | Creates custom header/footer script output for HTTP requests. |
| `Apache::Session` | Adds options for maintaining persistency across sessions. |
| `Apache::SSI` | Processes server-side includes using `mod_perl`. |
| `Apache::Status` | Provides information about the status of the Perl process during runtime. |
| `Apache::TransLDAP` | Uses LDAP to transform requests. |
| `Apache::Throttle` | Negotiates content based on connection speed. |

Many of the Apache::* modules are automatically installed as part of mod_perl. Other modules that aren't part of the package can be made available to mod_perl simply by installing them in the normal manner. After downloading them from CPAN (or wherever) and unbundling them, they're almost always installed by using the following commands in the unbundled directory:

```
perl Makefile.PL
make
make test
make install
```

# Installing mod_perl

The best way to install mod_perl is as a DSO (Dynamic Shared Object), which doesn't require that you have the source to your existing Apache installation. It also means that you don't need to rebuild your Apache binary just to add mod_perl to it.

To install mod_perl as a DSO, follow these steps:

1. Download and unbundle the source code in a subdirectory of the parent directory of the Apache source code (such as /usr/local/apache/src/modules/ mod_perl-1.21):

```
cd /usr/local/apache/src/modules
tar xzvf mod_perl-1.21.tar.gz
```

### Note

If you are on a system that doesn't have GNU *tar* as the default archiver (for example, Solaris), you may see a complaint about the z option. In that case, you will have to *gunzip* the source code first and then use tar to unbundle it:

```
gunzip mod_perl-1.21.tar.gz
tar -xvf mod_perl-1.21.tar
```

2. Switch to the mod_perl directory and run the standard Perl module install script, Makefile.PL:

```
cd mod_perl-1.21
perl Makefile.PL USE_APXS=1 WITH_APXS=/usr/local/apache/bin/apxs
    ➡EVERYTHING=1
```

The meanings of the options are as follows:

| | |
|---|---|
| `USE_APXS=1` | Use the apxs utility to install the Apache DSO module without Apache source. |
| `WITH_APXS=/path_to_apxs` | Let Perl know where to find apxs. If you have multiple Apache installations, you may also have multiple installations of apxs. |
| `EVERYTHING=1` | Enable all of `mod_perl`'s features and handler hooks. |

3. To complete the installation process, run the standard `make` commands:

```
make
make test
make install
```

4. To verify that `mod_perl` was successfully installed, restart the server and view the end of the Apache error log:

```
apachectl restart
tail /var/log/httpd/error_log
```

If the `mod_perl` module is correctly installed, you will see something similar to

```
[Mon Oct 1 00:02:19 1999] [Notice] Apache/1.3.9 (Unix)
➥mod_perl/1.21 configured -- resuming normal operations
```

You might want to install additional Apache/`mod_perl` modules. You can find a listing of the available modules at `http://perl.apache.org/src/apache-modlist.html`.

# Configuring `mod_perl`

To make `mod_perl` usable, you'll need to add lines like the following to your `httpd.conf` configuration files:

```
Alias /perl/ /home/httpd/perl/
<Location /perl>
    SetHandler perl-script
    PerlHandler Apache::Registry
    PerlSendHeader On
    Options +ExecCGI
</Location>
```

This will cause every file in the `/home/httpd/perl/` directory to be treated as a CGI script to be executed by `mod_perl`, specifically by the `Apache::Registry` capability. This is the short path to improving the performance of your existing Perl CGI scripts with `mod_perl`.

You can selectively enable the `Apache::Registry` performance improvement for particular scripts in your existing `/cgi-bin/` directory with something like the following:

```
ScriptAlias /cgi-bin/ /home/httpd/cgi-bin/
<Directory /home/httpd/cgi-bin>
    AllowOverride None
    Options None
    <Files just-this-script>
        SetHandler perl-script
        PerlHandler Apache::Registry
        Options +ExecCGI
    </Files>
</Directory>
```

In this case, the `/cgi-bin/just-this-script` script will be executed by the `Apache::Registry` Perl handler, improving performance for that script only, while all other scripts in the directory are executed by using the normal CGI method.

> **Note**
>
> Any scripts to be handled by `mod_perl` need to be within a scope that includes the `ExecCGI` option keyword.

Many `mod_perl` users like to have Apache handle CGI scripts differently based on the URL. For example, a Webmaster may want some scripts to run in `Apache::Registry` mode and others in `Apache::PerlRun` mode while still being able to run old CGI scripts unharmed. This flexible capability can be accomplished by the following directives in `httpd.conf`:

```
ScriptAlias /cgi-bin/ /home/httpd/cgi-bin/
Alias /perl/ /home/httpd/cgi-bin/
Alias /cgi-perl/ /home/httpd/cgi-bin/
```

The first directive, `ScriptAlias`, causes CGI scripts to be handled normally. The second uses `/perl/` as the URL prefix for well-behaved Perl scripts that can be handled with `Registry`. The third creates a `/cgi-perl/` URL prefix for use with `PerlRun`.

## Preloading Perl Modules

If your site makes active use of a database, you may want to preload Perl database modules. Otherwise, the modules will need to be reloaded on every invocation (which is likely to be a costly process). To accomplish preloading, use the `PerlModule` directive in your server configuration file:

```
PerlModule Apache::DBI DBD::Mysql
```

Database modules are used as an example here because they are often fairly substantial and reloading them has a noticeable impact on request latency. The same technique is appropriate for any modules that are used heavily and repeatedly in your Web server's output.

Modules listed on a `PerlModule` directive are located by the interpreter by looking in the usual `@INC` Perl include path. If you want to specify a path to a Perl script to be executed during this phase of processing, use the `PerlRequire` directive instead:

```
PerlRequire mod-perl/init-phase.pl
```

You can specify either an absolute or a relative path; if you use the latter, `mod_perl` will use the entries in the `@INC` array as anchors for the relative path and search for the script under each in turn.

> **Caution**
>
> Perl modules listed on the `PerlModule` or `PerlRequire` directive in the server configuration files are executed by the Apache server before it changes its identity. On Unix systems, this usually mean the server is still running as `root`, so the modules listed will have full superuser access to your system.

Both the `PerlModule` and `PerlRequire` directives can be used in `.htaccess` files, but modules and scripts listed in such directives will be loaded normally at request time rather than at startup time, since the server doesn't look for `.htaccess` files until a request has been translated to a file system path.

# Perl Module Phase Handlers

If you build `mod_perl` using the `EVERYTHING=1` option, all the module's capabilities are available to you—including the capability to declare a Perl module as a handler in any phase of server configuration and request processing. The standard format for this type of declaration is

```
PerlXXXHandler module-name [...]
```

The *XXX* can be null (for example, the directive is specified as `PerlHandler`) or any of `ChildInit`, `PostReadRequest`, `Init`, `Trans`, `HeaderParser`, `Access`, `Authen`, `Authz`, `Type`, `Fixup`, `Log`, `Cleanup`, `ChildExit`, `Dispatch`, or `Restart`. Each will install one or more Perl modules as handlers in the corresponding Apache API phase or `mod_perl` pseudo-phase.

The one phase that seems to be omitted is that of content generation, but it hasn't been left out—it's associated with the simple `PerlHandler` directive, the one that doesn't seem to include a phase name.

Each handler type is described very briefly in the following sections. In most cases, the arguments to the directives are module class names; mod_perl will load the module if it isn't already loaded and call the module's `handler()` method at the appropriate time during request processing. If a particular module can handle multiple phases, it is up to the `handler()` method to determine for which phase it's being invoked.

You can specify a method to be invoked instead of the `handler()` method, such as `Apache::Foo:generate_content`. If you use this technique to specify a method rather than a class or module name, you need to load the module yourself, such as with `PerlModule`, because mod_perl won't. If you reference a method from a module that isn't loaded, mod_perl will report an error in the server's error log. Because this is a common mistake, the `PerlXXXHandler` directives actually provide a means for loading the module: Just prefix the argument with +, as in `PerlHandler+Apache::Foo:generate_content`.

If multiple modules or methods are declared for a particular phase, how many of them are actually called depends on the phase itself. Some phases finish as soon as something returns success; some will continue calling modules until all have been invoked. (All phases automatically stop if any method returns an error.)

## PerlChildInitHandler: Dealing with Child Process Creation

In the Unix multiprocess model, requests are handled by children of the main Apache process. As these child processes are created, one of the first things they do is to invoke any Perl modules declared in `PerlChildInitHandler` directives. This gives you the opportunity to set up any process-wide resources or connections you need. On Windows systems, these modules will be called only once, since there is only one process.

All modules listed on the directive line will be called, unless one returns an error.

## PerlPostReadRequestHandler: Initial Request Handling

Modules listed on these directive lines will be invoked as soon as the Apache server has read the request header from the client. All the modules will be called in turn, unless one of them returns an error.

All modules named for this phase will be invoked until one returns an error or indicates that the request has been completely handled by returning DONE.

## PerlInitHandler: Initial Handler Alias

This directive isn't associated with a single phase. Rather, it's an alias for either the PerlPostReadRequestHandler or PerlHeaderParserHandler directive, depending on where the PerlInitHandler is found. If it's inside a `<Directory>` or `<Location>` container, it's the same as PerlHeaderParserHandler; otherwise, it's equivalent to PerlPostReadRequestHandler.

How many modules are invoked depends on the context; see the descriptions of the directives for which this is an alias for details.

## PerlTransHandler: Translating a Request URI into a Filename

Modules declared for this phase are given the opportunity to translate the requested URI into a file system location. This is how the Alias directive of the standard Apache mod_alias module functions. Since the translation hasn't been performed yet, it's meaningless (and not allowed) for this directive to appear in a `<Directory>` or `<Location>` container. And since the translation has *already* been performed by the time an .htaccess file is processed, it's equally meaningless (and disallowed) for it to appear there.

This phase finishes as soon as any module returns anything other than DECLINED. This means that only one module can actually perform this translation.

## PerlHeaderParserHandler: Reacting to a Request Header

Modules named in this directive are expected to determine whether to proceed with the request based on the contents of the request's header. This is very similar to the phase identified by the PerlPostReadRequest directive, except that additional processing has been performed and there's more information available to these modules for their decision-making.

This phase will call all modules listed on the directive until one returns either an error or DONE, signifying that the request processing has been completed.

## PerlAccessHandler: Checking Basic Access Control

Modules listed on this directive line will be invoked early in the processing of a request and have the duty of determining whether the request should be permitted to proceed, based on its origin. The only information available to the handlers are the contents of the request header and the attributes of the request, such as the client's IP address. The most common sort of access control is based on checking to see whether that address is permitted to access the document in question.

> **Note**
>
> No username or password information is available at this stage of request processing.

All modules in this phase are invoked until one returns something other than OK. If no module returns an error or OK (for example, all modules have returned DECLINED), the Apache server assumes failure and will forbid the request.

## PerlAuthenHandler: Validating Credentials

PerlAuthenHandler modules are invoked for the purpose of validating any user credentials that accompany the request. Usually this means looking them up in some sort of credential database, but it might be something simpler, such as verifying that they match some sort of pattern. Under normal circumstances, if no credentials are sent, no authentication module will report a successful lookup, and the server will tell the client that credentials are required—which should result in the client trying again, after obtaining credentials.

All modules declared for this phase will be invoked, unless one aborts the sequence by returning an error. As with the modules declared on the PerlAccessHandler directive, at least one module must return OK or else the server will abort the request.

## PerlAuthzHandler: Verifying Permission to Access a Document

After user credentials are validated (that is, found to match expected values), the request processing proceeds to the next phase, which involves checking to see whether the validated user is allowed to access the requested resource. This process is called *authorization*, which explains why the directive that declares modules to handle this phase is named PerlAuthzHandler.

This process is broken into two separate phases, because it's perfectly reasonable for a username and password to be valid but not allowed access to all documents. For example, all departments at a company might share the same user database, but only members of the Payroll department would be allowed to access the employee compensation records.

mod_perl will call all the modules for this phase until one returns OK. If no module accepts responsibility for the request by saying that the credentials are valid for the document, the Apache server will abort the request as being forbidden.

## `PerlTypeHandler`: Determining Content-Type of the Response

Modules declared with this directive are expected to use the information that has already been gathered about the request, such as the underlying filename, to determine and report the MIME content-type (that is, `text/html` or `image/jpeg`) of the response content that will be sent back to the client.

Module invocation for this phase stops as soon as a module returns `OK`.

## `PerlFixupHandler`: Making Last-Minute Request Changes

This phase permits modules to perform any last-minute verifications, validations, or modifications to the request before it's advanced to the content-generation phase. For example, since the filename that corresponds to the requested URI (if any) has been definitively determined by the time request processing has gotten to this point, the fixup phase provides an excellent opportunity for a module to adjust the response header, such as setting a `Last-Modified` or `Expires` value.

All modules declared for this phase are invoked unless one returns an error.

## `PerlHandler`: Generating Response Content

Modules listed on this directive are candidates for generating the actual content of the page to be delivered to the client—the response content. According to the Apache API, only one content handler can return `OK`, signifying that the content has been generated and sent, but Perl modules running under the auspices of `mod_perl` can actually be "chained" together, allowing multiple modules to contribute to the final result, or even pass the output from one handler as the input to the next.

The server will invoke all modules in this phase until one returns `OK`.

## `PerlLogHandler`: Logging the Completed Request

Any modules listed on a `PerlLogHandler` directive are invoked after the response is sent back to the client and are expected to record the transaction somehow, such as to a text file, a remote server, or a database.

All modules listed in this directive will be invoked unless one returns an error.

## `PerlCleanupHandler`: Final Per-Request Activity

This directive isn't directly associated with an Apache request processing phase. Rather, modules declared with this directive are invoked after a request is completely processed, with all phases having been executed (at least all that are going to be). Since it's actually declaring routines to be executed, the arguments should be actual method names, like `Apache::Foo::cleanup_request`, rather than the class names.

## `PerlChildExitHandler`: Dealing with Apache Child Deletion

As with the `PerlChildInitHandler` directive, this one allows you to declare Perl modules that should be invoked when the Apache child process is being affected—in this case, when it's being deleted from the system. As with `PerlCleanupHandler`, the arguments are methods rather than class names.

## `PerlDispatchHandler`

The `PerlDispatchHandler` directive is intended for use only by those who are very familiar with mod_perl and want to have detailed control over how the module deals with the various handlers. The use of this directive should be considered a very advanced topic and well beyond the scope of this chapter.

> **Caution**
>
> A minor error in this processing will completely break all phases of request processing.

## `PerlRestartHandler`

This directive isn't associated with an Apache phase. Instead, it identifies modules that should be invoked when the server is restarted. The arguments to this directive are method names instead of module class names.

# Viewing the Status of `mod_perl`

mod_perl has its own submodule, similar to Apache's mod_status, named `Apache::Status`. To use it, add the following directives to your configuration file:

```
<Location /perl-status>
    SetHandler perl-script
    PerlHandler Apache::Status
</Location>
```

Then you can view the status of mod_perl and your Perl modules by requesting a URL on your system, like `http://myhost/perl-status`. If you keep this module enabled, you'll almost certainly want to add deny/allow directives for access control, to keep from revealing too much about your configuration to casual (or malicious) observers.

> **Note**
>
> The `Apache::Status` module requires the `Devel::Symdump` Perl module, which may or may not be part of your Perl installation. If the status page doesn't display correctly, verify that you have this module installed. You can get it from CPAN.

# `mod_perl` Interaction with Databases

Perl provides an abstraction layer, called DBI, for interacting with most databases. The DBI module can be downloaded from any CPAN mirror listed on the `perl.com` Web site. To install it, issue the usual commands to install a CPAN Perl module:

```
perl Makefile.PL
make
make test
make install
```

To use DBI, you also need a low-level driver for your particular database. This is typically named DBD-*databasename* (DBD meaning *database driver*). During the install process, you may be asked questions about your database, including necessary authorization information to connect and run a test of DBI functions.

Accessing DBI from Apache requires `Apache::DBI`, which is part of mod_perl. You should preload the database connection module as well as `Apache::DBI` via a `PerlModule` directive.

To debug DBI connections from mod_perl, load the `Apache::DebugDBI` module.

# Debugging `mod_perl`

Most mod_perl scripts will leave output in the Apache error log if a serious problem occurs. In fact, nearly all sites monitor error logs to catch problems as they occur. Usually there will be either a compilation error message or notice about a system problem. Scripts frequently begin to fail after someone upgrades Perl and forgets to make sure that the old Perl modules are visible to existing applications.

The directive `PerlWarn` controls whether strict checking of Perl scripts is performed during compilation. If `PerlWarn` is set to `On`, these warnings are also sent to the error log. `PerlWarn` can be `On` during development and `Off` in production, when you feel comfortable that the module is functioning correctly.

You can use the Perl debugger, invoked with `perl -d`, to check a lengthy Perl script.

> **Tip**
>
> As with normal Perl programming, it's always a good idea when debugging to tell Perl to warn you explicitly about possible problems by declaring the following at the top of your script:
> ```
> #!/usr/bin/perl -w
> use strict;
> ```

# Performance Tuning

Web server performance is one of the primary reasons for using mod_perl. However, the sites that switch to mod_perl for performance gains generally already have performance problems and need to know how to optimize mod_perl for their needs.

Performance depends on a number of factors, but primarily on latency (how long it takes for the server to process each request). If the server is bogged down because it's trying to read/write too much data to disk, using excessive memory, or starting too many processes, you may have a problem that can be addressed by configuring Apache or mod_perl appropriately. Or it may be that the Perl application is functioning inefficiently and should be profiled and possibly rewritten.

If these efforts at performance tuning are insufficient, you may need to step down to the hardware level to improve performance, such as by adding memory or switching to a faster processor or disk controller.

It's important to plan your Web server for optimal traffic handling. If users complain of performance problems during peak periods, you may need to increase the maximum number of child processes. If memory usage is high during these periods but normal otherwise, you certainly need to add more memory. The idea is to get a good rough concept of your worst-case memory/child ratio and increase the maximum allowable number of children to well above the highest number of requests you expect to receive at any one time. It's common for Perl-based Web servers to require 128MB–1GB to handle traffic on dynamic sites.

Similarly, set the minimum number of children to a reasonable number. The StartServers value needs to be high enough that, when the server first starts up, visitors won't be kept waiting while new children start. Likewise, the difference between the maximum and minimum number of children needs to be large enough that the server isn't constantly adding or killing children under normal load. Each child action adds to visitor latency.

## Memory

mod_perl attempts to use shared memory—that is, have only one copy of Perl in memory while multiple child processes of the Apache server handle requests. Children are normally created or terminated when an arbitrary number of requests have been processed or there are too few or too many of them to handle the incoming requests.

Each child process uses its own small personal amount of memory in the system and can potentially create its own copy of the Perl module and script. The child uses this potential only when the request results in the child having to maintain private data or activate otherwise unused portions of script functionality.

To determine if there is a memory problem on a Unix Web server, the normal process is to have a system utility, such as vmstat, take and log periodic measurements of memory available over a prolonged period of time. It's common to see a small drop over periods of days and weeks but, if there are noticeable hourly differences or if the daily amount changes significantly, you might have a problem. The amount will fluctuate according to the server's traffic.

The PerlSetEnv directive can be used to set resource limits per child. Do you really want a single child to grow to 64MB+? If not, the following will disable it:

PerlSetEnv PERL_RLIMIT_DATA 48:64

In this case, 48MB is the soft limit and 64MB is the hard limit.

> **Note**
>
> If you suspect that you have a memory leak with a Perl script and can't debug it, one alternative is to decrease MaxRequestsPerChild so that a new child is created automatically before the old child reaches a significant size.

# Basic mod_perl Scripts and Uses

The most basic mod_perl scripts are those that are simply CGI scripts being processed through the Apache::Registry module. Apache::Registry is a PerlHandler content-handler that uses the information about the request to determine the name of the script being requested. If the script has never been executed before, Apache::Registry will load and compile it; if the script *has* been invoked before but hasn't been changed on disk since the last invocation, the already-compiled version will be used—otherwise, it will be reloaded and recompiled before being executed again. Since such on-disk changes tend to be much less frequent than the Web requests for the scripts, this means that the overhead of compilation is vastly reduced. Combine this with the performance improvement gained by not having to start up the Perl interpreter for each script, and the impact of using `Apache::Registry` to process your CGI scripts can be phenomenal.

As mentioned earlier, `mod_perl` allows you to do something that the Apache C API doesn't: stack or chain content handlers to allow the response content to be generated from multiple methods. This is done by specifying multiple modules on a `PerlHandler` directive. There are actually two aspects to this: serialized output and pipelined output.

For serialized output coming from multiple modules, each is called in turn and must do the appropriate tasks for its calling position in the sequence. For instance, the first content generator invoked has to send the response header by calling `$r->send_http_header()`, after which it can add content to the output stream using calls to `$r->print()`. Subsequent modules add to the content with their own calls to `$r->print()`.

Pipelined output involves modules working together so that each can accept input from an earlier content handler and pass its own output to another. This is done by overriding the binding of the filehandle to which the `$r->print()` method sends its arguments and providing a means for each module to obtain input from its predecessor. (Obviously, the `$r->print()` binding must be restored for the last content handler method, or else it won't reach the client!)

Pipelining content is very popular but, due to the restrictions of the Apache V1 API and the complexity of `mod_perl` and Perl's object-oriented programming, it's not as simple to implement as it is to describe. Finding new and better ways to accomplish pipelined output remains a hot topic in the `mod_perl` development community; for more information about the latest progress in this area, visit the `http://perl.apache.org/` Web site.

# The Perl Module Interface to `mod_perl`

To write Perl modules that take advantage of `mod_perl`'s capabilities, you need to be very conversant with Perl 5's object-oriented syntax and capabilities. Almost all the phases call module `handler` methods with an `Apache::Request` object as the argument; to gain access to this, you can use something like

```
sub handler {
    my($r) = @_;
```

or

```
sub handler {
    my $r = shift;
```

The Apache::Request object passed to the handler method is the gateway to all the other API structures you'll need, such as the Apache::Server or Apache::Connection object:

```
print $r->server()->server_hostname();
$client_ipaddr = $r->connection()->remote_addr();
```

Everything in the mod_perl Perl interface is done through objects, and the mod_perl API is at least as rich as the standard Apache C API—and just as prone to change and updating, if not more so. For the latest information, consult the http://perl.apache.or/ project Web site.

# Summary

In this chapter, you learned about mod_perl and the tremendous impact it can have on Web application performance and flexibility. We covered installation of mod_perl and several other Perl modules. You also learned many of the concepts behind mod_perl, including its architecture and important information about troubleshooting and performance tuning. In the next chapter, you learn about another server-side scripting module—PHP.

# Using the PHP Module

PHP is another popular Apache module of choice for many developers of dynamic Web pages. PHP has a rich set of features, good performance, and extensive database connectivity. And thanks to its seamless integration as a module in Apache's framework, it has won the hearts of many hard-core Perl programmers.

A vast number of Web-hosting services offer PHP 3 in conjunction with popular databases such as mSQL and MySQL, so the choice of PHP is nearly ideal for the task.

This chapter tells you how to install and configure PHP with Apache and dive into the language syntax. You'll then see a few examples of PHP in action.

> **Note**
>
> This chapter is meant to give you a taste of PHP 3 and some of its capabilities and by no means covers the subject in its entirety. Entire books have been written about PHP.

# The Purpose of PHP

PHP stands for Personal Home Page tools, although it also could easily be called a Portable Hypertext Programming language. PHP's purpose is to deliver dynamic content on the Web, and this is possible with a properly configured Apache Web server—although other Web servers do work as well—and the language's rich feature set.

You can embed PHP in your HTML pages or, if you prefer, use PHP to generate the entire HTML content. With PHP, you not only have the tools of a modern modular language with all its constructs, but also database connectivity, generation of on-the-fly graphics, access to I/O and disk access functions, powerful Perl-like regular expressions, and many string and mathematical functions, among others.

PHP also can adjust itself to your needs by means of dynamic loading of modules. This makes PHP an extendable language.

You can even put some of your object-oriented skills to use with PHP 3.0.

## History of PHP as a Server-Side Language

Rasmus Lerdorf is credited for the birth of PHP, the first version of which he released on the Web. In its original form it was but a simple macro replacement tool that would generate some HTML out of embedded commands and even SQL queries.

Little did he know that PHP would become what it has become today. As with all successful open source projects, people become hungry for functionality to fulfill more of their needs. Thanks to that hunger, PHP 2.0 was released in 1996 and included more language-like features with a new language parser. At that time it was already possible to use it to process HTML form data and perform database-related operations, thanks to its improved parser that featured the same constructs as any other modern modular language.

Back in October 1997, the first alpha release of PHP 3.0 came out, sporting yet another new interpreter by Zeev Suraski and Andi Gutmans, with help from Shane Caraveo, Stig Bakken, Jim Winstead, and countless others. The official production release of PHP 3.0 was in June 1998.

Development is still an ongoing process and, while there are still new releases of PHP 3.0, the 4.0 code line—code-named Zend—is already underway and undergoing testing. Again this new version will contain a new parser engine designed from scratch. One nice feature of version 4.0 is its capability to interpret byte codes. The use of byte codes will make it possible for PHP 4.0 Web site developers to deploy only byte code, as opposed to source code. This will most certainly be faster to execute than having to reinterpret the same PHP source code on every page hit.

The most recent Netcraft (`http://www.netcraft.com/`) usage statistics, shown at `http://www.php.net/usage.php3`, show more than a million domain names using a version of PHP.

## Why Not Plain Server-Side Includes?

Server-side includes (SSI) can be considered a precursor to what is today `mod_php`, `mod_perl`, and others. Server-side includes allow the inclusion of basic commands. These not only add flexibility to the design of your Web site, but also help reduce maintenance—for example, by including a standard footer rather than placing one on every page and having to update all of them every time.

While SSI is more than just inclusion of files, it isn't flexible enough to deliver dynamic content. Moreover, it doesn't offer the capability of connecting to databases and performing complex processing.

By using PHP as a server-side scripting language, it's possible to deliver content that varies according to the circumstances and even according to user choices. We can say that PHP is to SSI as C is to assembler programming.

## Module or CGI?

The common gateway interface (CGI) was how dynamic content was delivered on the Web in the beginning (Chapter 11, "CGI Programming," discusses CGI in more detail).

PHP can also be used with CGI, and in this form it's possible to use it with any CGI-capable Web server.

One disadvantage of the CGI method is that for every request (page hit) to that handler, a separate process is forked by the Web server. In the case of the CGI version of PHP, this separate process is the PHP interpreter. This incurs some overhead and its inherent performance penalty. FastCGI addressed this and other shortcomings, but it doesn't seem to have gained wide acceptance.

However, it's also possible to embed the PHP interpreter into the Apache executable or even by using Apache's Dynamic Shared Object (DSO) feature, in which the PHP module (in our case) is loaded when a PHP page is requested.

The dynamically loaded version of PHP 3.x is usually a file called `mod_php3.so`. This PHP interpreter can have any filename as a dynamically loaded module, because the actual file used is determined by the Apache `LoadModule` directive. This will be covered later, in the section "Building and Installing the PHP Interpreter."

By using the compiled or DSO version of PHP, we have the advantage that the Web server no longer needs to spawn a different process to handle PHP page requests. It's already there, ready for interpreting any PHP page.

# Latest Releases and Availability

The best place to go for current information about the development of PHP 3.x is `http://www.php.net/`, which is a very informative and well-designed site using PHP 3.0. There you can also fetch the latest release of PHP, learn what has changed since previous releases, submit bug reports, and find out which Internet service providers (ISPs) are using PHP.

Since the first official release of PHP 4 will happen shortly after the time of this writing, it's advisable to keep track of its current state at either the PHP site (`http://www.php.net/version4/`) or the official Zend site (`http://www.zend.org/`).

> **Note**
>
> Don't be confused about Zend and PHP. Although some may view Zend as a synonym of PHP 4, it's neither that nor a competitor. Zend is a complete rewrite of the PHP scripting engine and is just that—a powerful scripting engine. PHP 4 uses Zend, the scripting engine; as a result, it will be faster and downward compatible with PHP 3. In fact, Zend can be used by other products and not just PHP. By that I mean that you can concoct your own application and use Zend as the underlying scripting engine rather than develop your own.

# Installing and Configuring mod_php

If you are lucky, PHP is already installed on your system. However, it's possible that it isn't installed by default or that the default installation doesn't suit your needs. For example, Red Hat comes with optional PHP modules that you can install, but it doesn't include any database connectivity features.

This section assumes that you are going to develop a Web site that uses mSQL (http://www.hughes.com.au/) as its database, although it could be MySQL (http://www.mysql.com) or Postgres as well. (Chapter 23, "Other Well-Known Modules," discusses the Postgres database management server in a bit more detail.) We will rebuild PHP with support for one of these databases.

We will take you almost step by step into rebuilding PHP on a Red Hat Linux installation; paths may vary on other distributions.

## Building and Installing the PHP Interpreter

Assume that you already have an Apache installation, as described in the previous chapters, and that you have the PHP source code in the current directory. Usually it is best to get the configuration done before the actual build. You can find out which configuration options are available with

```
./configure --help
```

Now we are going to build the PHP interpreter in its module format rather than the CGI version:

```
./configure --with-msql=/usr/lib/Hughes \
  --enable-track-vars --with-apxs=/usr/sbin/apxs \
  --prefix=/usr --with-config-file-path=/etc/httpd \
  --with-exec-dir=/usr/bin
```

This means we are including support for the mSQL database and indicating the location of the (installed) Apache *apxs* program. Sometimes it's easier to use this rather than specify where Apache is located, especially if you don't have the Apache build tree anymore.

Paths may vary, depending on your system. The preceding configuration parameters assume that the Apache runtime configuration files are in the conf directory under /etc/httpd. It's in this directory that the php3.ini file (php.ini in version 4) will be installed.

If no errors are produced during this configuration step, you are ready to build the PHP interpreter by using `make` and installing it subsequently:

```
make
make install
```

The installed files are the PHP configuration file, the PHP interpreter, and whatever extra PHP modules are built with the above command.

> ### Tip
>
> It's definitely a good idea to read the INSTALL files provided in the distribution, especially if you are facing some build problems.

## `php.ini`: Configuring Your PHP Setup

After you build and install PHP on your system, you can find a default PHP configuration file in the `/etc/httpd/` directory on a Red Hat Linux box. The name of this PHP configuration file is `php3.ini` (on both Windows and Unix), although this has become just `php.ini` in PHP 4 so that the configuration filename doesn't contain a version number.

Many configuration parameters are set in this file, and a detailed explanation is beyond the scope of this book. The ones worth looking at in case your needs vary at some stage are described here.

Fortunately, in the great majority of cases the default values provided in the configuration file work just fine. However, it may be a good idea to take a look at it. You may find something interesting.

### Language Options

`short_open_tag` is normally on and enables the use of the `<?` tag in an HTML page; otherwise, only `<?php` and `<script>` are allowed. Although it is up to the user's preferences, it's advisable to use the `<?php` open tag, which is not only short but also specifies the type of script.

All the `highlight.*` options are used for specifying the font colors used when displaying PHP source code on a Web browser using the PHP `show_source()` command. This allows you to do syntax highlighting for strings, comments, keyword, and HTML, as well as the background color.

## Resource Limits Options

With `max_execution_time` you can specify the maximum time (in seconds) to be spent waiting for a PHP script to finish executing. This time defaults to 30 seconds, which is fine. If your script takes longer than that to execute, it's very likely that something is wrong. If not, this gives you the opportunity to tune the PHP interpreter.

Likewise, a script is bound to a maximum amount of memory it can claim; the default, about 8MB, should be more than enough for most applications. This is controlled by the `memory_limit` option.

## Data-Handling Options

You can control which file is always attached at the beginning and end of a PHP script by using the `auto_prepend_file` and `auto_append_file` options. These are normally left blank.

The most useful is the `track_vars` option, which is normally on. This means that all the HTML `POST` and `GET` form variables are available in arrays named `HTTP_POST_VARS` and `HTTP_GET_VARS`, respectively. The variables are indexed by the name given in the `NAME` attribute of the respective HTML tag. In the same manner, the cookies are available in the `HTTP_COOKIE_VARS` array.

## Miscellaneous Options

With PHP it's also possible to do file upload. You can control the maximum size of an uploaded file with the `upload_max_filesize` option. This defaults to about 2MB, which is normally sufficient.

The `extension_dir` option points to the directory containing dynamically loaded modules, while the `extension` option is used to indicate which module should be automatically loaded.

Early in PHP version 3, a primitive debugging facility was implemented. You can control whether you want debug information to be sent to a remote debugger with the `debugger.*` options. Normally it means local host port 7869 and is disabled. This can be overruled with the `debugger_on()` and `debugger_off()` statements.

# Configuring Apache for Use with PHP

If you're using the module version of PHP with Apache's DSO feature—as opposed to compiled into the Apache executable—it's necessary to enable this module in the Apache `httpd.conf` file. You should uncomment or add the following two directives:

```
LoadModule php3_module    modules/mod_php3.so
```

```
AddModule                    mod_php3.c
```

The module's entry must be in the same relative order in the `LoadModule` and `AddModule` sections.

In the `srm.conf` file (or `httpd.conf` in one-file systems), it's necessary to tell the Apache Web server which extensions are to be associated with the PHP3 interpreter:

```
AddType    application/x-httpd-php3        .php3
AddType    application/x-httpd-php3-source .phps
```

Given the first of the above directives, all files with the `.php3` extension will be processed by the PHP 3 interpreter. The second directive causes all files ending in `.phps` to be displayed on the browser, using PHP syntax highlighting, rather than be executed. In the same configuration file, you may want to modify the following directive for your convenience so that a PHP page can also be an index page:

```
DirectoryIndex index.html index.shtml index.php3
```

The subject of which file extension you use is a matter of personal choice, at least of the person administering the Apache server. Keep in mind that as of PHP 4, the application type will become `application/x-httpd-php` without the PHP version number.

# Syntax and Essentials of Using mod_php

When writing an active/dynamic page, you have the option of generating all the HTML output from the PHP script or embedding PHP code in the HTML. Your choice is a matter of personal taste. The beginning of a PHP script is usually delimited by the <?php...?> or <?...?> tags.

Syntax-wise, we can say that if you already know C or Perl, you will find it very easy to learn to program in PHP. PHP commands are separated with a semicolon just like C and Perl, and for comments you can use either the C++ (double forward slash) or the C style, as shown in Listing 22.1.

**LISTING 22.1** PHP Tags and Comments

```
<html>
<head><title>Example 22-1</title></head>
<body>

<?php
    /*
```

```
      * Example 22-1
      * Synopsis: PHP tags and comments
      */
      phpinfo(); // Show information about Apache/PHP
?>
</body>
</html>
```

# Identifiers, Constants, and Scope

An identifier can be a function, variable, or constant's name. It can be of any length and contain any letter or digit or the underscore character. The only constraint is that the first character of the identifier must be a letter or underscore.

All identifiers are case sensitive, with the exception of built-in functions. Identifiers that represent a variable are preceded by a dollar sign just like Perl scalar variables. Constants, on the other hand, are used without the dollar sign.

Variables aren't declared in PHP; you simply give them a value. The only times you need to declare variables are when specifying their scope with the `global` or `static` keyword or within a PHP class with the `var` keyword.

Variable scope is always local; what that means depends on whether variables are being used within a function, a class, or anywhere else on the script. Within a function you can use the `global` keyword to tell the interpreter that that variable (or list of variables) is a global variable rather than one with scope limited to the function. Likewise, the `static` keyword can be used just like in C to specify that the variable list will preserve its value even across function calls to the same function.

Rather than specify that an identifier is a constant by means of a modifying keyword, PHP uses a built-in function to accomplish the task using `define`. Constants can be of any type and can be declared as follows:

```
define("PI", 3.141592); // A floating point constant
```

Constants have a global scope, so they can be used within a function without using the `global` keyword. Because both `TRUE` and `FALSE` are also predefined, you can implement Boolean variables.

Listing 22.2 demonstrates some of the concepts introduced in this section. Notice that, even though the `my_global` variable in the `ShowVariables()` function has the same name as a global variable, because it wasn't declared as such inside the function, it becomes a local variable.

**LISTING 22.2**    Variables, Constants, and Scope

```php
<?php
    /*
     * Example 22-2
     * Synopsis: Variables, constants and scope
     */
    $my_global = 23;
    $my_float = 36.0;

    function ShowConstants() {
      echo("Constants have a global scope wherever " .
          "they are.\n");
      echo("PHP_VERSION: " . PHP_VERSION . "\n");
      echo("TRUE: " . TRUE . "\n");
      echo("FALSE: " . FALSE . "\n");
      echo("M_PI: " . M_PI . "\n");
      echo("__FILE__: " . __FILE__ . "\n");
      echo("__LINE__: " . __LINE__ . "\n");
    }

    function ShowVariables() {
      global $my_float;

      echo("Global variable (not imported): " .
          "my_global = $my_global\n");
      // Notice that this my_global is actually local!
      $my_global = 1963;
      echo("Local variable: my_global = $my_global\n");
      echo("Global variable (imported): " .
          "my_float = $my_float\n");
    }

    echo("Some built in constants");
    ShowConstants();
    echo("Scope demo");
    ShowVariables();
    ?>
```

# PHP Data Types

PHP uses three data types: floating point/real numbers, integers, and strings.

## Floating-Point Numbers

Floating-point numbers must always contain a decimal point even if the decimal part is zero. That way, PHP knows it to be a floating-point number.

```php
$weight = 67.45;
```

# Integers

Integers don't contain a decimal point, so they are just digits.

```php
$date_of_birth = 23;
```

# Strings

PHP strings are delimited by double (") or single (') quotes.

```php
$name = "Gandalf D' Grey"; // String
$city = 'Panama';          // Fixed string
```

Within a string you may need to escape certain special characters with a backslash. These are the double quotes and the backslash itself. You can also insert special codes such as newlines (\n), carriage returns (\r), tabs (\t), and any other character by using that character's hexadecimal code (\x20, for example, is the space character).

There are two ways to represent a string: use single quotes as in `$city` and double quotes as in `$name` in the preceding example. In this respect, PHP behaves like Perl; if the string is between single quotes, its value is taken exactly as is. If on the other hand the string appears between double quotes, PHP will perform variable interpolation. *Variable interpolation* means that any valid PHP variable within the string will be substituted by the variable's contents. Between double quotes you can also use escaped characters such as carriage returns. For example

```php
$age = 28;
$msg = "Age of the subject is $age\n";
```

As a result, the `$age` variable, `$msg`, will contain `Age of the subject is 28`. If we had used single quotes, neither the age nor the carriage return would be substituted, and the resulting value would be `Age of the subject is $age\n` just as it is, which is probably not what you wanted.

---

### Working with PHP Variables

You can say that PHP variables are kind of amorphous—they don't need to be declared of any particular type, they can be assigned any type, and their type is interpreted according to its context. This is unlike C but very much like Perl.

You can use some PHP statements to cast a value to another type by using `intval`, `doubleval`, and `strval`, which return a value of integer, floating point and string types, respectively. There's also a series of PHP statements for checking the current variable type: `is_array`, `is_double`, `is_float`, `is_integer`, `is_long`, `is_object`, `is_real`, and `is_type`.

# Operators and Expressions

There are three main types of operators: arithmetic, logical, and relational.

You will probably bump into a few other operators after you feel more comfortable with PHP. Of these miscellaneous operators, the most important at this level are the string concatenation operator (.), the variable reference operator (&), and the tertiary conditional operator (?). (See the later section "The if Statement and Tertiary Operator" for more information on the tertiary operator.)

## Arithmetic Operators

We are all familiar with the arithmetic operators, which have the following order of precedence:

| Operator | Description |
|----------|-------------|
| * | Multiplication |
| / | Division |
| % | Modulo division (integer remainder) |
| ++ | Pre/post increment |
| -- | Pre/post decrement |
| - | Subtraction |
| + | Addition |

The pre and post increment and decrement operators are a shorthand notation used to increment or decrement a variable by a value of 1. It has the same behavior as in C and Perl, meaning that when used in an expression, if the operator is before the variable, as in --$i and ++$i, the variable is updated before using its value in the expression. If it's after the variable ($i++ and $i--), the current value is used in the expression and the value of the variable is operated on afterward.

One of the most common uses of modulo division (but certainly not the only one) is to determine whether a value is odd or even by using a modulo division by two:

```
$value % 2
```

This would result in 0 if $value is even, 1 if it is odd.

## Logical Operators

Logical operators are used in what is known as *Boolean arithmetic*, where everything evaluates to either true or false (most of the time). These can be bitwise or just plain logical. The difference is that the former operates on every bit of the value independently, whereas the latter performs the operation on the whole value at once.

| Operator | Description |
|----------|-------------|
| AND && | AND |
| & | Bitwise AND |
| OR \|\| | OR |
| \| | Bitwise OR |
| XOR | Exclusive OR |
| ^ | Bitwise Exclusive OR |
| ! | Not |
| ~ | Bitwise negation (one's complement) |
| << | Shift all bits to the left |
| >> | Shift all bits to the right |

Usually the bitwise logical operators are used when dealing with multiple flags stored in a single value. They are very popular in embedded systems programming.

The bit-shifting operators may seem out of this world to some people, but they are very useful. Shifting left by one bit is equivalent to multiplying by two; shifting by one bit to the right accomplishes the opposite (divide by two). For a more detailed coverage of these operators, refer to a book on programming or digital logic.

## Relational Operators

Expressions aren't complete without relational operators. As the name indicates, a relational operator expresses the relation of values to the left and right of the operator.

| Operator | Description |
|----------|-------------|
| < | Less than |
| > | Greater than |
| <= | Less than or equal to |
| >= | Greater than or equal to |
| != | Not equal to |
| == | Equal to |

A common mistake by beginners is to use the assignment operator (=) in an expression rather than the "equal to" (==) operator. While it's also valid to use the assignment operator in an expression, it's not always what the programmer meant.

## Functions

PHP is also a modular language; it allows you to define functions. Putting functions to good use will give you a better overview of the software. Try to use meaningful names for the functions, and reading your code will be a bit more pleasurable. If you don't do it for yourself, do it for those who will read your code.

As you already saw in the code snippet of Listing 22.2, a function is declared by the `function` keyword, followed by the function's name and then, between parentheses, a list of *optional* comma-delimited formal parameters in the form of variable names:

```
function DoesSomething( $param1, $param2 ) {
    Static $remember_it;
    Global $from_outside;

    $param1 = 2 * $param2 + $remember_it;
    $remember_it = $param1;
    Return $param2;
}
```

The body of the function is delimited by braces; inside them you can have any valid PHP statement. This is a good time to remember that whatever variable is first used within a function is known only within that function, unless you declare it as having a global scope or as being static (persistent value).

Parameters are passed by value, but if you need to pass a variable by reference, on the function invocation prepend the variable name with an ampersand. For example, if we were going to call the `DoesSomething` function (which does nothing particularly interesting or meaningful) with the first parameter passed by reference, it would be done like this:

```
$result = DoesSomething( &$par_one, $par_two);
```

Notice that, while it's possible to return a value, there is neither a check for the type of the return value nor the availability of a return value. This freedom comes with a responsibility to know what you are doing. The same applies for the parameter list.

## Flow Control

Flow control is an important element of every programming language because it allows you to implement complex logic and control operations. This can be roughly divided into decision making and loop control statements.

In PHP, you can implement decision making with any of the three statement families: `if`, `switch`, and the tertiary operator. The name *tertiary* stems from the operator needing three parts: the condition and two expressions. One expression is executed when the condition evaluates to `true`, the other in the event of a `false`.

Loop control can be performed with the usual `for` statement and two forms of the `while` statement.

## The `if` Statement and Tertiary Operator

The most common way to implement decision logic into a program is to use the `if` statement in any of its three forms. The `if` statement operates the same as in a natural language—that is, after the keyword, a condition (any valid PHP expression) is stated. In its simplest form, the statement has the following syntax:

```
if ( expression ) statement;
```

You can also group multiple statements to be executed when the condition represented by *expression* is true by using braces to delimit a block of statements, each of which is delimited by a semicolon:

```
if ( expression ) { statement-block }
```

Often we run into situations when it's also desirable to perform a different statement (or series of statements) when the condition isn't fulfilled. In this case, we use an `if...else` statement. For example:

```
if ( expression ) { perform-if-true; }
else { perform-if-false; }
```

In some cases the operations to be performed with `if...else` can be expressed in a simple way, either by a simple statement or a function call. It's then possible to use the tertiary operator as follows:

```
$is_even = ( $value % 2 == 0) ? TRUE : FALSE;
```

The tertiary operator is often used in assignment statements, but its usage is a matter of personal choice. If the expression evaluates to `true` (any non-zero value), the statement between the question mark and the colon is executed; otherwise, the statement between the colon and the semicolon is executed.

There are also situations in which a decision tree is called for. Very often people opt for cascading `if` statements. The most portable way this works with any language that uses `if...else` statements is to use the `else` block to contain the cascaded `if`. Fortunately, some languages—and PHP is one of them—offer an extra keyword suitable for decision trees. In PHP you can use the `elseif` keyword, which usually has the advantage of reducing indentation levels. A cascaded `if` would then look like this:

```
if ( condition ) { perform-if-true; }
elseif ( another-condition ) { perform-this; }
else { perform-this-instead; }
```

## The `switch` Statement

Any seasoned programmer has run into a situation where things aren't quite black and white. In such cases, the result of the expression doesn't necessarily evaluate to `true` or `false` but has a set of possible outcomes. The `switch` statement is most useful in these cases. Some languages don't offer this statement, but fortunately PHP does and goes even further. Some languages, such as C, restrict the use of `switch` to either numeric or single character sets. In PHP, your decision sets can be of any valid type, even strings.

The syntax of the `switch` statement involves the evaluation of an expression and one or more cases that represent a different outcome. It also can use the catch-all `default` in case none of the explicit cases match the result of the expression.

```
switch ( expression ) {
    case value:
        Statement(s);
        break;
    case value:
        Statement(s);
        break;
    default:
        Statements(s);
        break;
}
```

Of course, you can use as many `case` statements as you want, but only one `default` statement.

The `break` statement delimits the end of a statement block for a given result. It can be omitted if the intention is to let the execution fall through to the next `case` statement. Likewise, it's possible to put two `case value` sets one after the other so that both results cause the same group of statements to be executed.

## The `for` Statement

This looping statement follows the same syntax used in C:

```
for ( initial-expression ; condition ; update ) {
    any statements
}
```

`for` loops are usually associated with an incrementing or decrementing counter used by the statements to perform a repetitive operation.

The initial expression is performed the first time we enter the loop; it's used to initialize the incrementing or decrementing variable. The condition is tested at the end of every loop, and the loop will continue for as long as this condition evaluates to `true`. Also, every time the condition evaluates to true and the loop is executed, the `update` part of the `for` statement is executed. This is usually an increment or decrement operation of the variable that is initialized in the initial expression.

It's perfectly valid to not have any statements inside the braces.

## The `while` Statement

You could say that this statement is redundant. You also could say that it allows you to have a bit more freedom in expressing your thoughts as you are being cast into a program. There are two ways of using the `while` statement. One is the usual

```
while ( condition ) {
    statement(s);
}
```

The statements, if any, are executed for as long as the condition is `true`. Obviously there must be a way that the values of the elements used in the condition are changed; this is usually accomplished by the statements performed in the loop.

In this first form, the statements are executed zero or more times; if the condition is `false` upon entry, these statements never get executed. In another form of the `while` statement, the statements within the braces get executed at least once because the condition is evaluated at the end rather than at the beginning:

```
do {
    statement(s);
} while ( condition );
```

# Using Arrays

An *array* is a collection of values that have something in common. For example, an array can be a collection of measurements or a list of colors. In these cases it is usually impractical, if not inefficient, to create a different variable for each element. Arrays allow you to group them under a single variable name.

In PHP, you can have *indexed arrays* and *associative arrays*. An indexed array, which is indexed by an integer value, is in such common use that it is available in almost all modern languages. In an associative array, a string value, called the *key*, is used to index the array.

An element within an array—regardless of its type—is referenced by using the variable name that corresponds to the array, followed by a set of square brackets that contains the index value.

```
$colors[6] = 'blue';         // an indexed array element
$colors['blue'] = '#0000ff'; // an associative element
```

This syntax is used both in the assignment of elements and in referencing them in an expression.

While the preceding syntax is the most common, it's very impractical if we have to initialize a relatively large array with a set of values. In these cases, it's best to use the PHP array statement to initialize the array. With this statement, all the array's elements are set between the parentheses and separated by a comma. The preceding example can then be expressed as

```
$colors = array( 6 => 'blue', 'blue' => '#0000ff' );
```

It's perfectly valid to mix numbers and strings in the index of the same array. Notice the use of the => operator, which associates a value to a particular index. When indexing by numbers, the default starting index is zero.

PHP offers a variety of statements to handle array data and to convert to and from arrays. The most important are reset, next, key, and current, but there are many more. All of these take an array variable as argument.

Every PHP array contains an internal pointer and by default points to the first element inserted in the array. The reset function resets the internal pointer to the first element in the array; the opposite is accomplished by the end function. The next and prev functions move the pointer forward and backward, respectively, and return the array element indicated by that index. The current function (same as pos) returns the element at the current internal pointer; key returns the index of the current pointer. For example, this code snippet

```
$attrArray = array( "bgcolor"=>"#00ffee",
                    "text" => "#aabbcc" );
for ( reset($attrArray);
    $attrname = key($attrArray);
next($attrArray)) {
    $attrvalue = current($attrArray);
    echo("$attrname = $attrvalue\n");
}
```

will achieve the following: given an array with attributes, it will first set the internal pointer to the first element, and then get each element and its associated value from the array, until there is no more.

There are also two other useful functions called join (or implode) and explode. The former converts an array into a string by delimiting its values with a user-selected string:

```
$words = array('the', 'slow', 'old',
            'turtle', 'swam', 'into', 'the', 'sea');
$phrase = join($words, " ");
```

This will result in the $phrase value the slow old turtle swam into the sea. Working from that result, we can revert to the array form by using explode:

```
$words = explode(" ", $phrase);
```

which comes in quite handy when reading a configuration file with comma-delimited fields, for example.

## Getting Input from Web Forms

Although you can use PHP to generate Web pages on demand, you can also use it to process input from Web forms. That is, rather than have a CGI script as the requested action of a form, you can use a PHP script. The syntax is the same, and you can use either the GET or the POST method.

If you have done CGI programming, you will find PHP much easier to use to process forms, because the PHP interpreter does a great deal for you behind the scenes. For example, it converts all GET/POST key/value sets into plain PHP variables.

HTML forms have several types of elements to represent user input. These can be hidden fields, text fields, text areas, radio groups, check box groups, and option selections. The first four types of entities (hidden fields, text fields, text areas, and radio groups) are converted to plain PHP variables, so if you have an HTML form element like this

```
<input type="text" name="vname" size="25">
```

the handler script, when invoked, will contain a PHP variable named $vname. You can use the isset function to test if the value has been set; alternatively, you can check for a null string.

The last two element types, checkbox and select, may have multiple items selected. Remember our discussion about arrays and how they are used in PHP to collect values? That is exactly what we must do with these two input entities. It is a common mistake of newbies to forget to tell the PHP interpreter that it's an array that is being input and not a simple variable. For example

```
<input type="checkbox" name="vfruits[]" value="papaya">
```

Notice that a pair of square brackets is included in the name attribute for the checkbox input element. That tells PHP to create an array named vfruits and set one of its elements to papaya if the user selects the element. Since there can be zero or more elements selected, you can use the count function to check how many elements are present in the array.

## Classes

PHP is constantly evolving, and while it's not meant as a real application programming language like C++, PHP took the leap into object-oriented programming (OOP) in version 3. Applying OOP principles to your PHP projects will help you greatly in making your code reusable, if based on a good design.

Don't expect world-class OOP features in PHP3; there are enough basic features to let you apply the concepts and devise PHP objects in an easy way. There is support for a constructor, although early in the development of version 3.0 there was no support for class constructors. There are no destructors either, nor function overloading (although the latter can be more or less emulated). However, what is available will get you very far.

A PHP class definition is an envelope that contains the variables and methods that implement the class. Within a class you can define class variables by using the var keyword at the top of the class. There's no concept of private, public, or protected class variables; in fact, you can access them from outside the class. Class variables and class methods are accessed by using the -> operator. A class can access its own member functions and class variables by using the this keyword. As an example, let us create a simple class that we will use later on, as shown in Listing 22.3.

**LISTING 22.3** A Base Class for an HTML Object (htmlbase.class.php3)

```php
<?php
/* File: 22example03.php3 aka htmlbase.class.php3 */
if (!defined(HTML_BASE)) {
    define("HTML_BASE", 0.1);

    class HtmlBase {
     Var $site = 'Coralys.com';

        cfunction HtmlBase( $title, $body ) {
                    echo("<html><head><title>$title</title></head>\n");
            $this->Tag('body', $body);
    }

    // Tag - A generic HTML tag output
    //    $h->Tag('td', array('colspan' => 2));
    //    $h->Tag('table', 'border=5 cellspacing=3');
    cfunction Tag( $tag, $attrArray ) {
        $html = "<$tag";
        if (is_array($attrArray)) {
        // Go through each of the items in the associative
        // array. These are in the form key=value
        for (reset($attrArray);
            $attrname = key($attrArray);
            next($attrArray)) {
            $attrvalue = pos($attrArray);
            $html .= " $attrname=\"$attrvalue\"";
        }
        } else {
        // We got all attributes in one string
        $html .= $attrArray;
        }
```

```
        echo("$html>\n");
    }

    cfunction Footer() {
        echo("<hr><font size=\"-1\">" .
            "Based on work for $this->site</font>\n");
        echo("</body></html>\n");
    }
    };
}
?>
```

Here we defined a class variable named $site. This variable is used in the Footer method. If we had used just $site in Footer, it would have referred to a local variable in the scope of the Footer method. What we actually want is the class variable, so we use the notation this->site to access it.

Listing 22.3 also defines a constructor method. The constructor method must have the same name as the class and might or might not have parameters. The constructor is invoked when the class is instantiated—that is, created with the new statement. A class can be defined without a constructor as well.

We have defined a couple of class methods, which are defined in the same way as functions, except that we have used the cfunction (class function) keyword. You can also use the function keyword.

We have also defined a constant at the top within a conditional to prevent a redefinition of the class in case the file is included more than once in the same file. However, this only defines the class; to use it, we must create an instance of the object. To do that, we use the new statement, followed by the class name and possibly parameters if a constructor with parameters was defined. We could instantiate an object of the above class with the following statement:

```
$html = new HtmlBase("Fruit Parlor", $bodyattributes);
```

This would execute the constructor method that we have defined. If we were to use the Footer method, provided that we already had the object, we would use the following construct:

```
$html->Footer(); // Footer method of object $html
```

Once an object of a given class is instantiated, you can't get rid of it, at least not in PHP 3.

# Simple `mod_php` Scripts

Now you know enough to get started on writing a relatively simple yet useful example. One of the most common tasks done by PHP 3 is Web form processing. Rather than have a CGI program do it, use your newly installed PHP3.

For this we need two things: a Web page displaying the form and a PHP 3 script to do the processing of user input. It's also possible to implement both into one (a script) but for the sake of simplicity we will have an HTML page as in Listing 22.4 to present the form.

**LISTING 22.4**    Web Form Source for the Fruit Parlor

```
<html>
<head><title>Natural Fruits Milkshakes</title></head>
<body bgcolor="#ffffff" text="#008b8b">

<!-- File 22example04.html Example 22-4 -->
<h1>Fruity Ice Cream Parlor</h1>
<form name="myfruits" action="fruits.php3" method="POST">
Name: <input type="text" name="vname"
        size="20" value="Drosophila Melanogaster">

<h2>Your order</h2>
The ice cream, the cup and the spoon are included in the base price. Please
select your options now.<P>
<!-- Select either a Milkshake or a Sundae -->
Which product?<br>
<ul>
<input type="radio" name="vproduct"
 value="milkshake" checked> Milkshake<br>
<input type="radio" name="vproduct"
 value="sundae"> Sundae<br>
</ul>

<!-- Select multiple fruits -->
Which fruits?<br>
<ul>
<input type="checkbox" name="vfruit[]"
 value="banana" checked> Banana<br>
<input type="checkbox" name="vfruit[]"
 value="orange"> Orange<br>
<input type="checkbox" name="vfruit[]"
 value="peach"> Peach<br>
<input type="checkbox" name="vfruit[]"
 value="papaya"> Papaya<br>
</ul>
```

```
<!-- The form buttons -->
<center>
 <input type="submit" name="send" value="Buy">
 <input type="reset" name="clear" value="Clear">
</center>
</form>
<hr>
</body>
</html>
```

When this form is displayed in a Web browser, we should see something like that in Figure 22.1.

**FIGURE 22.1**

*Fruit Parlor Web form display.*

How PHP handles form variables was discussed earlier in the section "Getting Input from Web Forms." Now when a user clicks the Buy button, the PHP script given in the ACTION attribute of the <FORM> tag is invoked. The source of this script is shown in Listing 22.5.

**LISTING 22.5**   Fruit Parlor Form Handler (*fruits.php3*)

```
<?php
   /*
    * File: 22example05.php3
    * Program: fruits.php3
    * Description:
    *        Handles the web form 22example04.html (Ice Cream Parlor)
    */
   include "htmlbase.class.php3";

   $prices = array(        // As an associative array
                "milkshake" => 1.10, "sundae" => 0.85,
                "banana"    => 0.45, "orange" => 0.20,
```

**Listing 22.5**    continued

```
                    "peach"     => 0.30, "papaya" => 0.50);
    $bodyattr = array(
                    "text"     => "#b22222",
                    "bgcolor"  => "#ffffff");

    function ProcessOrder( $ho, $total_price ) {
        global $vname, $vproduct, $vfruit;   // Form Variables
        global $prices;

        echo("<h1>Thank You!</h1>\n");
        echo("Good Day <b>$vname</b>!,<br>your " .
            "<b>$vproduct</b> is being prepared<P>\n");

        $total_price = $prices[$vproduct];

        $ho->Tag('table', array('border'=>0));

        echo("<tr>\n");
        $ho->Tag('td', array('colspan'=>2));
        echo("<b>Product:</b></td>\n");
        echo("</tr>\n");
        echo("<tr><td>$vproduct</td>\n");
        printf("<td>$ %3.02f</td></tr>", $total_price);

        echo("<tr>\n");
        $ho->Tag('td', array('colspan'=>2));
        echo("<b>Extra ingredients:</b></td>\n");
        echo("</tr>\n");

        // Check if there are any elements in the vfruit array
        if (count($vfruit) == 0) {
            // Nothing selected in this checkbox group
            echo("<tr>\n");
            echo("<td>none (vanilla)</td><td>$ 0.00</td>\n");
            echo("</tr>\n");
        } else {
            // Go through the array
            for ($i = 0; $i < count($vfruit); $i++) {
                $fruitname = $vfruit[$i];
                $fruitprice= $prices[$fruitname];
                echo("<tr>\n");
                echo("<td>$fruitname</td>\n");
                printf("<td>$ %3.02f</td>", $fruitprice);
                echo("</tr>\n");
                // Update the price for this order
                $total_price += $fruitprice;
            }
        }
        printf("<tr><td><b>Total:</b></td><td>$ %3.02f</td></tr>\n",
```

```
            $total_price);

    echo("</table>\n");
  }

  /* --------- Main Body --------- */
  $html = new HtmlBase("Fruit Parlor Checkout", $bodyattr);
  ProcessOrder( $html, &$pay );
  $html->Footer();
?>
```

First we introduce the `include` statement by which we include a class that was defined in Listing 22.3. At this time, all form variables are available to PHP. Next we create a new object. Then we process the order and generate some output. Notice how in `ProcessOrder` we pass two parameters: the object we have just created and a variable by reference.

Within the function we now access the methods of the object. We also calculate the price of the order and generate a detailed list of which ingredients were chosen and their prices. We use a global statement to access the form variables from within the function. An associative array is used to obtain the prices of the products and ingredients, and at some point we also iterate through the array of ingredients chosen by the user using the functions introduced in the "Using Arrays" section.

It's all very simple and, while this isn't complete coverage of PHP 3, we hope to have encouraged you to try PHP 3 with Apache all by yourself.

# Sites Using PHP and Information on the Web

Plenty of sites use PHP, many of which are Internet service providers that provide PHP either in module or CGI form for their clients. One site that relies on PHP almost exclusively is `http://www.coralys.com/`.

FreeMed (`http://www.freemed.org/`) not only uses PHP but is also the home page of the FreeMed project, which aims at developing an office management application for physicians, all by using PHP.

One obvious place for Linux/Unix software announcements is Freshmeat (`http://www.freshmeat.net/`), which uses PHP 3 to implement all the features of the site. This includes software announcements and a software database.

32 Bits Online (`http://32bit.com/`) is another Web site using PHP. This site deals with 32-bit software (probably until 64-bit becomes mainstream) for Windows, Linux, and so on. Here you find news as well as a software download section.

If you are looking for fonts, `http://fonts.linuxpower.org/` is a good place to find them and see PHP 3 put to good use as well.

It may be that your installation didn't include the PHP documentation. All the PHP documents are available online at `http://www.php.net/docs.php3`.

At some point you may find it useful to subscribe to the PHP 3 users list, `php3@lists.php.net`. This is a high volume mailing list, and I mean *high volume*. You can easily subscribe to this list at the `php.net` site at the touch of a button. If you don't want to subscribe, you can also browse the list archives at `http://www.phpbuilder.com/`. This is a good source of help when facing problems, because it is very likely somebody else already has found a solution.

And last but not least, PHPWizard (`http://phpwizard.net/`) is also using PHP 3. Here you can find PHP software components for your designs.

# Summary

In this chapter, you learned about the PHP module and what this could mean when used to provide dynamic content without sacrificing flexibility or performance. We have taken you through the installation and configuration of PHP. We have exposed you to the essentials of programming in PHP and provided several examples to aid in understanding its many features.

# Other Well-Known Modules

**CHAPTER 23**

Along with the standard modules that come packaged with Apache are numerous modules from external sources, both commercial and open source. You can even write your own, as you'll see in Chapter 24, "Working with the Apache API," and contribute to Apache's usefulness. (One central registry for nonstandard open-source Apache modules is `modules.apache.org`.)

Broadly speaking, there are three types of Apache modules:

- **Language support**   The module provides an interface for a programming language to the Apache API—similarly to the way the Apache API provides an interface for C and `mod_perl` provides an interface for Perl. The module is general purpose and doesn't provide any specific functionality itself (outside of what the language provides).

- **Application server**   The module provides a collection of features, including some type of programming, useful in building Web-based applications. The later section "Application Servers" goes into more detail about the features you can expect in an application server. Applications can be widely divided into those that use content-embedded scripting code such as PHP and those that use code outside the relevant content, such as Java servlets.

- **Utility module**   The module provides a single well-defined feature that's used principally as a helper to other modules or the generic Apache functionality and isn't meant to incorporate application-specific logic. In general, utility modules don't have their own programming or scripting languages. Most standard modules can be considered utility modules.

This chapter will discuss how to use a data security mechanism, SSL, with Apache.

# Language Support Modules

In addition to the `mod_perl` module for Perl language support and the native C support of the Apache API, there are modules that let you develop in Java and Python.

## Java and JavaScript

Java is a popular computer language with an object-oriented model, cross-platform portability, and various out-of-the-box functions. JavaScript is a scripting language with Java syntax and a less rigorous object-oriented model. Two current modules, `mod_fjord` and `mod_js`, provide a way to interface directly between these two languages and Apache.

The `mod_fjord` module connects the Apache API to the freely distributed Kaffe Java Virtual Machine, enabling developers to write applications in Java. This module doesn't allow access to the entire Apache API. It should be considered experimental and may be out of date with your current Apache setup. (See `www.ace.net/Objects/ApacheModule.html` for more information.)

---

**Note**

The Apache Group has started a project called `mod_java` to translate the entire Apache API directly into Java. It's currently only in the design phase.

---

The `mod_js` module allows a developer to program a subset of the Apache API in the JavaScript language. This module should also be considered experimental and may be out of date with your current Apache setup. (See `www.geocities.com/TimesSquare/Fortress/9743/binjs.html` for more information.)

In addition to these two modules, you can also use Java in the Java Servlet API (see the later section "Java Servlet API").

## Python: PyApache

Python is an easy-to-earn, interpreted, object-oriented scripting language. It's freely distributed, available for many operating systems, and surprisingly simple and powerful at the same time. For all these reasons, it's commonly compared to Perl.

Just as with any other language, you can use Python as a CGI script, but there's also an Apache in-process interpreter module, PyApache, which lets you access the Apache API without spawning a separate process.

Although PyApache is open source, it's relatively up-to-date with the newest Apache APIs, and its popularity is helping it become more stable and reliable. More info on PyApache is available at `www.msg.com.mx/pyapache/`.

# Application Servers

The basic credo of an application server is "We'll do the bookkeeping so that you don't have to."

Different vendors and developers give different definitions for what this *bookkeeping* is, so the term *application server* varies. It's important not to get too pedantic about the definition, however. Suffice it to say that an application server should help developers by providing them with out-of-the-box components useful to business application programming. The most common of the application server features are as follows:

- **Multitier architecture**   Most application server products follow a multitier architecture, running the Web server, which handles messaging with the various browsers, and the application server, which handles the business logic (as well as the database server, which handles the data storage, of course) in different server processes. All the server processes may, in turn, be located on different machines or clusters of machines, adding to the scalability and robustness of the entire system.

- **Data persistence layer**   A key area to many applications is the underlying data and how to access it efficiently and safely. All application servers and most languages provide support to a relational database. The solutions are many and varied. Java Servlets cooperating with Sun's Enterprise JavaBeans and WebObjects' Enterprise Objects Modeler go furthest in this regard with their application servers.

- **Session management**   One of the often-quoted disadvantages of HTTP is that it's a *stateless* protocol (although it's often said that this is an advantage as well). What this term means is that each interaction or connection is expected to process one atomic request and stop. An exception, of course, is Keep-Alive connections, which stay open long enough to enable a coherent set of requests such as images and frames to be met—but still, these connections will not be left open in any human sense. No information about the server or the client is stored by the other. Workarounds to stateless sessions are to use cookies and to pass state information through CGI parameters (through the GET method's QUERY_STRING or the POST method's standard input). Many application servers implement one or more of these devices and provide the developer with the convenient fiction that state is preserved across connections and that interaction with the client is really a continuous session.

- **User profiling**   User profiling means more than just knowing what the username and password are. It means knowing and possibly tailoring the content to fit the specific needs of the user. Although developers can implement this functionality themselves, application servers that have out-of-the-box user profiling solutions ease the development task.

- **Support for different Web servers**   Although we hate to think poorly of our beloved Apache, vendors and developers of application servers have other goals in mind. For them, casting a wide net and supporting different Web servers is beneficial.

- **General-purpose programming**   One key to application servers is that they don't specify which application you are serving. Therefore support for general-purpose programming is essential. Some application servers even support multiple languages. For example, WebObjects started with Objective-C support and has expanded it to C++ and Java; The imprecisely named JSP is an interface that doesn't specify an actual scripting language.

- **Development support**   Application servers can provide scaffolding to design, develop, test, and debug your application code, which increases the productivity of your development efforts.

As you may be able to tell, application servers turn the Apache-module relationship on its head. The Apache server may be seen as simply servicing the application server with HTTP requests and dispatching the application server's responses. It's the application server that finds itself firmly in the middle of the architecture, giving rise to another name for application servers—*middleware*.

# Java Servlets and Java Server Pages

Although initially touted as a language perfectly matched to the Internet, with few exceptions Java was used only for browser applets until its use in Sun Microsystems' Java Servlet and Java Server Pages APIs. These two APIs are becoming popular with Web developers because of Sun's open API development (or at least *perceived* as open), the large number of available implementations, the stability and reliability of many of these implementations, and the number of other Java APIs that allow additional functionality.

## Java Servlet API

Unlike the `mod_fjord module` or the `mod_java module that is under development`, the Java Servlet API is not simply a translation of the Apache API. For one thing, the Java Servlet API wasn't meant to be used only with Apache—any sufficiently modular Web server would do. Secondly, the Java Servlet API isn't an actual working piece of code—it's simply a description of how an actual Java Servlet implementation should work. Lastly, the process lifecycle is different, and the Java Servlet API doesn't support all the lifecycle steps (such as configuration steps or MIME handler) of the Apache API.

Briefly, the features of the current Java Servlet 2.2 API are as follows:

- **Session and application management**   Servlets (the core classes that interact with the Servlet API) can store data for the life of the session or the application.
- **HTTP utilities**   There is ready access to a variety of HTTP and HTML types and utilities, including cookies, HTTP headers, parameter parsing, character encoding, path translation, internal request forwarding, connection I/O buffering, and SSL certificates (in Java 1.2).
- **Multithreaded support**   Multithreaded execution of program code means a more responsive server environment.
- **Application-level packaging and safety**   One area that Java Servlet use lags in is large-scale multi-application environments—for example, at an ISP. To encourage developers, the API has recently been extended to include features that specifically

enable easy packaging and portability of servlet code, as well as safety by restricting access.

- **Distributed application support**    The Java Servlet API has recently added support for Web applications across multiple machines. This feature enhances the Web application's scalability and robustness.

More information about the Java Servlet API can be found on Sun's sites: `www.javasoft.com/products/servlet/index.html` and `http://java.sun.com/docs/books/tutorial/servlets/index.html`.

## Java Server Pages (JSP)

It's inaccurate to treat Java Server Pages as completely separate from Java Servlets. In fact, JSP is a natural complement to Java Servlets—both because JSP pages are usually translated into Java Servlets and because Java Servlets can use JSP pages as templates.

It may seem that translating a JSP page into a Java Servlet (it is almost literally transformed into a servlet with a bunch of `print()` statements) just to add a few bits of dynamic functionality is extreme. Actually, it mimics how high-performance Web servers serve static pages—by caching the files in RAM, either explicitly in the Web server (through the `mod_mmap` module) or implicitly, through the OS (which caches often-used files).

The basic features of JSP are as follows:

- **Content-embedded scripting**    JSP code is embedded as JSP tags into the HTML code as a parallel, XML-compliant extension to the language. JSP doesn't prescribe what programming language the scripting elements, the ones that perform in-place logic, must actually be, though almost all JSP implementations currently support only Java.

- **JavaBean support**    JSP interfaces with JavaBeans to access specific units of data.

- **Tag extensions**    The most recent JSP API allows developers to implement their own JSP tags to encapsulate areas of functionality and to keep the presentation content and business logic as separate as possible.

## Java Servlet and JSP Implementations

The following sections list the common commercial and freely distributed implementations of the Java Servlet and JSP APIs. Java Servlet implementations are usually called *servlet engines*. Also note that the Java Servlet API is fast moving and that, as of this writing (January 2000), none of the production-quality servlet engines are up to the 2.2 version features.

## Reference: JSWDK and Tomcat

Along with Java Server API documents, Sun provides a reference implementation, used in testing the soundness of the API and the correctness of other production-quality implementations. The name of this reference implementation was JSDWK until the 2.1 version of the Servlet API and the 1.0.1 version of the JSP API. Currently, Sun's Java Servlet 2.2 and JSP 1.1 reference implementations have been folded into Tomcat 3.0. Tomcat falls under the rubric of the Apache Group's Jakarta project. For more information, visit `www.javasoft.com/products/servlet/index.html` and `jakarta.apache.org/tomcat/index.html`.

## Apache Group's Jserv

The Apache Group also has the oldest production-quality Java Server implementation, called Jserv. It's freely distributable and open source. This is only a Java Servlet implementation, not a JSP implementation. However, you can use JSP with Jserv with a third-party component such as GNUJSP. Apache Group's Jakarta team is looking to have Tomcat succeed Jserv not only in terms of API features, but also with quality characteristics such as scalability and reliability.

## Allaire's JRun

Allaire's JRun is one of the oldest commercial servlet engines available. It implements the Java Servlet 2.1 and JSP 1.0 APIs. JRun also offers Web-based administration and application safety by running applications in separate JVMs. JRun is available on various platforms and for various Web servers and is compatible with various JVMs.

## IBM's WebSphere Application Server

IBM also has a robust and scalable servlet engine product, called WebSphere. WebSphere has support for Java Server 2.1 and JSP 1.0 APIs, an XML parser, a fast JIT compiler (on Windows NT), database pooling, user profiling and Web-based administration. It also integrates with other IBM products such as the IBM HTTP Server, VisualAge for Java, WebSphere Studio, and Tivoli-based tools. More information is available at `www-4.ibm.com/software/webservers/appserv/`.

## BEA's WebLogic

BEA's WebLogic product is not just a servlet engine—it supports connections from various sources. It supports Java Server 2.1 and JSP 1.0 APIs, Enterprise JavaBeans, CORBA, and SSL. It has been built with large-scale deployment in mind and is highly scalable and robust. More info is available at `www.beasys.com/products/weblogic/server/index.html`.

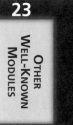

23

OTHER
WELL-KNOWN
MODULES

### New Atlanta's ServletExec

Like JRun, ServletExec is a popular, stable servlet engine. It implements Java Servlet 2.1 and JSP 1.0 APIs. ServletExec also offers Web-based administration and a runtime debugger that integrates with common IDEs.

### Caucho's Resin

Resin is a Java servlet engine with JSP support, which among other features has a stub Apache module to integrate with Apache. It currently supports Java Servlet 2.1 and JSP 1.0 APIs. For more info, visit `www.caucho.com/products/resin1.0/index.html`.

### GNUJSP

GNUJSP is an open source implementation of JSP 1.0 API. You can use it with Apache and Jserv to serve JSP pages. For more info, visit `www.klomp.org/gnujsp/`.

## Allaire's ColdFusion

ColdFusion is a mature multitiered application server product from Allaire. It's based on content-embedded scripting to glue templates to database access, session management, and user profiling features. It's popular because of its simplicity, its extensibility (for example, you can add customized scripting tags), and the variety of prebuilt ColdFusion applications. You can find more information about ColdFusion at `www.allaire.com`.

## Apple's WebObjects

Although not often considered, Apple's WebObjects is a mature (tracing its lineage back 10 years to being an application development framework for NeXT), stable, and powerful application server. And best of all, it works with Apache!

WebObjects uses a stub Apache module to interface with its own application server architecture.

It allows for powerful scalability and stability by allowing distribution of the work across multiple Web server machines, multiple application server machines and multiple database server machines, if that is needed.

WebObjects also provides a well-tested, feature-full development environment, a robust object persistence model to store long-term data in databases and support for code to be written in Objective-C, Java, and C++. WebObjects is available only for Solaris with Apache.

## Active Server Pages (ASP)

One of the more successful Web development platforms of the last few years has been Active Server Pages (ASP). It is architecture for content-embedded scripting, with various support features such as database connectivity, COM, user profiling, and session management.

For a long time, the use of ASP was limited to Microsoft's Internet Information Server, but that has changed recently.

Chili!Soft ASP implements ASP, allowing you to run on Apache software previously developed only for Microsoft's Internet Information Server. See `www.chilisoft.com` for more information.

Another ASP module available only for Windows NT is the OpenASP module, sponsored by the ActiveScripting Organization. See `www.activescripting.org` for more info.

You can also obtain ASP scripting capability with an experimental Perl Apache module, `Apache::ASP`. See `www.nodeworks.com/asp/` for more information.

## Zope

Zope is an open source Python-based application server that provides embedded content scripting, persistent object and content management, and administrative features. It is still immature and malleable. The content management piece of Zope used to be called Bobo.

More information can be found at `www.zope.org` and `weblogs.userland.com0/zopeNewbies/`.

# Utility Modules

Here are some common utility modules that are available for Apache. These modules vary widely in their functions, from access management to language translation to Web-based authoring.

## National Character Sets: `mod_fontxlate`

The `mod_fontxlate` module converts the character set of the response to the one sought in the request. For more info, visit `www.rcc-irc.si/eng/fontxlate`.

**23**

OTHER
WELL-KNOWN
MODULES

## Bandwidth Management: `mod_bandwidth`

The `mod_bandwidth` module controls the amount of bandwidth as defined by sizes of transmissions that users can have. It is quite configurable and useful, especially in hosting environments. More info can be found at `http://www.cohprog.com/mod_bandwidth.html`.

## The `mod_lock` Module

For more info, see `hpwww.ec-lyon.fr/~vincent/apache/mod_lock.html`.

## WebDAV: `mod_dav`

WebDAV is a set of HTTP extensions that supports distributed Web authoring (addressing issues of locks, versioning, and document properties). The `mod_dav` module implements much of the WebDAV interface. For more info, see `http:/www.webdav.org/mod_dav`.

## FTP: `mod_conv`

The `mod_conv` module lets you convert FTP archives into Web-viewable form.

More info is at `http://sunsite.mff.cuni.cz/web/local/mod_conv.0.2.1.tar.gz`.

## Oracle

A couple of Apache modules let you connect directly to Oracle PL/SQL. The two most popular are `mod_plsql` and `mod_owa`. These should be considered experimental.

More info is at `www.selfsort.com/progs/mod_plsql/` and `interntk.kada.lt:7777/pub/apache`.

## Postgres 95

Postgres 95 is an open source object-oriented database management server. One can store files in the database and use the `mod_blob_pg95` module to translate URIs and extract them. You can download Postgres 95 from `ftp://hachiman.vidya.com/pub/apache/mod_blob_pg95.tar.gz`.

## FrontPage Support

FrontPage is a popular HTML composition program developed by Microsoft. It allows the capability not only to modify HTML files in place—that is, on a client's computer—but also to compose and modify files across the network. It seems natural to use the HTTP protocol itself to open and save files, since the protocol does provide methods for changing files: PUT and DELETE. The only problem is that for security reasons these two methods are completely disabled in standard Apache—in fact, you need to go out of your way to enable them in Apache. The FrontPage module provides these two methods and the authentication and locking mechanisms necessary to work with the FrontPage 98 program.

For more information about downloading and installing the FrontPage module, see `http://www.rtr.com/fpsupport/`.

You will most likely want to have a measure of security with your FrontPage editing, so it makes sense to use a common security method: SSL. See `http://www.itma/lu/howto/apache` for information about how to set up Apache-SSL with the FrontPage extensions.

# Apache with SSL

Before going into the mechanics of Apache with Secure Sockets Layer (SSL), first let's outline why this combination may be necessary. The basic motivation is that you, the Webmaster, or your Web site users are concerned about someone else interfering with the information in your messages. Specifically, the three types of interference are as follows:

- Breaches of confidentiality, when information is available to someone it's not supposed to be available to.

- Breaches of authentication, when someone successfully pretends to be someone he is not.

- Breaches of data integrity, when someone corrupts your information and makes it unusable or, worse, incorrect.

Such caution is obviously necessary with such high-profile information as credit card information but is also the case whenever actions and information need to be protected.

You may think that since confidentiality, correct authentication, and data integrity are important to people, security should be built into the current HTTP standard. But on a practical basis, that ends up not being the case because extra precautions and security measures are expensive. It takes time to encrypt and decrypt information, and information is by far mostly harmless; either it is generic knowledge like most images and static HTML files or unrevealing such as your anonymous answers to an Internet poll. So it makes sense to separate the messages that need to be secure from the vast majority of messages that don't.

The method that is by far the most commonly used to achieve security on the World Wide Web is the HTTPS protocol—the regular HTTP protocol over secure sockets, the so-called Secure Sockets Layer (SSL). That is, there is no difference in the way the HTTP request/response mechanism works; it is simply that the underlying socket connections are assumed to be secure.

## How SSL Works

The Secure Sockets Layer was first devised by Netscape, and a full description of the current and stable 3.0 version can be found at Netscape's site (`www.netscape.com/eng/ssl3/draft302.txt`). Currently the standards community is working on a broader security mechanism, Transport Layer Security 1.0 (TLS). TLS will not be the same as SSL but will gracefully fall back to the SSL interface to ensure backward compatibility. Some SSL implementations (such as the venerable SSLeay, version 0.9.0) are misnamed because they've jumped ahead and implemented the current draft of the TLS protocol as well.

An outline of the SSL protocol follows. You can refer to the schematic in Figure 23.1 for more detail about the actual messages sent.

1. Identity is authenticated by using asymmetric cryptography (such as RSA, Diffie-Hellman) during an initial handshake sequence where public keys are exchanged.

2. The public keys themselves are verified by using a trusted certificate authority. These two steps secure against breaches of authentication.

3. When identity is authenticated, the connection is secured by using symmetric cryptography (such as IDEA, DEA, RC4, and Fortezza). That is, both parties are issued secret keys to use for the rest of the connection. Asymmetric cryptography isn't used throughout the connection because it's a slower method of encrypting and decrypting data. This step secures against breaches of confidentiality.

4. Encrypted messages are also summarized into a short digital digest (called a *message authentication code*, or MAC) that can be recomputed on both computers to assure no part of the original message is missing or has been changed. This is akin to making sure that two files are the same by comparing their sizes, except that the summarizing techniques are much harder to circumvent. Hashing or digest algorithms (such as MD5 or SHA) are used to produce the digital digest. This step secures against breaches of data integrity.

That's it. Everything else works as in HTTP. In fact, the SSL protocol isn't limited to HTTP and can be used with Telnet and FTP as well.

Usually HTTPS runs on port 443, but you can easily change that in the configuration files just as you can for HTTP.

**FIGURE 23.1**

*A scenario illustrating the SSL protocol.*

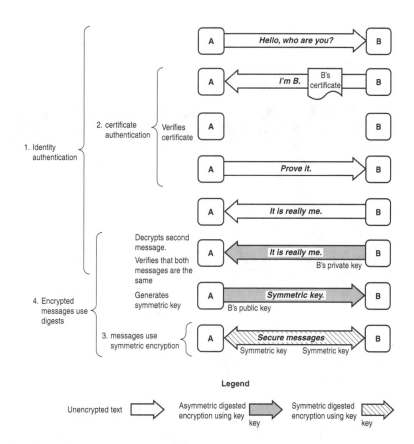

## Apache with SSL Implementations

Since the Apache community strongly favors open source and freely distributable software, one solution is to build an open source and freely distributable Apache with SSL, which is what Apache-SSL and `mod_ssl` are. Another path is to have commercial companies augment Apache with their own SSL code and/or licenses—usually selling SSL-enhanced Apache binaries. The advantages and disadvantages of these two solutions are the same as with other open source versus commercial software, with the only complication that the patents and national security issues concerning the underlying encryption algorithms prohibit use in some countries without a license or even at all.

Basically, if you want to use SSL inside the United States for commercial purposes, you need to obtain a license from RSA Security Inc. (see www.rsasecurity.com for more info) because that company is the patent holder on the most commonly used asymmetric cryptography algorithm. This applies not only to Apache but also to other Web servers such as Netscape Enterprise or Microsoft IIS. When you purchase either server, as well as a commercial Apache with SSL server, you obtain a license to use the underlying RSA algorithms. If you want to use the freely available implementations of Apache with SSL commercially, you need to contact RSA Security and purchase your own license.

> **Note**
>
> Building Apache with SSL and subsequently exporting it out of the country most likely infringes on export restrictions. We urge you to obtain legal counsel before doing so.

## Apache-SSL

Apache-SSL is an open source, freely distributed implementation of SSL for Apache. It's not a module—it's a patch to the core Apache files as well as some additional code files. It relies on the OpenSSL library and the RSA cryptography library. For more information on Apache-SSL, see www.apache-ssl.org and www.openssl.org.

## The `mod_ssl` Package

The `mod_ssl` package is another open source, freely distributable add-on to Apache. In many ways it's an evolutionary successor to the Apache-SSL.

Although the name may indicate that `mod_ssl` is just another Apache module, that isn't exactly the case. The `mod_ssl` package is a regular Apache module plus an extension to the Apache API, called Extended API (EAPI). The EAPI allows the `mod_ssl` Apache module to dig into the bowels of Apache in a way that the regular Apache API doesn't. The `mod_ssl` module then interfaces with OpenSSL, which in turn uses the cryptography algorithm libraries to do the actual encrypting, decrypting, and digesting of data. You can find more on this package at www.modssl.org.

## Stronghold

Stronghold by C2net is one of the more popular and longest available commercial SSL implementations. The company provides extensive service and even a free certificate. They make their source code available to promote better security and allow for easy extensions with other modules. Stronghold versions 2.3 and later are based on `mod_ssl`. For more information on this product, see www.c2.net/products/sh2/.

## IBM HTTP Server

IBM has enhanced the Apache server with its own SSL implementation, IBM HTTP Server. Features include browser-based configuration, LDAP and SNMP support, and product support from IBM. IBM HTTP Server is currently available for AIX, Windows NT, OS/390, AS/400, Solaris, and Linux. It is the most stable SSL implementation of Apache on the Windows NT platform. More information is at `www-4.ibm.com/software/webservers/httpservers/`.

## Raven

Raven is produced by Covalent Technologies, which provides support with its product. Because of security restrictions, it's available only to customers in the U.S. and Canada. It too is based on `mod_ssl`. For more details, visit `www.covalent.net/raven/ssl/`.

## Red Hat Secure Web Server

Red Hat, the popular Linux distributor, provides an SSL implementation with binary and code, called Secure Web Server, with its Red Hat Linux distribution. It too is based on `mod_ssl`. Find out more at `www.redhat.com`.

## Certificate Authorities

A *certificate authority* is a canonical place where your SSL server and a browser can agree on each other's identity. It's where public keys are stored and browsers go to confirm that the public key your SSL server is using is actually from you. A number of places offer the service of storing and handling certificates, including the following:

- **Thawte Consulting**   `www.thawte.com`
- **Verisign Inc.**   `www.verisign.com`
- **CertiSign Certificadora Digital Ltda.**   `www.certisign.com/br`
- **IKS GmbH.**   `www.iks-jena.de/produkte/ca`
- **BelSign NV/SA**   `www.belsign.be`
- **Entrust.net Ltd.**   `entrust.net`
- **Equifax Inc.**   `www.equifaxsecure.com`
- **NLSign BV**   `www.nlsign.nl`

23

OTHER WELL-KNOWN MODULES

# Summary

In this chapter, you looked at the common modules available for Apache, including language support, application servers, and utility modules. We also described the security mechanism provided by SSL and listed the implementations of Apache with SSL.

# Working with the Apache API

Apache is more than just a core with standard feature modules; it is also an extensive and powerful application programming interface (API) that allows the enterprising developer to extend Apache's functionality greatly. It is not a simple API, and we advise that you have solid experience with C, but its complexity is a function of its richness, of its high goals.

Once you become familiar with the Apache API, you will realize to what an extent the Apache development team has worked to help you, the developer, be able to write Apache modules that are quick to develop, powerful, and stable.

So let's begin with the basic architectural parts.

# Basic Module Architecture

A *module* is a collection of handlers called by the Apache core at crucial steps in the Apache process lifecycle. Broadly, whenever the Apache core has a choice of what to do, it asks, "What should be done?" and the modules respond.

More specifically, when a module is loaded, it registers itself and its handlers with the Apache core. When the Apache core reaches a handle situation, it goes to the modules for assistance. There are two types of handle situations:

- Only one handler will successfully handle an *exclusive* situation. In this case, the Apache core iterates through its list of handlers for this situation until one returns a decisive value (that is, a non-DECLINE status code; see the later section "Apache Handler Status Codes").

- In an *inclusive* situation, all the handlers will be called. This is the case with process endpoints—the creation and destruction of the process, with the four configuration handlers and with the header parser.

The Apache core iterates over the modules in the order they were compiled or loaded.

The Apache handle situations are described with their corresponding handle fields in the section "The module Structure," later in this chapter.

## Apache Handlers

First, let's look at Apache handlers. The Apache API provides the Apache handler with the following:

- A resource object (a pointer to a struct) that provides a mechanism to access data provided by the Apache core to the handlers and usually a pool. The various structures are discussed later in the section "Apache Data Structures".

- A memory management scheme through the use of pools (described later in the section "Resource Pools").
- Utility routines for HTTP, I/O, and Apache-specific processing.

The responsibility of the Apache handler is to

- Do something useful, usually at least one of the following:
    - Change one or more fields in the `resource` object
    - Send a request back to the Apache core (not as a return value, but by using the `ap_send_request()` routine)
    - Create a configuration data structure to be used by other handlers in the module (this technique is used by the four configuration handlers)
- Use pools for memory management.
- Return an informative status code.
- Not interfere with other modules unnecessarily.

> **Note**
>
> It's possible to "do something useful" by simply returning an informative status code, as is the case with the access control handlers that only calculate and return a status code reflecting the user's access permissions.

## Apache Process Lifecycle

Before we discuss the handlers, data structures, and pools in more detail, let's step back and review the Apache process lifecycle to see what the handler steps are. Figure 24.1 demonstrates the steps of the Apache process lifecycle.

Notice that in the request/response loop, if any of the handlers returns an error code, process control will stop and be handed over to the logger and subsequently to the cleanup handlers.

## The `module` Structure

The `module` structure reflects the Apache process lifecycle, though not necessarily in the order shown in the lifecycle in Figure 24.1 (the Apache API was developed over time to incorporate refinements in the process lifecycle). In Figure 24.1, each circled label corresponds to a handler situation. Listing 24.1 shows the `module` struct.

**FIGURE 24.1**

*The Apache process lifecycle.*

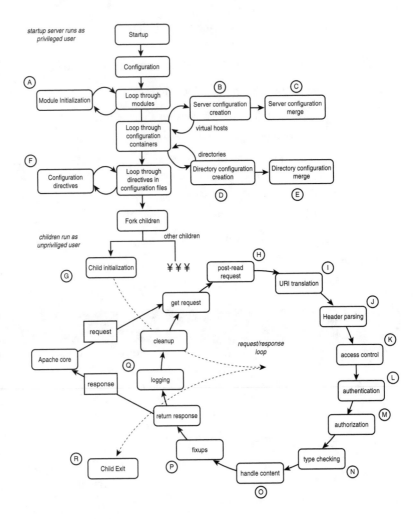

**LISTING 24.1** The *module* Struct

```
module MODULE_VAR_EXPORT name_module =
{
    STANDARD_MODULE_STUFF,
    init_modname,                    /* initializer handler */
    create_modname_dir_config,       /* directory config creator */
    merge_modname_dir_configs,       /* directory config merger */
    create_modname_server_configs,   /* server config creator */
    merge_modname_server_configs,    /* server config merger */
    modname_cmds,                    /* configuration directives table */
    modname_handlers,                /* MIME handlers */
    modname_translator,              /* URI translator */
```

```
    modname_check_user_id,          /* authentication handler*/
    modname_check_auth,             /* authority handler */
    modname_check_access,           /* access control handler */
    modname_type_checker,           /* type checker */
    modname_fixups,                 /* fixups handler */
    modname_logger,                 /* logger handler */
    modname_header,                 /* header parser */
    modname_child_init,             /* child initialization routine */
    modname_child_exit,             /* child exit routine */
    modname_postread                /* post read-request handler */
};
```

Replace the *modname* label with the actual name of your module. The labels are
merely suggestions; you can name the routines anything you want as long as the names
don't interfere with the names of other routines.

MODULE_VAR_EXPORT is a macro used by Win32 systems.

STANDARD_MODULE_STUFF is a boilerplate macro that swaps in standard module fields
such as API version number, module name, module runtime index number, DSO handler,
and module linked list pointer. You don't need to worry about any of these fields; they
are generated and used internally by the Apache core.

The following sections describe the other fields in the module struct. Most fields in the
struct are handlers—that is, function pointers. We give the expected signature of the
function for those fields. For the remaining fields, we give the types.

## Initializer Handler (A)

The initializer handler is called during module initialization right after the Apache server
is started:

```
void name_init(server_rec *s, pool *p);
```

It's expected that the module will use this handler to create and initialize any data
resources such as file descriptors, module-specific data structures, and so forth. In Unix
implementations, database connections shouldn't be initialized here, as they aren't stable
during the forking process; their initialization should be reserved for the child initialization step.

Under Unix systems, the data structures created here are copied into the forked children
and are independent of (and thus safe from) each other. Under Win32, the data structures
are the same across threads, and module authors need to ensure thread safety on their
own.

The server_rec argument provides the handler access to the necessary data.

24

WORKING WITH
THE APACHE API

The lifetime of the `pool` argument is the lifetime of the Apache server.

## Directory Config Creator (D)

The directory config creator handler creates the directory-specific configuration and passes it to the Apache core:

```
void *create_name_dir_config (pool *p, char *dir);
```

This handler is called once for every `<Directory>`, `<Location>`, and `AccessFileName`. Since the Apache core doesn't know about module-specific `typedefs`, it's up to the module author to typecast the pointer correctly. The handler is passed the name of the directory and a `pool` pointer to use for memory management. See the section "Resource Pools" for more about pools.

## Directory Config Merger

The directory config merger handler combines a directory configuration with its parent directory configuration:

```
void *create_name_dir_config (pool *p, void *base, void *new_conf);
```

It's called once per request. It's passed a pool for memory management and pointers to the parent directory and current directory configurations.

## Server Config Creator (B)

The server config creator handler creates the server-specific configuration and passes it to the Apache core:

```
void *create_name_server_config (pool *p, server_rec *s);
```

This handler is called once at server startup and once for each virtual server. Since the Apache core doesn't know about module-specific `typedefs`, it's up to the module author to typecast the pointer correctly. The handler is passed a `pool` pointer to use for memory management and a `server_rec` pointer to obtain necessary server data. See the section "Resource Pools" for more info about pools and the section "Server Struct (`server_rec`)" for more info about `server_rec`.

## Server Config Merger (C)

The server config merger handler combines a virtual host's configuration with that of the general Apache server:

```
void *create_name_server_config (pool *p, void *base, void *new_conf);
```

It's called once during the server initialization. The handler is passed a `pool` pointer to use for memory management and pointers to the server and virtual host configurations.

## Configuration Directives Table (F)

The configuration directives table points to an array of configuration directives that this module enables and that will be used to configure this module:

```
command_rec *modname_cmds or command_rec modname_cmds[]
```

> **Note**
>
> The last entry in the table needs to be {NULL}.

The `command_rec` struct is defined (in `httpd_config.h`) as shown in Listing 24.2.

**LISTING 24.2**    The `command_rec` Struct

```
typedef struct command_struct {
    const char *name;        /* Name of this command */
    const char *(*func) (); /* Function invoked */
    void *cmd_data;          /* Extra data, for functions which
                              * implement multiple commands...
                              */
    int req_override;        /* What overrides need to be allowed to
                              * enable this command.
                              */
    enum cmd_how args_how;   /* What the command expects as arguments */
    const char *errmsg;      /* 'usage' message, in case of syntax errors */
} command_rec;
```

These fields are as follows:

- `const char *name` is the name of the directive. This is the label used in the configuration file. It can't have whitespace.

- `const char *(*func) ()` is a pointer to a function to invoke for this directive. The function accepts parsed arguments (see the description of the `args_how` field later in this list) and changes this module's configuration accordingly. Normally, the function will return `NULL`. Any non-`NULL` string is treated as an error message.

- `void *cmd_data` is a pointer to a data block. It's used to share information among this module's directives.

**24**

**WORKING WITH THE APACHE API**

- `int req_override` determines the scope of this directive. Apache uses the scope to figure out where in the configuration it is meaningful to use this directive. It's the logical `OR` of any of the macros in Table 24.1.

**Table 24.1**   The `req_override` Constants

| Constant Label | Purpose |
| --- | --- |
| RSRC_CONF | Directive useful only in configuration files, outside of `<Directory>`, `<Location>`, and `<Files>` directives. Not allowed in `AccessFileName` files (that is, the ones usually called `.htaccess`). |
| ACCESS_CONF | Directive useful only in configuration files inside `<Directory>`, `<Location>`, and `<Files>` directives. Not allowed in `AccessFileName` files. |
| OR_NONE | This directive cannot be overridden by the `AllowOverride` directive. |
| OR_AUTHCFG | Same as `ACCESS_CONF` but lets the `AllowOverride` directive override it for `AccessFileName` files for current directory with the `AuthConfig` argument. |
| OR_LIMIT | Same as `OR_AUTHCFG` except the `AllowOverride` argument is `Limit`. |
| OR_OPTIONS | This directive is allowed anywhere in the configuration files and also in the `AccessFileName` file as long as `AllowOverride` is configured to `Options` for the current directory. |
| OR_FILEINFO | Same as `OR_OPTIONS` but `AllowOverride` must be set to `FileInfo` in the current directory. |
| OR_INDEXES | Same as `OR_OPTIONS` but `AllowOverride` must be set to `Indexes` in the current directory. |
| OR_ALL | Directive is allowed everywhere. |

- `enum cmd_how args_how` describes what format the argument list to the directive will take. The `args_how` constants, their meanings, and their function signatures are as follows:

| Constant | Description | Function Signature |
|---|---|---|
| NO_ARGS | Takes no arguments. | `funct(cmd_params *params, void *mconfig);` |
| FLAG | Takes a Boolean argument: either `On` or `Off`. The parameter parser changes this to the `int flag` argument: `0` for `Off`, nonzero for `On`. | `funct(cmd_params *params, void *mconfig, int flag);` |
| TAKE1 | Takes only one argument, which is passed as the `char *arg` value. | `funct(cmd_params *params, void *mconfig, const char *arg);` |
| TAKE2, TAKE12 | Accepts either exactly two arguments (`TAKE2`) or one or two arguments (`TAKE12`). In the latter case, if the second argument is missing, the value of the corresponding parameter will be `NULL`. The function signature is the same for both. | `funct(cmd_params *params, void *mconfig, const char *arg1, const char *arg2);` |
| TAKE3, TAKE23, TAKE123, TAKE13 | Accepts either exactly three arguments (`TAKE3`); either two or three arguments (`TAKE23`); either one, two or three arguments (`TAKE123`); or either one or three (but not two) arguments (`TAKE13`). If any of the arguments is missing, the value of the corresponding parameter will be `NULL`. The function signature is the same for all of these. | `funct(cmd_params *params, void *mconfig, const char arg1, *const char *arg2, const char *arg3);` |
| ITERATE | Accepts a list of arguments, all of which will be dealt with the same. The function will be called repeatedly for every argument in the configuration. Thus, the signature is quite simple. | `funct(cmd_params *params, void *mconfig, const char *arg);` |

**24**

| | | |
|---|---|---|
| `ITERATE2` | Takes one necessary argument followed by a list of similar ones. The function is called repeatedly, passing the same first argument and different second arguments each time. | `funct(cmd_params *params, void *mconfig, const c har *arg1, const char *arg2);` |
| `RAW_ARGS` | The arguments of the directive don't fit any of the above molds, and the Apache core can't help the directive in parsing them. Thus, the entire text argument string is passed directly to the directive handler in the args argument. | `funct(cmd_params *params, void *mconfig, const char *args);` |

Notice that the directive handler functions all contain the `cmd_params` and `mconfig` arguments. These standard data structures are passed in for every directive handler:

- The `cmd_params` argument is a generic parameter structure for directives and is described later in the section "The Rest of the API."
- The `mconfig` argument is a generic pointer to this module's per-directory configuration data as created by the directory config creator described above. More information comes later, in the section "Module Configuration Structure."

## Content Handlers Table (O)

The Apache core goes to the content handler tables of the modules to find the function to call for a particular content type:

`handler_rec modname_handlers[]`

or

`handler_rec *modname_handlers`

This is next to last in the request/response loop before the response is sent to the client; it's also where content-changing modules concentrate the bulk of their work. The content handlers table should end in a {NULL, NULL} entry.

Before we discuss content handlers in more detail, let's finish with the content handlers table. It's an array of `handler_rec` objects. The definition of `handler_rec` is as follows:

```
typedef struct {
    const char *content_type;
    int (*handler) (request_rec *);
} handler_rec;
```

The two fields of the `handler_rec` structure are as follows:

- `content_type` is the name of the content type: either a MIME type, an encoding, or an Apache content handling type. It must all be in lowercase letters.

  When the Apache core tries to match the content type of the request, it first checks for exact matches in the content handler tables. If an exact match isn't found, it treats the `content_type` string as a MIME type with wildcards and attempts to match the content type to these MIME types.

- `handler` is the function that will be called for this particular content type. As the preceding `typedef` struct indicates, the signature of the `handler` functions should be

  ```
  int handler (request_rec *r)
  ```

  The content handler is similar to the other Apache handlers. It's called with the `request_rec` object that will be modified, in most cases, and is expected to return an Apache status code.

> **Note**
>
> It's imperative that your handler send the HTTP headers to the client before returning. You can ensure that they do this by calling the `ap_send_http_header()` function, which is discussed in more detail in the section "HTTP Utilities."

## URI Translator (I)

The URI translator is called after a post-read request handler and before the header parser in the lifecycle sequence:

```
int modname_translator(request_rec *r)
```

Its responsibility is to take the URI in the request and translate it into an internal usable filename path. Often there's no need for any translation: A request for `/mydir/file.html` is a request for just that, the file called `file.html` in the `mydir` directory. But it's also useful to make URI naming more flexible to provide for simple aliases and redirects as well as an entire virtual file system. The URI translator is the core of the `mod_alias` and `mod_rewrite` modules.

URI translators function exclusively; the Apache core stops calling URI translators after one of them returns a non-DECLINE status. You can get around this by having a URI translator modify the URI but return a DECLINE status for others to finish the URI translation. Be careful if you do this, since you need to be finicky about the module order and make sure that at least one of the modules "catches" the task and returns a non-DECLINE status value.

## Authentication Handler (L)

The authentication handler determines whether the client user is who he purports to be:

```
int modname_check_user_id(request_rec *r)
```

The actual proofing or authenticating scheme is the responsibility of the authentication handler. The authentication scheme supported by most browsers is the Basic authentication scheme, described in RFC 2617, a simple clear text challenge/response mechanism. Authentication handlers usually return a status of OK if authentication has been confirmed and an HTTP error code of HTTP_UNAUTHORIZED if authentication hasn't been confirmed. If the handler can't process the request, it should return DECLINE to let other authentication handlers attempt authentication.

Authentication handlers function exclusively. When one has returned a definitive status code—OK or an HTTP status code—no further attempts at authentication are made.

## Authorization Handler (M)

The authorization handler determines if the identified user of this request is allowed the specific URI that he's requesting:

```
int modname_check_auth(request_rec *r)
```

The actual authorization mechanism that determines who can access what is the responsibility of the module author. The authorization handler returns an OK status code when authorization has been approved and an HTTP error code of HTTP_UNAUTHORIZED if authorization has not been approved.

Authorization handlers function exclusively. The first one to return an OK or an HTTP status code will prevent any others from attempting authorization.

## Access Control Handler (K)

The access control handler determines whether the URI requested by an HTTP request is allowed:

```
int modname_check_access(request_rec *r)
```

The handler can use non–user-specific criteria to make this determination. The difference between access control and authorization is that authorization makes a determination based on the user's identity, whereas access control doesn't. You can use any criteria you want to allow or limit access, and access control modules are some of the most common extensions to Apache. Access control handlers usually return an `HTTP_FORBIDDEN` status code to indicate denial of access.

Access handlers function inclusively. All handlers are called unless one returns an HTTP error code, which aborts the loop.

## Type Checker (N)

The type checker is used after the authentication handler to determine what type of content the response will have and to call the correct handler for that type:

```
int modname_type_checker(request_rec *r)
```

There are three types of content:

- A MIME type (for example, `image/gif`)
- An encoding (for example, `x-gzip`)
- An Apache-specific content-handling label set with the `SetHandler` directive (for example, `imap-file`)

The type checker determines the content-handling type by checking the filename's extension or checking the directory configuration of `<Directory>`, `<Location>`, `<Files>`, and `AccessFileName` directives.

## Fixups Handler (P)

The fixups handler is called after the content handler composes its HTTP response but before the response is shipped to the client:

```
int modname_fixups(request_rec *r)
```

It's used by modules to add or modify the response in a content type–neutral way. For example, the `mod_usertrack` module uses a fixups handler to handle cookie information.

Fixups handlers are called inclusively in a special way. The fixups handlers of any modules that have a handler for this response's content type are called in turn, unless one of them returns a `DONE` or HTTP error status code.

## Logger (Q)

The logger handler is called when the HTTP response is fully formed and after it is handed over for transfer to the Apache core:

```
int modname_logger(request_rec *r)
```

It's never skipped because, even in the event of errors at earlier steps in the lifecycle, control will still be handed over to it. The standard `mod_log_config` module uses it to append log information to log files. The `Apache::DBILogger` module uses the logger handler to log access information in an SQL database.

Logger handlers are similar to fixups handlers—they are called inclusively for all modules that have handlers for this response's content type. Only `DONE` terminates the loop through the loggers.

## Header Parser (J)

After the URI translation, control is passed to the module header parsers:

```
int modname_header(request_rec *r)
```

The name is a bit of a misnomer, since the HTTP headers are *parsed* (the text separated into a useful data struct) by the Apache core right after the request is received. The header parsers of the modules are used as a chain of filters: Each header parser gets a chance to do something useful with or to a request's HTTP headers before they are actually used by the other handlers in the Apache request/response loop.

Since the header parsers are used as a chain of filters, they function inclusively—the Apache core calls each one in turn. The exception to this rule is that a header parser can break out of the loop by returning a `DONE` or an HTTP error status code.

## Child Initialization Handler (G)

The child initialization handler initializes resources and does processing on a child process basis:

```
int modname_child_init(server_rec *r, pool *p)
```

It's called only once—after the creation of the child process. The `server_rec` argument is used to access server data. The resource pool can be used for memory management—it won't be released before the end of the process.

The child initialization handlers of all modules are called. The return values are not used.

> **Note**
>
> Because the Win32 Apache implementation uses multiple threads instead of multiple processes to accept requests, Win32 doesn't use the child initialization and child exit handlers. In the future, thread initialization and thread exit handlers may be added to the Apache API to support Win32 implementations and to utilize threads in Unix.

## Child Exit Handler (R)

The child exit handler is used to release resources that a module has been using; it should undo everything the initializer and child initialization handlers did:

```
int modname_child_init(server_rec *r, pool *p)
```

The `server_rec` argument is used to access server data. The resource pool can be used for memory management, but it won't be released before the end of the process.

The child exit handlers of all modules are called. The return values are not used.

## Post-Read Request Handler (H)

The post-read request handler is the first one to be called in a request/response loop:

```
int modname_postread(request_rec *r)
```

It's called immediately after the Apache child process determines that the request it received was a valid HTTP request and the HTTP headers are parsed. For example, a post-read request handler is used in the `mod_unique_id` module to generate a unique token for the user before anything else happens.

# Apache Handler Status Codes

Apache handler status codes are `int` values returned by the Apache handlers. The Apache API augments the standard HTTP status codes with a couple of its own, which are used internally.

## Apache Status Codes

Apache uses these status codes from Apache handlers to determine whether the handler has finished successfully:

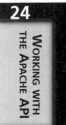

- `OK`  The Apache handler processed the callback successfully.
- `DECLINED`  The Apache handler, for one reason or another, doesn't want to process the callback.
- `DONE`  The Apache handler processed the callback successfully, and no more Apache handlers should process this lifecycle step.

## HTTP Status Codes

All HTTP status codes are in the Apache API. The macro names that the Apache API uses for the codes are derived from the status names used by HTTP/1.1, and the underlying integer values are the same. For example, the `HTTP_BAD_REQUEST` status code corresponds to the HTTP status 400, or "Bad Request." The HTTP status codes are delineated in Table 24.2.

**TABLE 24.2**  Apache API HTTP Status Codes

| *HTTP Status* | *Apache API Name* |
| --- | --- |
| 100 | HTTP_CONTINUE |
| 101 | HTTP_SWITCHING_PROTOCOLS |
| 102 | HTTP_PROCESSING |
| 200 | HTTP_OK |
| 201 | HTTP_CREATED |
| 202 | HTTP_ACCEPTED |
| 203 | HTTP_NON_AUTHORITATIVE |
| 204 | HTTP_NO_CONTENT |
| 205 | HTTP_RESET_CONTENT |
| 206 | HTTP_PARTIAL_CONTENT |
| 207 | HTTP_MULTI_STATUS |
| 300 | HTTP_MULTIPLE_CHOICES |
| 301 | HTTP_MOVED_PERMANENTLY |
| 302 | HTTP_MOVED_TEMPORARILY |
| 303 | HTTP_SEE_OTHER |
| 304 | HTTP_NOT_MODIFIED |
| 305 | HTTP_USE_PROXY |
| 307 | HTTP_TEMPORARY_REDIRECT |
| 400 | HTTP_BAD_REQUEST |
| 401 | HTTP_UNAUTHORIZED |
| 402 | HTTP_PAYMENT_REQUIRED |
| 403 | HTTP_FORBIDDEN |
| 404 | HTTP_NOT_FOUND |
| 405 | HTTP_METHOD_NOT_ALLOWED |
| 406 | HTTP_NOT_ACCEPTABLE |
| 407 | HTTP_PROXY_AUTHENTICATION_REQUIRED |
| 408 | HTTP_REQUEST_TIME_OUT |
| 409 | HTTP_CONFLICT |
| 410 | HTTP_GONE |
| 411 | HTTP_LENGTH_REQUIRED |
| 412 | HTTP_PRECONDITION_FAILED |
| 413 | HTTP_REQUEST_ENTITY_TOO_LARGE |

| HTTP Status | Apache API Name |
|---|---|
| 414 | HTTP_REQUEST_URI_TOO_LARGE |
| 415 | HTTP_UNSUPPORTED_MEDIA_TYPE |
| 416 | HTTP_RANGE_NOT_SATISFIABLE |
| 417 | HTTP_EXPECTATION_FAILED |
| 422 | HTTP_UNPROCESSABLE_ENTITY |
| 423 | HTTP_LOCKED |
| 424 | HTTP_FAILED_DEPENDENCY |
| 500 | HTTP_INTERNAL_SERVER_ERROR |
| 501 | HTTP_NOT_IMPLEMENTED |
| 502 | HTTP_BAD_GATEWAY |
| 503 | HTTP_SERVICE_UNAVAILABLE |
| 504 | HTTP_GATEWAY_TIME_OUT |
| 505 | HTTP_VERSION_NOT_SUPPORTED |
| 506 | HTTP_VARIANT_ALSO_VARIES |
| 507 | HTTP_INSUFFICIENT_STORAGE |
| 510 | HTTP_NOT_EXTENDED |

# Apache Data Structures

The module structure is only the beginning of the Apache API's collection of data structures. The following sections describe the provided request_rec, server_rec, and conn_rec structures, as well as the user-defined module configuration structure.

## Request Structure (request_rec)

The request_rec structure is the central data structure by which the Apache core exposes data to the Apache handlers. It allows the Apache handlers to access all pertinent information about the HTTP request.

Some of the request_rec structure's fields are for internal use. Below we describe the fields of interest to the module author. The full definition of request_rec can be found in the httpd.h header file, though we caution you against using the implicitly private fields.

- ap_pool *pool points to a pool of memory used with the memory management functions. The memory in the pool is guaranteed not to be released during the request's lifetime. See the section "Resource Pools" for information about pools.

- `conn_rec *connection` points to the connection structure of the current request. See the section "Connection Struct (`conn_rec`)," later in this chapter.

- `server_rec *server` points to the current server structure. See "Server Struct (`server_rec`)," later in this chapter.

- `request_rec *next` is a pointer to the request structure of an internally redirected request.

- `request_rec *prev` is a pointer to the request structure of the request from which it was internally redirected.

- `request_rec *main` is a pointer to the request structure of the topmost request if the request was redirected internally.

- `char *the_request` contains the first line of the request.

- `int proxyreq` is a proxy request if it's nonzero.

- `int header_only`, if nonzero, indicates that the request method was a HEAD.

- `char *protocol` contains the name and version number of the protocol—for example, HTTP/1.1.

- `const char *hostname` contains the name of the host from the Host header.

- `time_t request_time` indicates the time the request started as a C `time_t` struct.

- `const char *status_line` contains the full status text, such as 505 Internal Server Error.

- `int status` contains the numeric value of the status. Refer back to the section "HTTP Status Codes."

- `const char *method` contains the HTTP method—for example, POST.

- `int method_number` indicates the numeric value of the HTTP method. These values are internal to Apache; you should use the constants provided by the Apache API—M_GET, M_POST, and likewise—for the rest of the HTTP methods.

- `int allowed` is a bit vector representing which HTTP methods are allowed (set in the Allow header, where applicable). Use logical OR to indicate the methods you want your handler to be able to handle (using the constants M_GET, M_POST, and so on). For example

  `request->allowed = M_HEAD | M_GET;`

  allows only HEAD and GET requests.

- `long bytes_sent` indicates the number of bytes sent in the request, excluding the HTTP headers.

- `time_t mtime` indicates the time the requested file was last modified. Your module handlers should modify this value for greater efficiency with the

If-Last-Modified header fields. This value should be set with the ap_update_mtime() function.

- long clength indicates the number of bytes in the content of the response. This will be the Content-length header value.

- long remaining shows the number of bytes left to read in the request's content (initially set to the value of the request's Content-length header).

- long read_length indicates the number of bytes already read from the request's content.

- table *headers_in points to a table containing name/value pairs of the request's HTTP headers.

- table *headers_out points to a table containing name/value pairs of the response's HTTP headers.

- table *err_headers_out points to a table containing name/value pairs of the response's HTTP headers in case of an error.

- table *subprocess_env points to a table containing name/value pairs of the environment (for example, the PATH variable). This table will be used in composing the environment of forked processes, such as CGI scripts.

- table *notes points to a table containing name/value pairs. That's it—there is no predefined use for this field. Essentially, it's an easily accessible place where handlers can leave data during the request/response loop for other handlers.

- const char *content_type contains the MIME content type, in lowercase, of the response.

- const char *handler contains the Apache content handling label (for example, "server-parsed") in lowercase.

- const char *content_encoding contains the MIME content encoding of the response in lowercase.

- const char *content_language; contains the content language of the response (for example, "fr-ca") in lowercase.

- array_header *content_languages contains the array of content languages, in lowercase, if there's more than one content language for the response content.

- int no_cache, if nonzero, indicates that this document shouldn't be cached by the client (by setting the Expires header to the current date and time).

- char *unparsed_uri contains the raw URI of the request before URI translation is performed.

- char *uri contains the path part of the URI.

- `char *filename` contains the translated URI of the request.
- `char *path_info` contains the additional part of the path, after the translated filename.
- `char *args` contains the QUERY ARGUMENT of the URI request.
- `uri_components parsed_uri` contains the uri_component structure of the parsed URI.
- `void *per_dir_config` points to the directory configuration data structure.
- `void *request_config` points to the configuration data structure of this request.

## Server Struct (`server_rec`)

Like the `request_rec` structure, the `server_rec` structure contains information about the current server—specifically, information about the current virtual host, if applicable. You can access the `server_rec` structure through `request_rec` structure's `server` field or by having the `server_rec` passed directly into the handler in the arguments.

As was the case with `request_rec`, some of `server_rec` structure's fields are meant to be used internally. Here are the ones module authors will find useful:

- `server_rec *next` is a pointer to the next virtual host in the linked list of virtual hosts that the Apache core stores.
- `char *srm_confname` contains the full location of the resource file (usually `srm.conf`).
- `char *access_confname` contains the full location of the access control file (usually `access.conf`).
- `char *server_admin` contains the email address of the server administrator (set with the `ServerAdmin` directive).
- `char *server_hostname` contains the name of the server—the virtual name if this is a virtual host.
- `unsigned short port` contains the port that this server is listening on.
- `char *error_fname` contains the name of the error file.
- `FILE *error_log` contains a file descriptor open to the error file.
- `int loglevel` contains the logging level, which is indicated by a number from 1 to 8. This value is set with the `LogLevel` directive.
- `int is_virtual` shows nonzero if the server is a virtual host.
- `void *module_config` points to the module's configuration structure. See the section "Module Configuration Structure," later in this chapter.

- `int timeout` indicates the time in seconds the server should wait before timing out (set by the `Timeout` directive).

- `int keep_alive_timeout` shows the time in seconds to wait for another request during a `Keep-Alive` connection (set by the `KeepAliveTimeout` directive).

- `int keep_alive_max` indicates the maximum number of requests in a `Keep-Alive` connection (set by the `MaxKeepAliveRequests` directive).

- `int keep_alive` is nonzero if the server accepts `Keep-Alive` connections (set by the `KeepAlive` directive).

- `char *path` contains the server's path.

- `array_header *names` points to an array containing strings of exact aliases for this server (set with the `ServerAlias` directive).

- `array_header *wild_names` indicates an array containing strings of wildcard aliases for this server.

- `uid_t server_uid` indicates the user ID of the server.

- `gid_t server_gid` indicates the group ID of the server.

## Connection Struct (`conn_rec`)

The `conn_rec` structure is another useful data structure in the Apache API. It contains information specific to the current client/server HTTP connection.

As with `request_rec` and `server_rec`, some fields are for private use, but the ones useful to module authors are listed here:

- `ap_pool *pool` points to a pool of memory used with memory management functions. The memory in the pool is guaranteed not to be released during the connection's lifetime. See the "Resource Pools" section for information about pools.

- `server_rec *server` points to the server that is currently serving.

- `server_rec *base_server` points to the server the connection came in on.

- `BUFF *client` indicates a connection buffer object to the client.

- `struct sockaddr_in local_addr` shows the TCP/IP socket of the local address.

- `struct sockaddr_in remote_addr` indicates the TCP/IP socket of the local address.

- `char *remote_ip` contains the client's IP address.

- `char *remote_host` contains the client's hostname, if resolved. It's `NULL` if not checked and `""` if no address was found. Use `ap_get_remote_host()` to access this information.

24

WORKING WITH
THE APACHE API

- `char *remote_logname` contains the remote login name of the remote user. Use `ap_get_remote_logname()` to access this information.

- `char *user` contains the login name provided by the user, if an authentication check was made.

- `char *ap_auth_type` contains the authentication scheme name (for example, `Basic`), if an authentication check was made.

- `unsigned aborted` is nonzero if a timeout has occurred during the connection.

- `signed int keepalive` indicates whether `Keep-Alive` is being used. 1 is yes; 0 is undecided; and -1 is a fatal error.

- `unsigned keptalive` is nonzero if the connection used `Keep-Alive`.

- `signed int double_reverse` indicates whether the connection used a double reverse hostname lookup. 1 is yes; 0 is undecided; and -1 is a fatal error.

- `int keepalives` shows the number of requests processed during this `Keep-Alive` connection.

## Module Configuration Structure

A module configuration data structure isn't a predefined Apache struct, it's a data structure you need to define yourself if you'll be using configuration directives. Since the module configuration data struct is module specific, Apache core doesn't know about its `typedef` and must deal with the data generically—by a generic pointer, a `void *`. To pass it to the Apache core, the module routines need to cast it to `void *`. And when the data is retrieved from the Apache core, it will be passed as a `void *` and must be set to the configuration module struct `typedef`.

Here are some examples from the `mod_usertrack` module:

- An example of a module-specific configuration structure
  ```
  typedef struct {
      int enabled;
      char *cookie_name;
  } cookie_dir_rec;
  ```

- Creating the structure and passing it to the Apache core in the directory config creator handler:
  ```
  static void *make_cookie_dir(pool *p, char *d)
  {
      cookie_dir_rec *dcfg;
      dcfg = (cookie_dir_rec *) ap_pcalloc(p, sizeof(cookie_dir_rec));
      dcfg->cookie_name = COOKIE_NAME;
      dcfg->enabled = 0;
      return dcfg;
  }
  ```

- Retrieving the structure as a parameter in a directive handler:

```
static const char *set_cookie_enable(cmd_parms *cmd,
➥void *mconfig, int arg)
{
    cookie_dir_rec *dcfg = mconfig;
    dcfg->enabled = arg;
    return NULL;
}
```

- Retrieving it by using ap_get_module_config():

```
static int spot_cookie(request_rec *r)
{
    cookie_dir_rec *dcfg = ap_get_module_config(r->per_dir_config,
    ➥&usertrack_module);


    const char *cookie;
    char *value;

    if (!dcfg->enabled) {
      return DECLINED;
}
    /* more processing…
    */
}
```

# Resource Pools

One utility feature of the Apache API is the memory management mechanism. This is a way to control the orderly allocation and deallocation of memory, avoiding the memory leaks that could otherwise destroy the reliability and stability of the Apache server. The Apache developers found a stable and efficient memory management scheme necessary for their core development, so they opened it up to module authors as well.

Basically the way it works is that memory is partitioned into resource pools. These resource pools are used for all memory use. The resource pools are tied to the lifetimes of specific entities in Apache—they are created and destroyed with the beginning and end of these entities.

Although you can know the lifetime of a pool explicitly (by digging around in the API), you usually don't need to, because the lifetime of the resource pool available to you in your Apache handler is most likely the lifetime that you will need for the objects that you want to place inside that memory. For example, the resource pool available to you in the child initialization handler will last the lifetime of the child process, and the resource pool available to you in an Apache handler in the request/response loop will last the duration of the request/response loop. Voilà, just-in-time garbage collection!

There are two ways to access a resource pool inside your Apache handlers. The most obvious way is when the resource pool is passed into your handler directly through an argument—this is the case with Apache handlers such as the directory config creator. The other way is when a resource pool is available to you through a data structure, as is the case with the request_rec and conn_rec structures through their ap_pool fields.

In addition to creating regular data blocks in a resource pool, Apache handlers can create subpools within a resource pool to enable even finer-grained control over memory. The module handlers can destroy these subpools as you see fit without needing to worry about making a mistake in freeing memory—every pool will free the memory of its subpools when it's freed.

The following Apache API functions are used to manage pools:

- void *ap_palloc(struct pool *p, int nbytes) allocates nbytes bytes of memory from the pool's memory and returns a pointer to it. Works like malloc() except, as noted in the discussion about memory management, there's no need to free the memory explicitly.

- void *ap_pcalloc(struct pool *p, int nbytes) allocates nbytes bytes of memory filled in with '\0' bytes. Equivalent to the calloc() function.

- char *ap_pstrdup(struct pool *p, const char *s) copies the s string into new memory in the pool, returning a pointer to this memory. Equivalent to strdup().

- char *ap_pstrndup(struct pool *p, const char *s, int n)copies n bytes of the s string into new memory in the pool's memory, returning a pointer to this memory. Equivalent to strndup().

- char *ap_pstrcat(struct pool *p,...) joins a number of strings into a new one from the pool's memory. Returns a pointer to this concatenated string. The argument list is variable-length—all the arguments but the first must be strings (that is, char *). Similar to strcat().

- char *ap_psprintf(struct pool *p, const char *fmt, ...) uses the pool's memory to perform a sprintf(). See the standard C function, sprintf(), for more info about the arguments.

- struct pool ap_make_sub_pool(struct pool *p) returns a pool that's a subpool of the argument.

- void ap_destroy_pool(pool *p) destroys the specified pool. You should destroy only pools that you've created.

- void ap_clear_pool(struct pool *p) clears out the memory in a pool but leaves the pool available for further use.

- `pool* ap_find_pool(const void *block)` returns a pointer to the pool that owns this memory block.

- `int ap_pool_is_ancestor(pool *a, pool *b)` returns nonzero if pool *b* is an ancestor of pool *a*.

# The Rest of the API

The preceding sections have covered the major structures and functions of the Apache API. These will allow you to get started in writing your module. However, the Apache API is richer than just those structures and functions. The Apache development team has graced the module author with an abundance of other useful utility structures and functions. The following sections cover the rest of the Apache API.

## TCP/IP Utilities

The following three functions relate to basic TCP/IP features:

- `char *ap_get_local_host(pool *p)` returns the fully qualified domain for the local host.

- `unsigned long ap_get_virthost_addr(char *hostname,unsigned short *port)` converts the *hostname* and *port* into an IP address.

- `const char *ap_get_remote_host(conn_rec *connection, void *dir_config, int type)` returns the client's hostname or IP address. *dir_config* is the configuration structure of the request. The `type` argument is one of the following: `REMOTE_HOST` (return hostname or `NULL` if DNS failure), `REMOTE_NAME` (return hostname or IP address if DNS failure), `REMOTE_NOLOOKUP` (return IP without performing a DNS lookup), or `REMOTE_DOUBLE_REV` (do a double reverse DNS lookup; return hostname if successful, `NULL` otherwise).

## URI and URL Functions

It shouldn't be surprising that an HTTP server would have functions for processing URIs.

Listing 24.3 shows the type definition from the `httpd.h` header file of the salient `uri_components` data structure used by most of the functions that follow. Most fields should be obvious to someone familiar with the URI specification. Those fields that aren't as familiar have illuminating comments.

**24**

**WORKING WITH THE APACHE API**

**LISTING 24.3** The `uri_components` Structure

```
typedef struct {
    char *scheme;      /* scheme ("http"/"ftp"/...) */
    char *hostinfo;    /* combined [user[:password]@]host[:port] */
    char *user;        /* user name, as in http://user:passwd@host:port/ */
    char *password;    /* password, as in http://user:passwd@host:port/ */
    char *hostname;    /* hostname from URI (or from Host: header) */
    char *port_str;    /* port string value */
    char *path;        /* the request path (or "/" if none */
    char *query;       /* Everything after a '?' in the path, if present */
    char *fragment;    /* Trailing "#fragment" string, if present */
    struct hostent *hostent;
    unsigned short port;  /* integer representation of the port */
    unsigned is_initialized;
    unsigned dns_looked_up;
    unsigned dns_resolved;
```

The following functions use the `uri_component` structure to obtain or set URI-related information:

- `unsigned short ap_default_port_for_scheme(const char *scheme_str)` returns the default port for the given schema.

- `unsigned short ap_default_port_for_request(const request_rec *r)` returns the default port for the given request.

- `struct hostent *ap_pduphostent(pool *p, const struct hostent *hp)` copies the hostent structure using the pool for memory.

- `struct hostent *ap_pgethostbyname(pool *p, const char *hostname)` is similar to `gethostbyname()`, except the pool is used for memory allocation.

- `char *ap_unparse_uri_components(pool *p, const uri_components *uptr, unsigned flags)` makes a string in the pool out of the given `uri_components` structure. The `flags` variable gives format options as follows:

  | | |
  |---|---|
  | `UNP_OMITSITEPART` | Leave out everything before the path. |
  | `UNP_OMITUSER` | Leave out user. |
  | `UNP_OMITPASSWORD` | Leave out password. |
  | `UNP_OMITUSERINFO` | Leave out both user and password. |
  | `UNP_REVEALPASSWORD` | Show the actual password. |

- `int ap_parse_uri_components(pool *p, const char *uri, uri_components *uptr)` parses the `uri` string into the new `uri_component`, `uptr`, using the pool for memory allocation.

- `int ap_parse_hostinfo_components(pool *p, const char *hostinfo, uri_components *uptr)` parses the *hostinfo* string into the new `uri_component`, *uptr*, using the pool for memory allocation. It's assumed that *hostinfo* is just host and port data.

- `int ap_is_url(const char *u)` is nonzero if the given string is a valid URL.

- `int ap_unescape_url(char *url)` converts escape sequences in a URL back to the original character.

- `void ap_no2slash(char *name)` removes double slashes from a path.

- `void ap_getparents(char *name)` removes . and .. from the path.

- `char *ap_escape_path_segment(pool *p, const char *s)` returns the string with the characters escaped.

- `char* ap_escape_uri(pool *p, char *path)` returns an escaped path from the given string.

- `char *ap_escape_html(pool *p, const char *s)` returns escaped HTML from the given string.

- `char *ap_escape_shell_cmd(pool *p, const char *s)` returns an escaped shell command from the given string.

- `char *ap_make_dirstr(pool *p, const char *s, int n)` copies the given string in the pool, truncating after the *n*th slash.

- `char *ap_make_dirstr_parent(pool *p, const char *s)` makes a new string in the pool with the parent of the given string.

- `char *ap_make_dirstr_prefix(char *d, const char *s, int n)` copies the first *n* path elements of *s* to *d*.

- `int ap_count_dirs(const char *path)` returns the number of directories in a given string.

- `void ap_chdir_file(const char *file)` changes the current directory to the one *file* is in.

- `char *ap_construct_server(pool *p, const char *hostname, unsigned port, const request_rec *r)` returns fleshed-out server info (host and port number) if *port* is not the default port of `request_rec`.

## Log Utilities

Apache defines some commonly used logging functions:

- `void ap_log_error(const char *file, int line, int level, const server_rec *s, const char *fmt, ...)` logs an error for filename *file* at line

*line* of error severity *level*. The server_rec argument is used to find the correct error file to write to. The *fmt* string is used to format the rest of the argument (with the sprintf() rules for formatting).

- void ap_log_rerror(const char *file, int line, int level, const request_rec *r, const char *fmt, ...) is similar to ap_log_error() except that the request_rec argument is passed.

The possibilities for the severity level are as follows, logically ORed together as needed:

| | |
|---|---|
| APLOG_NOERRNO | Suppress showing errno variables. |
| APLOG_WIN32ERROR | Only for Win32, enables logging the value of the GetLastError() Windows system call. |
| APLOG_EMERG | Signifies an emergency condition. |
| APLOG_ALERT | Signifies an alert condition. |
| APLOG_CRIT | Signifies a critical problem. |
| APLOG_ERR | Signifies a noncritical error. |
| APLOG_WARN | Signifies a condition less severe than a noncritical error. |
| APLOG_NOTICE | Signifies a condition that is important but less severe than a warning. |
| APLOG_INFO | Signifies an information-level message. |
| APLOG_DEBUG | Signifies a debug-level message. |

# File and Socket Utilities

To protect the server from orphaned resources, the Apache API is very particular about how files and sockets are created and destroyed—specifically, file descriptors and socket connections are tied to pools so that they can be correctly closed when the pool is. The association between a pool and its file or socket is a cleanup function. The following Apache API functions accomplish these tasks:

- int ap_popenf(pool *p, const char *name, int flag, int mode) is similar to the C function open(), except that the opened file descriptor is tied to the given pool.

- int ap_pclosef(pool *p, int fd) is similar to fclose() and the C function close(). The file's cleanup function is removed from the pool.

- FILE *ap_pfopen(pool *p, const char *name, const char *mode) is similar to fopen() except that the file is tied to the given pool.

- FILE *ap_pfdopen(pool *p, int fd, const char *mode) is similar to fdopen() except that the file is tied to the given pool.

- `DIR *ap_popendir(pool *p, const char *name)` is similar to `opendir()` except that the open directory is tied to the pool.

- `void ap_pclosedir(pool *p, DIR *d)` is similar to `closedir()`. The directory's cleanup function is removed from the pool.

- `int ap_psocket(pool *p, int domain, int type, int protocol)` is similar to `socket()` except that the socket is tied to the given pool.

- `int ap_pclosesocket(pool *p, int sock)` is similar to `closesocket()`. The socket's cleanup function is removed from the pool.

# HTTP Utilities

The Apache API also provides the following HTTP-related functions:

- `void ap_send_http_header(request_rec *r)` sends the HTTP headers to the client.

- `void ap_send_http_size(size_t size, request_rec *r)` sends *size* to the client.

- `long ap_send_http_client_block(request_rec *r, char *buffer, int bufsiz)` reads up to *bufsiz* characters into *buffer* from the client.

- `long ap_send_fd(FILE *f, request_rec *r)` copies *f* into the client and returns the number of bytes sent.

- `ap_send_fd_length(FILE *f, request_rec *r, long length)` is similar to `ap_send_fd()`, except the transmission size is limited to *length* bytes.

- `long ap_send_fb(BUFF *b, request_rec *r)` is similar to `ap_send_fd()`, except a BUFF is sent.

- `ap_send_fb_length(BUFF *f, request_rec *r, long length)` is similar to `ap_send_fd_length()`, except a BUFF is sent.

- `int ap_rputc(int c, request_rec *r)` sends *c* to the client. Returns EOF if failure.

- `int ap_rwrite(const void *buf, int nbytes, request_rec *r)` sends *nbytes* bytes to the client. Returns -1 if failure.

- `int ap_rputs(const char *s, request_rec *r)` sends a given string to the client. Returns -1 if failure.

- `int ap_rprintf(request_rec *r, const char *fmt, ...)` sends a string to the client, formatted with the *fmt* string and the subsequent arguments (the formatting rules are the same as for `sprintf()`).

- `int ap_rflush(request_rec *r)` sends currently buffered data to the client. Returns -1 if failure.

- `int ap_set_content_length(request_rec *r, long length)` sets the response's `Content-length` header value.

- `int ap_set_etag(request_rec *r)` sets the `Etag` header of the response. See the HTTP specification for more information on the `Etag` header.

- `time_t ap_update_mtime(request_rec *r, time_t dependency_mtime)` sets what will be the response's `Last-modified` header to the given `time_t` value.

- `void ap_set_last_modified(request_rec *r)` sets the response's `Last-modified` header.

- `int ap_meets_conditions(request_rec *r)` returns `HTTP_NOT_MODIFIED` if the requested filename hasn't been modified according to the `If-Modified-Since`, `If-Unmodified-Since`, and `If-Match` conditions of the request. Otherwise, it returns `OK` or an HTTP error status code.

## Configuration Directive Utilities

With Apache, most everything is configurable. So it shouldn't be surprising that the Apache API provides you with a host of features to access configurations.

First, look at the `configfile_t` structure, which is a wrapper around the configuration mechanism (most commonly from files, but Apache has the flexibility to be configured in multiple ways) and has the following fields:

- `int (*getch) (void *param)` is a function that acts like `getc()`.

- `void *(*getstr) (void *buf, size_t bufsiz, void *param)` is a function that acts like `fgets()`.

- `int (*close) (void *param)` is a function that acts like `close()`.

- `void *param` specifies the argument data block passed to `getch()`, `getstr()`, and `close()`.

- `const char *name` indicates the filename or configuration description.

- `unsigned line_number` indicates the current line number, starting at 1.

Unless you write your own configuration mechanism (for example, from a database), you won't need to concern yourself with the details of the `configfile_t` structure too much—just treat the `getch()` function as `getc()`, and do the same with the other two function fields.

To work with `configfile_t` structures, the Apache API provides the following functions:

- `configfile_t *ap_pcfg_openfile(pool *p, const char *name)` opens a configuration named *name* using `pool` for resource memory and returning a pointer to a valid `configfile_t` structure of that file. The following

  ```
  configfile_t *ap_pcfg_open_custom(pool *p, const char *name,
      void *param, int(*getc_func)(void*),
      void *(*getstr_func) (void *buf, size_t bufsiz, void *param),
      int(*close_func)(void *param))
  ```

  creates a `configfile_t` structure from the pool with the `name`, `param`, `getc`, `getstr`, and `close` fields filled in from the argument list, in that order.

- `int ap_cfg_getline(char *buf, size_t bufsize, configfile_t *cfp)` reads one line from *cfp* and puts it in *buf*.

- `int ap_cfg_getc(configfile_t *cfp)` returns one read character from *cfp*. `EOF` signifies an error.

- `int ap_cfg_closefile(configfile_t *cfp)` closes the *cfp*.

Here is the main function that deals with the module's actual configuration data (supplied by the four creator and merger handlers of the module structure):

```
void *ap_get_module_config(void *conf_vector, module *m)
```

This function gets a module configuration of the given module, *m*. To get the per-directory configuration, do this:

```
my_dir_config *cfg = (my_dir_config *)
        ➥ap_get_module_config(r->per_dir_config, &my_module);
```

where *r* is the `request_rec` and *my_module* is a reference to your specific module.

To get the per-server configuration for a given module, you need to pass a reference to a `server_rec` structure's `module_config` field, either directly as a variable or from the `server` field in a `request_rec` reference. For example

```
my_server_config *cfg = (my_server_config *)
        ➥ap_get_module_config(r->server->module_config, &my_module);
```

# Memory Structure APIs

An interesting feature of the Apache API is the addition of memory structures, arrays, and tables. These structures aren't related to HTTP protocol or to Apache's internal process lifestyle—they were simply added by the Apache development team because of their general usefulness.

# Array API

The Apache developers found it useful to have a generic mechanism for dealing with variable length and variable type arrays. Thus, the Array API was born. It consists of an array_header structure with a set of functions to deal with this structure. The salient fields in the array_header are the nelts field, which is the number of data elements, and the elts field, which is a pointer to the data in the array. The elts field is a generic pointer, so it will need to be typecast to the correct type.

Here is a list of the Apache API functions used to deal with arrays:

- array_header *ap_make_array(pool *p, int *nelts*, int *elt_size*) allocates a new array from the resource pool with *nelts* elements each of *elt_size* bytes.
- void *ap_push_array(array_header *arr*) allocates space for a new element at the end of an array. The return value is a pointer to this new element.
- void ap_array_cat(array_header *dst*, const array_header *src*) concatenates the *src* array onto the end of the *dst* one.
- array_header *ap_append_arrays(pool *p, const array_header *dst*, const array_header *src*) creates a brand new array from the pool, concatenating the elements of *src* at the end of the elements of *dst*.
- char *ap_array_pstrcat(pool *p, const array_header *arr*, const char *sep*) builds a string out of the elements of the array using *sep* as a delimiter.
- array_header *ap_copy_array(pool *p, const array_header *src*) deep copies all the elements in one array into a new one. Returns a pointer to the new array.
- array_header *ap_copy_array_hdr(pool *p, const array_header *src*) shallow copies one array into a new one (that is, elements aren't copied). A deep copy is made only if the new array is extended.

# Table API

As with arrays, the Apache developers found it useful to have mechanisms for dealing with maps and lookup tables. Briefly, a map connects a name and a value. The Table API isn't entirely generic, since both the name and the value have to be strings. But these are still a useful couple of structures, along with table-handling routines.

The first structure you need to know about is table_entry. It's very simple, with only two fields. The first is the key field, which corresponds to the key in the mapping. The second is the value field, which corresponds to the value associated with the key. They are both strings. You shouldn't access these fields directly but use the Table API functions, detailed below.

The second structure is `table`. For all practical purposes, it's just an array of `table_entry` structures.

The following Apache API functions are used to deal with tables:

- `table *ap_make_table(pool *p, int `*`nelts`*`)` creates a new table in the pool with *nelts* initial elements.

- `table *ap_copy_table(pool *p, const table *t)` copies a table entry-by-entry into a new one using the memory in the pool. Returns a pointer to the new table.

- `void ap_clear_table(table *t)` deletes the entries in a table.

- `const char *ap_table_get(const table *t, const char *`*`key`*`)` fetches the value associated with *key* from the given table.

- `void ap_table_set(table *t, const char *`*`key`*`, const char *`*`val`*`)` sets a single-valued entry in the given table to the name/value pair of *key* and *val*, respectively. The values of *key* and *val* are copied.

- `void ap_table_setn(table *t, const char *`*`key`*`, const char *`*`val`*`)` is similar to `ap_table_set()` except the *key* and *val* strings aren't copied.

- `void ap_table_merge(table *t, const char *`*`key`*`, const char *`*`more_val`*`)` appends the *val* string to the value associated with the *key* key. Uses a comma and a space as a delimiter. Copies the values of *key* and *val*.

- `void ap_table_mergen(table *t, const char *`*`key`*`, const char *`*`more_val`*`)` is similar to `ap_table_merge` except the values of *key* and *val* aren't copied.

- `void ap_table_unset(table *t, const char *`*`key`*`)` deletes all entries from the table with *key*.

- `void ap_table_add(table *t, const char *`*`key`*`, const char *`*`val`*`)` adds an entry to the table with *key* and value *val*. Note that, unlike `ap_table_set()`, multiple entries with the same key can now exist. Copies the values of *key* and *val*.

- `void ap_table_addn(table *t, const char *`*`key`*`, const char *`*`val`*`)` is similar to `ap_table_add` except that the values of *key* and *val* aren't copied.

- `void ap_table_do(int (*comp) (void *, const char *, const char *), void *`*`rec`*`, const table *t, ...)` iterates through the table, calling a function on all the entries that match the given keys. This function is a bit involved. The table to iterate over is *t*. The keys to match are the strings that follow *t* in the argument list (the number of which might vary and which are ended by a NULL argument). The *rec* pointer is a pointer to some data that will be passed to the function. The first argument is the function itself. It should have this signature:

  ```
  int comp(void *rec, const char *key, const *val)
  ```

where *rec* is the same data pointer as *rec* in ap_table_do(), and *key* and *val* are the key and corresponding value of this particular iteration. The function should return 0 if it wants to break out of the iteration through the keys.

- table *ap_overlay_tables(pool *p, const table *overlay, const table *base) overlays the *overlay* table onto the *base* one, where the overlapping keys are taken from the *overlay* table. Creates a new table from the pool and returns a pointer to it.

- array_header *ap_table_elts(table *t) converts a table into an array_header of table_entry structures.

- int ap_is_empty_table(table *t) returns nonzero if the given table is empty; 0, if not.

## Miscellaneous Utilities

Finally, we have a couple of miscellaneous functions that convert date strings to time_t structures and back.

- char *ap_gm_timestr_822(pool *p, time_t t) returns an RFC 822–compliant date string given a time_t (using the memory from pool).

- time_t ap_parseHTTPdate(const char *date) returns a time_t structure from a given RFC 822–compliant standard date string. This is the opposite of ap_gm_timestr().

# Module Installation

This section covers the steps necessary to install your Apache module for use with Apache:

1. Make sure that your module code file includes the appropriate header files. The following list covers the header files for all the declarations we have dealt with in this chapter:

```
#include "httpd.h"
#include "http_config.h"
#include "http_core.h"
#include "http_log.h"
#include "http_protocol.h"
#include "util_script.h"
```

2. Create a place for it in the source tree. If you haven't done so already, create a directory for your modules—for example, src/modules/MyCompany/.

3. Make a Makefile.tmpl file in that directory. For example

```
$(OBJS) $(OBJS_PIC): Makefile
# DO NOT REMOVE
mod_mymodule.o: mod_mymodule.c \
 $(INCDIR)/httpd.h \
 $(INCDIR)/ap_config.h $(INCDIR)/ap_mmn.h \
 $(INCDIR)/ap_config_auto.h $(OSDIR)/os.h \
 $(INCDIR)/ap_ctype.h $(INCDIR)/hsregex.h \
 $(INCDIR)/alloc.h $(INCDIR)/buff.h $(INCDIR)/ap.h \
 $(INCDIR)/util_uri.h $(INCDIR)/http_config.h \
 $(INCDIR)/http_log.h $(INCDIR)/http_protocol.h \
 $(INCDIR)/http_request.h $(INCDIR)/http_core.h
```

4. Put your .c file into the directory, if you haven't done so already.

5. Configure Apache to link in your module by using Apache's configure program:

```
./configure --activate-module=src/modules/MyCompany/mod_mymodule.c -
        --enable-module=mymodule
```

6. Recompile Apache:

```
make
```

That's it. When you start (or restart) the Apache server, your module will be part of the server!

# References

For more information on the Apache API, you should

- Check out the Apache API documentation that comes with your installation of Apache.

- Read through the example module that can be found in src/modules/example. This example module implements a handler for every lifecycle step, just to show you where and how everything happens.

- As a more thorough measure, peruse the Apache source code yourself, starting at the header files and working your way to the actual implementation.

# Summary

This chapter took a journey to the center of Apache—well, not quite, but as far as you can go before stepping on the toes of the Apache core development team. You visited the Apache process lifecycle; saw the Apache API data structures and functions that you will be using; and learned about the procedure to install a module into Apache.

**24**

**WORKING WITH THE APACHE API**

# CHAPTER 25

# Contributing to Apache

The Apache HTTP server software is developed primarily by volunteers working on their own time with their own resources. Although they've accomplished wonders, that doesn't mean there's not plenty of opportunity for more volunteers—or more resources.

The name *Apache* originally referred to either the Apache Web server software or the people who developed it: the Apache Group, an informal collection of about 20 volunteers who worked on the Apache HTTP Server Project. In March 1999, though, the Apache Software Foundation was created and incorporated. Old habits die hard, and when *Apache* is used now it might mean the Web server software, the developers who work on it, or the Foundation itself.

The Apache Software Foundation was created for a number of reasons, including

- The desire to set up a framework that could foster other open-source projects and make available to them the infrastructure that has so successfully supported the Apache HTTP Server Project
- The need to create a corporate entity that could accept donations, register things like trademarks, and provide legal protections for individual developers

So now when we speak of *contributing to Apache*, it's not necessarily clear what's meant. The Apache HTTP Server Project is still one of the Foundation's projects and needs contributions as much as ever, but over time other projects will be coming to live under the Apache name and aegis and will need support as well.

# Donations

When the word *donation* appears in a conversation or in print, many people immediately think of charity fund drives, bake sales, and the like. The Apache Software Foundation is somewhat similar, with the beneficiaries of its efforts being users of computer software. The Foundation supports projects that develop open-source software, such as the Apache HTTP server, XML parsers, and other packages that are developed and distributed in the open with full access to and peer review of the source code.

But good software doesn't just spring into existence—it doesn't write itself. It needs programmers to create it, software to build it, and hardware on which to be built. Since the Foundation is a not-for-profit organization and doesn't sell any of the software created by its member projects, there are no paid programmers on staff, no software support contracts, no depreciating corporate computer centers; the only resources the Foundation has are those contributed by volunteers or donors.

As a consequence, one of the most valuable contributions you can make to a project such as the Apache HTTP server is of your time to help develop it.

Although organizations such as the Apache Software Foundation *can* use donations of hardware, software, or even money, they typically stand in much greater need of intangible donations. Of course, contributions of any sort are welcome and will be put to good use, so benefactors have complete leeway when it comes to the type of donation. The following sections describe some of the possibilities.

## Funds, Goods, or Services

Some things are intrinsically destined for individual use, such as a desktop development machine or a single software license. Others are suitable for shared use, such as a large multiuser server system, unlimited access to a software package, or a grant of money.

Unlike a contribution of time, the disposition of which you control totally (since you choose when and on which project you work), donations to the Apache Software Foundation of tangibles typically can't be targeted too specifically. In other words, if you donate a workstation to the Foundation, you can't say, "I want this to be assigned to John Foo, working on project Zed."

To find out more about making this sort of donation, contact the Foundation's treasurer at the following address:

> The Apache Software Foundation
> ATTN: Treasurer
> c/o Covalent Technologies, Inc.
> 1200 N Street, Suite 112
> Lincoln, NE  68508
> USA

You should also check the Foundation's Web site to verify the continued accuracy of this address and to see if there are any particular outstanding needs or updated procedures. You can find this information at the following URL:

```
http://www.apache.org/foundation/contributing.html
```

If you're interested in contributing in this manner, monetary donations obviously provide the most flexibility, because the Foundation can allocate portions at need. As of the autumn of 1999, the Apache Software Foundation is *not* a registered tax-exempt non-profit organization, so donations aren't tax deductible. This may have changed by the time you read this; check the preceding Web URL for the most current status.

The Apache Software Foundation uses its funds to pay for things such as overhead (corporate paperwork administration, backup media for the central software repository, and so on), developer meetings, press relations, legal fees, and additional needs determined

**25**

CONTRIBUTING TO APACHE

by the Foundation's projects (such as additional hardware or software). No funds are used to pay salaries to corporate directors or officers.

## Contributing Your Time

Development of open-source software is largely a matter of volunteers scratching itches. As with everything else, each person gets involved for his own reasons. It might be in order to gain fame (if not fortune) by getting his name on a list of contributors; a number of people have indicated that they have been hired for various positions *because* of their open-source involvement. Or it might be a sense of obligation; since they didn't pay for the software, contributing to its betterment (even if only a little) can replace formal payment. Or it might be a form of altruism; many contributors find themselves getting involved because they made a modification and offered it to the project just in case it would be useful to others. Or perhaps they work on the stuff just because they find it a fun hobby.

Whatever your motivation might be, and whatever you might have to offer in terms of your time, there's a good chance that your contribution would be welcome to one of the Apache Software Foundation projects.

There are four basic forms a donation of time might take:

- Working on the software itself
- Working on documentation
- Helping deal with bug reports
- Assisting with administrative issues, such as maintaining mailing lists or the like

Generally, help is needed in *all* these areas, so you can help out even if you can't write a line of code. The software is only part of what makes a successful or useful project.

Typical time contributions range from a few minutes a month to several hours a day; some people fiddle with stuff at night as a hobby, and others are actually paid by their employers to work on it. No contribution is too small—or too large, of course.

Because most people interested in any of the sorts of things the Apache Software Foundation is doing are likely to have their own computers and software, a donation of time *really is* the most valuable contribution you can make if you're so inclined.

# Different Apache Projects

Several different efforts are actually operating under the Foundation's aegis. Some of them are well established, such as the HTTP Server Project, and others are less so. All of them can always use more involvement than they have; even the HTTP Server Project is eager for people with knowledge of unusual or esoteric matters or system platforms. Because the Web server is the topic of this book, it's used as a sort of "poster project" in this chapter—but what applies to it most likely applies to other Apache projects as well.

The list of ASF projects fluctuates from time to time. To see what projects are active, check out the Foundation's project list on the following Web site:

```
http://www.apache.org/foundation/projects.html
```

You can see from the Web list whether there's a project that meets your interests more particularly than the HTTP Server Project (which is likely to remain a Foundation project as long as the Foundation exists).

The HTTP Server Project can always use more volunteers. If you want to get involved, one approach is to become familiar with the project by working on some of the less-glamorous aspects, such as documentation or bug reports.

Probably the most common path to participation in the development itself goes something like this:

1. Get interested in the software.
2. Find and ask one of the developers some questions, or send a bit of code you've found useful.
3. Get invited to join the development mailing list.
4. "Lurk" on the list for a few weeks (or months) to find out how things are done, who the developers are, and what the hot issues are.
5. Look at the list of open bug reports, develop a fix or two, and submit the fixes to the development list. (This also applies to documentation issues, such as locating and reporting/fixing typos or submitting new documentation in an area where it's lacking.)
6. Become accepted on the list as a participant.

Of course, each individual will find his own path to involvement, so the roadmap above is no more than a guide to how other people have gotten there.

# Source Code Development

Each development project has a different model when it comes to working on the source code itself. Some will give access to complete newcomers whom nobody knows; others may require a sort of "apprenticeship," during which new people must show themselves interested, capable, and possessed of enough persistence to do the work.

The Apache HTTP Server Project, for instance, follows the latter model. Everyone is free to download the source and modify it. Everyone is free to submit the changes back for possible inclusion in the base package. However, the ability to actually make the change to the master sources themselves is typically granted only after a period of a few months, during which the existing developers learn to trust the submitter. The idea is that there will be fewer mistakes in the code if changes can be made only by people who have themselves already gone through a sort of peer-review process. Whether this method actually accomplishes this goal is a matter of opinion; however, one definite effect it has had is that the number of people with direct access to the master sources is quite limited—fewer than two dozen people were "core developers" in mid-1999. Another effect is that most of the changes made originate with the core developers, rather than with outsiders, so the server features and implementation tend to reflect the opinions of a few people.

The PHP project, which evolved independently of the Apache HTTP Server Project, uses something more along the lines of the former model. It also has been quite successful at producing quality software—even though the development is done by more than a hundred people. Some of those people contribute a lot; others contribute just a small amount and then are never heard from again.

If you decide to volunteer some of your time toward working on an open-source project, some attributes you'll probably need are persistence and assertiveness—and possibly a thick skin. You'll be joining a group of people who have already established their credentials and opinions on what should be done and how. Unless you're a known expert in the area of the project (such as Web servers and the Apache code itself for the HTTP Server Project), chances are that *your* opinions will be challenged and you'll have to defend your positions.

Many development issues are discussed on mailing lists, and some of those lists can get pretty high octane. It's not uncommon for a newcomer who joins a list and voices an opinion in the middle of a discussion to get flamed to a crisp. Another common occurrence is for such cheeky newcomers to simply be ignored. Less common than either of these, unfortunately, is for a newcomer's suggestions and comments to be welcomed and discussed.

When joining a development mailing list, it's a good idea to lurk for a few weeks and just read the mail traffic so that you can get an idea of what the project's current issues are and who the various participants on the list are. If the mailing list has archives, perusing them is a good idea, too, although for a large and long-running project the archives may consist of hundreds of megabytes.

If you can find someone already involved in the project to act as a mentor for you, so much the better. Unless you already know the person, a good approach is probably to pick someone from the current development discussions whose opinions are respected (that is, someone who doesn't get flamed) and who doesn't seem strongly opinionated to a fault. This is unfortunately a bit of a Catch-22; you may not be able to locate such a person without joining the development list, which is one of the things you want the person to help you do.

As an alternative to finding a mentor through the mailing list, though, there are the Usenet news groups. Many open-source projects have one or more newsgroups in which the project is discussed; for instance, users and developers of the Apache HTTP server hang out in the `comp.infosystems.www.servers.*` newsgroups. A disadvantage to locating a mentor through this path, however, is that you might end up approaching someone who's knowledgeable about the source, personable, friendly, and helpful—but isn't one of the actual developers. He might be able to recommend someone on the development team to you, though.

Another way in which you can "earn merit" and gain respect is to look through the list of bugs in the software (most projects have a bug database of some sort) and figure out fixes for some of them. Submit your fixes to the development team for possible implementation. The more bugs for which you provide fixes, the better your reputation will become.

Yet another possibility for gaining acceptance is to pick a particular less-well-maintained area of the project, such as an Apache module or a specific area of functionality, and become the expert in that area. If you can fix bugs in that area or provide feature or performance enhancements for it, you'll be showing your value to the project.

If fixing bugs or maintaining a lesser-known piece of the software isn't your cup of tea, don't rule out these methods—after you're accepted as a member of the development team, you can always branch out into your *real* areas of interest.

# Help with Bug Reports

One area in which almost all projects can use help is in dealing with reports of bugs, problems, and inconsistencies in the source code. It's quite common for most of the primary and long-involved developers on a project to be quite narrowly focused on new features or the future and not feel much call to work on bugs. This is particularly true of bugs that were introduced by someone *else*, and even more so if the bug's author has moved on and is no longer associated with the project.

Because open-source project work is done mostly as a volunteer effort, that attitude really can't be criticized. The developers work on what they want to work on, or else they don't work on the project at all. Unfortunately, this can mean that the number of outstanding problems with the software grows gradually over time, if none of the active developers find fixing them to be attractive.

This is an excellent opportunity for "new blood"—people who want to become involved with a project. Not only does the software benefit from bugs getting fixed, but the new volunteer becomes more familiar with the code as a consequence of having to understand it in order to fix it. And the existing development team will probably come to know and appreciate the new person because of the quality of his work and his willingness to take on a necessary task that the long-time developers themselves probably don't want to deal with (guilt can be good).

Each project has its own means of recording bug reports. Figure 25.1 shows a snapshot of the Apache HTTP Server Project's bug search form; you can see from the size of the slider in the pop-up box that bugs can fall into many different categories. As of October 1999, more than 5,000 bug reports had been filed against the software, so the user community is active in reporting problems they encounter. Unfortunately, almost 20 percent of them are still open or unresolved, so you can see that this is an area in which contributions would be very welcome.

**FIGURE 25.1**

*Apache HTTP server bug database.*

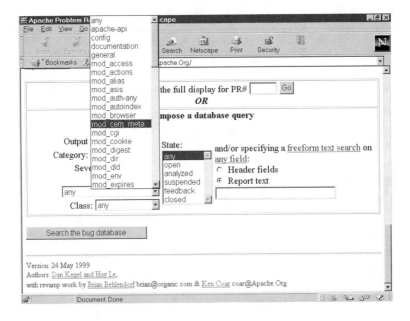

As a contrast, Figure 25.2 shows the top page from the bug reporting system of the open-source PHP project (`http://www.php.net/`), including a corresponding partial list of the available bug categories. In October 1999, the PHP bug database had roughly 2,400 entries; of these, again, almost 20 percent were still open.

**FIGURE 25.2**

*PHP project bug database.*

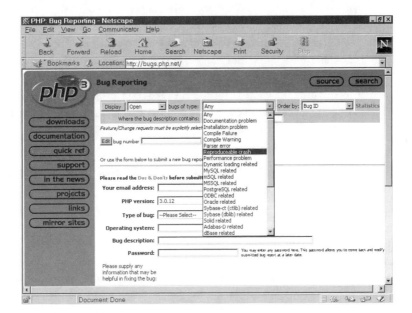

With about every fifth bug report still open, bug tracking and repair is clearly a fertile field of endeavor, at least for these two projects—and there's no reason to think it's not an area in which almost any project would gladly welcome assistance.

# Help by Testing the Software

Software projects can almost always benefit by having the software tested by people other than those who develop it. This is variously called *alpha*, *beta*, or *field* testing. Alpha and beta testing refer to the expected stability of the software being tested; alpha-quality software is usually considered highly experimental, and some (or many) features may not work correctly or be altogether broken. Beta-quality software is generally considered pretty stable; all the features *should* work, although there are probably some minor issues. There's also an excellent chance that new features will be added to the software between an alpha version and the final stable release; this also applies to beta-quality software, but to a lesser extent. Features you find in beta-quality code are virtually certain to be in the final release; that may or may not be true for alpha software. Field-testing is a more general term that covers both alpha and beta testing.

Although most new code is checked pretty carefully for bugs when it's added, there are always a few bugs that sneak in here and there. Even more insidious than bugs in the new functionality are the inadvertent interactions with existing features that may cause problems. If a piece of software no longer works the way it used to, it is said to have *regressed*, and the changed behavior is called a *regression*. Regressions are among the nastiest of bugs, because they elude the focused testing of new features, cropping up instead in areas that usually seem unrelated and are considered stable. Testing that records a wide (if not complete) range of expected software behavior and then measures a new version against those expectations is known as a *regression test suite*, and at the time of this writing none exists for the HTTP Server Project software. Regression test suites are vastly desirable; even regression tests that measure only certain facets of software operation are welcome bits of support.

The Apache HTTP Server Project in particular maintains two mailing lists of people who have volunteered to test the server and provide bug reports to the developers:

- `stable-testers`
- `current-testers`

The `stable-testers` people are contacted by the server project's current release manager when a new release is being assembled; the hope is that they'll test the about-to-be-packaged server in their environments and report any functional regressions back to the release manager or the development list. In a perfect world, the `stable-testers` won't find anything; in reality, they usually turn up one or two last-minute bugs that need to either be fixed or at least noted in the documentation for the release. Once in a while they locate a serious regression that either stalls the release or requires some frantic release-noting.

The `current-testers` list is comprised of volunteers who occasionally test the latest development version of the server, whether or not it's being prepared for release. This list, too, is contacted by the release manager during package preparation but, by virtue of being on this list, the `current-testers` should be providing semi-regular feedback to the developers even during the development cycle.

To join either list, you just need to send a message such as the following and respond to the instructions in the confirmation message you'll receive:

```
To: majordomo@Apache.Org
Subject: joining stable-testers list

Subscribe stable-testers
```

Make the appropriate changes to join the `current-testers` list instead.

That's how things stand with the HTTP Server Project, at least. Other Apache projects may or may not have parallel mechanisms for software testing; check with someone on the core development team of the appropriate project to find out.

# Documentation

Software developers are widely known for being resistant, as a group, to writing documentation. There are outstanding exceptions, of course, but the general rule is that developers prefer to write code rather than write *about* code.

A natural consequence of this is that the documentation for a particular piece of software developed by volunteers has a tendency to be somewhat out-of-date at best and woefully spotty and inadequate—if not altogether absent—at worst. So helping out with project documentation is another sort of contribution that's likely to be welcomed with glad cries.

Some projects make it easy to contribute to the documentation effort; for instance, as shown in Figure 25.3, the PHP project (`http://www.php.net`) makes it as easy as adding text on a Web page. Every so often, the PHP developers collect all the comments and make appropriate changes to the documentation. When the result is published again, the comments are cleared, and new ones can be made.

**FIGURE 25.3**

*Commenting on PHP online documentation.*

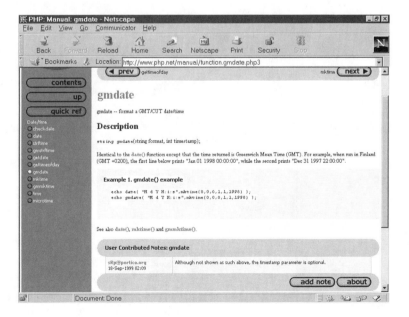

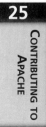

25

CONTRIBUTING TO APACHE

Other projects have more complex procedures.

Depending on the project, more than one type of documentation might be involved. For instance, the Apache HTTP Server Project has documentation about how to actually *use* the server and how to modify and enhance it. The latter is called the API (Application Programming Interface) documentation, and what's available can be as complete as that shown in Figure 25.4 or as sparse as that in Figure 25.5.

**FIGURE 25.4**

*A moderately good example of Apache API documentation.*

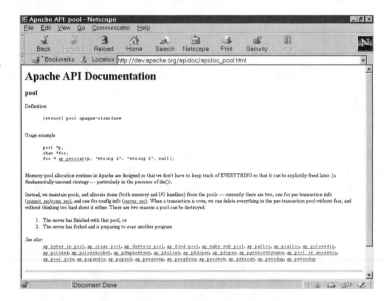

**FIGURE 25.5**

*A woefully inadequate documentation example.*

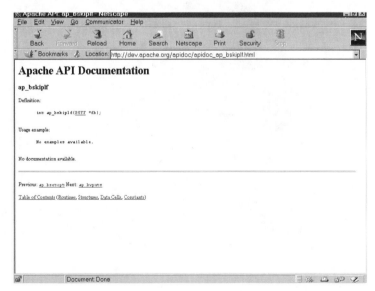

The API documentation tends to be more in need of updating than the main server documentation on an ongoing basis, as a natural consequence of its tracking the internal workings of the software.

Working on the API documentation is definitely a contribution appreciated by hundreds or thousands of people, that being the number of people worldwide who actually deal with the intricacies of enhancing the Apache server. Of course, it's also not for the faint of heart, requiring some expertise in the detailed operation of the code.

> **Note**
>
> If you're going to volunteer to work on the documentation, you should at least be familiar with the thing you're documenting. In the case of something as technical as API descriptions, you're probably going to already be involved in the development of the source code itself.

# Donating Tangibles

Tangible donations should be given to the Apache Software Foundation, even those intended to further a specific purpose. Since the Foundation is providing support for all the different projects, it maintains a sort of "pool" of resources and allocates them to projects according to need. If a gift is made with the intention of supporting a particular project or purpose, the Foundation makes a good-faith best effort to see that it gets there—but it can't guarantee it. That might lead to popular and well-known projects getting all the support, possibly even more than they needed, while smaller but equally deserving ones would get starved.

Some examples of tangible donations include

- *Licensed software*, such as an installation builder or development suite. Enough copies or licenses should be provided for more than one user; otherwise, things can stall as the software is passed around.

- *Services*, such as legal assistance, data trend analyses, trademark searches, network connectivity for project hardware or even individual developers, or the like. These aren't *really* tangible, but they aren't the same as volunteering to work on a project, either.

- *Computer hardware*, such as disks, CD writers, network cards, monitors, laptops, or even desktop workstations or server-level systems.

When contributing things of this sort, remember that the developers are scattered all around the world—and passing a particular piece of hardware or software from one person to the next is generally not as simple as walking down the hall to his office.

If you intend to donate computer hardware, it's best to consult the Foundation's treasurer first to see whether there are any outstanding needs.

# Summary

The Apache Software Foundation is a not-for-profit organization that develops and distributes quality software for free. It's supported solely by donations and volunteer efforts, and every little bit helps. If you want to help out, any contribution you care to make will almost certainly be gladly welcomed. If you feel your life or work has been improved at all by any of the Foundation's projects, please consider donating something so they can keep up the good work.

# Appendixes

## PART VI

# The Apache License

This software consists of voluntary contributions made by many individuals on behalf of the Apache Group and was originally based on public domain software written at the National Center for Supercomputing Applications, University of Illinois, Urbana-Champaign. For more information on the Apache Group and the Apache HTTP server project, please see `http://www.apache.org/`.

# Apache Version History

The following is a rough timeline of the Apache project:

- **Oct 28, 1991:** Tim Berners-Lee sends first message over the WWW-Talk mailing list. Later that week, he announces a public Web server, at CERN, that you can access via Telnet. See the archives at `http://www.webhistory.org/www.lists/`.

- **December 13, 1991:** Pei Y. Wei announces on WWW-Talk that he has a graphical Web browser working.

- **December 1, 1992:** Marc Andreesen posts to WWW-Talk, announcing that he is working on an HTTP server at NCSA.

- **January 23, 1993:** Marc Andreesen announces the first public release of the Mosaic Web browser.

- **April 22, 1993:** Rob McCool announces the 0.3 beta release of NCSA's HTTP server.

- **February 1995:** Brian Behlendorf and Cliff Skolnick put together developer resources on space donated by HotWired and begin to collect patches from various people using the NCSA HTTPd server. These patches are applied to the 1.3 version of the NCSA server.

- **March 1995:** Apache Server 0.6.2 released to the public—the first public release.

- **May-June 1995:** Robert Thau works on a rewrite of the server, code-named Shambhala.

- **August 1995:** Apache 0.8.8, based on Robert Thau's work, released. New features include a modular structure that's still in use today.

- **December 1, 1995:** Apache 1.0 released.

- **April 1996:** Apache passes NCSA as the most popular Web server in use.

- **July 1996:** Apache 1.1 released. Major new features include the implementation of HTTP/1.1 keep-alive connections, name-based virtual hosts, and handlers.

- **January 18, 1997:** mod_perl 0.10 beta released. See `http://perl.apache.org/`.

- **June 1997:** Apache 1.2 released.

- **February 1998:** Netcraft reports that more than half of the Web servers on the Internet run Apache or some derivative of Apache. See `http://www.netcraft.com/survey/`.

- **February 19, 1998:** Apache 1.2.6 released.

- **March 1998:** Apache 1.3 released with support for Microsoft Windows NT.

- **June 12, 1998:** mod_perl 1.0.0 released.

- **June 22, 1998:** IBM and The Apache Group announce a partnership to work on the Apache Web server. This makes IBM the first major company to openly endorse an Open Source project. Several other companies announce Open Source projects in the following months. See `http://www.apacheweek.com/issues/98-06-19#ibm`.

- **October 14-16, 1998:** ApacheCon 98, the first Apache conference, is held at the San Francisco Hilton. See `http://www.apachecon.com/`.

- **August 21-24, 1999:** The O'Reilly Apache Conference at the O'Reilly Open Source Convention in Monterey. See `http://conference.oreilly.com/convention99.html`.

- **Early 2000:** Apache 2.0 release expected.

# APPENDIX C

# Configuration File Listings

When you first set up your server, you can just go with most of the default values in the configuration files, and things will work just fine. Some things won't be optimal for your needs, and you might want some features disabled, but the server should at least run.

You will find that the default configuration files are heavily commented and very clearly explain what each directive does, usually providing an example setting. If you don't understand a particular section, chances are pretty good that you don't need to change it. What follows are the default configuration files that come with Apache 1.3.9.

There are two versions of `httpd.conf`, the main server configuration file. The first one, in Listing C.1, is the Unix version of the file; the second version, in Listing C.2, is for Microsoft Windows. The main differences are in the modules section.

Sprinkled throughout the `httpd.conf` files is `@@ServerRoot@@`, which is replaced when you compile and install the server with the location of your `ServerRoot`. On Unix systems by default this is `/usr/local/apache`; on Microsoft Windows it is `c:\Program Files\Apache Group\Apache`. However, both settings can be changed during installation. See Chapter 3, "Compiling and Installing Apache," for more information on the installation process for Unix and Microsoft Windows.

Following the `httpd.conf` file listings are the `srm.conf` and `access.conf` file listings. These files are listed for historical reasons only and contain nothing more than comments stating why they are there.

**Listing C.1**   `httpd.conf-dist` for Unix Installations

```
#
# Based upon the NCSA server configuration files originally by Rob McCool.
#
# This is the main Apache server configuration file. It contains the
# configuration directives that give the server its instructions.
# See <URL:http://www.apache.org/docs/> for detailed information about
# the directives.
#
# Do NOT simply read the instructions in here without understanding
# what they do. They're here only as hints or reminders. If you are unsure
# consult the online docs. You have been warned.
#
# After this file is processed, the server will look for and process
# @@ServerRoot@@/conf/srm.conf and then @@ServerRoot@@/conf/access.conf
# unless you have overridden these with ResourceConfig and/or
# AccessConfig directives here.
#
# The configuration directives are grouped into three basic sections:
#  1. Directives that control the operation of the Apache server process as a
#     whole (the 'global environment').
```

# APPENDIX C

# Configuration File Listings

```
# 2. Directives that define the parameters of the 'main' or 'default' server,
#    which responds to requests that aren't handled by a virtual host.
#    These directives also provide default values for the settings
#    of all virtual hosts.
# 3. Settings for virtual hosts, which allow Web requests to be sent to
#    different IP addresses or hostnames and have them handled by the
#    same Apache server process.
#
# Configuration and logfile names: If the filenames you specify for many
# of the server's control files begin with "/" (or "drive:/" for Win32), the
# server will use that explicit path. If the filenames do *not* begin
# with "/", the value of ServerRoot is prepended -- so "logs/foo.log"
# with ServerRoot set to "/usr/local/apache" will be interpreted by the
# server as "/usr/local/apache/logs/foo.log".
#

### Section 1: Global Environment
#
# The directives in this section affect the overall operation of Apache,
# such as the number of concurrent requests it can handle or where it
# can find its configuration files.
#

#
# ServerType is either inetd or standalone. Inetd mode is only supported on
# Unix platforms.
#
ServerType standalone

#
# ServerRoot: The top of the directory tree under which the server's
# configuration, error, and log files are kept.
#
# NOTE! If you intend to place this on an NFS (or otherwise network)
# mounted file system then please read the LockFile documentation
# (available at <URL:http://www.apache.org/docs/mod/core.html#lockfile>);
# you will save yourself a lot of trouble.
#
# Do NOT add a slash at the end of the directory path.
#
ServerRoot "@@ServerRoot@@"

#
# The LockFile directive sets the path to the lockfile used when Apache
# is compiled with either USE_FCNTL_SERIALIZED_ACCEPT or
# USE_FLOCK_SERIALIZED_ACCEPT. This directive should normally be left at
# its default value. The main reason for changing it is if the logs
# directory is NFS mounted, since the lockfile MUST BE STORED ON A LOCAL
# DISK. The PID of the main server process is automatically appended to
```

*continues*

**LISTING C.1**    continued

```
# the filename.
#
#LockFile logs/accept.lock


#
# PidFile: The file in which the server should record its process
# identification number when it starts.
#
PidFile logs/httpd.pid


#
# ScoreBoardFile: File used to store internal server process information.
# Not all architectures require this. But if yours does (you'll know because
# this file will be created when you run Apache) then you *must* ensure that
# no two invocations of Apache share the same scoreboard file.
#
ScoreBoardFile logs/apache_runtime_status


#
# In the standard configuration, the server will process this file,
# srm.conf, and access.conf in that order. The latter two files are
# now distributed empty, as it is recommended that all directives
# be kept in a single file for simplicity. The commented-out values
# below are the built-in defaults. You can have the server ignore
# these files altogether by using "/dev/null" (for Unix) or
# "nul" (for Win32) for the arguments to the directives.
#
#ResourceConfig conf/srm.conf
#AccessConfig conf/access.conf


#
# Timeout: The number of seconds before receives and sends time out.
#
Timeout 300


#
# KeepAlive: Whether or not to allow persistent connections (more than
# one request per connection). Set to "Off" to deactivate.
#
KeepAlive On


#
# MaxKeepAliveRequests: The maximum number of requests to allow
# during a persistent connection. Set to 0 to allow an unlimited amount.
# We recommend you leave this number high, for maximum performance.
#
MaxKeepAliveRequests 100


#
```

```
# KeepAliveTimeout: Number of seconds to wait for the next request from the
# same client on the same connection.
#
KeepAliveTimeout 15


#
# Server-pool size regulation. Rather than making you guess how many
# server processes you need, Apache dynamically adapts to the load it
# sees --- that is, it tries to maintain enough server processes to
# handle the current load, plus a few spare servers to handle transient
# load spikes (e.g., multiple simultaneous requests from a single
# Netscape browser).
#
# It does this by periodically checking how many servers are waiting
# for a request. If there are fewer than MinSpareServers, it creates
# a new spare. If there are more than MaxSpareServers, some of the
# spares die off. The default values are probably OK for most sites.
#
MinSpareServers 5
MaxSpareServers 10


#
# Number of servers to start initially --- should be a reasonable ballpark
# figure.
#
StartServers 5


#
# Limit on total number of servers running, i.e., limit on the number
# of clients who can simultaneously connect --- if this limit is ever
# reached, clients will be LOCKED OUT, so it should NOT BE SET TOO LOW.
# It is intended mainly as a brake to keep a runaway server from taking
# the system with it as it spirals down...
#
MaxClients 150


#
# MaxRequestsPerChild: the number of requests each child process is
# allowed to process before the child dies. The child will exit so
# as to avoid problems after prolonged use when Apache (and maybe the
# libraries it uses) leak memory or other resources. On most systems, this
# isn't really needed, but a few (such as Solaris) do have notable leaks
# in the libraries. For these platforms, set to something like 10000
# or so; a setting of 0 means unlimited.
#
# NOTE: This value does not include keepalive requests after the initial
#       request per connection. For example, if a child process handles
#       an initial request and 10 subsequent "keptalive" requests, it
#       would only count as 1 request towards this limit.
```

*continues*

**LISTING C.1** continued

```
#
MaxRequestsPerChild 0

#
# Listen: Allows you to bind Apache to specific IP addresses and/or
# ports, in addition to the default. See also the <VirtualHost>
# directive.
#
#Listen 3000
#Listen 12.34.56.78:80

#
# BindAddress: You can support virtual hosts with this option. This directive
# is used to tell the server which IP address to listen to. It can either
# contain "*", an IP address, or a fully qualified Internet domain name.
# See also the <VirtualHost> and Listen directives.
#
#BindAddress *

#
# Dynamic Shared Object (DSO) Support
#
# To be able to use the functionality of a module which was built as a DSO you
# have to place corresponding 'LoadModule' lines at this location so the
# directives contained in it are actually available _before_ they are used.
# Please read the file README.DSO in the Apache 1.3 distribution for more
# details about the DSO mechanism and run 'httpd -l' for the list of already
# built-in (statically linked and thus always available) modules in your httpd
# binary.
#
# Note: The order is which modules are loaded is important. Don't change
# the order below without expert advice.
#
# Example:
# LoadModule foo_module libexec/mod_foo.so

#
# ExtendedStatus controls whether Apache will generate "full" status
# information (ExtendedStatus On) or just basic information (ExtendedStatus
# Off) when the "server-status" handler is called. The default is Off.
#
#ExtendedStatus On

### Section 2: 'Main' server configuration
#
# The directives in this section set up the values used by the 'main'
# server, which responds to any requests that aren't handled by a
# <VirtualHost> definition. These values also provide defaults for
# any <VirtualHost> containers you may define later in the file.
```

```
#
# All of these directives may appear inside <VirtualHost> containers,
# in which case these default settings will be overridden for the
# virtual host being defined.
#


#
# If your ServerType directive (set earlier in the 'Global Environment'
# section) is set to "inetd", the next few directives don't have any
# effect since their settings are defined by the inetd configuration.
# Skip ahead to the ServerAdmin directive.
#


#
# Port: The port to which the standalone server listens. For
# ports < 1023, you will need httpd to be run as root initially.
#
Port 80


#
# If you wish httpd to run as a different user or group, you must run
# httpd as root initially and it will switch.
#
# User/Group: The name (or #number) of the user/group to run httpd as.
#  . On SCO (ODT 3) use "User nouser" and "Group nogroup".
#  . On HPUX you may not be able to use shared memory as nobody, and the
#    suggested workaround is to create a user www and use that user.
#  NOTE that some kernels refuse to setgid(Group) or semctl(IPC_SET)
#  when the value of (unsigned)Group is above 60000;
#  don't use Group #-1 on these systems!
#
User nobody
Group #-1


#
# ServerAdmin: Your address, where problems with the server should be
# e-mailed. This address appears on some server-generated pages, such
# as error documents.
#
ServerAdmin you@your.address


#
# ServerName allows you to set a host name which is sent back to clients for
# your server if it's different than the one the program would get (i.e., use
# "www" instead of the host's real name).
#
# Note: You cannot just invent host names and hope they work. The name you
# define here must be a valid DNS name for your host. If you don't understand
# this, ask your network administrator.
```

*continues*

**LISTING C.1**    continued

```
# If your host doesn't have a registered DNS name, enter its IP address here.
# You will have to access it by its address (e.g., http://123.45.67.89/)
# anyway, and this will make redirections work in a sensible way.
#
#ServerName new.host.name


#
# DocumentRoot: The directory out of which you will serve your
# documents. By default, all requests are taken from this directory, but
# symbolic links and aliases may be used to point to other locations.
#
DocumentRoot "@@ServerRoot@@/htdocs"


#
# Each directory to which Apache has access, can be configured with respect
# to which services and features are allowed and/or disabled in that
# directory (and its subdirectories).
#
# First, we configure the "default" to be a very restrictive set of
# permissions.
#
<Directory />
    Options FollowSymLinks
    AllowOverride None
</Directory>


#
# Note that from this point forward you must specifically allow
# particular features to be enabled - so if something's not working as
# you might expect, make sure that you have specifically enabled it
# below.
#


#
# This should be changed to whatever you set DocumentRoot to.
#
<Directory "@@ServerRoot@@/htdocs">


#
# This may also be "None", "All", or any combination of "Indexes",
# "Includes", "FollowSymLinks", "ExecCGI", or "MultiViews".
#
# Note that "MultiViews" must be named *explicitly* --- "Options All"
# doesn't give it to you.
#
    Options Indexes FollowSymLinks


#
# This controls which options the .htaccess files in directories can
```

```
# override. Can also be "All", or any combination of "Options", "FileInfo",
# "AuthConfig", and "Limit"
#
    AllowOverride None


#
# Controls who can get stuff from this server.
#
    Order allow,deny
    Allow from all
</Directory>


#
# UserDir: The name of the directory which is appended onto a user's home
# directory if a ~user request is received.
#
UserDir public_html


#
# Control access to UserDir directories. The following is an example
# for a site where these directories are restricted to read-only.
#
#<Directory /home/*/public_html>
#    AllowOverride FileInfo AuthConfig Limit
#    Options MultiViews Indexes SymLinksIfOwnerMatch IncludesNoExec
#    <Limit GET POST OPTIONS PROPFIND>
#        Order allow,deny
#        Allow from all
#    </Limit>
#    <Limit PUT DELETE PATCH PROPPATCH MKCOL COPY MOVE LOCK UNLOCK>
#        Order deny,allow
#        Deny from all
#    </Limit>
#</Directory>


#
# DirectoryIndex: Name of the file or files to use as a pre-written HTML
# directory index. Separate multiple entries with spaces.
#
DirectoryIndex index.html


#
# AccessFileName: The name of the file to look for in each directory
# for access control information.
#
AccessFileName .htaccess


#
# The following lines prevent .htaccess files from being viewed by
```

*continues*

**LISTING C.1** continued

```
# Web clients. Since .htaccess files often contain authorization
# information, access is disallowed for security reasons. Comment
# these lines out if you want Web visitors to see the contents of
# .htaccess files. If you change the AccessFileName directive above,
# be sure to make the corresponding changes here.
#
# Also, folks tend to use names such as .htpasswd for password
# files, so this will protect those as well.
#
<Files ~ "^\.ht">
    Order allow,deny
    Deny from all
</Files>


#
# CacheNegotiatedDocs: By default, Apache sends "Pragma: no-cache" with each
# document that was negotiated on the basis of content. This asks proxy
# servers not to cache the document. Uncommenting the following line disables
# this behavior, and proxies will be allowed to cache the documents.
#
#CacheNegotiatedDocs


#
# UseCanonicalName: (new for 1.3) With this setting turned on, whenever
# Apache needs to construct a self-referencing URL (a URL that refers back
# to the server the response is coming from) it will use ServerName and
# Port to form a "canonical" name. With this setting off, Apache will
# use the hostname:port that the client supplied, when possible. This
# also affects SERVER_NAME and SERVER_PORT in CGI scripts.
#
UseCanonicalName On


#
# TypesConfig describes where the mime.types file (or equivalent) is
# to be found.
#
TypesConfig conf/mime.types


#
# DefaultType is the default MIME type the server will use for a document
# if it cannot otherwise determine one, such as from filename extensions.
# If your server contains mostly text or HTML documents, "text/plain" is
# a good value. If most of your content is binary, such as applications
# or images, you may want to use "application/octet-stream" instead to
# keep browsers from trying to display binary files as though they are
# text.
#
DefaultType text/plain
```

```
#
# The mod_mime_magic module allows the server to use various hints from the
# contents of the file itself to determine its type. The MIMEMagicFile
# directive tells the module where the hint definitions are located.
# mod_mime_magic is not part of the default server (you have to add
# it yourself with a LoadModule [see the DSO paragraph in the 'Global
# Environment' section], or recompile the server and include mod_mime_magic
# as part of the configuration), so it's enclosed in an <IfModule> container.
# This means that the MIMEMagicFile directive will only be processed if the
# module is part of the server.
#
<IfModule mod_mime_magic.c>
    MIMEMagicFile conf/magic
</IfModule>


#
# HostnameLookups: Log the names of clients or just their IP addresses
# e.g., www.apache.org (on) or 204.62.129.132 (off).
# The default is off because it'd be overall better for the net if people
# had to knowingly turn this feature on, since enabling it means that
# each client request will result in AT LEAST one lookup request to the
# nameserver.
#
HostnameLookups Off


#
# ErrorLog: The location of the error log file.
# If you do not specify an ErrorLog directive within a <VirtualHost>
# container, error messages relating to that virtual host will be
# logged here. If you *do* define an error logfile for a <VirtualHost>
# container, that host's errors will be logged there and not here.
#
ErrorLog logs/error_log


#
# LogLevel: Control the number of messages logged to the error_log.
# Possible values include: debug, info, notice, warn, error, crit,
# alert, emerg.
#
LogLevel warn


#
# The following directives define some format nicknames for use with
# a CustomLog directive (see below).
#
LogFormat "%h %l %u %t \"%r\" %>s %b \"%{Referer}i\" \"%{User-Agent}i\""
➥combined
LogFormat "%h %l %u %t \"%r\" %>s %b" common
LogFormat "%{Referer}i -> %U" referer
LogFormat "%{User-agent}i" agent
```

*continues*

**LISTING C.1** continued

```
#
# The location and format of the access logfile (Common Logfile Format).
# If you do not define any access logfiles within a <VirtualHost>
# container, they will be logged here. Contrariwise, if you *do*
# define per-<VirtualHost> access logfiles, transactions will be
# logged therein and *not* in this file.
#
CustomLog logs/access_log common


#
# If you would like to have agent and referer logfiles, uncomment the
# following directives.
#
#CustomLog logs/referer_log referer
#CustomLog logs/agent_log agent


#
# If you prefer a single logfile with access, agent, and referer information
# (Combined Logfile Format) you can use the following directive.
#
#CustomLog logs/access_log combined


#
# Optionally add a line containing the server version and virtual host
# name to server-generated pages (error documents, FTP directory listings,
# mod_status and mod_info output etc., but not CGI generated documents).
# Set to "EMail" to also include a mailto: link to the ServerAdmin.
# Set to one of: On | Off | EMail
#
ServerSignature On


#
# Aliases: Add here as many aliases as you need (with no limit). The format is
# Alias fakename realname
#
# Note that if you include a trailing / on fakename then the server will
# require it to be present in the URL. So "/icons" isn't aliased in this
# example, only "/icons/"..
#
Alias /icons/ "@@ServerRoot@@/icons/"

<Directory "@@ServerRoot@@/icons">
    Options Indexes MultiViews
    AllowOverride None
    Order allow,deny
    Allow from all
</Directory>


#
```

```
# ScriptAlias: This controls which directories contain server scripts.
# ScriptAliases are essentially the same as Aliases, except that
# documents in the realname directory are treated as applications and
# run by the server when requested rather than as documents sent to the client.
# The same rules about trailing "/" apply to ScriptAlias directives as to
# Alias.
#
ScriptAlias /cgi-bin/ "@@ServerRoot@@/cgi-bin/"


#
# "@@ServerRoot@@/cgi-bin" should be changed to whatever your ScriptAliased
# CGI directory exists, if you have that configured.
#
<Directory "@@ServerRoot@@/cgi-bin">
    AllowOverride None
    Options None
    Order allow,deny
    Allow from all
</Directory>


#
# Redirect allows you to tell clients about documents which used to exist in
# your server's namespace, but do not anymore. This allows you to tell the
# clients where to look for the relocated document.
# Format: Redirect old-URI new-URL
#


#
# Directives controlling the display of server-generated directory listings.
#


#
# FancyIndexing is whether you want fancy directory indexing or standard
#
IndexOptions FancyIndexing


#
# AddIcon* directives tell the server which icon to show for different
# files or filename extensions. These are only displayed for
# FancyIndexed directories.
#
AddIconByEncoding (CMP,/icons/compressed.gif) x-compress x-gzip

AddIconByType (TXT,/icons/text.gif) text/*
AddIconByType (IMG,/icons/image2.gif) image/*
AddIconByType (SND,/icons/sound2.gif) audio/*
AddIconByType (VID,/icons/movie.gif) video/*

AddIcon /icons/binary.gif .bin .exe
```

*continues*

**LISTING C.1**  continued

```
AddIcon /icons/binhex.gif .hqx
AddIcon /icons/tar.gif .tar
AddIcon /icons/world2.gif .wrl .wrl.gz .vrml .vrm .iv
AddIcon /icons/compressed.gif .Z .z .tgz .gz .zip
AddIcon /icons/a.gif .ps .ai .eps
AddIcon /icons/layout.gif .html .shtml .htm .pdf
AddIcon /icons/text.gif .txt
AddIcon /icons/c.gif .c
AddIcon /icons/p.gif .pl .py
AddIcon /icons/f.gif .for
AddIcon /icons/dvi.gif .dvi
AddIcon /icons/uuencoded.gif .uu
AddIcon /icons/script.gif .conf .sh .shar .csh .ksh .tcl
AddIcon /icons/tex.gif .tex
AddIcon /icons/bomb.gif core

AddIcon /icons/back.gif ..
AddIcon /icons/hand.right.gif README
AddIcon /icons/folder.gif ^^DIRECTORY^^
AddIcon /icons/blank.gif ^^BLANKICON^^

#
# DefaultIcon is which icon to show for files which do not have an icon
# explicitly set.
#
DefaultIcon /icons/unknown.gif

#
# AddDescription allows you to place a short description after a file in
# server-generated indexes. These are only displayed for FancyIndexed
# directories.
# Format: AddDescription "description" filename
#
#AddDescription "GZIP compressed document" .gz
#AddDescription "tar archive" .tar
#AddDescription "GZIP compressed tar archive" .tgz

#
# ReadmeName is the name of the README file the server will look for by
# default, and append to directory listings.
#
# HeaderName is the name of a file which should be prepended to
# directory indexes.
#
# The server will first look for name.html and include it if found.
# If name.html doesn't exist, the server will then look for name.txt
# and include it as plaintext if found.
#
ReadmeName README
```

```
HeaderName HEADER

#
# IndexIgnore is a set of filenames which directory indexing should ignore
# and not include in the listing. Shell-style wildcarding is permitted.
#
IndexIgnore .??* *~ *# HEADER* README* RCS CVS *,v *,t


#
# AddEncoding allows you to have certain browsers (Mosaic/X 2.1+) uncompress
# information on the fly. Note: Not all browsers support this.
# Despite the name similarity, the following Add* directives have nothing
# to do with the FancyIndexing customization directives above.
#
AddEncoding x-compress Z
AddEncoding x-gzip gz tgz


#
# AddLanguage allows you to specify the language of a document. You can
# then use content negotiation to give a browser a file in a language
# it can understand. Note that the suffix does not have to be the same
# as the language keyword --- those with documents in Polish (whose
# net-standard language code is pl) may wish to use "AddLanguage pl .po"
# to avoid the ambiguity with the common suffix for perl scripts.
#
AddLanguage en .en
AddLanguage fr .fr
AddLanguage de .de
AddLanguage da .da
AddLanguage el .el
AddLanguage it .it


#
# LanguagePriority allows you to give precedence to some languages
# in case of a tie during content negotiation.
# Just list the languages in decreasing order of preference.
#
LanguagePriority en fr de


#
# AddType allows you to tweak mime.types without actually editing it, or to
# make certain files to be certain types.
#
# For example, the PHP3 module (not part of the Apache distribution - see
# http://www.php.net) will typically use:
#
#AddType application/x-httpd-php3 .php3
#AddType application/x-httpd-php3-source .phps
```

*continues*

**LISTING C.1**   continued

```
AddType application/x-tar .tgz


#
# AddHandler allows you to map certain file extensions to "handlers",
# actions unrelated to filetype. These can be either built into the server
# or added with the Action command (see below)
#
# If you want to use server side includes, or CGI outside
# ScriptAliased directories, uncomment the following lines.
#
# To use CGI scripts:
#
#AddHandler cgi-script .cgi


#
# To use server-parsed HTML files
#
#AddType text/html .shtml
#AddHandler server-parsed .shtml


#
# Uncomment the following line to enable Apache's send-asis HTTP file
# feature
#
#AddHandler send-as-is asis


#
# If you wish to use server-parsed imagemap files, use
#
#AddHandler imap-file map


#
# To enable type maps, you might want to use
#
#AddHandler type-map var


#
# Action lets you define media types that will execute a script whenever
# a matching file is called. This eliminates the need for repeated URL
# pathnames for oft-used CGI file processors.
# Format: Action media/type /cgi-script/location
# Format: Action handler-name /cgi-script/location
#


#
# MetaDir: specifies the name of the directory in which Apache can find
# meta information files. These files contain additional HTTP headers
# to include when sending the document
#
```

```
#MetaDir .web

#
# MetaSuffix: specifies the file name suffix for the file containing the
# meta information.
#
#MetaSuffix .meta


#
# Customizable error response (Apache style)
#   these come in three flavors
#
#     1) plain text
#ErrorDocument 500 "The server made a boo boo.
# n.b. the (") marks it as text, it does not get output
#
#     2) local redirects
#ErrorDocument 404 /missing.html
# to redirect to local URL /missing.html
#ErrorDocument 404 /cgi-bin/missing_handler.pl
# N.B.: You can redirect to a script or a document using server-side-includes.
#
#     3) external redirects
#ErrorDocument 402 http://some.other_server.com/subscription_info.html
# N.B.: Many of the environment variables associated with the original
# request will *not* be available to such a script.


#
# The following directives modify normal HTTP response behavior.
# The first directive disables keepalive for Netscape 2.x and browsers that
# spoof it. There are known problems with these browser implementations.
# The second directive is for Microsoft Internet Explorer 4.0b2
# which has a broken HTTP/1.1 implementation and does not properly
# support keepalive when it is used on 301 or 302 (redirect) responses.
#
BrowserMatch "Mozilla/2" nokeepalive
BrowserMatch "MSIE 4\.0b2;" nokeepalive downgrade-1.0 force-response-1.0


#
# The following directive disables HTTP/1.1 responses to browsers which
# are in violation of the HTTP/1.0 spec by not being able to grok a
# basic 1.1 response.
#
BrowserMatch "RealPlayer 4\.0" force-response-1.0
BrowserMatch "Java/1\.0" force-response-1.0
BrowserMatch "JDK/1\.0" force-response-1.0


#
# Allow server status reports, with the URL of http://servername/server-status
```

*continues*

**LISTING C.1**   continued

```
# Change the ".your_domain.com" to match your domain to enable.
#
#<Location /server-status>
#    SetHandler server-status
#    Order deny,allow
#    Deny from all
#    Allow from .your_domain.com
#</Location>

#
# Allow remote server configuration reports, with the URL of
#  http://servername/server-info (requires that mod_info.c be loaded).
# Change the ".your_domain.com" to match your domain to enable.
#
#<Location /server-info>
#    SetHandler server-info
#    Order deny,allow
#    Deny from all
#    Allow from .your_domain.com
#</Location>

#
# There have been reports of people trying to abuse an old bug from pre-1.1
# days. This bug involved a CGI script distributed as a part of Apache.
# By uncommenting these lines you can redirect these attacks to a logging
# script on phf.apache.org. Or, you can record them yourself, using the script
# support/phf_abuse_log.cgi.
#
#<Location /cgi-bin/phf*>
#    Deny from all
#    ErrorDocument 403 http://phf.apache.org/phf_abuse_log.cgi
#</Location>

#
# Proxy Server directives. Uncomment the following lines to
# enable the proxy server:
#
#<IfModule mod_proxy.c>
#ProxyRequests On
#
#<Directory proxy:*>
#    Order deny,allow
#    Deny from all
#    Allow from .your_domain.com
#</Directory>

#
# Enable/disable the handling of HTTP/1.1 "Via:" headers.
# ("Full" adds the server version; "Block" removes all outgoing Via: headers)
```

```
# Set to one of: Off | On | Full | Block
#
#ProxyVia On


#
# To enable the cache as well, edit and uncomment the following lines:
# (no cacheing without CacheRoot)
#
#CacheRoot "@@ServerRoot@@/proxy"
#CacheSize 5
#CacheGcInterval 4
#CacheMaxExpire 24
#CacheLastModifiedFactor 0.1
#CacheDefaultExpire 1
#NoCache a_domain.com another_domain.edu joes.garage_sale.com


#</IfModule>
# End of proxy directives.


### Section 3: Virtual Hosts
#
# VirtualHost: If you want to maintain multiple domains/hostnames on your
# machine you can setup VirtualHost containers for them.
# Please see the documentation at <URL:http://www.apache.org/docs/vhosts/>
# for further details before you try to setup virtual hosts.
# You may use the command line option '-S' to verify your virtual host
# configuration.


#
# If you want to use name-based virtual hosts you need to define at
# least one IP address (and port number) for them.
#
#NameVirtualHost 12.34.56.78:80
#NameVirtualHost 12.34.56.78


#
# VirtualHost example:
# Almost any Apache directive may go into a VirtualHost container.
#
#<VirtualHost ip.address.of.host.some_domain.com>
#    ServerAdmin webmaster@host.some_domain.com
#    DocumentRoot /www/docs/host.some_domain.com
#    ServerName host.some_domain.com
#    ErrorLog logs/host.some_domain.com-error_log
#    CustomLog logs/host.some_domain.com-access_log common
#</VirtualHost>

#<VirtualHost _default_:*>
#</VirtualHost>
```

**LISTING C.2** `httpd.conf-dist-win` for Windows Installations

```
#
# Based upon the NCSA server configuration files originally by Rob McCool.
#
# This is the main Apache server configuration file. It contains the
# configuration directives that give the server its instructions.
# See <URL:http://www.apache.org/docs/> for detailed information about
# the directives.
#
# Do NOT simply read the instructions in here without understanding
# what they do. They're here only as hints or reminders. If you are unsure
# consult the online docs. You have been warned.
#
# After this file is processed, the server will look for and process
# @@ServerRoot@@/conf/srm.conf and then @@ServerRoot@@/conf/access.conf
# unless you have overridden these with ResourceConfig and/or
# AccessConfig directives here.
#
# The configuration directives are grouped into three basic sections:
#  1. Directives that control the operation of the Apache server process as a
#     whole (the 'global environment').
#  2. Directives that define the parameters of the 'main' or 'default' server,
#     which responds to requests that aren't handled by a virtual host.
#     These directives also provide default values for the settings
#     of all virtual hosts.
#  3. Settings for virtual hosts, which allow Web requests to be sent to
#     different IP addresses or hostnames and have them handled by the
#     same Apache server process.
#
# Configuration and logfile names: If the filenames you specify for many
# of the server's control files begin with "/" (or "drive:/" for Win32), the
# server will use that explicit path. If the filenames do *not* begin
# with "/", the value of ServerRoot is prepended -- so "logs/foo.log"
# with ServerRoot set to "/usr/local/apache" will be interpreted by the
# server as "/usr/local/apache/logs/foo.log".
#
# NOTE: Where filenames are specified, you must use forward slashes
# instead of backslashes (e.g., "c:/apache" instead of "c:\apache").
# If a drive letter is omitted, the drive on which Apache.exe is located
# will be used by default. It is recommended that you always supply
# an explicit drive letter in absolute paths, however, to avoid
# confusion.
#


### Section 1: Global Environment
#
# The directives in this section affect the overall operation of Apache,
# such as the number of concurrent requests it can handle or where it
# can find its configuration files.
#
```

```
#
# ServerType is either inetd, or standalone. Inetd mode is only supported on
# Unix platforms.
#
ServerType standalone

#
# ServerRoot: The top of the directory tree under which the server's
# configuration, error, and log files are kept.
#
# Do NOT add a slash at the end of the directory path.
#
ServerRoot "@@ServerRoot@@"

#
# PidFile: The file in which the server should record its process
# identification number when it starts.
#
PidFile logs/httpd.pid

#
# ScoreBoardFile: File used to store internal server process information.
# Not all architectures require this. But if yours does (you'll know because
# this file will be created when you run Apache) then you *must* ensure that
# no two invocations of Apache share the same scoreboard file.
#
ScoreBoardFile logs/apache_status

#
# In the standard configuration, the server will process httpd.conf,
# srm.conf, and access.conf in that order. The latter two files are
# now distributed empty, as it is recommended that all directives
# be kept in a single file for simplicity. The commented-out values
# below are the built-in defaults. You can have the server ignore
# these files altogether by using "/dev/null" (for Unix) or
# "nul" (for Win32) for the arguments to the directives.
#
#ResourceConfig conf/srm.conf
#AccessConfig conf/access.conf

#
# Timeout: The number of seconds before receives and sends time out.
#
Timeout 300

#
# KeepAlive: Whether or not to allow persistent connections (more than
# one request per connection). Set to "Off" to deactivate.
```

*continues*

**LISTING C.2**    continued

```
#
KeepAlive On

#
# MaxKeepAliveRequests: The maximum number of requests to allow
# during a persistent connection. Set to 0 to allow an unlimited amount.
# We reccomend you leave this number high, for maximum performance.
#
MaxKeepAliveRequests 100

#
# KeepAliveTimeout: Number of seconds to wait for the next request from the
# same client on the same connection.
#
KeepAliveTimeout 15

#
# Apache on Win32 always creates one child process to handle requests. If it
# dies, another child process is created automatically. Within the child
# process multiple threads handle incoming requests. The next two
# directives control the behaviour of the threads and processes.
#

#
# MaxRequestsPerChild: the number of requests each child process is
# allowed to process before the child dies. The child will exit so
# as to avoid problems after prolonged use when Apache (and maybe the
# libraries it uses) leak memory or other resources. On most systems, this
# isn't really needed, but a few (such as Solaris) do have notable leaks
# in the libraries. For Win32, set this value to zero (unlimited)
# unless advised otherwise.
#
MaxRequestsPerChild 0

#
# Number of concurrent threads (i.e., requests) the server will allow.
# Set this value according to the responsiveness of the server (more
# requests active at once means they're all handled more slowly) and
# the amount of system resources you'll allow the server to consume.
#
ThreadsPerChild 50

#
# Listen: Allows you to bind Apache to specific IP addresses and/or
# ports, in addition to the default. See also the <VirtualHost>
# directive.
#
#Listen 3000
#Listen 12.34.56.78:80
```

```
#
# BindAddress: You can support virtual hosts with this option. This directive
# is used to tell the server which IP address to listen to. It can either
# contain "*", an IP address, or a fully qualified Internet domain name.
# See also the <VirtualHost> and Listen directives.
#
#BindAddress *


#
# Dynamic Shared Object (DSO) Support
#
# To be able to use the functionality of a module which was built as a DSO you
# have to place corresponding 'LoadModule' lines at this location so the
# directives contained in it are actually available _before_ they are used.
# Please read the file README.DSO in the Apache 1.3 distribution for more
# details about the DSO mechanism and run 'apache -l' for the list of already
# built-in (statically linked and thus always available) modules in your Apache
# binary.
#
# Note: The order in which modules are loaded is important. Don't change
# the order below without expert advice.
#
#LoadModule anon_auth_module modules/ApacheModuleAuthAnon.dll
#LoadModule cern_meta_module modules/ApacheModuleCERNMeta.dll
#LoadModule digest_module modules/ApacheModuleDigest.dll
#LoadModule expires_module modules/ApacheModuleExpires.dll
#LoadModule headers_module modules/ApacheModuleHeaders.dll
#LoadModule proxy_module modules/ApacheModuleProxy.dll
#LoadModule rewrite_module modules/ApacheModuleRewrite.dll
#LoadModule speling_module modules/ApacheModuleSpeling.dll
#LoadModule status_module modules/ApacheModuleStatus.dll
#LoadModule usertrack_module modules/ApacheModuleUserTrack.dll


#
# ExtendedStatus controls whether Apache will generate "full" status
# information (ExtendedStatus On) or just basic information (ExtendedStatus
# Off) when the "server-status" handler is called. The default is Off.
#
#ExtendedStatus On

### Section 2: 'Main' server configuration
#
# The directives in this section set up the values used by the 'main'
# server, which responds to any requests that aren't handled by a
# <VirtualHost> definition. These values also provide defaults for
# any <VirtualHost> containers you may define later in the file.
#
# All of these directives may appear inside <VirtualHost> containers,
```

**C**

CONFIGURATION
FILE LISTINGS

*continues*

**LISTING C.2    continued**

```
# in which case these default settings will be overridden for the
# virtual host being defined.
#


#
# If your ServerType directive (set earlier in the 'Global Environment'
# section) is set to "inetd", the next few directives don't have any
# effect since their settings are defined by the inetd configuration.
# Skip ahead to the ServerAdmin directive.
#


#
# Port: The port to which the standalone server listens.
#
Port 80


#
# ServerAdmin: Your address, where problems with the server should be
# e-mailed. This address appears on some server-generated pages, such
# as error documents.
#
ServerAdmin you@your.address


#
# ServerName allows you to set a host name which is sent back to clients for
# your server if it's different than the one the program would get (i.e., use
# "www" instead of the host's real name).
#
# Note: You cannot just invent host names and hope they work. The name you
# define here must be a valid DNS name for your host. If you don't understand
# this, ask your network administrator.
# If your host doesn't have a registered DNS name, enter its IP address here.
# You will have to access it by its address (e.g., http://123.45.67.89/)
# anyway, and this will make redirections work in a sensible way.
#
#ServerName new.host.name


#
# DocumentRoot: The directory out of which you will serve your
# documents. By default, all requests are taken from this directory, but
# symbolic links and aliases may be used to point to other locations.
#
DocumentRoot "@@ServerRoot@@/htdocs"


#
# Each directory to which Apache has access, can be configured with respect
# to which services and features are allowed and/or disabled in that
# directory (and its subdirectories).
#
```

```
# First, we configure the "default" to be a very restrictive set of
# permissions.
#
<Directory />
    Options FollowSymLinks
    AllowOverride None
</Directory>


#
# Note that from this point forward you must specifically allow
# particular features to be enabled - so if something's not working as
# you might expect, make sure that you have specifically enabled it
# below.
#


#
# This should be changed to whatever you set DocumentRoot to.
#
<Directory "@@ServerRoot@@/htdocs">

#
# This may also be "None", "All", or any combination of "Indexes",
# "Includes", "FollowSymLinks", "ExecCGI", or "MultiViews".
#
# Note that "MultiViews" must be named *explicitly* --- "Options All"
# doesn't give it to you.
#
    Options Indexes FollowSymLinks


#
# This controls which options the .htaccess files in directories can
# override. Can also be "All", or any combination of "Options", "FileInfo",
# "AuthConfig", and "Limit"
#
    AllowOverride None


#
# Controls who can get stuff from this server.
#
    Order allow,deny
    Allow from all
</Directory>


#
# UserDir: The name of the directory which is appended onto a user's home
# directory if a ~user request is received.
#
# Under Win32, we do not currently try to determine the home directory of
# a Windows login, so a format such as that below needs to be used. See
```

*continues*

**LISTING C.2**   continued

```
# the UserDir documentation for details.
#
UserDir "@@ServerRoot@@/users/"


#
# DirectoryIndex: Name of the file or files to use as a pre-written HTML
# directory index. Separate multiple entries with spaces.
#
DirectoryIndex index.html


#
# AccessFileName: The name of the file to look for in each directory
# for access control information.
#
AccessFileName .htaccess


#
# The following lines prevent .htaccess files from being viewed by
# Web clients. Since .htaccess files often contain authorization
# information, access is disallowed for security reasons. Comment
# these lines out if you want Web visitors to see the contents of
# .htaccess files. If you change the AccessFileName directive above,
# be sure to make the corresponding changes here.
#
<Files .htaccess>
    Order allow,deny
    Deny from all
</Files>


#
# CacheNegotiatedDocs: By default, Apache sends "Pragma: no-cache" with each
# document that was negotiated on the basis of content. This asks proxy
# servers not to cache the document. Uncommenting the following line disables
# this behavior, and proxies will be allowed to cache the documents.
#
#CacheNegotiatedDocs


#
# UseCanonicalName: (new for 1.3) With this setting turned on, whenever
# Apache needs to construct a self-referencing URL (a URL that refers back
# to the server the response is coming from) it will use ServerName and
# Port to form a "canonical" name. With this setting off, Apache will
# use the hostname:port that the client supplied, when possible. This
# also affects SERVER_NAME and SERVER_PORT in CGI scripts.
#
UseCanonicalName On


#
# TypesConfig describes where the mime.types file (or equivalent) is
```

```
# to be found.
#
TypesConfig conf/mime.types


#
# DefaultType is the default MIME type the server will use for a document
# if it cannot otherwise determine one, such as from filename extensions.
# If your server contains mostly text or HTML documents, "text/plain" is
# a good value. If most of your content is binary, such as applications
# or images, you may want to use "application/octet-stream" instead to
# keep browsers from trying to display binary files as though they are
# text.
#
DefaultType text/plain


#
# The mod_mime_magic module allows the server to use various hints from the
# contents of the file itself to determine its type. The MIMEMagicFile
# directive tells the module where the hint definitions are located.
# mod_mime_magic is not part of the default server (you have to add
# it yourself with a LoadModule [see the DSO paragraph in the 'Global
# Environment' section], or recompile the server and include mod_mime_magic
# as part of the configuration), so it's enclosed in an <IfModule> container.
# This means that the MIMEMagicFile directive will only be processed if the
# module is part of the server.
#
<IfModule mod_mime_magic.c>
    MIMEMagicFile conf/magic
</IfModule>


#
# HostnameLookups: Log the names of clients or just their IP addresses
# e.g., www.apache.org (on) or 204.62.129.132 (off).
# The default is off because it'd be overall better for the net if people
# had to knowingly turn this feature on, since enabling it means that
# each client request will result in AT LEAST one lookup request to the
# nameserver.
#
HostnameLookups Off


#
# ErrorLog: The location of the error log file.
# If you do not specify an ErrorLog directive within a <VirtualHost>
# container, error messages relating to that virtual host will be
# logged here. If you *do* define an error logfile for a <VirtualHost>
# container, that host's errors will be logged there and not here.
#
ErrorLog logs/error.log
```

*continues*

**LISTING C.2**    continued

```
#
# LogLevel: Control the number of messages logged to the error.log.
# Possible values include: debug, info, notice, warn, error, crit,
# alert, emerg.
#
LogLevel warn


#
# The following directives define some format nicknames for use with
# a CustomLog directive (see below).
#
LogFormat "%h %l %u %t \"%r\" %>s %b \"%{Referer}i\" \"%{User-Agent}i\""
➥combined
LogFormat "%h %l %u %t \"%r\" %>s %b" common
LogFormat "%{Referer}i -> %U" referer
LogFormat "%{User-agent}i" agent


#
# The location and format of the access logfile (Common Logfile Format).
# If you do not define any access logfiles within a <VirtualHost>
# container, they will be logged here. Contrariwise, if you *do*
# define per-<VirtualHost> access logfiles, transactions will be
# logged therein and *not* in this file.
#
CustomLog logs/access.log common


#
# If you would like to have agent and referer logfiles, uncomment the
# following directives.
#
#CustomLog logs/referer.log referer
#CustomLog logs/agent.log agent


#
# If you prefer a single logfile with access, agent, and referer information
# (Combined Logfile Format) you can use the following directive.
#
#CustomLog logs/access.log combined


#
# Optionally add a line containing the server version and virtual host
# name to server-generated pages (error documents, FTP directory listings,
# mod_status and mod_info output etc., but not CGI generated documents).
# Set to "EMail" to also include a mailto: link to the ServerAdmin.
# Set to one of: On | Off | EMail
#
ServerSignature On


#
```

```
# Aliases: Add here as many aliases as you need (with no limit). The format is
# Alias fakename realname
#
# Note that if you include a trailing / on fakename then the server will
# require it to be present in the URL. So "/icons" isn't aliased in this
# example, only "/icons/"..
#
Alias /icons/ "@@ServerRoot@@/icons/"


#
# ScriptAlias: This controls which directories contain server scripts.
# ScriptAliases are essentially the same as Aliases, except that
# documents in the realname directory are treated as applications and
# run by the server when requested rather than as documents sent to the client.
# The same rules about trailing "/" apply to ScriptAlias directives as to
# Alias.
#
ScriptAlias /cgi-bin "@@ServerRoot@@/cgi-bin/"


#
# "@@ServerRoot@@/cgi-bin" should be changed to whatever your ScriptAliased
# CGI directory exists, if you have that configured.
#
<Directory "@@ServerRoot@@/cgi-bin">
    AllowOverride None
    Options None
</Directory>


#
# Redirect allows you to tell clients about documents which used to exist in
# your server's namespace, but do not anymore. This allows you to tell the
# clients where to look for the relocated document.
# Format: Redirect old-URI new-URL
#


#
# Directives controlling the display of server-generated directory listings.
#


#
# FancyIndexing is whether you want fancy directory indexing or standard
#
IndexOptions FancyIndexing


#
# AddIcon* directives tell the server which icon to show for different
# files or filename extensions. These are only displayed for
# FancyIndexed directories.
#
```

*continues*

**LISTING C.2**   continued

```
AddIconByEncoding (CMP,/icons/compressed.gif) x-compress x-gzip

AddIconByType (TXT,/icons/text.gif) text/*
AddIconByType (IMG,/icons/image2.gif) image/*
AddIconByType (SND,/icons/sound2.gif) audio/*
AddIconByType (VID,/icons/movie.gif) video/*

AddIcon /icons/binary.gif .bin .exe
AddIcon /icons/binhex.gif .hqx
AddIcon /icons/tar.gif .tar
AddIcon /icons/world2.gif .wrl .wrl.gz .vrml .vrm .iv
AddIcon /icons/compressed.gif .Z .z .tgz .gz .zip
AddIcon /icons/a.gif .ps .ai .eps
AddIcon /icons/layout.gif .html .shtml .htm .pdf
AddIcon /icons/text.gif .txt
AddIcon /icons/c.gif .c
AddIcon /icons/p.gif .pl .py
AddIcon /icons/f.gif .for
AddIcon /icons/dvi.gif .dvi
AddIcon /icons/uuencoded.gif .uu
AddIcon /icons/script.gif .conf .sh .shar .csh .ksh .tcl
AddIcon /icons/tex.gif .tex
AddIcon /icons/bomb.gif core

AddIcon /icons/back.gif ..
AddIcon /icons/hand.right.gif README
AddIcon /icons/folder.gif ^^DIRECTORY^^
AddIcon /icons/blank.gif ^^BLANKICON^^

#
# DefaultIcon is which icon to show for files which do not have an icon
# explicitly set.
#
DefaultIcon /icons/unknown.gif

#
# AddDescription allows you to place a short description after a file in
# server-generated indexes. These are only displayed for FancyIndexed
# directories.
# Format: AddDescription "description" filename
#
#AddDescription "GZIP compressed document" .gz
#AddDescription "tar archive" .tar
#AddDescription "GZIP compressed tar archive" .tgz

#
# ReadmeName is the name of the README file the server will look for by
# default, and append to directory listings.
#
```

```
# HeaderName is the name of a file which should be prepended to
# directory indexes.
#
# The server will first look for name.html and include it if found.
# If name.html doesn't exist, the server will then look for name.txt
# and include it as plaintext if found.
#
ReadmeName README
HeaderName HEADER


#
# IndexIgnore is a set of filenames which directory indexing should ignore
# and not include in the listing. Shell-style wildcarding is permitted.
#
IndexIgnore .??* *~ *# HEADER* README* RCS CVS *,v *,t


#
# AddEncoding allows you to have certain browsers (Mosaic/X 2.1+) uncompress
# information on the fly. Note: Not all browsers support this.
# Despite the name similarity, the following Add* directives have nothing
# to do with the FancyIndexing customisation directives above.
#
AddEncoding x-compress Z
AddEncoding x-gzip gz tgz


#
# AddLanguage allows you to specify the language of a document. You can
# then use content negotiation to give a browser a file in a language
# it can understand. Note that the suffix does not have to be the same
# as the language keyword --- those with documents in Polish (whose
# net-standard language code is pl) may wish to use "AddLanguage pl .po"
# to avoid the ambiguity with the common suffix for perl scripts.
#
AddLanguage en .en
AddLanguage fr .fr
AddLanguage de .de
AddLanguage da .da
AddLanguage el .el
AddLanguage it .it


#
# LanguagePriority allows you to give precedence to some languages
# in case of a tie during content negotiation.
# Just list the languages in decreasing order of preference.
#
LanguagePriority en fr de


#
# AddType allows you to tweak mime.types without actually editing it, or to
```

*continues*

**LISTING C.2** continued

```
# make certain files to be certain types.
#
# For example, the PHP3 module (not part of the Apache distribution)
# will typically use:
#
#AddType application/x-httpd-php3 .phtml
#AddType application/x-httpd-php3-source .phps

AddType application/x-tar .tgz


#
# AddHandler allows you to map certain file extensions to "handlers",
# actions unrelated to filetype. These can be either built into the server
# or added with the Action command (see below)
#
# If you want to use server side includes, or CGI outside
# ScriptAliased directories, uncomment the following lines.
#
# To use CGI scripts:
#
#AddHandler cgi-script .cgi


#
# To use server-parsed HTML files
#
#AddType text/html .shtml
#AddHandler server-parsed .shtml


#
# Uncomment the following line to enable Apache's send-asis HTTP file
# feature
#
#AddHandler send-as-is asis


#
# If you wish to use server-parsed imagemap files, use
#
#AddHandler imap-file map


#
# To enable type maps, you might want to use
#
#AddHandler type-map var


#
# Action lets you define media types that will execute a script whenever
# a matching file is called. This eliminates the need for repeated URL
# pathnames for oft-used CGI file processors.
# Format: Action media/type /cgi-script/location
```

```
# Format: Action handler-name /cgi-script/location
#

#
# MetaDir: specifies the name of the directory in which Apache can find
# meta information files. These files contain additional HTTP headers
# to include when sending the document
#
#MetaDir .web

#
# MetaSuffix: specifies the file name suffix for the file containing the
# meta information.
#
#MetaSuffix .meta

#
# Customizable error response (Apache style)
#   these come in three flavors
#
#     1) plain text
#ErrorDocument 500 "The server made a boo boo.
#  n.b.   the (") marks it as text, it does not get output
#
#     2) local redirects
#ErrorDocument 404 /missing.html
#  to redirect to local URL /missing.html
#ErrorDocument 404 /cgi-bin/missing_handler.pl
#  N.B.: You can redirect to a script or a document using server-side-includes.
#
#     3) external redirects
#ErrorDocument 402 http://some.other_server.com/subscription_info.html
#  N.B.: Many of the environment variables associated with the original
#  request will *not* be available to such a script.

#
# The following directives disable keepalives and HTTP header flushes.
# The first directive disables it for Netscape 2.x and browsers which
# spoof it. There are known problems with these.
# The second directive is for Microsoft Internet Explorer 4.0b2
# which has a broken HTTP/1.1 implementation and does not properly
# support keepalive when it is used on 301 or 302 (redirect) responses.
#
BrowserMatch "Mozilla/2" nokeepalive
BrowserMatch "MSIE 4\.0b2;" nokeepalive downgrade-1.0 force-response-1.0

#
# The following directive disables HTTP/1.1 responses to browsers which
# are in violation of the HTTP/1.0 spec by not being able to grok a
```

*continues*

**LISTING C.2**    continued

```
# basic 1.1 response.
#
BrowserMatch "RealPlayer 4\.0" force-response-1.0
BrowserMatch "Java/1\.0" force-response-1.0
BrowserMatch "JDK/1\.0" force-response-1.0


#
# Allow server status reports, with the URL of http://servername/server-status
# Change the ".your_domain.com" to match your domain to enable.
#
#<Location /server-status>
#    SetHandler server-status
#    Order deny,allow
#    Deny from all
#    Allow from .your_domain.com
#</Location>


#
# Allow remote server configuration reports, with the URL of
#  http://servername/server-info (requires that mod_info.c be loaded).
# Change the ".your_domain.com" to match your domain to enable.
#
#<Location /server-info>
#    SetHandler server-info
#    Order deny,allow
#    Deny from all
#    Allow from .your_domain.com
#</Location>


#
# There have been reports of people trying to abuse an old bug from pre-1.1
# days. This bug involved a CGI script distributed as a part of Apache.
# By uncommenting these lines you can redirect these attacks to a logging
# script on phf.apache.org. Or, you can record them yourself, using the script
# support/phf_abuse_log.cgi.
#
#<Location /cgi-bin/phf*>
#    Deny from all
#    ErrorDocument 403 http://phf.apache.org/phf_abuse_log.cgi
#</Location>


#
# Proxy Server directives. Uncomment the following line to
# enable the proxy server:
#
#ProxyRequests On


#
# Enable/disable the handling of HTTP/1.1 "Via:" headers.
```

```
# ("Full" adds the server version; "Block" removes all outgoing Via: headers)
# Set to one of: Off | On | Full | Block
#
#ProxyVia On


#
# To enable the cache as well, edit and uncomment the following lines:
# (no cacheing without CacheRoot)
#
#CacheRoot "@@ServerRoot@@/proxy"
#CacheSize 5
#CacheGcInterval 4
#CacheMaxExpire 24
#CacheLastModifiedFactor 0.1
#CacheDefaultExpire 1
#NoCache a_domain.com another_domain.edu joes.garage_sale.com


### Section 3: Virtual Hosts
#
# VirtualHost: If you want to maintain multiple domains/hostnames on your
# machine you can setup VirtualHost containers for them.
# Please see the documentation at <URL:http://www.apache.org/docs/vhosts/>
# for further details before you try to setup virtual hosts.
# You may use the command line option '-S' to verify your virtual host
# configuration.


#
# If you want to use name-based virtual hosts you need to define at
# least one IP address (and port number) for them.
#
#NameVirtualHost 12.34.56.78:80
#NameVirtualHost 12.34.56.78


#
# VirtualHost example:
# Almost any Apache directive may go into a VirtualHost container.
#
#<VirtualHost ip.address.of.host.some_domain.com>
#    ServerAdmin webmaster@host.some_domain.com
#    DocumentRoot /www/docs/host.some_domain.com
#    ServerName host.some_domain.com
#    ErrorLog logs/host.some_domain.com-error_log
#    CustomLog logs/host.some_domain.com-access_log common
#</VirtualHost>

#<VirtualHost _default_:*>
#</VirtualHost>
```

The `srm.conf-dist` file is the default file for the `ResourceConfig` directive in `httpd.conf`; `access.conf-dist` is the default file for the `AccessConfig` directive. Rather than use either file, you should put all your server directives into `httpd.conf` and leave these two files empty (except for the comment text that they already contain). These files are included in Listings C.3 and C.4 for completeness.

**LISTING C.3**  `srm.conf-dist`

```
#
# This is the default file for the ResourceConfig directive in httpd.conf.
# It is processed after httpd.conf but before access.conf.
#
# To avoid confusion, it is recommended that you put all of your
# Apache server directives into the httpd.conf file and leave this
# one essentially empty.
#
```

**LISTING C.4**  `access.conf-dist`

```
#
# This is the default file for the AccessConfig directive in httpd.conf.
# It is processed after httpd.conf and srm.conf.
#
# To avoid confusion, it is recommended that you put all of your
# Apache server directives into the httpd.conf file and leave this
# one essentially empty.
#
```

# Where to Get More Information

**APPENDIX D**

There's no shortage of available information about the Apache server. Most of this information is available online in one form or another. This appendix attempts to point out all available online resources about Apache in the form of Web sites, mailing lists, and Usenet groups.

# Web Sites

The following Web sites provide excellent information about the Apache server and related topics.

## ApacheUnleashed.com

The companion Web site for this book, `http://www.ApacheUnleashed.com/`, contains links to related resources, information about the authors, and errata for this book.

## The Apache Server Project

The Apache Group's Web site at `http://www.apache.org/httpd.html` is, of course, the primary source for information about the Apache Web server. This is also the primary location for downloading source code and binaries for the server.

A particularly important part of the site is the page that lists known bugs in the product (`http://www.apache.org/info/known_bugs.html`). Always check here before submitting a bug report.

This site is part of a larger site, `http://www.apache.org/`, which contains various other projects that the Apache Software Foundation is involved in, such as `mod_perl`, Jakarta, and `mod_php`.

## *Apache Week*

*Apache Week* is, as its name suggests, a weekly online publication about Apache (`http://www.apacheweek.com/`). It's the best way for the average user to find out what's happening with Apache. Information includes the latest bugs that have been found, what patches are available, and what the schedule is looking like for the next release.

*Apache Week* can also be delivered to you via email.

## NSCA HTTPd

Interesting for purely historical reasons, the NCSA HTTPd Web site at `http://hoohoo.ncsa.uiuc.edu/` contains documentation and history about the HTTPd project. This site also contains resources on CGI, server-side includes, and security, which are still valuable even though the documents are rather dated and occasionally obsolete.

## World Wide Web Consortium (W3C)

The W3C (`http://www.w3.org/`) is largely responsible for the Web existing in the first place. Tim Berners-Lee, director of the W3C, invented the World Wide Web in 1990 and defined URLs, HTTP, and HTML.

# Mailing Lists

The following mailing lists, in part or in whole, are devoted to the operation of the Apache Web server and answering questions about its use.

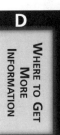

## Apache Week

As mentioned earlier, Apache Week is available via email. You can get it in plain text or in an HTML version. This is a read-only list (that is, you can't send anything back to the list). To subscribe, send email to `majordomo@apacheweek.com`. If you want to receive the plain text format, put the following text in the body of your email message:

```
subscribe apacheweek
```

If you want to receive the HTML version, say `subscribe apacheweek-html`. You can unsubscribe from the list in the same way, just replacing the word `subscribe` with the word `unsubscribe`.

## apache-announce

The `apache-announce` mailing list is "to inform people of new releases, bug fixes, security fixes, and general news and information about the Apache server." You can subscribe to the list by sending email to `apache-announce-request@apache.org` and putting the text `subscribe` in the body of your message.

This read-only list is sent out only when there's something worth telling you about.

## HWG-servers

The `HWG-servers` mailing list is operated by the HTML Writers Guild and deals with all sorts of issues surrounding running a Web server, including CGI programming and Web server configuration. The list is fairly low traffic, with 2 to 10 messages a day.

You can find more information about the list at `http://www.hwg.org/lists/hwg-servers/index.html`. Please read the list charter and netiquette guidelines before posting to the list. Failure to do so might result in a note from the List Guide (that's me).

To subscribe to the list, send email to `hwg-servers-request@hwg.org`, with the word `subscribe` in the body of your message. To unsubscribe, send email to the same address, with the word `unsubscribe` in the body of your message.

The list is available in a once-a-day digest format. To subscribe to (and unsubscribe from) that version of the list, just replace `hwg-servers-request` with `hwg-servers-digest-request` in the instructions above.

# Usenet

The following Usenet groups are valuable resources when you're trying to find more information about the Apache server.

If you want to post a question about your server to Usenet, be sure to post as much information as possible. Specifically, you should mention what version of Apache you are running, what operating system you are running it on, whether you did anything other than a default installation and, if so, what modules you added or removed.

Avoid statements such as "It does not work." You should very specifically state what's happening and how this is different from what you expected to happen.

Try to make your subject line meaningful. A post with a title of `Help!!! Urgent!!!` is much less likely to receive a meaningful answer than one titled `Installing Apache as a WinNT service`, even if the contents of the posts are identical.

## comp.infosystems.www.servers

`c.i.w.s` is generically about Web servers. There's some discussion of Apache here. Much of the traffic from this group has moved to the following two groups, which deal specifically with servers on Unix (and Unix-like) or Win32 systems:

- `comp.infosystems.www.servers.unix` is devoted to Web servers on Unix (and Unix-like) operating systems. Make sure that you specify on what Unix flavor you are running.

- `comp.infosystems.www.servers.mswindows` is devoted to Web servers on Microsoft Windows operating systems (Windows 3.1, Windows 95, Windows NT, Windows 98, and Windows 2000). Make sure that you specify what version of Windows you are running.

## comp.infosystems.www.authoring.cgi

As discussed in the chapter on CGI programming, many problems that people experience with CGI programs occur because the server is configured incorrectly. Consequently, much of the discussion on `c.i.w.a.c` is more related to Web servers than to CGI programming.

# INDEX

# Other Related Titles

# Installing the CD for *Apache Server Unleashed*

## Windows 95/98/NT/2000 Installation Instructions

1. Insert the CD-ROM disc into your CD-ROM drive.

2. From the Windows desktop, double-click the My Computer icon.

3. Double-click the icon representing your CD-ROM drive.

4. Double-click the file README.TXT to find out what's on the CD-ROM.

## Linux and Unix Installation Instructions

These installation instructions assume that you have a passing familiarity with Unix commands and the basic setup of your machine. Unix has many flavors, and only generic commands are used. If you have any problems with the commands, please consult the appropriate man page or your system administrator.

1. Insert the CD-ROM in the CD drive.

2. If you have a volume manager, mounting of the CD-ROM will be automatic. If you don't have a volume manager, you can mount the CD-ROM by typing

   ```
   mount -tiso9660 /dev/cdrom /mnt/cdrom
   ```

> **Note**
>
> /mnt/cdrom is just a mount point, but it must exist when you issue the mount command. You can also use any empty directory for a mount point if you don't want to use /mnt/cdrom.

3. Navigate to the root directory of your CD-ROM. If your mount point matches the preceding example, type

   ```
   cd /mnt/cdrom
   ```

4. Open the file README.TXT with your favorite text editor to find out what's on the CD-ROM.